Human Rights in Canadian Foreign Policy

EDITED BY
ROBERT O. MATTHEWS
AND
CRANFORD PRATT

McGill-Queen's University Press
Kingston and Montreal

©McGill-Queen's University Press 1988
ISBN 0-7735-0667-5 (cloth)
ISBN 0-7735-0683-7 (paper)

Legal deposit fourth quarter 1988
Bibliothèque nationale du Québec

∞

Printed in Canada on acid-free paper

Canadian Cataloguing in Publication Data

Main entry under title:
Human rights in Canadian foreign policy
   Includes bibliographical references and an index.
   ISBN 0-7735-0667-5 (bound) -
   ISBN 0-7735-0683-7 (pbk.).
   1. Canada – Foreign relations – 1945-
   2. Human rights.
   I. Matthews, Robert O.
   II. Pratt, Cranford, 1926-
   FC242.H94 1988   327.71   C88-090220-5
   F1029.H94 1988

FC242 .H86 1988

0134106927160

Human rights in Canadian
foreign policy /
c1988.

Contents

Preface vii

1 Introduction: Concepts and Instruments /
ROBERT O. MATTHEWS and CRANFORD PRATT 3

PART ONE   DOMESTIC CONTEXT

2 Human Rights in Domestic Politics and
Policy / RONALD MANZER 23

3 Cabin'd, Cribb'd, Confin'd?: Canada's Interest
in Human Rights / KIM RICHARD NOSSAL 46

4 Human Rights and Foreign Policy–Making /
VICTORIA BERRY and ALLAN MC CHESNEY 59

PART TWO   INTERNATIONAL FORUMS

5 The UN Commission on Human Rights /
JOHN W. FOSTER 79

6 The Human Rights Committee /
CATHAL J. NOLAN 101

7 The International Labour Organization /
KALMEN KAPLANSKY 115

8 The Helsinki Process / H. GORDON SKILLING 135

9 International Financial Institutions /
RENATE PRATT 159

PART THREE BILATERAL DIPLOMACY

10 Development Assistance / T.A. KEENLEYSIDE   187

11 Military Sales / ERNIE REGEHR   209

12 "America's Backyard": Central America / FRANCES ARBOUR   221

13 The Polish Case / STEFANIA SZLEK MILLER   246

14 Black Africa and South Africa / RHODA E. HOWARD   265

15 Conclusion: Questions and Prospects / ROBERT O. MATTHEWS and CRANFORD PRATT   285

Notes   313

Index   369

Contributors   376

Preface

This volume has had a long prehistory. In the academic year 1984–5, a group of some 20 individuals met recurrently in Toronto to discuss human rights and Canadian foreign policy. The group included academics and activists from non-governmental organizations involved in human rights issues. In addition to most of the contributors to this volume, Edward Appathurai, Christian Bay, Nibaldo Galleguillos, André Gombay, Bonnie Greene, and Moira Hutchinson actively participated. Those meetings culminated in a two-day conference on human rights and Canadian foreign policy in June 1985 which included the members of the original study group along with about 20 individuals we felt would be interested in and able to contribute to the discussion. The conference was so successful that we undertook to organize this volume.

The volume, to our pleasure and its own advantage, continues to reflect the participation of academics and activists. It is a fruitful and rewarding mode of collaboration that we are happy to recommend.

We are pleased to acknowledge support from the Development Studies Program (DSP) of the University of Toronto, which drew on a Connaught Development Grant received from the University of Toronto, the Canadian Institute for International Peace and Security (CIIPS), and the Social Sciences and Humanities Research Council. We wish to express our appreciation in particular to Professor Richard Sandbrook, director of the DSP, David Cox, of CIIPS, Jack Donnelly, Philip Alston, and Philippe LeBlanc for their encouragement and sustaining support. We wish to thank Susan Roberts, until recently administrative secretary of the DSP, for her assistance, which took many forms and was extended unfailingly with cheerful good humour. We are much indebted to Marion Magee and to John Parry, who skilfully and meticulously edited this volume. Finally we thank Martha and Renate, who accepted with such supportive goodwill the many intrusions of this volume into our lives.

Robert O. Matthews
Cranford Pratt
Department of Political Science
University of Toronto

Human Rights in Canadian Foreign Policy

CHAPTER ONE

Introduction: Concepts and Instruments

ROBERT O. MATTHEWS and
CRANFORD PRATT

It is an axiom of social scientists, important to their self-esteem, that they think carefully about the concepts and normative assumptions that they use when they discuss public policy. In this volume the authors discuss foreign policies that Canada is following or might follow in order to promote human rights in countries where there is much oppression. This chapter therefore strives to define human rights and Canada's obligations in this regard. That done, we then describe the form and range of instruments that Canada has employed to promote human rights abroad.

HUMAN RIGHTS

There is, despite the International Bill of Rights, a remarkable lack of consensus about the importance to be attached to the various rights included in the bill. This lack of agreement is particularly apparent in international politics. There, human rights have been caught in the propaganda and rhetoric of superpower contention, with the United States affirming the paramountcy of civil and political rights, which it believes are severely denied in communist countries, and the Soviet Union and its allies championing economic and social rights, which they believe under-acknowledged in capitalist states. Moreover, the lack of consensus is not confined to diplomacy. It, and much disagreement about the justification for human rights claims, feature as well in scholarly writing.

We begin, therefore, with definitions. What is a human right, be it to subsistence or to freedom from torture? There is no one correct, true response. Some responses clarify and largely coincide with widespread understanding of the term; others are innovative and seek to convince. We seek a coherent and concise definition that will strike a chord with readers; we shall then draw out nuances and implications of this definition.

A human right is, in our view, a justified entitlement that any person may claim because of being human and that ought to be socially guaranteed. Ensuring human rights requires institutions committed to their promotion and enforcement. This requirement explains the final clause of our definition.

Many rights are specific to a context – a product of promises made, of benefits received, of endeavours shared, of damages suffered. *Human* rights generate moral obligations toward individuals because they are human.[1]

Our definition omits reference to who is obligated. Many philosophic definitions of human rights regard the obligations to be as universal as the rights themselves. For rights that are affirmations of individual liberties, this seems reasonable. One could hardly argue that an obligation not to torture applies only to the torturing of fellow nationals. Or, to make the same point from the claimant's viewpoint, one would be unlikely to assert the right not to be tortured by one's own government but concede the legitimacy of being tortured by a foreign authority. However, in addition to the duty they entail that others ought not to violate those rights, human rights have two other important dimensions – the need for institutions to ensure them and the obligations they create on others to take positive action (for example, to provide food to the hungry or create institutions to prevent non-judicial detention). It is not self-evident that these obligations are universal. In many cases certainly, the obligation to ensure enforcement will fall primarily on governments. It is reasonable to accept the existence of human rights and to concede that obligations in regard to them fall primarily on one's own state and its institutions. We do not, however, build this viewpoint into our definition. We wish to ask whether and to what extent human rights in one country are the legitimate concern of other nations and peoples. These seem meaningful questions. We therefore prefer a definition that does not appear to prejudge the answers.

But what are human rights? Popular usage seems to use three categories. First, some human rights are viewed as justified claims to essential personal liberties. In the Western constitutional democratic tradition, these are the essential personal liberties and civil and political rights which constrain abuses of power by governments. The classical liberal view, in which the primary threat to citizens' rights appears to come from an oppressive state, emphasizes these civil and political rights, sometimes to the exclusion of others.

Second, some rights emphasize economic and social entitlements – the right, for example, to employment, to a living wage, or to reasonable habitation. These entitlements are individually experienced but require positive acts by others, particularly the state, if they are to be assured. Many people see them as standing in sharp contrast to civil and political rights – socialist rather than liberal rights. We do not find this distinction helpful. It is hard to draw any sharp line between the two sets, either by calling civil and political rights negative and economic and social rights positive or by seeing one set as having logical or political priority over the other. The safeguarding of both sets of rights requires positive action by the state and effective institutions. As well, achievement of economic and social rights is likely to require widespread acceptance of civil and political liberties, which help to ensure that rulers do not lose sight of the needs of the poor. Economic and social rights can thus better be seen as a further elaboration of human rights. Civil and political rights, by themselves, will not help someone in despair about his or her next meal, health, or where to sleep and live. Similarly, well-fed and healthy individuals whose personal liberty and civil rights are in jeopardy will be insecure about their current economic and social entitlements. The two sets of rights are interdependent, perhaps indivisible, and each set requires effective governmental institutions to be realized.

Third, there are human rights that are essentially collective rather than individual. One has long been acknowledged – the right to national self-determination – but most have only recently been articulated – the right to clean air, for example, or to peace.

Most people, we believe, would not argue that individuals have an entitlement, a just claim against others, to all that constitutes a desirable life. This state should be within their grasp as a consequence of personal effort, but no one else is obliged to make it available. People should be aided, say, to live a culturally enriched life or to enjoy a free press, but the language of human rights seems inappropriate for the wide range of advantageous and desirable social arrangements. It is better used for the essential prerequisites of a moral and decent life.

If this is accepted, the concept retains a strong individualist flavour. This is unavoidable and, indeed, desirable. Human rights are about the essential freedoms and, we believe, the social and personal prerequisites for a life of minimal dignity. They are concerned with permitting persons to pursue their chosen objectives. To use "human rights" in this way assumes that individual freedom is highly valued and that the meeting of many human needs should remain in the arena of autonomous human action. This individualistic component could diminish the recognition that we are social individuals, living in, needing, and much influenced by societies. Its liberal twist could diminish recognition of the collective nature of some human rights and the collective character of the effort needed to ensure them, But this need not be. Human rights in the usage we propose can combine easily with strong convictions about the positive role of the state. Such convictions are not in conflict with the belief that the welfare and development of individuals and the quality of their life remain the yardstick by which to judge social arrangements. The concept of human rights seems naturally and in actual usage to refer back to individuals.

Many moral and political philosophers use human rights in the general sense that we are proposing. Their detailed elaborations of the concept differ, but each is seeking to identify "the necessary conditions of human action" or the important humans needs, "whether a freedom, a good or a benefit of crucial importance to human life."[2] By defining a human right as an entitlement that every individual may justifiably claim on the grounds of her or his humanity and that ought to be socially ensured, we are placing ourselves within their ranks. We are accepting as a first axiomatic premise that all human beings have certain essential and fundamental needs that are so important to their existence as human beings that they may legitimately claim against others that these needs be met. To speak of human rights is to accept as self-evident the moral validity of such claims.[3]

In recent years the concept of "basic" rights has crept into the literature.[4] It might be taken as an alternative to human rights, as each concept refers to the essential minimum claims that individuals, as individuals, can make. Indeed Henry Shue speaks of "basic," not "human" rights, while Gewirth does the opposite. In our view, and in the view of some of our contributors, it is useful to employ both concepts.

Shue argues, convincingly, that basic rights include the right to security of person and to subsistence. Without a far wider range of rights, a decent and moral life is not possible, but without these two, no other right can be enjoyed. "Basic" rights, then, are those human rights without which no other rights can conceivably be enjoyed. We shall mean by basic rights (1) the right to basic subsistence and related needs required for sustaining life; (2) freedom from arbitrary arrest and detention without trial; (3) freedom from torture; and (4) freedom from extrajudicial execution.

CANADA'S OBLIGATIONS

We come now to the first of the harder questions: have people duties beyond their country's borders vis-à-vis others' basic rights? We believe that Canada has duties of this sort, and this is the general view of the contributors to this volume. We need to be clear about the grounds for this view.[5]

It would be feasible to argue that one's obligation to ensure human rights relates only to one's community. Moral consciousness for most people does not reach beyond those with whom they have ties of natural sentiments. Those who would argue this case need not claim that the nation-state is the largest community within which most people share some sense of identity. Religion, national origin, and race often generate a sense of community that extends beyond the state. There is also emerging a sense of shared destiny with all humankind. Nevertheless, human rights are primarily realizable through political institutions and within political communities, and no institutions yet exist beyond the nation-state that can directly protect and enforce these rights. The claim on others that human rights give to anyone is thus directed first and primarily to fellow citizens and one's own state.

International realities provide some support for the view that states should be left to exercise their responsibility for human rights within their own borders. Indeed, Kim Nossal argues in this volume that respect for sovereignty has left Canadian officials hesitant to emphasize human rights in foreign policy. He clearly finds this view persuasive. We concede only that it is forceful.

These considerations we view more as cautions against too extended a championing of a wide range of human rights than as a justification for denying obligations when there are gross, systematic, and continuous violations of basic human rights in particular states. Growing global interdependence makes assertion of the moral autonomy of nation-states less and less convincing. Communications and media technologies give many in the world intimate knowledge of the suffering of others about which they would have known nothing in other eras. This planet is, to some extent, now a global community. People have begun to acknowledge international values and a concern for the welfare of fellow human beings of all nationalities. In this world community, there are the beginnings of institutions to keep human rights issues under review. Even Michael Walzer, who is very sensitive to the moral worth of national societies, writes: "Perhaps every victim of authoritarianism and bigotry is the moral comrade of a liberal citizen; that is an argument I would like to make."[6] This tide of opinion explains widespread concern for human rights.

There are, we believe, compelling reasons why, in the words of a special joint committee of the Canadian Parliament, Canada should be actively concerned when "systematic, gross and continuous violations of basic human rights occur and can reasonably be ascribed to state policy."[7] There is widespread acknowledgment that there are rights so fundamental that no one should be denied them. These rights have become an international quasi-common law and are embodied in international declarations and covenants. They appear in national bills of rights. Very few states deny their validity. There has emerged a widespread conviction that these rights are so important that states that systematically abuse them must anticipate criticism and mounting pressure from individual countries, international institutions, and international non-governmental organizations. These rights constitute a minimal code of behaviour for a state toward its citizens which the world is increasingly insisting every government must follow. We accept that Canada has a moral obligation to attach high priority to helping consolidate international acceptance of these rights.

This consideration is paramount. However, it is reinforced by other arguments of a different kind. Surely a world in which human rights are widely respected is preferable for liberal and pacific middle powers such as Canada. Promotion of such an order is therefore in Canada's interest. Finally, as is often argued, a country's foreign policy should reflect its most fundamental values. These values may not remain vital and compelling within Canadian society if they are not reflected in Canada's international role.

We therefore conclude that it is a legitimate, desirable, and morally compelling foreign policy objective to contribute to the international consolidation of basic human rights; to support international structures that review these rights and discuss, investigate, and mediate alleged abuses of them; and to use Canada's influence in bilateral foreign policy relations to seek reforms in states that grossly and persistently violate these rights.

FOREIGN POLICY AND NON-BASIC HUMAN RIGHTS

Focusing on systematic violators of basic human rights makes the argument for a human rights component to foreign policy more compelling. If Canada can contribute to international acceptance of a minimal standard of decent behaviour by states toward their citizens, it will have made a valuable contribution to human welfare and to a more civil world. This explains and, we hope, justifies this volume's emphasis on basic human rights.

Nevertheless greater concern for basic human rights does not exhaust the legitimate expectations of those who seek a more active human rights component in foreign policy. Consider each of these observations.

(1) Two collective rights, of national communities to self-determination and of states to live at peace with their neighbours, have a sub-

stantial history, an important place in international law, and solid international acceptance. Each can easily be transcribed into the language of human rights. The first becomes the right to live in a self-determining national community, and the second the right to live in a state that is not assaulted by neighbours. Each, it might even be argued, is a basic right: when a people is denied either, it often moves rapidly to active resistance. These two classic collective rights can be set off from the basic, individualist rights, but their importance can hardly be denied.

(2) Basic human rights as we define them do not include civil and political rights. Nevertheless, they have, at minimum, a high instrumental value in helping to ensure governmental concern for the protection of basic rights. They are important components of democracy as Canadians practise and understand it. In Western and in democratic political culture, at least since universal suffrage has been common, these rights are regarded as essential to a life of dignity and self-respect. Canada's foreign policy is influenced by its citizens' commitment to these rights.

(3) We have argued that obligations regarding the rights of others emerge naturally within a community. The community of sentiments shared by people of the same national origin cuts across state boundaries. This community unites immigrants and their descendants with those living in their homeland. Where there is severe denial of civil and political rights in their countries of origin, immigrants and descendants are bound to be particularly concerned. In Canada, where many citizens are still attached by ties of memory and affection to their mother countries, or to national communities within them, this factor reinforces the more purely ethical or ideological predisposition to ensure that Canadian foreign policy expresses concern for civil and political rights.

(4) The international community has formally and unanimously endorsed both civil and political rights and economic and social rights in the Universal Declaration of Human Rights, the International Covenant on Economic, Social and Cultural Rights, and the International Covenant on Civil and Political Rights. The United Nations Commission on Human Rights and the United Nations Committee on Human Rights have monitored international respect for the wide range of rights covered by the covenants, as have other international structures such as the International Labour Organization. Canadian foreign policy, as it surely should, stresses strengthening of these institutions, using these arenas to mobilize international opinion against states that severely violate human rights.

We therefore conclude that Canada has legitimate foreign policy concerns with regard to a wide range of human rights. That this is widely accepted in Canada within both government and community is demonstrated in the chapters that follow. We shall return in our concluding chapter to the comparative importance of concern for basic human rights and concern for a far wider range of rights.

DELIMITING OBLIGATIONS

The literature on international human rights contains an interesting and largely unexplored disagreement. If the right to subsistence is a basic right, will not acceptance of an obligation in regard to global starvation overwhelm most individuals with duties that are beyond anyone but a saint to fulfil?

Among writers who accept that individuals have obligations regarding human rights in the world at large, some argue that these obligations would not assume dimensions that would overwhelm us. Gewirth, for example, says: "It may be objected that if individuals' rights to freedom and property may be invaded whenever this is needed to prevent harm to other persons, then there will be no limit to such invasion and hence in effect no rights. This slippery-slope contention fails, however, because in the present argument the harms in question are limited to interference with basic goods."[8]

This judgment, however, is a minority opinion. Indeed, we think Gewirth's own analysis points in the other direction. For him the prevention of starvation is a universal obligation that takes precedence over a nation's other rights: if a country has a food surplus and knows of starvation elsewhere, it must transfer food to the starving. How is Gewirth able nevertheless to conclude that obligations toward the starving do not have intimidating dimensions?

It is, certainly, James Fishkin's view that these obligations are overwhelming. The central theme of his *The Limits of Obligation* is the unavoidable conflict between general obligations ("what can be demanded of anyone by anyone") and the assumption that "a substantial proportion of any individual's action falls appropriately within the zone of indifference or permissible free personal choice."[9] Fishkin does not resolve the dilemma but persuades one that it is real. Ordinary people cannot be asked to make sacrifices of the order reserved for saints or heroes. Most people must have "a robust arena of indifference" within which morality has no say and in which they can pursue their interests as they wish. However, if one accepts general obligations (relating to basic human rights), little will be left of that "robust arena." Henry Shue's argument leads in a similar direction. He writes: "To deny a helpless person material resources that would save the person's life or vitality in order to protect material resources controlled but not needed so desperately by one or more other persons is to inflict a profound indignity

– not to mention probable death – upon the person whose urgent needs are denied."

Even though the logic of their arguments pushes toward heavy obligations on the rich and powerful, these writers seem to flinch at this conclusion. Limiting and constraining adjectives are interjected. Shue talks of fairness so that equivalent sacrifices are made internationally in the effort to assist those being denied their basic human rights.[10] Fishkin writes: "Anyone who can save a human life at minor cost is obliged to do so."[11] Other writers insert the requirement of reasonableness to limit the sacrifices implied by the logic of their moral philosophy. Rawls, for example, talks of "the duty of helping another where he is in need or jeopardy provided that one can do so without excessive risk or loss to oneself."[12]

It is easy to admit the realism of such phrases as "fairness," "without excessive risk," and "at minor cost," when talking about the international obligations of states. Yet when one thinks more concretely and specifically, the grounds for limiting obligations begin to sound specious. Why should the satisfaction of our non-essential, if not indulgent, interests count for more than famine assistance to Africa? Similarly, can homeless and despairing refugees be excluded in order possibly to preserve the quality of life of the Canadian nation?

This dilemma, we think, cannot be resolved. Morality puts impossible demands on the morally sensitive. It suggests international commitments that far exceed what citizens will judge reasonable. The world is not an easy place for caring people. Individuals and states determine the character and moral quality of their lives by their decisions in such matters. What is important in assessing Canadian human rights policy, therefore, is the weight it gives to human rights in contrast to other objectives and interests and the imagination, resources, and energy it devotes to the implementation of human rights. How Canada resolves these questions provides a measure of the sort of people Canadians are.

WHAT CAN BE DONE?

In deciding how to act, a government must not lose sight of its actual goals. If a state's primary goal in regard to human rights internationally is to end complicity in the deprivation of others' rights, then the most appropriate response might be what Jack Donnelly termed a "strategy of nonintervention" – "the gradual phasing out of all relations with the human rights-violating regime."[13] If the purpose is to assist other peoples against human rights violations perpetrated by their own governments, actions would be different. A state might contemplate severing relations (diplomatic, economic, and military) and would presumably want to "interfere" as well: through diplomatic representations, appeals to international bodies, public denunciations, and, in the most extreme instances, military action. If the goal is primarily to help the victims, then policies would centre on humanitarian support to those who have fled oppression, opening the door to refugees and, secondarily, drawing the attention of world public opinion to the underlying causes of the crises.

Our understanding of Canadian values (and our reading also of the contributions to this volume) suggest that Canadians desire a human rights foreign policy that would include all three of these expressions – a concern not to contribute to the violation of the human rights of others; a wish to influence positively situations where basic rights are grossly and systematically violated; and a willingness to help those who have directly suffered.

A nation's selection of instruments will also be influenced by their likely effectiveness, with minimal damage to its other interests. Selection of means must be tied closely to ends, and a careful estimate made of costs and benefits associated with instruments selected. A human rights policy is not designed solely to influence an offensive régime. It serves also as evidence of the continued concern of the international community about severe abuse of human rights. Even if international pressures were unlikely to have much effect, there still would be cause to censure a régime that consistently violates basic human rights and to make it clear that Canada regards this internal oppression as unacceptable.

A final consideration involves the distinction between punishments (sanctions) and rewards (inducements). As sanctions may provoke a hardening of attitudes within the violating country and, if applied unilaterally, are likely to be ineffective, rewards may better encourage change. Instead of threatening to cancel aid to a country with an abysmal human rights record, one might offer aid (or increased aid) if its human rights performance improved. Similarly, trade preferences might be extended to developing countries that took human rights seriously. Governments should not limit themselves to considering punishments; inducements may prove as or more effective.

Multilateral Measures

In expressing concern for human rights, governments have shown a distinct preference for using international forums to define rights, to negotiate legal instruments that set out internationally agreed norms, and to establish mechanisms for investigating alleged abuses and, ideally, making effective judicial arbitration. Steps taken in intergovernmental bodies bear the world's approval; they cannot be interpreted as representing the narrow interests of one country, ideology, or culture. Operating within international organizations avoids the charge of intervention in the domestic affairs of a sovereign state: the international community can legitimately draw the dividing line between domestic matters and those of international concern and decide what kind of behaviour constitutes unjustifiable intervention. Finally, only with widespread international agreement can new standards be established and new legal conventions negotiated.

Thus governments should be encouraged to continue support for human rights in the United Nations and its related bodies as well as within the Conference on Security and Cooperation in Europe (the Helsinki framework). In particular, states that have not yet done so should be pressed to ratify existing human rights instruments, especially the two international covenants, the optional protocol, and the recently negotiated Convention on Torture. In addition, all efforts should continue to set new standards for human rights by the development of new conventions.

International institutions have made considerable progress in setting standards and promoting human rights, but their implementation of those norms has been less satisfactory.[14] Developing effective procedures is bound to be a long process, marked by setbacks and frustrated by political and ideological divisions. This should not weaken the resolve of governments, particularly Canada's.

Bilateral Measures

Even though the United Nations has expanded its concern for human rights violations beyond the triad of South Africa, Israel, and Chile and is now able to name countries publicly and to denounce them roundly, its methods remain essentially investigation, review, and publicity, while its powers of enforcement are limited to persuasion, moral pressure, and the influence of informed public opinion.[15] Partly because of the weakness and ineffectiveness of the United Nations, governments have come under increasing pressure to undertake unilateral and collaborative initiatives to further human rights. Governments serious about human rights cannot restrict their actions to international forums. Failure to act unilaterally will be interpreted as a sign of lack of serious intent, while carrying on normal relations with a violator country may dilute or undermine positive results in Geneva or New York.

Expectations ran high, particularly during the early years of the Carter administration, when human rights were given a high rank in US priorities. Human rights appeared to be coming of age, moving from the margins of international relations to centre stage. And why not? There is an enormous range of instruments available to governments to

TABLE 1
Typology of Human Rights Measures

MULTILATERAL

Encouraging wider participation in existing international instruments
Pressing for development of new instruments
Supporting strengthening of existing means and creating of new ones for implementation
Supporting or initiating calls in such bodies as the UN Commission on Human Rights for investigation of serious situations
Supporting or initiating sanctions (diplomatic, economic, military) in international organizations
Encouraging and supporting governments that promote human rights

BILATERAL

Diplomatic and Political

Executing quiet diplomacy
Making public statements
Performing symbolic acts to identify with victims and those actively resisting violations
Cancelling or postponing official visits
Reducing size and/or status of diplomatic representation
Breaking off diplomatic relations
Strengthening relations with states seeking to improve conditions
Establishing links with opposition groups within offending states

Cultural and Communications

Reducing educational, cultural, and scientific exchanges where this would reflect adversely on the régime
Increasing exchanges that strengthen social forces and values threatened by the régime
Reducing or cancelling sporting events
Banning tourism (both ways)
Withdrawing visas
Restricting, suspending, or cancelling communications links
Assisting rights-related activities, such as ombudsmen, editorial commissions, and judiciary

TABLE 1 (continued)
Typology of Human Rights Measures

Economic

Reducing or cancelling aid (military and economic)
Reducing or cancelling credit
Imposing limited trade and/or investment sanctions
Imposing comprehensive trade and/or investment sanctions
Taking positive measures (aid, trade conventions), conditional on improvements

Military

Banning sale of arms
Halting all military assistance
Assisting in human rights training of police and armed forces
Providing military assistance to opposition groups
Using military force

TRANSNATIONAL

Co-ordinating activities – information gathering, expression of public outrage, foreign assistance, and support to liberation movements
Establishing codes of conduct
Discouraging or banning new investment

---

press for human rights improvements (see table 1). Except in the realm of force, there are no legal constraints on what states can do. The only obstacles are practical and political, rather than legal. Will these instruments be effective in achieving human rights objectives? What impact, if any, will their use have on the state's other goals (or values)? And will conflicts among state purposes be resolved in favour of human rights?

Most governments have apparently concluded that unilateral initiatives are ineffective or conflict with other, more important goals. Anxious not to tread on the sensitive toes of other sovereigns, most states seem to prefer harmonious relations. Where geopolitcal interests seem likely also to be served, criticisms are often strongly voiced. But where economic or political interests might be jeopardized, there seems general reluctance to make direct representations, sometimes even quiet ones, to governments that openly violate human rights. Gordon Skilling's chapter on Canada's role in the Conference on Security and Co-operation in Europe illustrates how much more vigorous are Canada's criticisms of violations in Eastern-bloc countries than of those by allied states.

Yet direct representations (private and public) to violating governments can affect domestic behaviour. If, as Evan Luard remarks, violators are "made to feel that the whole texture of their international relationship may be affected, they may be more willing to consider radical changes in policy." And if such protests are made with no obvious political motive, adding to criticisms already being made and stimulating others to add their voice, the risk of damaging bilateral relations is surely slight.

Many of the initiatives we discuss are largely symbolic, designed to communicate to various publics disapproval of certain policies and practices and identification with and sympathy for victims. Beyond such steps are reduction or severance of all ties (diplomatic, cultural, and economic). Although such actions have symbolic value, their main thrust is punitive – to hurt the target country by denying it some benefit previously extended. However, the initiating state is bound to suffer as well. Any state that wishes to press a violator country will likely have to pay a cost, forgo a benefit, possibly sacrifice another interest. Steps adopted will, therefore, depend on circumstances, on whether particular measures are likely to be effective, and on the importance of promoting basic human rights relative to other foreign policy objectives.

Diplomatic. Many analysts have argued that total isolation of a régime, however offensive, is undesirable and counterproductive. Such a step would leave the initiating state impotent (without information and influence) and would isolate opposition groups and victims in the target state. This argument seems to rest on the assumption that impotence is the result only of isolation; in fact it seems to be the norm for states involved in "constructive engagement." And pursuing a strategy of isolation does not mean abandoning the opposition; one can favour the complete isolation of the white régime in South Africa and support the African National Congress and other reform and revolutionary groups inside and outside South Africa.

Short of total isolation, however, there are other steps. Instead of breaking off diplomatic ties altogether, a state could cancel or postpone official visits to and from the offender, recall its ambassador for consultation, or reduce the size or status of its representation. Such steps might be largely symbolic but would signal disapproval. Some sort of response might be anticipated, but if it were limited to a diplomatic riposte, the costs would be minimal. The costs of not taking such action might be more substantial, even if only in terms of the reaction of one's own public.[17]

Cultural. The case for action in the cultural field is not self-evident. Maintenance of cultural links is often viewed as tantamount to recognition and approval. Those who sharply criticize sporting visits to South Africa and by South African teams to other countries fear that such exchanges constitute recognition or at least acceptance of apartheid. Excluding South Africans from world sporting events adds to international pressure on Pretoria in an arena of particular interest to South African whites.

There may be a strong case for cultural exchanges with countries that violate human rights. Unofficial links between professional, academic, and religious groups may strengthen resistance and encourage those who seek greater liberty.[18] Such a calculation has encouraged Western cultural exchanges with the Soviet Union. To disrupt these links might only further isolate elements that are a potential source of change and resistance.

There is no single appropriate response. Action will vary from country to country, taking into account whether exchanges touch on basic human rights and whether the oppressive régime is seriously threatened or is virtually unassailable.

Economic. A state may have recourse to a number of economic measures to put pressure on human rights violators. The main focus in this volume, as in public discussion, is on three: the use of foreign aid, the use of controls on trade and investment, and making human rights a co-determinant of loan and credit decisions of international financial institutions.

Cancelling or reducing aid to a serious violator is, as is argued by Keenleyside in this volume and by others elsewhere,[19] fraught with difficulties. Cutting aid may further harm the people human rights policy is designed to assist.[20] It could cause the oppressive régime to stiffen its policies, thus making the cut in aid ineffective and counterproductive. Under régimes that systematically deny basic human rights, however, the poor and downtrodden receive few benefits from so-called development programs – infrastructural projects such as roads and telecommunications systems. The authorities can use these developments to tighten the arm of the law and reduce freedom.

A government can channel assistance through small, narrowly defined projects more likely to assist the poor. It can use non-governmental organizations as a conduit for aid. Finally, a donor can reduce the status of an aid recipient from core country (or country of concentration) to occasional recipient.

Surely, as Keenleyside argues, few general rules are possible, and the adequacy and appropriateness of aid policies toward oppressing countries will depend on the understanding and sympathy of those shaping the policies. Concern to help the poor and oppressed should remain the dominant motivation.

States are generally sceptical about the use of trade sanctions. Clearly, the record is not encouraging. Nevertheless, sanctions had an influence (over the Dominican Republic in 1961) or were likely a contributing cause to change (Rhodesia, 1965–79) However, more often than not, they have not influenced a régime or contributed to its downfall. One should not discount other possible adverse effects: sanctions may harm innocent people and neighbouring states, to cite two arguments current in the debate over South African sanctions. And they may undermine the international trading system. However, sanctions may contribute to an international effort to secure change, show that the world has not forgotten, and encourage those actively fighting oppression.

Although there should be extreme caution in the use of sanctions, we do not conclude that they should never be used. Circumstances can justify their use and enhance the chances of their success. As black resistance increases in South Africa, strong economic sanctions may be one of the few ways for the outside world to assist the struggle and minimize bloodshed. Uganda under Idi Amin seemed to offer another example: his régime persistently and grossly violated basic rights. The Ugandan economy was dependent on the sale of coffee – four-fifths of exports. Since most of this coffee was bought by only seven Western countries – the United States bought one-third – considerable leverage existed. And because an embargo would have affected the régime and its supporters more than the vast majority of Ugandans, the costs might have been slight.

Only the largest economic powers can apply sufficient pressure on their own on violator states to force them to change their ways. For countries the size of Canada, as a former secretary of state for external affairs pointed out, cutting off trade relations "is unlikely to be effective unless part of a concerted international approach to the problem."[21] It is hard to disagree. However, Ottawa should not rule out such a campaign where basic rights are openly and grossly violated – whether South Africa today or some other country in the future.

As with foreign assistance, there are a number of unilateral steps short of a partial or total trade embargo. A state can withdraw trade commissioners and halt government loans to facilitate exports and trade insurance schemes and export promotional programs. More severe would be repeal of special trading status (most-favoured-nation or a general preferential rate).

Military. One of the first measures a state is likely to entertain when confronted by a régime that has clearly abused basic rights is to end all military assistance and halt the supply of arms, whether provided by governments or sold privately. This ban could be defined narrowly or could include dual-purpose equipment, such as computers that can be used by police and armed forces and aircraft that can serve military and civilian functions. There are, of course, more forceful instruments. A state can provide non-military or military assistance to those resisting oppression; have a clearly visible presence in neighbouring states that the violator régime threatens; and even intervene directly with military force, unlikely save in the most extreme circumstances, as we shall discuss.

Transnational Measures

Private groups or non-governmental organizations (NGOs) have been active in human rights. They can be more effective than governments: they can speak out more freely, are not subject to obvious political bias, and can establish closer relations with the poor and oppressed in violator countries. A country with human rights central to its foreign policy can co-ordinate its activities closely with that of NGOs and assist their work.

Governments are at a disadvantage in securing reliable information concerning human rights violations. Diplomatic circles do not often include the oppressed. Because groups promoting human rights in a violator state tend to be portrayed as "subversive," foreign diplomats are hesitant to establish close relations with them. They risk damaging relations with the government. By contrast, many NGOs have links with these groups and with the oppressed themselves. They can secure comprehensive and reliable information about human rights violations over long periods. Governments interested in human rights can learn much from NGOs.

When governments are reluctant to speak out or to take action for fear of damaging other interests, NGOs may serve as the conscience of the nation. A government may welcome wide public expression of revulsion toward a violator. Indeed, such an outpouring may force its hand, by providing it with good reason to approach the violator itself. If a government cuts back on aid to express concern, it may ask NGOs to channel government funds. In this way, it can reduce official relations while maintaining aid to those who need it most. It can use NGOs to channel funds to liberation groups.

Investments are usually private matters and thus fall within "transnational" society. However, since they do affect state-to-state relations, governments cannot ignore them in deciding what to do about human rights violations. It is inconsistent to condemn a government for its human rights performance and ignore financial and moral support that domestic corporations often extend to the offending régime. Faced with this contradiction, governments can contemplate options ranging from codes of conduct for investors, through encouragement of disinvestment, to prevention or discouragement of loans and new investments.

CONCLUSION

We have argued that Canada has an obligation to contribute to the international consolidation of basic rights as well as legitimate foreign policy concerns in regard to a far wider range of human rights. We have laid out the range of instruments (multilateral, bilateral, and transnational) available in pursuit of those obligations. This volume analyses Canada's human rights behaviour in five different international forums (chapters 4–8) and in bilateral diplomacy (9–13) – in two policy areas (9 and 10) and in three bilateral relationships (11–13).

As these studies will amply demonstrate, Canada has shown over the last decade or so a genuine interest in the promotion of human rights throughout the world. However, this interest has not been without limits. At home, Canada has had a fairly good record on human rights. And yet its achievements in this field are recent and limited primarily to political and civil rights. National sovereignty, legitimate competing objectives, and the concern for effectiveness are genuine enough constraints on Canada's foreign policy, though they are often conceded more force than necessary. Because these pressures form the limits within which Canada's human rights foreign policy is formulated, an attempt will be made in chapters 2–4 to identify these constraints and to assess their importance. We return to these issues in our conclusion.

PART ONE

Domestic Context

CHAPTER TWO

Human Rights in Domestic Politics and Policy

RONALD MANZER

A claim to a human right can be, and very often is, issued in the form of a political demand. It also can be advanced as the justification for a public policy. When advanced as political demands or incorporated in public policies, human rights are controversial in at least four ways. First, the existence of a right is not the only rational basis or convincing justification for making a political demand or deciding a public policy. In this role, majority preference, economic efficiency, average welfare, cultural enrichment, and national security may compete with rights, or complement them. Second, there may be conflict over which rights are recognized as legitimate and what each one means in principle and in practice. Third, there is the question of who is obligated by a right — which individual or group ought to assume the duties entailed by its existence. Fourth, there is the issue of what social institutions and practices can provide appropriate guarantees of rights.

Consideration of human rights in Canadian domestic politics and public policies must deal with each of these issues. The first two sections examine individual rights and collective rights, respectively, look at the ways in which they have been used as a basis for making political demands in Canada, and characterize the types of rights that have been claimed. The third section describes the extent to which human rights have been met by public policies in Canada and analyses the main approaches to guaranteeing them. The fourth section assesses their place in Canadian domestic politics and in public policy and considers the implications of this domestic experience for Canadian foreign policy.

INDIVIDUAL RIGHTS AS POLITICAL DEMANDS

At least three different doctrines or ideologies of individual rights can be found in Canadian political discourse. First, in the mainstream, individual rights have been claimed as traditional political and civil rights which individuals are assumed to enjoy and to which they are entitled as a heritage of the British constitutional tradition. Second, adopting the assumptions of the American Declaration of Independence or the French Declaration of the Rights of Man, political and civil rights have been held to belong to individuals as natural rights which are not abrogated in civil society but rather form the foundation and define the limits of the social contract. Third, in modern Canadian politics radical democrats and socialists have advocated a doctrine of human rights, based on a developmental theory of human needs, that makes a comprehensive claim not only to political and civil rights but also to economic, social and cultural rights.

Traditional Political and Civil Rights

The first political demands in Canada for the recognition and protection of individual rights were made by the British traders who moved into Quebec following the defeat of the French in 1760. In 1764 a petition from the British traders complained that "with Peace we trusted to enjoy the Blessing of British Liberty, and happily reap the fruits of our Industry." Rather than the open trade promised by the Royal Proclamation of 1763, the petitioners found "the Enacting Ordinances Vexatious, Oppressive, unconstitutional, injurious to civil Liberty and the Protestant Cause."[1] Two decades later, 501 British colonists signed a petition to the king to "relieve them from the Anarchy and Confusion, which at present prevail" because of the application of French civil law and "to Concur in establishing your affectionate Subjects of this Province, in the full Enjoyment, of their civil Rights as British Subjects; and in granting them a Free, Elective House of Assembly."[2]

The campaign for self-government was waged in Canada during the 1820s and 1830s. Arguments based on expediency and utility were as much, if not more, in evidence as arguments based on rights. When the claim of rights was made, however, it was phrased in terms of the established principles of the British constitution and the political rights of British subjects. In a letter to Lord Glenelg in July 1836, for example, the moderate reformer Robert Baldwin pressed for responsible government "not only as *expedient*, but *necessary* for the preservation of the Connexion between this Country and Upper Canada," but also argued that such a reform would ensure "that the People should feel that they had sufficient influence upon their Government to secure attention to their rights – and respect for their feelings and prejudices."[3] Similarly, Joseph Howe, writing to Lord John Russell in September 1839, prior to passage of the Act of Union, advanced elaborate arguments based on utility and necessity to support his defence of responsible government; but he also stated his belief that every colonist had the right to insist on the principles of the British constitution: "If then our right to inherit the Constitution be clear; if our capacity to maintain and enjoy it cannot be questioned; have we done anything to justify the alienation of our birthright? ... Am I not then justified, my Lord, in claiming for my countrymen that Constitution, which can be withheld from them by no plea but one unworthy of a British statesman – the tyrant's plea of power? I know that I am; and I feel also, that this is not the race that can be hoodwinked with sophistry, or made to submit to injustice without complaint. All suspicion of disloyalty we cast aside, as the product of ignorance or cupidity; we seek for nothing more than British subjects are entitled to; but we will be contented with nothing less."[4]

Ever since, in Canadian political discourse involving individual rights, it has usually been the doctrine of traditional British rights that is invoked. This tradition can be illustrated by the words of two great prime ministers. John A. Macdonald, winding up his speech in February 1865 on the Quebec resolutions to establish a federal union, emphasized the British heritage: "So long as that alliance is maintained, we enjoy, under her protection, the privileges of constitutional liberty according to the British system. We will enjoy here that which is the great test of constitutional freedom – we will have the rights of the minority respected."[5] Wilfrid Laurier, defending his political ideology and his party against attacks by the ultramontanist hierarchy of the Catholic church in Quebec, argued in 1877 that French-Canadian liberalism was not the anti-Catholic and anti-clerical liberalism of Europe but the tolerant political liberalism of Britain: "We are a free people; we are a minority, but we have retained all our rights and our privileges. Now, what is the cause to which we owe this liberty? It is the constitution that was won for us by our fathers and that we enjoy today ... We are a happy and a free people; and we are happy and free thanks to the liberal institutions that govern us, institutions which we owe to the exertions of our fathers and the wisdom of the mother country."[6]

Natural Political and Civil Rights

Under the British colonial régime, French-speaking Canadians could make no claim to a British heritage. Instead they appealed for protection of their language, religion, and customs as a matter of natural justice. Thus, against the claims of British traders in 1764, French colonists appealed to the natural justice of retaining French civil law and a French lower court: "How would Justice be administered if those who understand neither our Language nor our Customs should become our Judges, through the Medium of Interpreters ... Instead of the favoured Subjects of Your Majesty, we should become veritable Slaves."[7] In 1784 they opposed the English petition that a representative assembly "be indifferently composed of the ancient and new Subjects." "This article requires more explanation: for, from this word *indifferently* there might be as many and even more ancient than new Subjects in the House, which would be contrary to natural right, as there are twenty Canadians to one ancient Subject. What would become of our rights if they were entrusted to Strangers to our Laws?"[8]

The claim of natural right was simple and unspecific; there was none of the depth and eloquence of the Declaration of Independence or the Declaration of the Rights of Man. In the prelude to the 1837 rebellions, however, the radical reformers (in contrast to moderate reformers like Baldwin and Howe) turned to the American and French traditions of natural rights to back their political demands.

In William Lyon Mackenzie's draft constitution, published three weeks before the rebellions, the influence of the Declaration of Independence is evident. The preamble asserts that the people of Upper and Lower Canada have seen "our rights usurped" and protests ignored. Accordingly, "We, the people of the State of Upper Canada, acknowledging with gratitude the grace and beneficence of God, in permitting us to make choice of our form of government, and in order to establish justice, ensure domestic tranquility, provide for the common defence, promote the general welfare, and secure the blessings of civil and religious liberty to ourselves and our posterity, do establish this constitution."[9]

Undoubtedly the strongest language in the campaign for responsible government was used in the Six Counties Address adopted at a mass meeting at St. Charles in October 1837. Here the demand for responsible government was linked directly to "the wise and immortal framers" of the Declaration of Independence: "In common with the various nations of North and South America who have adopted the principles contained in that Declaration, we hold the same holy and self-evident doctrines: that GOD created no artificial distinctions between man and man, that government is but a mere human institution formed by those who are subject to its good or evil action, intended for the benefit of all who may consent to come, or remain under, its protection and control; and therefore, that its form may be changed whenever it ceases to accomplish the ends for which such government was established."[10]

The address and the draft constitution represent the high point in nineteenth-century Canadian politics of the justification of political demands by reference to individual political rights and civil liberties. It is impossible to know how much popular support such a view of natural rights had in 1837, but it seems to have been the work of a radical minority which was quickly defeated in the ensuing rebellions. The late-nineteenth- and early-twentieth- century campaigns of workers for the right to organize and of women for the right to vote invoked the traditional concept of British constitutional rights or the nascent concept of social rights.[11] Although the American approach of a written bill of rights would be revived after the Second World War, the American doctrine of natural rights as justification for political demands apparently died with the defeat of the rebels in 1837.[12]

Natural Economic and Social Rights

A doctrine of individual rights that involves claims to "social" or "economic and social" rights has been part of the left-wing tradition in Canadian politics but has been only weakly articulated and generally subordinate in political discourse to the mainstream liberal doctrine, which focuses on traditional political and civil rights.

For radicals in the workers' movement, the Winnipeg general strike of 1919 was equivalent in the campaign for economic democracy to the 1837 rebellions in the campaign for political democracy. Rejecting the policy of the Trades and Labour Congress to use collective bargaining rather than political action to remedy workers' grievances, the Winnipeg strikers' minimal demands showed a clear extension of political rights and civil liberties to include elementary economic rights: collective bargaining, a living wage, and the reinstatement of all strikers without prejudice. But the strike failed, and, with it, the radical One Big Union folded.

Claims for economic and social rights also found advocates in the 1910s and 1920s in the radical Christian wing of the social gospel movement, which based its political advocacy on "the two great Christian principles of democracy and brotherhood." Its leading intellectual exponent, Salem Bland, admired the evolution of the democratic principle in the British constitutional tradition but found it checked by capitalist control of industry. A new social order, a "labour Christianity," was needed; one of its essential principles would be "the right of every worker to a living wage." For Bland this social right was crucial: "This is nothing other than the assertion, in the only form that makes it more than iridescent froth, of the great Christian principle of the worth of the soul."[13]

In the midst of the Depression the ideals of trade union radicalism and the social gospel movement combined with the radical majoritarian democracy of the farmers' Progressive movement to form the philosophy of the Co-operative Commonwealth Federation (CCF). The Regina Manifesto, adopted at the CCF's second convention in July 1933, stated that the new party's goal was to replace a social order based on making profits with one founded on satisfying human needs. Its language explicitly expanded the doctrine of natural rights from political and civil to economic and social rights – not only freedom of speech and of assembly and equal treatment before the law irrespective of race, nationality, or religious or political beliefs but "security of tenure for the farmer upon his farm on conditions to be laid down by individual provinces" and a "National Labour Code to secure for the worker maximum income and leisure, insurance covering illness, accident, old age, and unemployment, freedom of association and effective participation in the management of his industry or profession."[14]

The Depression and the social idealism of the Second World War strengthened social liberal and social democratic politics in Canada and broadened the appeal for individual rights from political and civil rights to include an array of economic and social rights. In post-war Canadian politics claims to human rights have been both more comprehensively conceived and more commonly used to back political demands, reflecting two important changes. The language of human rights has become increasingly important in international discourse. The principles articulated by the Atlantic allies during the Second World War, the charter of the United Nations, and the Universal Declaration of Human Rights gave a new and enduring prominence to human rights as a legitimate political demand. And public policy has increasingly looked for models to the United States, where rights doctrines are prominent.[15]

Under these influences Canadian politics has seen the emergence of a human rights "political constituency," encompassing Parliament, public interest groups, and national parties.[16] For example, the Universal Declaration of Human Rights led directly to hearings by a joint committee of the Senate and House of Commons in 1947–8 and a Special Senate Committee in 1950 to study the protection of human rights and fundamental freedoms in Canada in the light of new international law. Prominent at these hearings were human rights organizations that had begun to form before the Second World War and were reorganized and strengthened after the war. They included the Association for Civil Liberties (now the Canadian Civil Liberties Association), which originated as separate groups in major cities during the late 1930s and early 1940s; at the end of the war these groups organized the national association, and reorganized in 1949, to make the Universal Declaration of Human Rights the basis of its advocacy. They also included the Canadian Jewish Congress and B'nai B'rith, both originating in the mid-1930s to counter discrimination against Jews, and the Jewish Labour Committee, created by Jewish trade union members to assist in settling war refugees. Other prominent public interest groups were the Canadian Bar As-

TABLE 2
References to Individual and Collective Rights in National Party Platforms, 1867–1968

Period	Individual Rights	Collective Rights	Total References by Period[*]
1867–91	2.2	2.2	4.5
1896–1917	1.5	2.2	3.7
1921–40	6.7	0.0	6.7
1945–53	24.6	3.7	28.4
1957–62	19.4	9.0	28.4
1963–8	20.1	8.2	28.4
Total references by type of rights[*]	74.6	25.4	100.0

Source: Owen D. Carrigan, *Canadian Party Platforms 1867–1968* (Urbana: University of Illinois Press 1968).

[*]Cell percentages may not add, horizontally and/or vertically, to the totals shown because of rounding.

sociation, which in 1943 established a section to study governmental encroachments on civil liberties and make annual reports to CBA meetings, and the Committee against Racial Intolerance, formed in 1944 by the Canadian Congress of Labour and the Trades and Labour Congress.

After 1945 there was a marked increase in recognition of individual (and collective) rights as principles of political commitment and as justifications for government action in national party platforms. As Table 2 shows, 85 per cent of the 134 references to individual and collective rights in national party platforms from 1867 to 1968 occurred after 1945. Left-wing parties, the CCF and the Labour Progressives, were responsible for two-thirds of the references to rights 1945–53 (see Table 3). Governing parties (Liberals, 1945–57; Conservatives 1957–63) seem less inclined than those in opposition to refer to rights in their platforms. By the early 1960s, however, at the outset of a two-decade debate on the place of individual and collective rights in the Canadian constitution – which began with the Canadian Bill of Rights in 1960, was given a decisive thrust forward in 1968 by the white paper on the Canadian Charter of Human Rights, and culminated in the Constitution Act, 1982 (see below) – doctrines of individual rights had become widely adopted as part of Canadian political discourse.

COLLECTIVE RIGHTS AS POLITICAL DEMANDS

Three types of claims for collective rights have dominated Canadian politics. First, claims for provincial rights have been justified by reference to Confederation as a compact or treaty among self-governing colonies of British North America. Second, claims for French-Canadian

TABLE 3
References to Individual and Collective Rights in National Party Platforms, 1867–1968

Period	Party*	Individual Rights†					Collective Rights			Total references by period
		Political	Civil	Economic	Social	Cultural	Provincial	French Canadian	Aboriginal	
1867–91	Conservative	0	0	0	0	0	0	0	0	0
	Liberal	2	1	0	0	0	3	0	0	6
1896–1917	Conservative	0	0	0	0	0	2	1	0	3
	Liberal	2	0	0	0	0	0	0	0	2
1921–40	Conservative	0	0	0	0	0	0	0	0	0
	Liberal	2	0	1	0	0	0	0	0	3
	Progressive	1	0	0	0	0	0	0	0	1
	Communist	0	0	2	0	0	0	0	0	2
	CCF	1	1	1	0	0	0	0	0	3
1945–53	Conservative	2	2	4	1	0	0	0	0	9
	Liberal	0	0	0	1	0	1	0	0	2
	Communist	5	2	3	1	0	1	0	1	13
	CCF	4	3	2	1	2	1	0	0	13
	Social Credit	0	0	1	0	0	0	0	0	1
1957–62	Conservative	1	0	0	0	0	1	1	0	3
	Liberal	2	1	3	2	0	0	1	0	9
	Communist	2	0	0	0	0	2	2	2	9
	CCF/NDP	4	3	3	2	2	2	2	1	17
	Social Credit	0	0	0	0	0	0	0	0	0
1963–8	Conservative	2	2	0	0	1	1	1	0	7
	Liberal	3	1	1	0	0	1	1	0	7
	Communist	3	0	3	0	0	0	2	2	11
	NDP	0	1	2	0	0	0	1	1	5
	Social Credit	2	2	3	0	0	1	0	0	8
Total references by type of right		38	21	29	7	5	14	12	8	134

Source: See Table 2.
* The Communist party was the Labour Progressive party in elections of 1945 to 1958. The CCF became the New Democratic Party (NDP) in elections from 1962 onward.
† Individual rights have been classified as political, civil, economic, social or cultural following the model of the International Covenant on Civil and Political Rights and the International Covenant on Economic, Social and Cultural Rights.

cultural rights have been justified by reference to Confederation as a "racial" compact between two founding peoples, French and English, designed to protect equally their existence and development as separate cultural groups. Third, claims for aboriginal rights have been made by Indian and Inuit peoples who occupied Canada before the French and English colonizations and who still maintain separate collective identities.

Provincial Rights

The British North America Act, 1867, essentially endowed the dominion government with the tutelary powers formerly exercised by the imperial government, including powers to reserve and to disallow provincial legislation. Provincial rights were advanced initially by the government of Ontario and later by that of Quebec to justify the claim for provincial responsible government, that is, the right to exercise fully the legislative and administrative powers of their constitutional jurisdiction without being subject to review by the federal government.

Undoubtedly the leading provincial politician in the campaign for provincial autonomy was Oliver Mowat, and the controversy raged over a wide range of dominion-provincial relations while he was premier of Ontario from 1872 to 1896. In the latter stages of the dispute, Mowat's position was strengthened by the election of a Liberal government in Quebec led by Honoré Mercier. Mercier was the proponent of a doctrine developed by Judge T.J.J. Loranger, that held that Confederation was a compact entered into by the provinces and that their rights to exercise legislative powers derived from that strictly limited agreement.

Western claims for provincial rights focused on demands for local autonomy and provincial status up to 1905, when Alberta and Saskatchewan were created. There followed a politics of agrarian protest which attacked the power of "special interests" such as monopolistic banks and railways and demanded democratic political and economic reform. Some critics were prepared to go further, however, including E.A. Partridge, a long-time activist in the grain growers' association: "In the case of the Prairie Provinces there has been the most bare-faced robbery of their provincial rights in the matter of their lands, including resources of timber, minerals, fishing waters, and sources of natural power, which were filched from them by the Dominion in its character of Trustee of these for the already conceived but still unborn sisters of the family, the older members of which were in full enjoyment of their own natural heritage."[17] Partridge concluded that western Canada should secede from Confederation.

After the First World War the Maritime provinces were faced with drastic changes in federal transportation policy and indifference to their demands for changes in federal subsidies. A Maritime rights movement arose, and the legalistic and patronizing response of Arthur Meighen's government only increased the intensity of demands. Typical was an editorial in the *Halifax Herald* in July 1922 which held out the model of western Progressive MPs: "We want to say that it is time for the people of the Maritime Provinces to put shoulder to shoulder and fight for their rights and cease not until those right(s) are acquired. We have the lesson of the Western Members of Parliament who stand like a rock and compelled the government to DELIVER THE GOODS."[18]

A royal commission on Maritime rights chaired by Sir Andrew Rae Duncan was appointed in 1926. It rejected any claim of Maritime rights but recognized that grievances did exist and recommended a revision of provincial subsidies based on some criterion of fiscal need.[19] The commission's definition of the problem prevailed, and claims to federal subsidies based on provincial rights were abandoned in favour of demands based on evidence of comparative fiscal need and revenue capacity.

Claims of provincial rights did not disappear. Stronger federal leadership in the development of a welfare state and managed economy quickly evoked provincial opposition. In the 1940s and 1950s Maurice Duplessis argued that a balanced distribution of powers was a vital safeguard of Canadian democracy: "Autonomy is desirable for all Provinces and particularly for the Province of Quebec which forms a minority within the Canadian State ... It claims not only respect for its own rights but absolute sovereignty for the rights of other Provinces as well."[20] Similarly, western governments have claimed provincial rights in order to prevent what they perceive as exploitation to serve the interests of central Canadian manufacturers, workers, and consumers. "This retreat behind the ramparts of provincial rights parallels a similar move in Quebec in the later nineteenth century and was undertaken for the same basic reason. Western Canadians in the last years have felt themselves surrounded by a generally unsympathetic and occasionally actively hostile Canadian majority. One way to thwart the national majority was to turn to means of limiting that majority by dividing its jurisdiction into its provincial components."[21]

French-Canadian Rights

The claim of French-Canadian rights based on Confederation as a "racial" compact received its initial expression in Henri Bourassa's critique of the Laurier government's language policies. Speaking in the House of Commons debates on the Alberta and Saskatchewan acts in 1905, Bourassa argued that the fathers of Confederation had made a compact between "the two great groups of the Canadian nation." In particular, "in establishing the Dominion Parliament, they did so on a basis in harmony with the rights and traditions of the two elements which make up the Canadian nation; and that is why they provided that the French and English tongues would be, on equal terms, the official language of Canada."[22] That collective cultural right led to insertion of section 23 protecting language rights, in the Manitoba Act, 1870, and was, Bourassa argued, essential for Alberta and Saskatchewan.

The doctrine of French-Canadian rights was given a more extended and mature articulation in the nationalist philosophy of Canon Lionel Groulx in the 1930s. Groulx believed that French-Canadian nationality could be adequately protected only in a French state. If Confederation impeded the achievement of a French state, its commitments should be abandoned. "No political institution has the right to prevent a group of human beings from obtaining its own good. No province, no nationality is obliged to accept being governed against itself."[23]

In the flowering of Quebec nationalism during the Quiet Revolution of the 1960s, the concept of French cultural sovereignty protected by a strong, growing Quebec state became a widely accepted assumption of Quebec political life; claims for a collective "right to live" were correspondingly strengthened. A correspondent to *Cité libre* in 1960 wrote: "There is a people here demanding to live, to live in peace with the world, and it *has the right* to do so. Since when does a nation not have the right to live as one?"[24] Similarly, when René Lévesque split with the Quebec Liberal party in 1967 and founded the separatist Parti québécois he explained his belief in a sovereign Quebec in terms of the right of a "collective personality" to cultural security and liberty. "For our own good, we must dare to seize for ourselves complete liberty in Quebec, the right to all the essential components of independence, i.e., the complete mastery of every last area of basic collective decision-making. This means that Quebec must become sovereign as soon as possible."[25]

Aboriginal Rights

In considering aboriginal rights as a basis for political demands, attention inevitably falls first on the claims made by the Métis of Manitoba and the Northwest Territories from 1869 to 1885. Their territory was on the verge of entering Confederation as the province of Manitoba, and fears of the Métis and Indians for the protection of their traditional rights in occupation and use of the land reached a critical point. Inspired by the leadership of Louis Riel, the Red River insurrection at first attempted to unite all elements in the territory in presenting their demands to the Canadian government. A convention of Métis, Indians, and settlers, both French-speaking and English-speaking, adopted a bill of rights; but when the English-speaking delegates proved reluctant to present it to the Canadian government, Riel disgustedly told them to go back to their farms: "Mais regardez-nous agir. Nous allons travailler et obtenir la guarantie de nos droits et des vôtres."[26]

As a result of the insurrection of 1869–70, the Manitoba Act did recognize the existence of aboriginal title and provided for its extinguishment by land grants to the Métis. Administration of the land grants was consistently incompetent and often corrupt, however; and the pressure of European settlement continued to mount. In 1884 another Settlers' Union bill of rights was drawn up and forwarded to Ottawa. In March 1885 John A. Macdonald, in the House of Commons, denied knowledge of a bill of rights. Riel, called back from exile, proclaimed a provisional government which was quickly ended by a dominion military expedition, and Riel was hanged for treason.

From the 1830s to the 1960s British and then Canadian aboriginal policies were based on the assumption of a gradual transition of Indians and Inuit from "primitive society" to "civilization" and assimilation. A hundred years after Riel's first insurrection, the Trudeau government's 1969 white paper on Indian policy rejected gradualism in favour of rapid integration. The white paper was fiercely attacked by native groups, and the government was forced to develop a new policy toward land claims based on acknowledgment of collective aboriginal identities and interests and settlement of both comprehensive and specific claims by direct negotiation with aboriginal claimants.

One important result of the campaign of native groups against the white paper, as well as subsequent negotiations over land claims, has been a clear statement of the doctrine of aboriginal rights. Declarations of aboriginal rights have showed a strong consensus on the rights of native peoples to occupy and use the land and to preserve and enhance their cultural heritage. They have also agreed that the political rights of self-determination and self-government are indispensable conditions for land and cultural rights. Thus, the statement of rights passed by a joint assembly of the Indian Brotherhood and the Métis Association of the Northwest Territories in July 1975 insisted on the Dene people's "right to be regarded by ourselves and the world as a nation … What we seek then is independence and self-determination and shall continue – in the tradition of Louis Riel – to express this right as equal partners in Confederation" and also "that we are a people with a right to a special status in Confederation." The declaration issued by the Assembly of First Nations in 1980 grounded aboriginal rights in natural law: "We the original Peoples of this Land know the Creator put us here ... The Laws of the Creator defined our rights and responsibilities." Among those rights, "the Creator has given us the right to govern ourselves and the right to self-determination."[27]

HUMAN RIGHTS AS PUBLIC POLICY

To the extent that state authorities seek to protect human rights, public policies will reflect which rights are recognized as legitimate grounds requiring action by state authorities and what form their social guarantee should take. In Canada, political discourse on public policies has not in general been marked by references to the principle of human rights. However, in practice human rights have been recognized and guaranteed in three main forms of public policy: judicial protection of rights in the common law; legislative protection of rights in public statutes; and entrenchment of rights in the constitution.

Common Law

One way to understand the role of the common law as the social guarantee of individual rights in Canada is by reference to Sir William Blackstone's classic *Commentaries on the Laws of England*, published in four volumes from 1765 to 1769, just about the time the common law was coming into force in Canada.[28] After reviewing the rights incorporated in Magna Carta, the Petition of Right, the Habeas Corpus Act, the Bill of Rights, and the Act of Settlement, Blackstone concluded that the rights of the people of England "may be reduced to three principal or primary articles: the right of personal security, the right of personal liberty, and the right of private property: because as there is no known method of compulsion, or of abridging man's natural free will, but by an infringement or diminution of one or other of these important rights, the preservation of these, inviolate, may justly be said to include the preservation of our civil immunities in their largest and most extensive sense."[29]

The protection of individual rights of personal security and personal liberty has been an enduring legacy of the common law tradition. Prominent among the ancient principles or rules of the common law are the tradition of an independent neutral judiciary; recognition of the state in cases of public crimes as simply a plaintiff suing the defendant, with the burden of proof resting on the plaintiff and the defendant presumed innocent until guilt is proved; the right to a speedy trial; the institution of the jury; and the strict monopoly of judges over interpretation of the law. Sir Frederick Pollock summarized the significance of these ancient procedural rules: "These are the principles of which we find the rudiments in the earliest justice of our ancestors; which were maintained and developed through all political vicissitudes in English history, and crossed the Atlantic with the institutions and traditions of the mother country; and which still distinguish the administration of law in every quarter of the world and every jurisdiction where the Common Law has taken root."[30]

Common law protection of the right of private property has been more problematical. At the beginning of the nineteenth century the common law was not particularly well suited to a rapid and inexpensive development of industrial capitalism.[31] Pre-industrial doctrines of property law, nuisance, and riparian rights, for example, permitted small landholders to enjoin and exact damages from new industries that interfered with traditional rights. Between about 1775 and 1850, however, judicial decisions in England and the United States changed the substance of the common law to facilitate economic development.[32] Similarly, in Canada, by the mid-nineteenth century the common law had substantially settled on values of individual initiative and individual responsibility. The law was intended to facilitate and encourage private initiative in economic activities, based on the assumption that each individual should have responsibility for his or her own fate.[33]

Economic growth and immigration in the late nineteenth and early twentieth centuries transformed Canada into an urban, industrial, pluralistic society in which many people encountered new threats to their basic needs for subsistence, security, and dignity. The common law tradition not only proved unable to alleviate these threats but became a major instrument used by the entrepreneurial and capitalist class to block reform. As the justice of the common law came increasingly into question statutory remedies were sought and gradually conceded.

To give one example, the common law doctrine prohibiting conspiracies in restraint of trade was used to impede the organization of trade unions. In the most important case, twenty-four union members were convicted and jailed during a printers' strike in 1872. The Macdonald government passed the Trade Union Act and amended the criminal law so as to provide limited protection from conspiracy charges for members of trade unions registered under the act, but from the 1870s to the 1940s workers seeking to strengthen their bargaining position worked for removal of restrictions placed by the common law (and criminal statutes) on their rights to organize unions and to express their grievances by peaceful picketing.

As another example, in the second half of the nineteenth century a person injured at work had only a very small chance of receiving adequate compensation. Under the fellow-servant rule of the common law, employers were generally liable for the negligence of their workers but not for their workers' negligence that caused injury to fellow workers. R.C.B. Risk's study of workers' compensation in Ontario has shown that from the 1860s to the 1880s, prior to the enactment of limited protective legislation, workers' civil suits for compensation failed in almost all cases. Following enactment of the first provincial protective legislation, in particular the Workmen's Compensation Act, 1886, which modified the common law on employers' liability, workers' claims were successful in more than half the cases; but the amounts recovered were usually not sufficient to replace income, and only a tiny portion of injured workers brought actions.[34] The Ontario Workmen's Compensation Act, 1914, established compulsory public insurance while ending workers' right to bring civil suits against employers.

Racial discrimination provides a third example of the failure of judicial protection under the common law. After the First World War a number of attempts were made to invoke the common law against discriminatory private conduct in public places.[35] In *Loew's Montreal Theatres Limited* v. *Reynolds* in 1919 the plaintiff sued for damages, contending that the defendant had refused to sell him an orchestra seat because of his colour; the Supreme Court held that "the management has the right to assign particular seats to different races and classes of men and women as it sees fit." In *Franklin* v. *Evans* (1924) an action against a London restaurant keeper who refused to serve a black man was dismissed, and in *Rogers* v. *Clarence Hotel Co Ltd* (1940) the BC court of appeal ruled that a beer parlour operator was within his rights in refusing to serve a black man. By 1940 it was clear that the common law tradition would not be invoked against racial discrimination. As Ian Hunter has concluded: "The judiciary had not lacked opportunities to advance equality but had preferred to advance commerce; judgements had adumbrated a code of mercantile privilege rather than a code of human rights."[36] After the Second World War public policy turned to fair employment and fair accommodation laws and then codes of human rights in order to create protection against racial discrimination.

Statutory Protections

In Canada the major statutory protections of individual rights were created during two periods of legislative reform. First, the original core of civil liberties embedded in the common law was decisively expanded from approximately the 1830s to the 1870s. Basic political rights to self-determination and popular government were achieved, criminal policy and administration were reformed from arbitrary procedures and cruel punishments to more impartial and proportionate justice, and universal provision was made for elementary schooling. Second, the trauma of the Depression and the Second World War unblocked reform and opened the way for creating, to the 1970s, significant statutory protections for a wide range of social rights. The rights to organize trade unions and to bargain collectively were at last fully recognized in legislation; rights to food, shelter, health, and social security found expression in extensive programs of social assistance and public insurance; educational reform and development were premissed on the principles of equal opportunity and individual self-actualization; and policies intended to nurture Canadian cultural development and equalize individual access to cultural institutions and activities emerged from the invisible margin of Canadian politics to become a major subject of public policy-making at all levels of government.[37]

A concept of human rights is seen most clearly in the development of anti-discrimination laws and human rights codes after the Second World War. The first statute was Ontario's Racial Discrimination Act, 1944, which made it an offence to publish or display signs, symbols, or other representations expressing racial or religious discrimination. The much more ambitious Saskatchewan Bill of Rights, 1947, protected traditional political rights and civil liberties and recognized specific egalitarian rights to engage in any occupation or business, buy or sell property, join a trade union or other occupational association, and obtain an education without discrimination because of race, creed, religion, colour, or ethnic national origin. Provincial and federal legislation in the 1950s prohibited discrimination in employment, trade union membership, and public accommodation. Because enforcement in the courts proved difficult, these statutes generally opted for investigation by a public official and appointment of conciliation boards to settle complaints, with prosecution undertaken as a last resort. In 1962 the Ontario Human Rights Code consolidated and extended previous categorical legislation on fair employment practices, fair accommodation practices, and equal pay; and the Ontario Human Rights Commission was given responsibility not only for enforcing the code but also for promoting equality through public information, educational programs, and research. Subsequently, all other provinces and, finally in 1977, the federal government set up similar human rights codes and commissions.

Statutory protection of human rights was the declared purpose of anti-discrimination legislation and human rights codes, but rights of social security, dignity, and opportunity for self-development also have found social guarantees in legislation for economic stability, social welfare, criminal justice, educational access and cultural development. Canada's reports on implementation of the International Covenant on Civil and Political Rights and on articles 6–9 and 10–12 of the International Covenant on Economic, Social and Cultural Rights reveal the extensive and complex range of provincial and federal statutory protections of human rights.[38]

What is uncertain, particularly in economic, social and cultural legislation, is whether politicians, administrators, and other citizens perceive these statutes as public responses to the existence of rights or think of them as guaranteeing recognized rights. In some legislation a concept of rights has been articulated; but the primary justification for legislation appears to be not statutory protection of rights but functional necessity, community welfare, collective responsibility, or even majority preferences. These criteria, for example, provided the philosophical basis in 1940 for the Royal Commission on Dominion-Provincial Relations (Rowell-Sirois) to advocate expanded state intervention, and they do not seem to have changed much since then. On state medicine and public health, the commission recognized the primitive condition of public policy and administration in 1867:

But the economic and social changes of the past seventy years ... have made necessary state activities and state expenditures on health matters to an extent undreamed of by the Fathers. The mobility of modern society due to the speed and ease of travel; the growth of urban and metropolitan communities; the interdependence for food and water supplies between widely separated geographical areas; the occupational diseases and physical hazards of high-speed, industrialized production; the loss in self-sufficiency of the family incident to the trend toward a wage-earning society; these and many other social changes have compelled governments at all levels to be concerned with the health of their citizens. It may be confidently predicted that the health activities of governments are indeed only beginning, and that expenditures in this field are likely to increase rapidly in Canada.[39]

The brief of the Canadian Teachers' Federation advanced the right to education as a justification for federal aid; the commission rejected it as denying "the right of each province to decide the relative importance of expenditure on education and expenditure on other competing services." The commission preferred to equalize the financial position of the provinces; and after that "it seems to us best that education, like every other form of welfare service in a democratic community, should have to fight for its life, and that a generous provision for the education of the children of the nation should depend, not on any arbitrary constitutional provision, but on the persistent conviction of the mass of the people that they must be ready to deny themselves some of the good things of life in order to deal fairly with their children."[40]

Constitutional Guarantees

In Canada the British tradition of common and statute law dominated protection of individual rights in the nineteenth and early twentieth centuries. The British North America (BNA) Act, 1867, guaranteed the right of self-determination and gave limited protection to the political, civil, and educational rights of linguistic and religious minority groups; but it gave no specific protection to universal individual rights in the manner of the first ten amendments to the American constitution (the Bill of Rights). As concern about protection of human rights intensified in Canada after 1945, however, proposals for constitutional guarantees won growing support. This trend culminated in 1982 with entrenchment of fundamental political, civil, egalitarian, and language rights in the Canadian Charter of Rights and Freedoms.

Three federal codes attempted to define basic rights: the Canadian Bill of Rights, 1960, for which John Diefenbaker desired constitutional entrenchment but lacked provincial support; the Canadian Charter of Human Rights, proposed in a 1958 federal white paper, amended by dropping sections on anti-discrimination rights and eventually nullified by Quebec; and the Canadian Charter of Rights and Freedoms, which became part of the constitution with approval of the Canada Act by the British Parliament and proclamation in April 1982 by the Queen.[41] The three codes differ considerably in detail but reveal a consensus on guarantees of rights.

First, all three documents guarantee freedom of conscience and religion; freedom of thought, belief, opinion and speech; and freedom of the press, assembly, and association. Following federal-provincial negotiation the charter approved at the 1971 Victoria conference also covered democratic rights of citizens to vote, popular election of the House of Commons at least once every five years, and annual sessions of Parliament; and these democratic rights were also included in the Charter of Rights and Freedoms.

Second, all three codes protect the civil liberties found in Magna Carta, the Petition of Right, the Bill of Rights, and the American Bill of Rights: rights to life, liberty, and security of the person and protection against unreasonable search and seizure, arbitrary detention or punishment, and cruel or unusual punishment. Specific guarantees include the right to be informed promptly of the reasons for arrest, to retain and instruct counsel, to habeas corpus, to protection against self-incrimination, to be presumed innocent until proved guilty, to bail on reasonable conditions, to trial by an independent and impartial tribunal, and to an interpreter.

Third, on discrimination, the Canadian Bill of Rights merely recognized the existence of basic political and legal rights "without discrimination by reason of race, national origin, colour, religion or sex." The 1968 white paper went much further, following provincial codes in prohibiting discrimination because of race, national or ethnic origin, colour, religion, and sex with respect to employment, membership in occupational and professional associations, education, property rental and ownership, contracting with public agencies, use of public accommodation and services, and eligibility to vote and hold public office; but these provisions were not approved at the Victoria conference. Finally, section 15(1) of the Canadian Charter of Rights and Freedoms states: "Every individual is equal before and under the law and has the right to the equal protection and equal benefit of the law without discrimination and, in particular, without discrimination based on race, national or ethnic origin, colour, religion, sex, age or mental or physical disability."

Constitutional protection of minority language rights was a major objective of both the white paper and the Charter. The Charter declares English and French to be official languages of Canada, and it extends section 133 of the BNA Act to include the New Brunswick legislature and courts but not, as the Trudeau government had hoped, the Ontario legislature and courts. Section 20, which entitles any Canadian to communicate with federal agencies in English or French, and section 23, which sets out minority language educational rights, both appear to involve collective rights: individual entitlement exists in general only where there is a "significant demand" or "the number of citizens who have such a right is sufficient to warrant the provision to them."

Four other statements of rights in the Charter should be mentioned. First, by section 6, every Canadian has the right to enter, remain in, and leave Canada, to move and take up residence in any province, and to seek a livelihood in any province. These mobility rights are similar to the rights in article 13 of the Universal Declaration of Human Rights and article 12 of the International Covenant on Civil and Political Rights. Second, aboriginal rights are recognized in section 25, but those rights are in no way specified, let alone protected. The negotiation of aboriginal claims and the entrenchment of aboriginal rights in the Charter remain the most important unfinished business of the constitutional negotiations. Third, in specific recognition of the rights of women, section 28 provides that "notwithstanding anything in this Charter, the rights and freedoms referred to in it are guaranteed equally to male and female persons." Fourth, section 27 provides that "this Charter shall be interpreted in a manner consistent with the preservation and enhancement of the multicultural heritage of Canada."

RIGHTS, POLITICS, AND FOREIGN POLICY

According to C.B. Macpherson, any doctrine of human rights must be in some sense a doctrine of natural rights. "Human rights can only be asserted as a species of natural rights, in the sense that they must be deduced from the nature (i.e., the needs and capacities) of men as such, whether of men as they now are or of men as they are thought capable of becoming. To say this, is simply to recognize that neither legal rights nor customary rights are a sufficient basis for human rights."[42] If Macpherson is correct, then at least until very recently the mainstream of Canadian politics has lacked a true doctrine of human rights.

Political discourse in Canada has not been oriented by a doctrine of human rights. In making political demands or justifying public policies, Canadians have more often adopted a utilitarian or a collective welfare argument, advancing economic necessity, national prosperity, majority preference, charitable obligations, social welfare, and national unity. Nonetheless, the concept of rights has had a significant place both as justification for political demands and as rationale for public policies.

Human Rights in Politics

Canadian political discourse is dominated by a concept of political and civil rights derived from the British constitutional tradition. Both "ancient" and "new" subjects have claimed their rights as British subjects, and even as they have moved to entrench these rights, Canadians have not abandoned this concept for one based on natural rights.

A radical Christian and social democratic tradition served to broaden British doctrine to include social rights but since the 1930s has been used inconsistently in making political demands and rarely cited explicitly as a warrant for public policies. Political and legal justice often have been guaranteed in Canada, but economic and social justice are more often seen as collective goods to be provided rather than individual rights to be protected.

A separation between constitutional guarantees and statutory protections in Canada corresponds almost exactly to the International Covenant on Civil and Political Rights and the International Covenant on Economic, Social, and Cultural Rights, respectively. Although common law and statutory protections determine many details of individual rights, the Charter guarantees civil and political rights. In contrast, economic, social, and cultural rights depend on statutory protection.

Political controversies in Canada have concerned collective more often than individual rights. Since the 1840s, demands for collective provincial, French-Canadian, and aboriginal rights have marked critical junctures. While claims of individual rights undoubtedly will become more visible, collective rights have continued to dominate the political controversies of the 1970s and 1980s.

Human Rights and Foreign Policy

Given the place of human rights in Canadian politics and public policies, what are the implications for Canadian foreign policy? Any response must be highly speculative.

First, there is a rising concern for human rights. Human rights are generally accorded low salience and little influence in making Canadian foreign policy, but from the Second World War, and especially since the mid-1970s, references to enhancement of human rights as a goal and as a justification for particular actions have increased. This shift is consistent with post-war experience in domestic politics and policy. To the extent that the Charter reorients domestic politics and policy-making, it cannot help but affect both élite and popular expectations about Canadian foreign policy.

Second, Canada now has at home a comparatively good and improving record on human rights. It appears to be in a position to advocate human rights in its foreign policy without fear of being seriously embarrassed by its domestic policies. However, the fairly recent achievement of this condition should be a reminder of the need for modesty in pressing human rights abroad.

Third, the collective rights of self-determination and self-government have had a special place in Canadian history. In international politics, the claims of subnational groups intrude continually as moral issues and occasionally quite abruptly as threats to peace. The Canadian record here is not unblemished, but Canada could construct from its long and generally useful experience a foreign policy stressing the legitimacy of subnational groups and the protection of their rights. Of course, Canada may be charged with meddling in the domestic affairs of other countries, and other countries may do the same in Canadian affairs. Advocacy of subnational groups abroad has been constrained by concern about the implications for the claims of subnational groups in Canada, particularly by French Canadians in Quebec. The open and vigorous debate over Quebec's sovereignty has revealed greater tolerance and maturity, however, and strengthened any Canadian claim to have its experience considered and its counsel taken seriously.

Fourth, one problem with high visibility and great potential for embarrassment is the unresolved issue of aboriginal rights. Probably the federal government and certainly several provinces are not yet prepared to recognize as a basis for policy the rights of aboriginal self-determination and self-government. Until this timid approach is remedied, the credibility of a foreign policy based on rights is vulnerable.

Fifth, human rights have a powerful legitimacy because of their roots in the traditional rights of the British constitutional heritage; but the Canadian concept of human rights has been restricted as a result, giving primacy to political and civil rights at the expense of social rights. The same limited understanding led the US government to press for the splitting of the Universal Declaration of Human Rights into separate covenants on political and civil and on economic, social, and cultural rights. Such a bifurcation in Canadian doctrine probably makes it difficult to develop a foreign policy that would give proper priority to basic rights of subsistence and security; and it also could undermine Canada's advocacy of human rights in countries that reject such a split. However, the Canadian political tradition does include the minor but historically significant movement based on social democracy and radical Christianity. It has been primarily supported by the political left, but all parties have contributed at one time or another. Foreign policy-makers might draw on it in order to legitimize the advocacy of social rights.

Sixth, the relationship of domestic to international politics is not one way; they interact. Canadian domestic human rights policies have been strongly shaped by memories of a world war against fascist dictatorships that systematically violated individual and collective rights, by the doctrines of human rights advocated as the foundation of the Atlantic alliance and the United Nations, and by the growing realization that – as in the wartime internment of Japanese Canadians – the Canadian government could violate accepted international standards of human rights. They also have been affected by Canada's transformation into a multicultural, pluralistic society, reflecting both the humanitarian opening to refugees and the termination of racial discrimination in immigration. Standards of human rights developed in international organizations have been adopted by Canadian legislation. For example, the rights of labour set by the International Labour Organization were pressed at home by Canadian trade unions and eventually recognized in federal and provincial legislation. Similarly, the Universal Declaration of Human Rights and the covenants spurred constitutional entrenchment of rights in Canada. Even the struggle of Third World countries for political and economic independence, one of today's primary expressions of claims to basic rights, resonated in Canada where an analogy has been asserted to back claims for both French-Canadian and aboriginal rights.

To conclude, despite the limitations of the mainstream doctrine of individual rights, politics and public policies in Canada provide a favourable and generally improving context for making human rights a more important factor in Canadian foreign policy. Moreover, if the historical record is any guide, a greater concern for human rights in making foreign policy will also enhance human rights in Canadian politics and public policies.

CHAPTER THREE

Cabin'd, Cribb'd, Confin'd?: Canada's Interests in Human Rights

KIM RICHARD NOSSAL

In his discussion of fate and will in foreign policy, James Eayrs noted that those charged with the conduct of statecraft tend to bemoan the milieu in which they are forced to operate. The typical foreign policy-maker, Eayrs wrote, "dwells gloomily upon drawbacks and difficulties" and laments "how hard it is to be a foreign minister, how narrow is his room to manoeuvre, how few his options are, how manifold the constraints, and oh! how heavy. He no longer depicts himself bestriding the narrow world; he depicts himself cabin'd, cribb'd, confin'd, bound in."[1] The Canadian government's position on human rights provides an interesting example of such a mentality at work. For that is how policy-makers have tended to characterize the constraints and impediments to an active policy to secure the protection of human rights by other states.

This chapter explores Canada's interests in human rights policy. The first section surveys the government's own public perceptions of the impediments to, and the opportunities for, an active human rights policy. I then explore the degree to which other external objectives – strategic, diplomatic, and economic – constrain Canadian activism in human rights. The second section looks at a number of limiting factors, including strategic and commercial interests and Ottawa's continuing attachment to the doctrine of state sovereignty. The third section considers the effect of the politics of international coalitions. A brief conclusion follows.

GOVERNMENT PERCEPTIONS

Since human rights achieved greater prominence on foreign policy agendas in the 1970s, Canadian governments have frequently been criticized for passivity and lack of forcefulness in protecting rights in other countries. The trenchant criticisms of Sheldon Gordon are indicative. "The prevailing pattern," he wrote in 1983, "from the Prime Minister on down, has been one of timidity and often appalling indifference." He criticized the Department of External Affairs for its "lacklustre approach," and for being even "less attentive" to human rights than ministers. He also took the government to task for refusing to use Canadian bilateral and multilateral development assistance to further human rights.[2] Gordon's view is not isolated: allegations of rights violations in Chile, El Salvador, Guatemala, Indonesia, Kampuchea, Poland, South Africa, Sri Lanka, Uganda, the Soviet Union, and Vietnam have brought the same critical refrain: the Canadian government could always do more to protect rights.[3]

In response to such criticism, the government's public explanations of its positions have featured a number of common themes. Canadian ministers and bureaucrats have avoided an ultra-realist conception of international politics, which in its most extreme and brutal form denies morality any part in the craft of state and therefore rejects a legitimate role for human rights considerations in the formulation of foreign policy.[4] On the contrary, in their public statements, political leaders and departmental officials stress that they are shocked and disturbed by evidence of human rights violations by other governments; that they believe that such behaviour is morally wrong; and that Canada, in its foreign policy, is obligated to involve itself in the issue. On numerous occasions since the Liberal government of Pierre Elliott Trudeau committed Ottawa to a "positive and vigorous" approach to human rights in its 1970 white paper,[5] senior policy-makers have echoed the sentiments of Don Jamieson, secretary of state for external affairs in 1977: "Canada will continue to uphold internationally the course of human rights, in the legitimate hope that we can eventually ameliorate the conditions of our fellow man."[6] This rhetorical commitment has been embraced by both major parties: the Progressive Conservative governments of both Joe Clark (1979–80) and Brian Mulroney (from 1984) shared this view.[7] Thus, there appears a great deal of desire for active involvement in human rights: the government casts itself as genuinely committed to human rights objectives, broadly construed.

The government's potential effectiveness in human rights, however, is rarely cast in anything but gloomy terms. Four themes emerge from public statements by political leaders and senior officials at External Affairs over the last decade.[8] First, the words used to describe the issue of human rights suggest thorniness: "complex," "difficult," or "complicated." Second, the international environment poses great difficulties for rights activists. The absence of universally agreed definitions of human rights, of a supranational judicial process, and of enforcement apparatus is said to represent "less than favourable" conditions. Third, Canada tends to be characterized as weak, vulnerable, unable by itself to affect other states or to alleviate human rights abuses. Too few states are dependent on Canada to enable Ottawa to use power to achieve its objectives; only influence can be used, and only when the bilateral relationship is close can influence achieve ends. Finally, human rights is one of a number of often contending interests and objectives. For these reasons, therefore, words like "intractable," "tangled," and "arduous" are summoned to describe the problems Canadian foreign policy-makers face in achieving human rights objectives. There are no easy answers or simple solutions, only dilemmas with horns on which to be squarely caught, and "the difficulties," as Allan MacEachen, secretary of state for external affairs, put it in 1983, "of promoting human rights effectively in a tougher, more hostile world."

With such perceived difficulties, admonitions about being "careful," "prudent," "pragmatic," and "realistic" flow naturally. Certainly Canadian policy-makers feel a need to avoid "ineffective," "inappropriate," or "self-indulgent," initiatives. A premium is placed on effectiveness: "If we take unilateral action," Jamieson asked rhetorically in 1977, "and it accomplishes nothing, what have we gained?"

In short, the government sees few possibilities for human rights activism.[9] While it projects concern for how states treat their citizens, it tends to be so pessimistic about success that it is often hesitant to take even modest measures.

ECONOMIC AND STRATEGIC INTERESTS

How can we best understand what Margaret Doxey has called the "rhetoric gap" in Canadian human rights policy[10] – that distance between expression of concern and actual government behaviour? Why has Ottawa, for all its rhetorical commitment, consistently refused to use all the available tools of statecraft? This chapter seeks to examine the factors that influence Canadian decision-makers on human rights. The argument is developed deductively, drawing not only on what policy-makers have said (and not said) but also on case studies. It will be argued that the Canadian government's interest in human rights is considerably diluted by other interests.

Commercial Interests

It is commonly argued that the commercial objectives pursued by national governments constrain and diminish their willingness to embrace an active human rights policy. As Matthews and Pratt have noted, using economic tools of statecraft to coerce offending governments into observing basic rights usually harms the economic interests of the state employing them. In Canada's case, how do interests created by economic intercourse with other states affect its human rights policies? It seems to fashion human rights policies with an eye firmly fixed on commercial interests.[11] In an examination of Canadian policy toward South Africa, Uganda, Argentina, Chile, and South Korea, Keenleyside and Taylor found general reluctance to engage in economic sanctions against violators "with which Canada has substantial and growing commercial relations."[12] Fear of damage to the Canadian economy apparently limits the government's willingness to use economic coercion.

The web of economic linkages between Canada and violators may affect human rights policy, since interruption in trade, investment, or development assistance affects some individual Canadians, and thus the Canadian economy writ large. But the economic argument is not as compelling as it may at first seem. Although based on rational notions of maximized self-interest, it makes little sense from a rational perspective, for it includes no assessment of the magnitude of the economic costs to Canada of measures used by Ottawa to further human rights.

The structure of the economy, and the direction of trade, make it unlikely that Ottawa would rationally regard the interruption in economic intercourse with violators as a serious impediment to action if other interests warranted it. External trade accounts for nearly 30 per cent of Canada's gross national product. But Canada trades almost exclusively with other capitalist states – which are unlikely to violate human rights grossly and persistently or to be targets of Canadian sanctions. Trade with these states accounts for nearly 95 per cent of all external trade. As a result, Canada's economic links with any single state in the east or the south that violates human rights (indeed, even with all such violators combined) represent a tiny percentage of overall external trade, and thus an even tinier percentage of GNP. In commercial or economic terms, sanctions against a state in the Second or Third worlds would represent minuscule "damage" to the Canadian economy.

Decision-makers in Ottawa are unlikely to be constrained by these commercial links alone in fashioning human rights policies. While economic links undoubtedly contribute to the mix of policy motives, concern for Canada's economic well-being probably does not play the cardinal role so commonly assumed in limiting government human rights policy. Other, more potent, factors must also be considered.

Interests in Sovereignty

How does the issue of national sovereignty affect Canadian decision-makers in human rights policy? Since the end of the Second World War Canadian policy-makers have tended to accept the normative idea that states ought not to be able to claim that human rights fall within "domestic jurisdiction." Soon after the war, the Canadian government was faced with a dilemma on domestic jurisdiction. John Holmes, a senior Canadian diplomat during this period, put it this way: "The Charter forbade interference in matters of domestic jurisdiction, and there was a strong argument for maintaining that principle. It provided a framework for the weak and, if not preserved, the UN could be swamped in irreconcilable conflict. On the other hand, the obligation to promote self-government and human rights was hamstrung if the provision was too literally interpreted." "The paradox," asserts Holmes, not uncharacteristically, "had to be lived with." Lived with, to be sure, but also resolved in practice, leading to what Holmes has termed "a cautious and conservative attitude" on the interpretation of article 2(7),[13] which outlines obligations on domestic jurisdiction.

Thus, for example, in 1955, the Canadian representative at the United Nations argued that because apartheid violated principles of the charter, it was "a matter of deep concern to member states." As a result, Canada had not argued "against the Assembly's right to discuss it."

It has become apparent, however, that some delegations are disposed to press the matter far beyond mere discussion. Action has been proposed which seems to us to undermine another basic principle of the Charter, that is, the sovereign equality of all the members of the United Nations. We have in mind the decision supported by a majority of members to establish the United Nations Commission on the Racial Situation in the Union of South Africa ...

From its inception we have doubted the wisdom of the procedure. Aware that the Government of South Africa was not disposed to cooperate with the Commission, we viewed its establishment ... as bordering on the kind of intervention which the Charter prohibits.[14]

The statement demonstrates Ottawa's uneasiness about tinkering with an accepted cornerstone of international order. Such concerns lingered into the 1960s. For example, in 1968, responding to criticism of Ottawa's refusal to stop dealing only with the federal government in Lagos during the Nigerian civil war, Mitchell Sharp, secretary of state for external affairs, stressed that the ideal of sovereignty was essential to Canadian thinking:

Canada's whole policy towards African and other newly emerging countries in recent years has been built on a spirit of co-operation rather than intervention. African history is ripe with examples of domination and intervention by peoples from other continents, and Africans are rightly sensitive about their hard-won sovereignty and their right to manage their own affairs.

Canada has earned a good name in Africa ... Why do we have a good reputation? Because we observe these principles of co-operation and non-intervention ... We have been welcome because our policy has been to assist Africans and not to tell them how to run their affairs.[15]

Even when human rights were propelled into sharper relief in the 1970s, Canadian rhetoric still reflected the concerns of sovereignty. In 1977, Don Jamieson, secretary of state for external affairs, stressed that "although Canada's approach to international human rights reflects our traditions, the ethics and moral codes of a Western Christian society, our approach is *only one of many* , and, I should add, *not* an approach that enjoys majority support internationally." He added: "There are no firm and fixed rules for raising and discussing what are essentially the domestic concerns of other states."[16]

A year later, however, the Canadian position had changed considerably. While still acknowledging little universal agreement on human rights, Jamieson claimed: "The Charter of the United Nations establishes as one of its key purposes the promotion and encouragement of respect for human rights ... In adhering to the Charter, Canada and all other member states have incurred obligations to support that objective. No country can contend with any justification that its performance is a purely domestic matter in which the international community has no right to intercede."[17] Likewise, Yvon Beaulne, Canada's representative to the UN Commission on Human Rights, declared in 1980: "It is not possible to maintain seriously today, as certain jurists have done in a less enlightened age, that the manner in which a state treats its citizens concerns it alone."[18] Mark MacGuigan and Allan MacEachen, Liberal secretaries of state for external affairs in the early 1980s, and Joe Clark, Conservative foreign minister, expressed similar views.

The shift in interpretation can be attributed to a number of developments. First, the increased interest in human rights in the United States, stemming from the events that led to the Helsinki Final Act and the Carter administration's more vigorous policies on human rights, affected the Canadian government. Second, the change coincided with Canada's term on the UN Security Council. That body was invoking chapter VII enforcement measures against South Africa, and Canada did not want its rhetoric on human rights and domestic jurisdiction to conflict with the justifications being offered for UN measures. Third, particularly gross and persistent violations were receiving considerable global attention: apartheid in South Africa, genocide in Kampuchea, and the brutality of the Amin régime in Uganda.

The change in view represented a distancing from Canadian governments of the 1950s on the legitimacy of human rights as an international concern. The effects of this shift should not, however, be magnified, for policy – and policy-makers – remain committed to state sovereignty.

One indicator of such a commitment is how Canada deals with governments accused of violating rights. There, the imperatives of diplomacy combine with sensitivity about the sovereign ideal to dampen human rights activism. Thus, for example, when Pierre Trudeau visited the Soviet Union in 1971, he did not raise human rights issues though widely urged to do so; indeed, he couched the reasons for his reticence in the language of national sovereignty.[19] Likewise, at a press conference during his January 1983 trip to Southeast Asia, he was asked whether he was going to raise human rights concerns with his hosts. "I don't visit other countries with the intention of telling them how they should run their own affairs," he was quoted as responding. "I don't have the authority to do so." Sheldon Gordon notes that the prime minister added that he had no intention of "trying to right any wrongs ... no more than I would like visitors to Canada to tell us how we should have dealt with the FLQ crisis."[20] When the presidents of Pakistan, South Korea, and Equatorial Guinea visited Canada in 1982, "Mr. Trudeau was," in Gordon's words, "tight-lipped, publicly and privately, about their oppressive rule."[21] Indeed, numerous other opportunities to urge oppressive governments to stop violating rights were not taken.

There is also general resistance to measures that would break down the assumptions underlying the sovereign ideal. Most obviously, the Canadian government has refused to consider legislating the behaviour of Canadians in other jurisdictions for human rights purposes. For example, the Canadian code of conduct for firms operating in South Africa, introduced in 1978, was a strictly voluntary measure; when the Conservative government moved in 1985 to "tighten" operation of the code, notably by appointing an administrator, it did not make adherence mandatory. Quite clearly, making it illegal to perform an act in another jurisdiction where such an act was legal would be to embrace something long anathema to Canadian policy-makers of all persuasions – extraterritoriality. On this the government will not be moved, for to do so would be to give up the ability to rebuff attempts at the extraterritorial application of US law to the many transnational corporations operating in Canada.

To be sure, the Canadian government's attachment to the doctrine of state sovereignty is not absolute. It tends to be selective and heavily influenced by parochial definitions of Canadian interest. Thus, for example, policy-makers have not shown the same interest in sovereignty as it affects some states. In particular, Canada has for a decade supported the policies of the World Bank and the International Monetary Fund which make financing to less developed countries conditional on changes in domestic fiscal policy.[22]

While Canada's position on sovereignty has not been entirely consistent, and while the interpretation of domestic jurisdiction in human rights has shifted since the late 1970s, Ottawa's continuing commitment to state sovereignty inhibits forceful action on human rights.

Strategic Interests

Case studies of Canada's relations with human rights violators suggest that Ottawa's policies are motivated by conceptions of Canada's "strategic" interests.[23] These are both direct (essential to Canada's economic or military security) and indirect (essential to the security interests of states to which Canadian policy contributes). Thus, for example, it is not uncommon to attribute Canada's policy toward South Africa to indirect strategic interests. The macro-strategic arguments of both structural Marxists and strategic analysts stress Canada's tendency to act in concert with other Western states because Ottawa shares conceptions of a "Western interest" developed in Washington or in other capitals of "leading" members of the alliance.

Structural Marxists argue that the Canadian government has a coincident interest with governments of other capitalist states in the maintenance of the capitalist system. This means participation in a broad coalition of capitalist states that have an interest in doing nothing that will precipitate collapse of the capitalist system in South Africa. The strategic studies approach has different assumptions: East-West rivalry and (assuming that white South Africa is on "our" side) the importance of denying the Soviet Union political hegemony in southern Africa and control over South Africa's strategic minerals, sea lanes, or ship repair facilities.[24] In both broad perspectives, which share some common analytical ground, the Canadian government is seen as bound and constrained by its perceptions of a threatening international environment.

Do Canadian policy-makers subordinate concerns about rights violations because of such strategic concerns? There would appear to be a relationship between the strategic importance of a state and Canada's propensity to pursue an activist policy on human rights. In the major cases of violations in the last decade, where "strategic concerns" have largely been absent, as in Uganda, Kampuchea, or Sri Lanka, Ottawa has taken a stiff stand against violations; where clearly identifiable strategic interests exist, it tended to play down violations. Canada's "considerable ambivalence" on South Africa,[25] or its relatively muted expressions of concern about Indonesia's political prisoners and its invasion of East Timor,[26] or its quiet diplomacy on human rights violations in

Central America, or its indifference to violations in Iran in the 1970s can be linked to the strategic importance of the states involved.

But the "interests" generated by such strategic importance are not Canada's directly. More commonly, they are defined by other states. The Canadian government may wish to be sensitive to the strategic and economic concerns of other governments in shaping its approach to human rights, but that is not the same as saying that Canada's human rights policies are motivated by strategic and economic interests. To understand the link between the strategic and economic interests of other states and Canadian policy, we must go beyond the editors' formulation and examine the dynamics of international coalitions and the interests that arise from membership.

INTERNATIONAL COALITIONS

I have argued that Canada's attachment to the idea of national sovereignty constrains Canadian advocacy of human rights. Commercial interests appear to dampen activism, but not as much as foreign policy and strategic interests. To understand how strategic and economic interests affect Canada's human rights policies, we must examine Canada's membership in a variety of international coalitions. Ottawa tends to define tactics on rights violations so as to maximize its abiding interests in coalition membership.

Canada belongs to, and interacts in, a number of coalitions. These groupings of states involve cross-cutting and overlapping memberships. One is a formal military alliance: the North Atlantic Treaty Organization (NATO). Another is the "economic" coalition of democratic capitalist states; its members meet in the Organization for Economic Co-operation and Development (OECD), in the "Summit Seven" and its financial subgroup, G-7, and on the boards of development banks. Yet another is the Commonwealth – a loose association of states of both North and South. There are also temporary coalitions of "like-minded" states created in particular forums, as during the law of the sea conferences or the Conference on Security and Cooperation in Europe, or on particular issues, as a "like-minded" coalition of Nordic and Antipodean states on the South African issue. Finally, there is a dominant and pervasive economic, military, and diplomatic relationship with the United States,[27] though it is not a coalition, properly speaking. It is hypothesized here that Ottawa's human rights policies are affected by membership in these various coalitions.

The dynamic is integral to any political coalition, whether of states, legislators, or members of an academic department. It has two strands. First, a junior, less powerful member has an interest in subordinating "real," or true, policy preferences and in moulding behaviour to fit within parameters set by dominant members of the coalition. Second, a junior member also has a broad interest in maintaining the coalition, and its behaviour may sometimes be impelled by concern for the coalition's survival.

Leaders of coalitions tend to have conceptions of interest that they wish pursued or maintained, conceptions that they typically impose, by transference, on the group. Junior members are not obligated to identify with, or share, these conceptions but are forced to work within the boundaries, or parameters, established by the leaders if they wish to remain members in good standing. Junior members who differ on an issue may try to alter, by private discussion, the leaders' definition of the group's interest. If such attempts fail, however, they must weigh the importance of taking action that will more properly reflect their definition of interest but will conflict with the leaders'. Independent action on an issue important to the leaders may be costly.

First, leaders will be concerned that independent action will undermine their own policies and objectives. Second, breaking ranks may precipitate or facilitate a bandwagon effect among like-minded members; leaders are likely to act against a recalcitrant member to demonstrate the substantial costs attached to defection. For example, European and US actions against Canada in the late 1960s and American actions against New Zealand in the mid-1980s appear to have been motivated by such a concern. Third, leaders view public expression of disunity with discomfort; dissent undermines their self-perceptions of, and claims to, effective leadership. Finally, defection on an issue important to the leader will likely have spillover effects. Not only will the leader regard the defector as untrustworthy, thus affecting the latter's influence, but dealings on other issues will probably be affected. Clearly, membership in a coalition will powerfully constrain independent initiatives by junior members.[28]

But the dynamic should not be cast simply in subordinate-superordinate terms, where the interest for the junior member is limited to deterring retaliation. It also gives rise to interests in the coalition per se. A member, by virtue of membership, has an abiding interest in maintenance of the coalition. When the coalition is threatened, a junior member may act on its behalf, even through policies that diverge from the leaders' preferences.

It is difficult to demonstrate such dynamics in Canada's human rights policy. The degree to which the solidarity of Canada's coalitions affects human rights policy is not discussed publicly. Indeed, in the government's explanations of its human rights policies, in particular cases and in general, intra-coalition considerations are not mentioned.

An argument about the dynamics of coalitions can be made only by inference and set against competing explanations. Consider Canadian policy toward South Africa. When viewed through the prism of coalition dynamics, it reveals both vertical and horizontal dimensions at work. For years, the Canadian government remained indifferent to the use of bilateral sanctions against South Africa to promote rights there. It preferred to declare abhorrence and embrace a multilateral approach; if and when the international community moved on apartheid, Canada would join. Then, in 1977, following the Soweto uprising and the death of Steve Biko, Pierre Trudeau's government adopted economic measures against South Africa. These were, however, never fully or carefully implemented. The Conservative government of Brian Mulroney adopted new sanctions in July and September 1985, and additional measures in June and August 1986, despite opposition from the United States, Britain, and West Germany.

It can be argued that until June 1986 the Canadian government, in its South African policy, was responding to the interests and initiatives of leaders of a number of coalitions to which Canada belonged. Neither the United States, with its strategic stake in the status quo with the "devil it knew," nor Britain, with a comparable economic stake, had any interest in seeing, much less taking, precipitous action. The Canadian government had no direct stake of consequence in South Africa and thus had little interest in conflict with Washington (bilaterally or multilaterally) or London (multilaterally, in the Commonwealth or NATO) by stepping outside the parameters established by the coalition leaders on this issue.

As a result, Canadian sanctions against South Africa, from the UN measure of the early 1960s to the wide-ranging moves of the mid-1980s, mirror almost exactly the actions taken by the leaders, particularly the United States. The initiatives of December 1977 were introduced in anticipation of strong measures by the Carter administration. And when President Reagan embraced "constructive engagement," Canada's interest in pursing an active policy quietly waned. With the 1985 sanctions, Canada was in even closer step with American policy. While Mulroney's rhetorical flourishes against apartheid were stronger and more pronounced than those of his Liberal predecessors, Ottawa's policy moves followed Washington: the punitive measures of July and September were announced days after the United States announced its own.

But by mid-1986 Canadian policy was far outreaching British and American policy.[29] Why? Canada's interest in not moving too far ahead of Washington was eclipsed by a more urgent, and important, interest – maintaining the Commonwealth. The continued refusal of Margaret's Thatcher's government to adopt economic sanctions against South Africa was leading African and Asian members to speak of withdrawal from the Commonwealth. Canada's measures of June and August 1986, and its leadership on this issue at the Commonwealth Heads of Government Meeting in Vancouver in October 1987, were probably motivated by a desire to prod London into sufficient action to avert the threat to the Commonwealth.

Similar arguments could account for Canada's human rights policies toward other violators. Uganda or Kampuchea were cases where Ottawa had a great deal of latitude to shape policy, because senior members of the Western alliance – or members of the Commonwealth – had no clear interests, economic or strategic. Likewise, it has had a relatively free hand to fashion policy on Soviet violations. By contrast, with violations by Western-leaning states in Southeast Asia, or by governments in Central or South America, it has been much more tightly constrained. The United States has clear strategic and economic interests and a very narrow definition of what divergence it will tolerate without invoking costs against defectors. Sensitivity to the strategic interests of the coalition leader promotes indifference to violations by some governments. While Ottawa may privately be concerned about violations in Saudi Arabia, Indonesia, or China, a sustained diplomatic effort to promote human rights in those countries would be very costly, given US definitions of its interests there.

Finally, there are cases where Canada will be active, in an effort to moderate the position of the coalition leader. Its efforts in 1986 on South Africa have been mentioned; likewise, the analysis in chapter 13, below, suggests that Canadian policy on the Polish crisis of 1981 was motivated by a comparable desire for moderation.

CONCLUSIONS

This chapter has argued that we can understand how and why the Canadian government's policies on human rights have fallen short of what the government's rhetoric would lead us to expect. Although policy-makers have an interest in human rights, their perceptions of Canadian interests create significant, self-imposed constraints on policy alternatives. These perceptions dampen enthusiasm for activism and greatly reduce the government's interest in grasping the nettle.

An interest in national sovereignty strongly influences human rights policies. The government does not regard the doctrine as immutable: we have seen its willingness, at least rhetorically, to modify slightly its view of domestic jurisdiction and human rights. Likewise, it has embraced chapter VII enforcement measures against South Africa. But Ottawa continues to embrace the ideal, diminishing its willingness to adopt policies that would diminish the doctrine. Sovereignty remains for Canada, as for other states, a self-confining obstacle to meaningful action on human rights.

But even if that obstacle were removed, Canada's membership in a number of coalitions, and the dynamics of coalitions, would limit interest in, and scope for, independent and forceful policies. The argument is tentative and inductive, but it is proffered as a complement to factors outlined in chapter 15. It does not deny the existence of other motives in the policy mix; rather, it suggests that the factors outlined by Matthews and Pratt are, by themselves, incomplete and do not fully explain why the Canadian government is so little interested in an active human rights policy using the range of tools available.

CHAPTER FOUR

Human Rights and Foreign Policy–Making

VICTORIA BERRY and
ALLAN MC CHESNEY

HUMAN RIGHTS IN THE 1970S

Canada's external relations are based on largely unchallenged presuppositions that determine the day-to-day parameters of decision-making at virtually all levels. These priorities include further growth as a trade-dependent capitalist country; membership in various Western military, political, and economic alliances; successful management of the relationship with the United States. These assumptions allow Canada, as two observers have said, "only limited manoeuvrability, with opportunities for change more at the margin than at the core of foreign policy decision making."[1] An awareness of limitations on action may help Canadians to manage responses to world development in specific areas and to reconsider the primacy of these assumptions.

The three presuppositions are reflected in policies and administrative structures. They form an operating environment and perspective so deeply ingrained in training, procedures, and evaluation processes that other possible objectives receive little serious, sustained attention. This environment clearly constrains the consideration of human rights.

For over two decades the Canadian public has expressed rising interest in the place of human rights in foreign policy. Senior cabinet members, most notably a number of secretaries of state for external affairs, have supported a significant role for human rights in foreign policy. Yet in the foreign policy apparatus there is minimal understanding of the role that human rights could play in formulating and conditioning Canada's international relations.

This chapter will describe how the foreign policy process deals with human rights and seek to show that despite the slight change in "atmosphere" – encouraging verbal support for human rights – in practice, human rights considerations are largely isolated and marginal in policy-making and in the day-to-day minutiae of implementation. In the absence of a policy framework incorporating human rights as a major element, the role of human rights will be ad hoc, sporadic, and highly dependent on individual policy-makers and bureaucrats.

Chapters 2, 6, and 7 confirm our own findings that until the 1970s human rights were unimportant at the national and international levels. During that decade a number of factors heightened the profile of human rights on foreign policy agendas. Every jurisdiction in Canada passed anti-discrimination statutes.[2] Individual Canadian parliamentarians sought to link development aid to human rights in 1977-8.[3] Canada became a party to the UN convention on racial discrimination and international covenants on economic, social, and cultural rights and civil and political rights, and federal-provincial discussions preceded their adoption. The Congress and President Carter took initiatives on external human rights policy. The Conference on Security and Co-operation in Europe led to the Helsinki Final Act of 1975. And there was a perceived need to respond to human rights crises in communist states and in other countries with gross and persistent violations.

The ministerial conference of December 1975 that led to Canada's accession to the international covenants also established a federal-provincial committee to maintain liaison on domestic and international human rights issues.[4] At that time, the Department of the Secretary of State took the lead role. However, as human rights became increasingly important internationally, External Affairs gradually took over human rights in foreign policy, leaving Secretary of State to monitor domestic implementation of international conventions and to organize federal-provincial consultation.

Canada's accession to every major human rights instrument, as well as its support for related UN "decades" (e.g. "to combat racism") and ad hoc groups studying particular issues (e.g. "disappearances"), also contributed to the public formation and expression of policy. With uneven but increasing frequency, from the mid-1970s officials have had to prepare speeches for ministers commemorating anniversaries of international human rights initiatives. Ministerial addresses became standard at annual events of such organizations as the International Commission of Jurists and the Canadian Human Rights Foundation.

Each January, in Ottawa, External Affairs organizes a two-day "consultation" (open forum) with non-governmental organizations. These sessions precede the principal meetings of the UN Commission on Human Rights. For these consultations, as well as the occasions mentioned above, External Affairs staff must review policy and prepare a text for senior officials and ministers to approve and perhaps build on. This mundane process has helped maintain, shape, promote, and occasionally subtly enhance human rights principles in Canadian foreign policy.

Speeches by external affairs secretaries provide important insight into government thinking on human rights in foreign policy. Over the past decade there has been a relatively consistent pattern in both approach and content. Several overall goals were presented: widespread ratification of existing international instruments, expansion of protections,[5] and improvement of means to promote and protect rights through better publicity and more effective international mechanisms. Speeches also refer to the need for "effectiveness," "realism," and "flexibility of approach." The ministerial statements stress that actions must be appropriate, and Canada cannot be involved to the same degree in each problem.[6] Canadian policy must "remain rooted in a certain realism," whether the real world of international politics, of Canadian-US relations, or of Canada's interests as a trading nation. "Flexibility" may permit wide scope for discretionary action, but veteran civil servants prefer to see it as ensuring that the circumstances of each case are duly weighed.

On occasion, ministerial statements suggested that human rights would receive higher status. In 1983 Allan MacEachen spoke of "its place as one of the main principles of Canadian foreign policy." In 1984 Minister for External Relations Jean-Luc Pepin stated "it has been the government's objective to integrate human rights into our whole system of relationships, to let the preoccupation permeate the entire structure." However, MacEachen added a hedge concerning "realism," and Pepin appears to have been rationalizing disbandment of the department's only human rights office.[7] Neither promised to give human rights increased importance in policy-making; nor did this occur.

Earlier speeches tended to suppose that civil and political rights were a Western concept; it was understandable if the Third World placed economic needs ahead of (other) rights, "attaching a greater priority to the duties of citizens than to their rights." Canada's international approach reflected its own traditions, but it was "only one of many," and "there were no firm rules" for raising "essentially the domestic concerns of other states."[8] Later speeches argued that all human rights were "indivisible" and some were not to be "sacrificed in favour of others."[9]

Ministers' speeches often stressed that Canada's human rights stance must be credible in the international arena. Canada must commit money and resources "if disparities are to be eliminated and if all forms of human rights are to be protected." Canada's domestic human rights record, capped by the Charter of Rights and Freedoms, gave it "a credible voice ... in the international community."[10]

Human rights have clearly entered the rhetoric of Canada's external affairs secretaries. Until the Hockin-Simard and Winegard reports and the government responses of the latter 1980s, these speeches were virtually the only comprehensive sources of government policy available.

THE FOREIGN POLICY PROCESS

Decision-making in Canadian foreign policy operates on the assumption that international relations should be left to officials: they will do what is best, quietly and behind closed doors, in support of "national security" and the "national interest." The involvement of minister, prime minister, and cabinet is shrouded in secrecy. Decision-making processes themselves change constantly to reflect the priorities of elected officials and civil servants.

In general, foreign policy–making in Canada is reactive, short-term, ad hoc, and diffuse. As a small state in a big world, Canada cannot attempt to plan foreign policy rationally: as a result, Nossal believes that "both ministers and their civil servants are left to concentrate on the day-to-day problems of Canadian diplomacy–"policy" at its lowest level."[11] Broad or lofty principles have a rough time working their way through the bureaucracy to or from the minister. The minister depends on the department's information and organizational wisdom; bureaucrats weigh the many steps in implementing a particular idea against a wide range of competing ideas and departmental activities.[12]

Where and how is Canadian foreign policy developed and administered? The central and most visible institution is the Department of External Affairs, which over the years has increasingly co-ordinated the many facets of foreign policy. The department has enjoyed an illustrious place in Canada's short history. In the post-war years, particularly prior to the 1960s, its members emerged as respected statesmen: their knowledge and skill raised Canada's profile in international affairs much beyond that warranted by its status. In this era, when diplomacy and largely political inter-state relations were prominent, the department was at its zenith. During the last two decades, however, the department has been challenged by growing awareness of economic interdependence – Canada has to sell its wares in world markets. In 1982, in response to a period of "crunching integration" in the world economy, the department absorbed the international functions of Industry, Trade and Commerce, thereby gaining major responsibility for overseas trade facilitation and promotion. "It was treated as a matter of national survival that the department's capacity in economics should be substantially increased." Integration of trade promotion into the department has affected Canada's international relations, particularly in human rights. Ambitious people entering the department look to trade and international economic relations, where the "real work" is being done. Many officials have gone to the trade side, "to the exclusion of other perspectives, and External's old forte, political analysis, appears to have lost much of its following."[13]

Since 1983 the department has increased its emphasis on regional organization. Each region of the world is covered by a branch, headed by an assistant deputy minister. Most branches are divided into bureaux, each with at least three operating divisions – trade development, political relations, and programs.

While External Affairs is the principal player, other departments and agencies have independent responsibilities which they jealously guard. Although interdepartmental committees no longer operate, departments consult regularly at various levels on major issues. Amalgamation and rationalization over the last decade have left Finance, National Defence, and Agriculture, the Canadian International Development Agency (CIDA), and the Bank of Canada as the other major actors; Justice and certain crown corporations perform supportive functions not discussed in this chapter. Finance plays second fiddle in foreign relations. National Defence is the lead department in Canada's various military alliances and security agreements. Agriculture maintains a significant international division which concentrates on trade in and transfer of Canadian foodstuffs and agricultural technologies and expertise. CIDA is of considerable interest to an aid-conscious Canadian public but falls under the external affairs secretary (and his or her junior minister).

As "custodian of at least some, if not all, of the Canadian government's highest priority goals," Finance can deploy "an enormous range of policy instruments and a vast amount of expertise;" it enjoys a "large measure of both *de facto* and *de jure* autonomy. Ministers and officials from other departments simply cannot challenge Finance in a number of areas in which that department possesses virtually all the available knowledge." Responsibility for the budget provides Finance with a "[unique] instrument for understanding major initiatives."[14] Finance assigns Canada's representatives to the World Bank and the International Monetary Fund.

Foreign policy guide-lines are formulated and mediated by three bodies: the Prime Minister's Office (PMO), the Privy Council Office (PCO), and the cabinet. The PMO's role varies with a prime minister's interest in and understanding of foreign affairs and the expertise he establishes in the PMO and the PCO. Because of ideological tensions within any ruling party, a prime minister ought to "establish an overarching policy framework or philosophic vision into which foreign policy can fit and from which its ministerial custodian can draw sustenance."[15] A prime minister's world view can determine the approach and political resources dedicated to a particular issue. An example would be Brian Mulroney's attention to the Commonwealth. The PCO acts as cabinet secretariat. It oversees government policies and looks out for issues likely to require cabinet guidance. It is central in long-term policy development, assessing policy trade-offs, tactics, and effects.[16]

The cabinet is at the core of the policy process. There ministers engage in trade-offs or forge a consensus from conflicting departmental policies and programs. Generally, foreign policy is dealt with in the Cabinet Committee on Foreign and Defence Policy. The committee meets twice monthly, with the external affairs secretary in the chair and the minister of national defence as vice-chair; External Affairs does most of the preparatory work. Important issues arising from meetings are referred to the key cabinet committee on Priorities and Planning and, if necessary, to the full cabinet.

Finally, although outside the decision-making process per se, members of Parliament (MPs) may influence foreign policy. They can call officials and ministers before House committees, raising issues and eliciting information otherwise bound up in departmental or governmental secrecy. Further, a question in the House to a minister, or a direct inquiry to an official, may set in motion a series of steps by which the government will attempt to clarify publicly its position and to quieten public unease. Within committees, MPs and senators review foreign policy questions, sometimes creating political pressure that may lead to policy changes. However, because these reviews are peripheral to the daily mechanics of foreign policy-making, ministers and, by extension, External Affairs often regard this work as unimportant.

The Conservative government and the present external affairs secretary, Joe Clark, have nonetheless sought to open the foreign policy process to greater parliamentary and public input. Following the 1985 release of a green paper, *Competitiveness and Security: Directions for Canada's International Relations,* a Special Joint Committee of the House of Commons and the Senate conducted extensive hearings across the country on Canada's international relations and released its report in 1986, hoping to set major new directions for Canadian foreign policy.

We maintain that the mechanisms for analysis, policy-making, and implementation of human rights policy in Canada's international relations are inadequate – particularly in light of the government's claim that human rights influence foreign policy because of Canadians' interest and concern. There are two main reasons for this inadequacy: the priority given to well-established objectives such as national security, economic development, and international peace, and the inherent difficulties in making new criteria operational at the departmental level.

Our discussion continues with an examination of the roles of External Affairs and of its minister, the principal actors (along with the prime minister) in foreign policy. We next describe the place of human rights in daily operations at External Affairs. We then look at how the Canadian public acts through non-governmental organizations and the media and at how MPs occasionally highlight human rights issues in foreign policy; we also review briefly the highest levels of governmental decision-making (PMO, PCO, and cabinet).

HUMAN RIGHTS AT EXTERNAL AFFAIRS

In the Department

What profile and importance are given to human rights within External Affairs? How are relevant issues handled within and between its various divisions and levels? Are they treated as an established and integral part of Canadian foreign policy?

Numerous off-the-record conversations with officials show that "human rights" are vaguely defined within the department. Most interviewees affirmed departmental sensitivity to human rights in foreign policy. Yet despite apparent general concern, only perfunctory effort is undertaken. The officials who prepared the government's 1985 foreign policy paper felt that there was no debate over the importance of human rights in foreign policy and gave the subject little space and consideration in a document intended to raise questions in contentious areas. It is possible that general support for human rights principles made the subject "non-contentious," but it is more likely that the lack of attention reflected insufficient interest within the department.

A generally accepted but loosely defined consensus cannot ensure that human rights are considered in foreign policy. Where human rights are vaguely defined, with everyone somehow responsible, too often no one will accept responsibility for them. Without administrative mechanisms to ensure consistent consideration they may be ignored in the face of competing political pressures. Good will is not enough in a department responsible primarily for international trade and security.

Consideration of human rights thus depends on the awareness, analysis, power, and commitment of individuals in the department. Yet most officials lacked formal expertise in human rights, and were uninterested in mechanisms to ensure proper treatment of the subject. There was no formal training in human rights for recruits prior to late 1986, and most officials are preoccupied with economic and security matters. Moreover, the External Affairs tradition of rotational appointments works against continuity of personnel in human rights, and demonstrated expertise does not lead to posts related to the area.

Officials interviewed spoke again and again of the need for "effectiveness" in implementation of foreign policies dealing with rights. They believed that considerations of human rights were likely to hamper unduly the normal give-and-take of diplomacy. They feared self-defeating posturing and wanted flexibility in responding to an ever-changing world. This attitude reflects an inadequate and undeveloped understanding of what might be involved in giving fuller consideration to human rights. Many officials tended to see human rights as "all or nothing" – whether or not to curtail political or economic relations. They had apparently not considered the many alternatives explored and developed over the last decade by practically minded non-governmental organizations and academics.

The Canadian government could develop practical ways of monitoring rights internationally and of judging the effect of Canadian policies in a wide range of situations. Analytical and administrative frameworks are needed. Without them, embassy reporting on abuses will often be haphazard, subject to the inclinations of the reporting office and of marginal significance.

Departmental officials cited five sources of information on human rights: departmental officials, Canadian missions overseas, non-governmental organizations (NGOs), the media, and foreign representatives. Each has shortcomings.

(1) *Departmental officials.* Given the dearth of training and expertise in human rights and its low value in terms of resources and career opportunities, it would be unclear whom and what to ask and what reliance to place on information received.

(2) *Canadian missions overseas.* It is hard to assess human rights information sent from overseas posts. The quality of information and analysis missions supply may be limited; few officials have received training on information gathering. Comprehensive human rights courses commenced only in 1987, and there are no defined categories of violations on which to report. In general, officials are expected to keep track of and report on "the overall human condition" of a given country. This is a far cry from the detailed definitions and fact-finding techniques employed by UN agencies and well-respected NGOs like Amnesty International.

(3) *Non-governmental organizations.* NGOs supply more and more human rights data and intelligence to the department. Most officials we talked to had an informal idea of which NGOs gave reliable information, although any such data would be thoroughly vetted against other sources.

(4) *The media.* They appear the most effective means of securing a hearing within the department. A front-page article in, for example, the

Globe and Mail or *Le Devoir* will likely lead to at least one question by an MP during question period, obliging even the most reticent minister and his/her department to examine and defend the government's position on an issue.

(5) *Foreign representatives.* Officials interviewed said that information is often obtained from representatives of other countries. Such information may be important, especially given Canada's close, congenial, and "like-minded" relations with US representatives in international settings. A report in the *Ottawa Citizen* on 1 June 1985 shows that American information can take precedence over that from other sources. On resumption of Canadian aid to El Salvador, External Affairs officials made it clear that their political bosses accepted the Reagan administration's viewpoint on the improvement of human rights in that country, despite ample evidence to the contrary from Canadian and international NGOs.

Analytically and procedurally the treatment of rights is highly compartmentalized within External Affairs. In spite of organizational refinements resulting from the meshing of trade and foreign policy, human rights is treated separately. A classic example occurs in a March 1981 letter from Prime Minister Trudeau. The Rev. Clark Raymond had asked why a government delegation to a conference on trade with Latin America did not query massive abuses by certain South American trading partners. Trudeau responded that, although rights are an important element of foreign policy, the conference did not address the whole range of Canadian relations with Latin America, since it was designed to explore commercial possibilities.[17] Clearly the government believed that overseas trade (even if facilitated or protected by taxpayers' money) is so important that human rights considerations should not hamper it.

This compartmentalization is reflected in the department's administrative structures and procedures. Established referral links between divisions on human rights are few and weak. Which division takes the lead varies from issue to issue. On a matter involving the general human rights "tone" of Canada's international relations, the International Organizations Bureau may do so in consultation with various posts and regional desks. On a particular country, responsibility may fall solely on the regional desk. Geographic desks may take their cues from one another. For example, the decision to suspend official trade promotion programs with South Africa affected the desk level of relations with other countries.

Let us follow a human rights issue through the policy process. Typically, an inquiry to, or pressure on, the minister produces a request for information from the minister's office to the relevant geographic desk. There is little responsiveness to public concerns, little sharing of experience or diagnoses with other desks, and no input by anyone responsible for and/or knowledgeable about the human rights dimension of the question. Further, any overall sense of the level of public concern or understanding becomes diffused. (There may also be a referral to the International Organizations Bureau.) Clarification and information are returned to the minister from the geographic desk. The minister may make a policy statement or response or refer the issue to cabinet.

Within this basic model, human rights aspects of aid and trade are handled differently. On a trade question the geographic desk prepares a response for the minister, after which the human rights unit of the International Organizations Bureau may be contacted. If the issue receives further attention (for instance, a prominent newspaper editorial), other relevant divisions will be brought in for consultation. To illustrate, on export credits to a Canadian company exporting to a developing country that is a human rights violator, the division on Economic Relations with Developing Countries would become involved, as well as the minister for international trade, the minister for regional industrial expansion, and possibly some other minister, if the exporting company is in his or her riding.

In an aid program, a decision to limit aid would be taken by the external affairs secretary in consultation with the minister for external relations (also in charge of CIDA) and other interested ministers. The secretary would communicate the decision in a statement to cabinet and perhaps to Parliament and through dissemination of a written memorandum. In the fall of 1985 discrimination in Sri Lanka against the Tamil minority affected sharing of the benefits of Canadian aid. In response to public attention resulting from a story in the *Globe and Mail* and concern within External Affairs, Joe Clark circulated a ministerial directive setting human rights preconditions on further aid to Sri Lanka.[18]

Although CIDA has little capacity to deal systematically with the issue, it has examined the relation between aid and human rights. Over the last several years the agency has both investigated and asserted a connection between official development assistance, basic needs, and human rights.[19]

Role of the Minister

Within a large bureaucracy that avoids innovation or risk in taking policy decisions, the secretary of state for external affairs is one of very few people who can ensure that human rights are promoted in Canadian foreign policy. The minister sets the "tone" for the department. A bureaucracy tends to act on the basis of past experience and judgments and will carry on as before unless told to do otherwise. Because most decisions are in the end "political," there is a tendency to "bump issues up" to the minister. We were assured time and again in External Affairs that if a minister is interested in something it would work its way through the bureaucracy and that if the minister showed an interest in human rights, officials would "spend time being very conscious of human rights."

The minister's office acts as a crucial "switching centre" for information coming out of and going into the department. Under the present minister a relatively large political staff watches the work of the bureaucracy and keeps the minister informed of important information coming from newspapers, constituents, MPs, and correspondence. The current staff sits in on departmental policy meetings whenever the minister has expressed interest in the issues under discussion. One member of the staff has responsibility for human rights. Allan MacEachen, external affairs secretary (1982-4) while also deputy prime minister, spent barely half a day a week at the department and had only one staff person.

The minister's speeches, statements in the House, and even correspondence often constitute policy on a given issue. Though these are often drafted by officials, the minister takes responsibility for them and sometimes insists on shaping them. For example, in June 1985 Nelson Riis questioned Clark in the Commons regarding his department's approval of the export of military equipment to Chile. There had apparently been little if any consultation within the department on the human rights implications of this sale. A resulting review by the minister's office of policies and procedures led to revisions to the Export-Import Control Act. Moreover, Clark's explanatory letter to Riis was for some time the only official, publicly accessible evidence of how the act would be modified.[20]

The minister therefore sets the context for the department's consideration of policy issues. If the minister is not interested in human rights, then there are few, if any, avenues to follow or resources with which departmental staff could pursue them.

Joe Clark has clearly set a positive tone concerning human rights and foreign policy, evident in the government's response to two reports by parliamentary committees in 1985 and 1986.[21] A 1985 telegram from the minister to Canada's ambassador to Guatemala stated that further aid to that country must be predicated on a reduction in violations. We are told that the telegram included instructions on how to assess whether abuses were declining.[22]

Human Rights in Daily Operations

Only two offices in External Affairs have a mandate to cover human rights, and both are oriented toward international bodies and multilateral institutions. The human rights unit is buried within the Human Rights and Social Affairs Division of the International Organizations Bureau, in turn part of the Political and International Security Affairs Branch. Although they have shown a constant interest in human rights, directors of the bureau have nonetheless had to weigh this interest against their other responsibilities, including Canada's relations with the Commonwealth and the United Nations. Much of the daily work of monitoring and managing the department's interests in human rights within multilateral institutions therefore falls to the three (generally) officers who make up the human rights unit. Because of personnel changes the unit has at times been staffed by only one officer.

The unit was established approximately ten years ago and has had a tenuous existence. In the early 1980s there was some thought given to doing away with it altogether on the ground that human rights were being covered adequately throughout the department and did not require specific attention. In what was not the first such effort, the bureau tried in the early 1980s to regularize the monitoring and implementation of human rights within the department by proposing an internal review that would include matters such as consultation with NGOs, staffing of the human rights unit, relations with parliamentary committees, and the selection of delegates to UN human rights meetings. Nothing has yet come of these suggestions. They foundered when others in the department raised commercial considerations and put forward objections related to the specific application of human rights norms to bilateral relations, to aid, and to the dealings of international financial institutions.

Much of the bureau's time is taken up with co-ordinating Canada's role in such multilateral bodies as the UN Commission on Human Rights and the Third Committee of the UN General Assembly. In connection with the former, there has been the only attempt to institutionalize consideration of human rights within departmental operations. For the last several years the bureau has organized an annual departmental consultation with NGOs prior to the Canadian delegation's departure to the commission's meeting in Geneva. NGOs present extensive briefs on abuses in countries under present or potential examination by the commission and question officials on Canada's planned positions at the meeting. NGOs also can request details on the government's relations with specific countries over the past year. In this way the bureau has tried to co-ordinate NGO interaction with the department on human rights and to raise issues beyond interactions with individual desk officers.

Otherwise, the bureau shies away from human rights within bilateral relations, as the issue is considered just one part of relations with a given country. It sees its role as ensuring that human rights are not "swept under the carpet." However, if bilateral divisions are doing their job, there is no need to bother them. But how does anybody know or keep track of just what the desks are doing in monitoring and promoting human rights? Formal, institutionalized, mandatory lines of communication and reference on human rights are few and far between.

The other office with a specific human rights reference is the United Nations Human Rights, Peace and Security Unit within the Legal Operations Division of the Legal Affairs Bureau. Consideration of human rights is placed solidly within the context of Canadian policies within multilateral institutions.

Other than these two offices, operationalization of human rights concerns is diffused throughout the department. The former Policy Coordination Branch helped prepare policy statements on rights, particularly in the 1985 green paper, *Competitiveness and Security*. Various officers on geographic desks are called upon to address human rights matters, but this normally involves little, if any, communication with human rights units. The importance given to rights considerations varies from desk to desk, according to the country's situation, the expertise and interests of the desk officer, outside pressures, and the concerns of the minister.

Eastern European divisions appear to look at human rights cases more regularly. Ethnic organizations are in "constant interaction" with the department over specific cases and are "significant sources" of information. Officers working in this area believe that human rights are more than adequately looked after and feel no need to consult with the department's human rights experts.

Although many other bureaux deal with matters that have a human rights component, no intradepartmental consultation is required. Most communication on human rights among External Affairs divisions is done informally. The International Organizations Bureau reports informally to other bureaux about what is going on; in turn the bureau hears from other sections on items such as applications for permits to trade with countries on the Export Control List. So unstructured a procedure can hardly ensure adequate consideration of human rights dimensions. We saw little evidence of systematic intradepartmental consultation on human rights. Neither the geographic desks, the first point of reference on a human rights question, nor the International Organizations Bureau is the guardian of human rights.

PUBLIC PRESSURE

NGOs and the Media

In their attempts to infuse foreign policy and practice with human rights considerations, NGOs and the media operate under a shared constraint.

Because so much of foreign policy is decided behind closed doors, they rarely know fully what External Affairs or the government has done or intends to do on any human rights issue. The public and its most visible representatives, NGOs and the media, operate on the basis of selectively supplied information, supplemented by contacts, informants, and associates. We found it difficult to assess the effect of media and NGOs pressure on human rights in foreign policy decisions.

Nonetheless, many public servants observed that NGOs raised the profile of human rights in foreign policy.[23] NGOs make their concerns known in a variety of ways: individual letters and letter-writing campaigns, detailed reports on abuses, and representations to and constant personal exchanges with MPs, senators, external affairs secretaries and departmental officials. The continuity of NGO action on human rights and of NGO representations to the government has helped keep human rights on the foreign policy agenda, in theory if not in practice, regardless of the government of the day.[24]

NGOs' briefs to ministers and parliamentary committees contain some of the most complete and coherent thinking on why and how human rights considerations should be integrated into foreign policy. Their suggestions help to form a background for policy debates between MPs and, to a lesser extent, within the bureaucracy. Equally important, NGOs are often extremely well informed about violations because of their wide networks of contacts, unconstrained by restrictions hampering members of the diplomatic corps.

NGOs represent a wide range of human rights interests and perceptions. In general, organizations such as the Inter-Church Committee on Human Rights in Latin America, which have concentrated on abuses in developing countries, have stressed gross and systematic violations in situations of extreme inequality. Eastern European organizations have raised many individual cases of violations in the Eastern bloc and maintained awareness of the denial of civil and political rights there. Other organizations, such as Amnesty International, focus on individual cases of extreme deprivation of basic rights.

The media also give rights issues a higher profile, though their attention is sporadic. A "newsworthy" issue, however, will certainly be more likely to attract the attention of policy-makers. Many topics raised in question period in the House are drawn from newspaper or television reports. High-profile news items receive the attention of the external affairs secretary, who must anticipate media and parliamentary questions at any time. NGO mobilization of support for a human rights issue – a Soviet scientist unjustly held in a psychiatric ward, a Chilean trade unionist who has "disappeared," or increased sanctions against South Africa – is unlikely to succeed unless it has aroused media interest.

Parliament

Over the last decade MPs and senators, responding to constituency pressure, NGO lobbying, and their own consciences, have shown increasing interest in international human rights. Reviews of the work of External Affairs and its minister by committees and by individual MPs constitute an important source for our knowledge of policy directions. In addition, some parliamentarians have formed watchdog groups on human rights; the most prominent is the Senate's Helsinki Human Rights Committee.

What impact do parliamentary committees have on human rights in foreign policy? We would argue that they have laid the groundwork for, and confirmed public interest in, a more prominent and systematic role for human rights in Canadian foreign policy-making. Interested parliamentarians and the public have explored a range of international human rights concerns during Committee hearings. Committee-related travel to violator countries and numerous submissions from NGOs have revealed to MPs and senators the increasing public interest and expertise and the nature and extent of violations.

The Sub-Committee on Canada's Relations with the Caribbean and Latin America was particularly important. Despite the entreaties of the minister, Mark MacGuigan, not to give "undue" attention to human rights in the face of more "important" and "practical" trade issues, the final report contains some of the strongest, most comprehensive, and far-reaching human rights analysis yet to emerge from the House of Commons.[25] Unfortunately, the government treated the report with disinterest, if not contempt, assigning a junior foreign service officer to draft cursory, insubstantial responses to the sub-committee's recommendations. Parliamentary interest was sustained, however, and in 1985 the report was quoted at length in the report of the Special Joint Committee on Canada's International Relations. The latter committee, like the sub-committee, stated that aid should not be given to countries with "gross and systematic" violations of human rights.[26]

In the spring of 1986, the House of Commons committee system was significantly changed. Smaller standing committees (10 or fewer members) were established to "mirror" each department of government. It was assumed that these changes would allow members to become expert in a particular area. International human rights issues are partly the responsibility of the Standing Committee on External Affairs. One of only three general committees is the new Standing Committee on Human Rights, which has the authority to examine domestic and international human rights policies and procedures, no matter which department is responsible for them. The seeds of the idea for the committee can be found in several NGO submissions to parliamentary committees.[27] Deliberations and appearances before this new committee by government officials and NGOs provide a unique opportunity to democratize the foreign policy process. More information can become available and links drawn between Canada's foreign and domestic human rights policies, making them more consistent.

Finally, individual MPs have been effective. David MacDonald's 1978 private member's bill on human rights and foreign aid conditionality, "helped focus criticism on the human rights component of Canada's aid policy."[28] Other MPs have brought constant attention to Canadian policy toward South Africa and in 1981 put pressure on the government when it sought to avoid taking a stand on violations in El Salvador and in Guatemala.

PMO, PCO, and Cabinet

In human rights, as in other policy areas, we know little about the inner workings of the policy-making centres in Canadian government. We know that foreign policy questions with a human rights component have been referred to cabinet. How a policy initiative changes in its journey from External Affairs to cabinet is difficult to ascertain. We cannot generalize about whether reference to the cabinet is likely to reinforce or weaken the human rights component in a policy. Working for greater responsiveness are likely to be those ministers, including the prime minister, responsible for Canada's international role and image. In contrast, ministers concerned primarily with trade and related matters tend to play down human rights considerations. Once a foreign policy issue that relates to human rights has aroused extensive public interest, domestic political considerations are also bound to be influential.

Because the Privy Council Office (PCO) is responsible for policy coordination and development, any major attempt to apply human rights criteria to foreign policy would clearly require its input and participation. Nothing discovered in our research suggested regular engagement with this issue, indicating its still highly tentative treatment in international relations.

As key players in foreign policy, the prime minister and external affairs secretary signal to the bureaucracy the profile to be given human rights considerations. On some international human rights issues, Brian Mulroney has strongly supported changes in foreign policy and has provided positive rhetorical leadership. Nowhere was this more evident than before and during recent Commonwealth heads-of-government meetings, where he pressed for unanimous condemnation of apartheid and pressure for change in South Africa. Apparently Mulroney and Joe Clark pursued these goals over more reticent tendencies within the Conservative caucus. According to Kirton, the two men united in their moral outrage over South Africa and called for "fast and severe measures." "Their party colleagues, seeing where the prime minister's preferences lay, retreated into silence. External Affairs was left to transform these preferences into a sophisticated long-term strategy."[29] It should be recalled, however, that the department minimized implementation of the measures toward South Africa announced by the then minister in December 1977. The department's subsequent record did not justify early expectations.[30]

One should carefully distinguish between words and deeds. Statements by political leaders have an important role to play in raising the profile of human rights in Canadian foreign policy. The test, however, is whether and to what extent their positions are realized in day-to-day policy implementation within External Affairs.

CONCLUSION

There is clearly general support within some parts of the government and the bureaucracy for attaching increased importance to human rights in Canadian foreign policy. However, our evidence and that of others in this volume indicate that general support and good will are insufficient. Human rights concerns must compete against powerful, more established foreign policy interests. The priority attached to economic considerations and military security is firmly rooted and reflected in governmental decision-making and administrative structures. Innumerable offices and officers with inter-related functions consult with a view to enhancing and protecting Canada's ability to sell abroad and to keep its boundaries secure. Achievement of human rights goals requires a commensurate level of attention and investment of resources.

Support for international rights objectives remains far below that devoted to more established goals. Human rights issues normally attract concern only when strong public interest is brought to bear on a particular problem. Even then, the kind and degree of official response, both rhetorical and practical, will depend greatly on the particular interests of individual politicians and bureaucrats.

Increasingly strong and sophisticated public and parliamentary interest in and commitment to international human rights warrants a more systematic approach to these concerns in foreign policy decision-making.[31] Such an approach would require clearly defined responsibilities, carefully formulated consultative procedures within and between departments, and mechanisms for systematically gathering, receiving, vetting and acting on human rights data.[32] Responsible incorporation of human rights concerns in Canada's international relations would include entrenchment of the means by which an interested public could gain information, so that it could know whether human rights criteria were considered on a particular issue and why they were given more or less weight in the formulation of a policy response.

PART TWO

International

Forums

CHAPTER FIVE

The UN Commission on Human Rights

JOHN W. FOSTER

The collective expression of international concern for human rights, foreshadowed in the Covenant of the League of Nations and the formation of the International Labour Organization following the First World War, became a fundamental reference point for the statements of the alliance against fascism during the Second World War. References to human rights and justice characterized the declaration of the United Nations in 1942, the Dumbarton Oaks proposals of 1944, and the UN charter.

The new international body included among its purposes "promoting and encouraging respect for human rights and for fundamental freedoms for all without distinction as to race, sex, language, or religion." The preamble and many of the articles of the charter reaffirm this commitment, and the functions and powers of the general assembly and of the Economic and Social Council (ECOSOC) include the explicit responsibility to assist the realization of human rights and to promote respect for and observance of these rights. ECOSOC, shortly after its formation, not only established the Commission on Human Rights but referred to it the task of drafting "an international bill of human rights."[1]

The Universal Declaration of Human Rights, adopted and proclaimed by the general assembly on 10 December 1948, and the companion international covenants on Economic, Social, and Cultural Rights and on Civil and Political Rights, together with the latter's Optional Protocol (1966), provide common "standards of achievement" for all nations. These instruments and a variety of other legally binding agreements have ensured that the promotion and protection of human rights remain a fundamental theme in the life and work of the United Nations. Whether the means provided for implementing that concern are efficient and the resources adequate has been asked with great urgency in the past two or three years. Nevertheless, a wide variety of UN bodies and agencies, including those that deal with labour, race and racism, children, the disabled, women, and self-determination, have human rights as part of their mandates. The work of developing international standards has continued since 1948 and is embodied in a long succession of international declarations and treaties. These in turn have influenced the development of regional human rights agreements and bodies and national bills of rights, charters, and constitutions.

THE COMMISSION

The Commission on Human Rights, the central UN policy organ in human rights, was established in 1946 and is based on article 68 of the UN charter. Its 43 members are elected at ECOSOC for three-year terms. It meets annually for five to six weeks. In 1947 the commission created the Sub-Commission on Prevention of Discrimination and Protection of Minorities (renamed in 1986 the Sub-Commission of Experts on Human Rights). The sub-commission is composed of experts serving in their personal capacity who are nominated by governments and elected by the commission for three-year terms. Each body has created a variety of means to undertake studies and investigations and to implement decisions.[2]

The UN secretariat provides staff and support for the commission, the sub-commission, and their subsidiary bodies. Originally termed the Division of Human Rights, this agency was renamed the United Nations Centre for Human Rights in 1982 and is located in Geneva, with a liaison office at the New York headquarters. The first director was a Canadian, John Humphrey, who served from 1946 to 1966 and was instrumental in drafting the Universal Declaration. The centre was, until recently, headed by an assistant deputy secretary-general. The last person to hold this position was Kurt Herndl. Following his resignation in 1986, the centre has been administered as part of the responsibility of a deputy secretary-general but has lacked a full-time director. Forty years after its inception, the centre's capacity and resources remain inadequate for the task represented by its elevated standards and at least theoretical universal applicability. With less than 1 per cent of the UN budget, the centre, commission, and sub-commission cannot adequately review communications, analyse complex situations, and provide redress.[3] A recent director, Theo van Boven, commented: "It should be kept in mind that very significant differences exist between various domestic human rights forums and UN human rights forums. Although the UN has developed a comprehensive set of international norms for the promotion and protection of human rights, its system of actual implementation and supervision is still rudimentary."[4]

The vulnerability of the staff of the centre and of the commission to political and other pressures should not be underestimated. Newly elected Secretary-General Javier Pérez de Cuéllar's termination of van Boven's mandate in 1982 seemed to contradict and undercut Perez's pledges to support human rights. Perez removed a forthright and courageous international civil servant who had provoked the ire of dictatorial régimes, particularly those in Argentina and Guatemala, as well as the annoyance of both superpowers.[5]

The Cycle of Consideration

The annual meetings of the commission, normally for six weeks in February and March, cannot be considered in isolation. Each meeting reviews reports of a variety of activities in the previous year; the most important is the report of the sub-commission.[6] This expert group, which normally meets for three weeks in August, considers and screens communications (appeals and complaints regarding human rights violations) and publishes lists thereof. The sub-commission has established, in addition to its Working Group on Communications, a continuing Working Group on Slavery and one on indigenous populations and sessional working groups on such issues as the rights of the detained or imprisoned and of those detained on the grounds of mental ill health.[7] As an expert body, the sub-commission has had greater liberty – in its own right and in response to communications – to initiate new areas of consideration and to bring new country situations onto the agenda. In recent years the international community of non-governmental organizations (NGOs) has made increasing use of the sub-commission to bring forward their urgent concerns. Meetings of the Working Group on Indigenous Populations have become a virtual international forum of organizations and representatives of indigenous peoples in the Americas, Europe, and elsewhere. The sub-commission prepares resolutions and decisions for the consideration of the commission.[8]

The commission has established, in addition to the sub-commission, working groups that meet periodically as continuing bodies or on a sessional basis immediately prior to or during the commission's sessions. The groups are instrumental to the advancement of the commission's agenda.

The commission's consideration often leads not only to recommendations to ECOSOC but to initiatives that affect debates in the general assembly. At each session, the general assembly, through its third committee, receives a report on the work of the commission. The assembly may also have before it interim reports by commission special rapporteurs on gross and systematic violations of human rights. General assembly resolutions initiated in October or November on such countries as Chile, El Salvador, and Guatemala may be informed by reports from rapporteurs appointed by the commission the previous March. The commission's agenda may be affected by decisions taken at ECOSOC or the general assembly the previous year.

Activities

The history of the UN Commission on Human Rights may usefully be subdivided into three broad phases: normative, from its founding until 1954; promotional, involving workshops and seminars around the world, 1954–66; and current, with its emphasis on protection, from 1966.[9] The general assembly's adoption of the two covenants and the Optional Protocol on 19 December 1966 and their coming into force in 1976 (Social and Economic Rights on 3 January and Civil and Political Rights and the Optional Protocol on 23 March) mark a further evolution in the UN approach to human rights. Together with the Universal Declaration these documents make up the International Bill of Human Rights. With their completion and ratification by a significant number of states, the Human Rights Committee was established in 1977 to review states' performance and specific cases of appeal. Energies were then freed for the difficult political work of developing support for implementation measures at the commission and elsewhere.

The period since 1966 may be further divided at 1975, when the commission picked up a reference from the general assembly about human rights in Chile, two years after the coup d'état in that country. The period 1975–82 saw a broadening agenda, growth in number and diversity of violator countries considered, and development of new instruments for investigation, documentation, and limited rapid intervention. The transition from van Boven to Herndl in 1982 ushered in a phase of retrenchment and insecurity.

The agenda of the commission typically includes three major categories: normative or standard-setting activities; investigation and action on gross and systematic violations; and other aspects of implementation, including structural proposals and advisory services.

In standard-setting, three activities highlight the past decade. In 1977, the commission was asked by the general assembly to draw up a draft convention on torture which would embody the principles stated in the 1977 Declaration on the Protection of All Persons from Being Subjected to Torture and Other Cruel, Inhuman or Degrading Treatment or Punishment. Working groups met each year 1980–4 to complete the task. Finally, the convention was adopted by the general assembly on 10 December 1984. After considerable debate, an investigatory mechanism –

a special rapporteur on torture – was established by the commission in 1985. The careful first report of the special rapporteur, P. Kooijmans, a former representative of the Netherlands to the commission, was presented to the commission in March 1986 and his mandate renewed for another year.[10]

In 1978 Poland submitted a draft declaration on the rights of the child to the general assembly; an amended version went to the commission in 1979. A working group was established by the commission and met in 1980, with further work in each succeeding year. By the end of 1985 a preamble and 21 articles of a draft convention had been completed, but the 1986 session was not able to finish the document and resolved to renew work on it in 1987.

The subject of religious intolerance has been before the commission in one form or another since 1962. When it proved impossible, after ten years of effort, to draft a convention on religious intolerance, energies were diverted to a declaration. The Declaration on the Elimination of All Forms of Intolerance and of Discrimination Based on Religion or Belief was completed in 1981. The Canadian role remains one of the proudest achievements in Yvon Beaulne's career.[11] In 1985 the general assembly requested the commission to consider measures for the implementation of the declaration. The commission decided to encourage a study already in progress in the sub-commission and to appoint for one year a special rapporteur to inquire into governmental actions "which are inconsistent with the provisions of the Declaration."[12]

In treating violations of human rights, the commission has, since the early 1970s, examined certain national or regional "situations" to ascertain whether consistent gross and systematic violation has occurred. In recent years, the commission has developed a typology according to theme: torture, involuntary disappearance, summary or arbitrary execution, and mass exodus. Consideration of actual situations of rights violations can, in turn be divided into three categories: those itemized on the agenda, those that emerge under agenda item "Study of situations which appear to reveal a consistent pattern of gross violations of human rights," and those treated under the confidential procedures of ECOSOC resolution 1503 (1973).

The "question of the violation of human rights in the occupied Arab territories, including Palestine" has been on the agenda since the 24th session (1968). Apartheid has also been treated separately: first as "violations of human rights in Southern Africa: report of the Ad Hoc Working Group of Experts" (established in 1967); then as "the adverse consequences for the enjoyment of human rights of political, military, economic and other forms of assistance given to colonial and racist regimes in southern Africa" (since 1974); and, finally, under the agenda item dealing with the "right of peoples to self-determination." Since 1975 the commission has maintained a particular agenda item on the "question of human rights in Chile." The "Question of human rights in Cyprus" has been maintained by the commission since its 32nd session (1976).[13]

These virtually permanent items excite varying amounts of interest and different results. Debates on the occupied Arab territories are often lengthy and heated. They repeat not only previous commission debates but discussions in parallel UN bodies. The studies put in motion with regard to South Africa have on occasion proved very useful to the international community, but because a number of UN bodies deal with related issues, the commission's debates often rehearse or repeat what is said elsewhere. The item on Cyprus occasionally flares into debate but is more of a "watching brief" on a relatively static situation. The question of Chile merited establishment of an active working group in the late 1970s, succeeded by a model special rapporteur in the early 1980s. In recent years Chile's Western friends have attempted to end the special attention given to the Pinochet dictatorship. A spirited US attempt in 1986 yielded the promise that the question of changing the status of the commission's treatment of Chile would top the agenda in 1987.[14]

The general item on situations, often coming up for debate in the fifth week of the six-week commission session, frequently excites tension and considerable diplomatic effort. The public treatment of situations of concern arises out of general assembly, sub-commission, and previous commission actions. During the past decade the list of countries subject to such public discussion has grown considerably, although often at a regrettably slow pace. Kampuchea, Equatorial Guinea, the Central African Empire, and Uganda were all examined in the late 1970s, but "the real work of the Commission with respect to these countries did not start until after the offensive regimes were overthrown."[15] Nicaragua was also subject to a public resolution in 1979, just before the overthrow of the Somoza dictatorship. Bolivia, El Salvador, and Guatemala were added in the early 1980s, along with Poland, Afghanistan, and the Islamic Republic of Iran. Additional countries – including Kampuchea and Western Sahara – have been examined under self-determination. The re-emergence of democratic government in Bolivia removed that country from consideration. Poland's non-co-operation and its allies' strong support have removed it from the list, while US pressure has weakened resolutions on Guatemala and El Salvador and may succeed in removing them.

While the geographic and political variety of offenders under review has increased, a number of acknowledged gross and systematic violators have not had to face public scrutiny by the commission. During the years of dictatorship and massive disappearances, Argentina escaped treatment, as did the neighbouring dictatorship in Uruguay and as does Paraguay to this day. Energetic efforts by NGOs to provoke public investigation and debate on the Philippines under President Marcos or on Sri Lanka prior to 1987 did not receive the requisite support.[16] Further, while a wide range of countries has merited examination under the commission's confidential procedures, those very procedures may provide a delaying and defensive mechanism for repressive régimes seeking to escape more direct and public examination.

While the naming and investigation of specific country situations have often proved extremely difficult and slow, another technique has permitted indirect investigation of alleged severe abuses. If the commission agrees to investigation of a widespread type of violation, then the process can be used to highlight particular country situations. For example, in the mid- and late 1970s it seemed impossible to bring the military dictatorship of Argentina before the commission as a violator régime. Yet the systematic disappearance of thousands of Argentinian citizens, as well as parallel occurrences in Chile and Uruguay and increasing evidence relating to El Salvador and Guatemala, did excite international concern.

In 1978 the general assembly noted the urgency of the problem of "disappeared persons," and while the issue was postponed from the commission's 1979 session, ECOSOC referred it to the sub-commission, which late in 1979 published a study of the problem in Chile. International concern was stimulated by the families and friends of the disappeared in several countries, and various NGOs provided documentation and pressure. France prepared a draft resolution for the commission, and the US Congress discussed the phenomenon and called for presidential action. Despite energetic objections from Argentina and prolonged debate, a consensus resolution setting up a Working Group on Enforced or Involuntary Disappearances was passed. The five-member group began operations in June 1980,[17] and six years later it continued to receive appeals, make investigations, and issue reports. It has also made several on-site visits to countries under investigation. During 1985 the working group received over 4,500 reports of disappearances and referred 2,200 to the governments of 22 countries. The report submitted in 1986 expresses concern for a new, but increasingly important phenomenon – the disappearance of persons already in jail.[18]

A related matter – the widespread practice of summary or arbitrary execution – gained the general assembly's attention in 1981. As a result, the commission's 1982 session appointed a special rapporteur, Amos Wako, to study the matter. Wako presented his fourth report in 1986. It detailed a wide variety of communications with governments alleged to be contemplating imminent or threatened summary or arbitrary executions. It noted no lessening in the number of executions, even though awareness of them has increased. It expressed particular concern at the increased number of deaths of people already in custody. A particularly poignant example of the international community's restricted ability to prevent such death occurred at the 1983 session of the commission, which received news of a planned series of summary executions in Guatemala. Despite the commission's appeal to Rios Montt, the Guatemalan dictator proceeded with the executions.[19] While some governments continue to refuse to respond to Wako's inquiries, and executions continue, relatives of victims and defenders of human rights gain some satisfaction from the fact that the governments concerned are named and the cases documented. Should political change provide the opportunity for fuller investigation, the responsible figures may be held to account through regular processes of justice.

The commission also addressed mass exodus. The relation between rights violations and large exoduses provoked action by the commission and the general assembly in 1980. The commission appointed a special rapporteur, Sadruddin Aga Khan, to investigate and make recommendations. In 1982 it received his report on the causes and nature of mass exoduses and considered his recommendations, including establishment of a "distant early warning system" involving possible movements of a corps of humanitarian observers to monitor situations and help ease tensions. The commission referred the matter to the Group of Governmental Experts on International Cooperation to Avert New Flows of Refugees.[20]

These thematic investigations, along with actions to implement the Convention on Torture, show on balance a strengthening of the commission's capacity for systematic review of alleged serious violations. The quality and forthrightness of reports vary considerably. Further, the resources available for meeting and communication, together with the necessary staff, have been limited and are currently threatened with severe reduction. Nevertheless, the precedents established, and the credibility gained for a UN investigative body through on-site visits to some alleged violator countries, are a net gain for the commission and the cause of human rights.

An Evolving Instrument

There were dramatic changes in the composition and atmosphere of the commission during the 1970s. Until mid-decade, it had been an "expert body" in emphasis, with delegations limited in size and having a significant amount of discretion. The commission later became more of a "council," with more governments seeking membership, delegations growing in size, a broader agenda, and more directly political debates. As Theo van Boven put it, "The Commission became a major organ, you *had* to be there." The first meeting of the sub-commission's Working Group on Communications in 1972, creation of the Ad Hoc Working Group on the Situation of Human Rights in Chile in 1975, and the high profile given to human rights in US foreign policy by the Carter administration all contributed to the growing attention given the commission. The issue of self-determination interested a number of African states. China, while not expressing particular interest in human rights, was interested because Kampuchea and Vietnam were considered by the commission. With the inclusion of Chile on the agenda, the Eastern bloc found it difficult to oppose both the addition of new situations and the growing activity of NGOs at the commission.

During the 1970s, the participation of NGOs changed remarkably. They discovered that the commission was a useful forum and platform for raising urgent concerns, like Chile and disappeared persons. The NGOs in turn affected the commission's atmosphere, increasing the range and specificity of interventions and discussions.[21] At first they were not permitted to mention specific countries: doing so provoked lengthy objections from representatives of offended (and often offending) states, like Argentina.[22] The rule simply was "eroded," first with regard to Chile and then over other states. NGOs intervened not only with verbal statements, but with written communications as well.[23] In recent years, the presence of several dozen NGO delegations has helped ensure that certain situations and thematic concerns gain attention. Repeated mention of a given country by NGOs, persistent pressure on national delegations to do the same, assistance in circulating and discussing draft resolutions, and pressure on home governments regarding wording and votes on resolutions have all increased attention on countries like Chile, Guatemala, and the Philippines and on disappearance and torture.

The maturing of the commission has led to changes in the way in which countries handle business at the annual sessions. With an extensive agenda, and sessions that often run far overtime, delegations appear more dependent on instruction from home ministries. International political and diplomatic activity related to specific agenda items has been increasingly apparent and controversial: US State Department initiatives to alter and reduce action on El Salvador in 1981, including visits to many capitals and representations to van Boven; US organizing of support for the initiative on Poland in 1982; and US activity to seek support for resolutions on religious intolerance (successful) and Ethiopia (unsuccessful) at the 1986 session. As one experienced Western delegate said, following the 1986 session: "There was an unacceptable level of pressure applied this year by the United States; you had to do what the Americans wanted."[24] US manipulation is particularly disturbing because of its own and its allies' frequent pledges of commitment to human rights. The Soviet delegation and its allies have on occasion obstructed progress and prevented or delayed consideration of sensitive situations or themes. The coincidence of interest between the Soviets and Arab delegations with sizeable numbers of supporting African and Asian votes ensures extensive consideration for certain high-priority agenda items of limited productivity.

The complexity and extent of the agenda have brought about a more highly organized division of labour among delegations. Regional groups meet regularly. The Western European and Others (WEO) delegations meet each morning. The group's New York personnel met at the close of the 1985 general assembly to allocate responsibilities in preparation for the 1986 commission session. One country is chosen chair, and specific personnel are selected to co-ordinate the group on particular agenda items and on situations in particular countries. Thus, at a session in the early 1980s, the Netherlands took responsibility for the Guatemala draft and the Canadians for that on Bolivia. The group system does not enforce consensus but certainly works toward it. It tends as well to reinforce North-South and East-West divisions.[25]

The Commission and Victims

Coincident with elaboration of agenda and structure in the past 20 years, the commission has become a recipient of complaints and a platform for the injured. Commission and members took refuge from complainants in the early years, stressing that their mandate include "no power to take any action in regard to any complaints concerning human rights," but two ECOSOC resolutions dramatically eroded this refuge. In 1967, ECOSOC resolution 1235 gave the commission power to "recommend and adopt general and specific measures to deal with violations of human rights" and to use communications (complaints) to this end; resolution 1503, in 1973, set up a procedure for dealing with communications relating to violations of human rights and fundamental freedoms. With the establishment of the Working Group on Communications (1971) a three-stage approach to complaints began. The working group screens communications, referring those that appear to reveal a consistent pattern of violations to the sub-commission, which reviews the matter and may refer it to the commission. The commission in turn can investigate and/or report. Communications from NGOs have become recognized and accepted in the 1503 process, in part because of the political limitations and functional overload of the small staff at the UN Centre for Human

Rights. Confronted by tens of thousands of appeals, the staff has had neither the mandate nor capacity to study appeals and to report consistent patterns to the working group. In the face of this scandal, the considered and well-documented submissions of recognized NGOs, whether Amnesty International or Canada's Inter-Church Committee on Human Rights in Latin America, provide alternative, evaluated information for sub-commission expert members.[26] The commission reserves time in confidential session for review of countries raised under 1503 and reports to a full public session only the names of those considered and whether action is continued or dropped.

The 1503 procedure, while a "crack in the citadel" of state sovereignty,[27] is not the only avenue used by injured parties or their representatives. From time to time NGO delegations may include victims, their relatives, or affiliated organizations defending victims in a particular situation. On the floor and in the coffee lounge, these people often find a sympathetic hearing among delegation members.

Victims and their organizations have also frequently used instruments set up by the commission. The Ad Hoc Working Group on the Situation of Human Rights in Chile (1975–8) and the later special rapporteurs on Chile received hundreds of individual and institutional communications on violations. Similarly, the Working Group on Enforced or Involuntary Disappearances has received appeals for urgent action and interviewed relatives of victims and human rights organizations. This working group developed the capacity for quick response with telegrams of inquiry in individual cases. Whether the special rapporteur dealing with torture will develop a similar capacity is unclear.[28]

While the commission's capacity to respond was increasing in the late 1970s and early 1980s, the capacity and variety of organizations able to make such appeals heard at the international level developed as well: the legal operations of the Vicariate of Solidarity in Chile; independent human rights commissions and legal aid services in Argentina, Guatemala, El Salvador, Honduras, the Philippines, Sri Lanka, and many other countries; and new organizations like the Federation of Families of the Disappeared (FEDEFAM). Older bodies like Amnesty International were strengthened. As a result, the frequency and sophistication of representations to the commission and its various subsidiary organs increased greatly, raising the commission's visibility and public expectations of its actions. Theo van Boven's public leadership also contributed to the rise in expectations.[29] However, the conduct of the assistant deputy secretary-general for human rights, together with the at least one-year interruption of sub-commission meetings and the system for dealing with communications because of the 1986 budget cuts, places a large question mark over this evolution.

CANADA AND THE COMMISSION

Canadian Participation

Canada became a member of the commission for one three-year term in 1963, with Margaret Aitken as delegate, and was again elected in 1976, serving for three terms ending with the 40th session in 1984. Yvon Beaulne, for much of the period Canada's ambassador to the Holy See, led the Canadian delegation during these last nine sessions. During 1985 and 1986, Canada was an observer at the commission, with the delegation led in the first year by Robert Middleton, an External Affairs official, and in the second by Gordon Fairweather, Canada's human rights commissioner. Canada's failure to gain re-election to the commission at the May 1986 meeting of ECOSOC meant that it would be represented for at least one more year by an observer.

Canada's delegation to the commission has been large, ranking in size with the Soviet Union's and France's but smaller than that of the United States. It has included, in addition to Beaulne, a senior official and one or more junior officials of the human rights and humanitarian division of External Affairs and a member of the Legal Bureau of the Department.[30] It also normally included at least one member of Canada's permanent missions to the United Nations in Geneva and New York, a representative of Secretary of State, and a representative of one or two of the provincial commissions of human rights. On occasion expert personnel from consulates in Europe, in particular those in Strasbourg and Marseilles, were added.

A Canadian expert, Judge Jules Deschenes, and alternate, Rita Cadieux, were elected to a three-year term on the sub-commission at the 40th session (1984) of the commission. Canadian personnel at the commission have been active participants in the sessional working groups, although none to date has been a member of a continuing working group or has served as a special rapporteur. Beaulne served as chairman of the commission during the 35th session (1979). The Canadian delegation to the general assembly has usually included one or more prospective members of the delegation at the commission.[31]

The 37th Session (1981)

When Canada was elected to membership in the commission in 1976, support at home for effective participation was mixed. The process of building agreement in Canada for ratification of the covenants, under the leadership of the Department of the Secretary of State, had improved federal-provincial co-ordination in the field and led to creation of continuing structures. However, External Affairs devoted little in terms of resources and personnel to human rights. The career diplomat appointed to head Canada's delegation at the commission, Yvon Beaulne, has termed the period "heroic times": human rights received one-twelfth of an Ottawa desk officer's time together with a portion of the time of an official at the permanent mission in Geneva.[32] In the following decade Canada was twice re-elected to the commission, with Beaulne serving a term as chairman and gaining a reputation for energetic, concerned, and effective delegation leadership. External Affairs increased the resources available to human rights, developing a division with a director and a small staff.

The approach, participation, and record of the Canadian delegation during this period can be put in perspective by examining briefly Canada's role in one session, the 37th, in 1981.[33]

The Canadian delegation took a particular interest in several aspects of the normative work, as well as helping develop thematic approaches to systematic violation so the effort of several sessions on a Declaration on Religious Intolerance was successfully concluded. Canadian delegates expressed delight at its completion, despite sustained resistance from eastern Europe, but they recognized the artful leadership of Abdoulaye Diéye of Senegal. Beaulne was delighted with Third World involvement in development and approval of the declaration, which Canada co-sponsored.[34] Concern for the Soviet dissident Andrei Sakharov and growing worry about human rights defenders in other countries led to work toward a declaration on the right of individuals and groups to promote human rights. A Canadian resolution asking the sub-commission to study this subject and recommend further action was passed by consensus. Canada co-sponsored a resolution asking the sub-committee to undertake another study, on the right to conscientious objection. Further, Canada participated in negotiations regarding a resolution on the right to development and with France, Algeria, and Senegal sponsored a resolution that most Western governments could support.

The 37th session received the first report of the Working Group on Involuntary Disappearances. The Canadian delegation had been instrumental in gaining backing for the group in the previous session and strongly supported renewal of the group's mandate. It spent a great deal of time and energy building on the previous year's resolution regarding the relation between mass exoduses and human rights. Canadian delegate Richard MacKinnon dedicated considerable effort to ensuring passage of a consensus resolution calling for a study of mass exoduses by a special rapporteur. The chairman appointed as special rapporteur former UN High Commissioner for Refugees Prince Sadruddin Aga Khan. The Canadian effort in this matter, despite the somewhat ambiguous definition of the enterprise, was a masterful exercise in the diplomatic game at the commission.[35]

The Canadian delegation worked hard on specific situations, but it was here that the limits of Canada's support for human rights became evident. Latin America highlighted the difficulties. The Canadian government was under increasing pressure at home to address the urgent situation of human rights violations and war in Central America as well as continuing pressure regarding human rights, political prisoners, and disappearances in Chile, Argentina, and Uruguay. Indeed, just as the 37th session ended, the government announced a special study of Canada's relations with Latin America and the Caribbean by the Commons Standing Committee on External Affairs and National Defence. The US government was pushing bilaterally and multilaterally to defuse concern about its client government in El Salvador and the military dictatorships in Guatemala and the southern cone. The Canadian delegation faced in Latin America four public situations of concern – Bolivia, Chile, El Salvador, and Guatemala – and others in confidential procedures under 1503.

Bolivia was the least controversial, and Canada introduced a resolution. The Netherlands took up public leadership on behalf of a resolution on Guatemala of specific concern to Yvon Beaulne. Guatemala had ignored and postponed a response to previous UN action, which had requested the secretary-general to establish contacts with the Guatemalan authorities and draw to their attention the extent of international concern regarding human rights. The commission resolution, which Canada co-sponsored, simply asked the secretary-general to pursue direct contacts, collect information, and present an interim report to the general assembly and a final report to the next session of the commission. In conversations with church representatives, Beaulne maintained that Canada was "all alone" and "courageous" in forwarding the initiative on Guatemala, at a time when most Latin American states opposed any action. The resolution was not, however, as critical of the Guatemalan authorities as many human rights agencies felt the evidence warranted, and no special rapporteur was established.

The resolution on El Salvador, initiated by France and Mexico, was much more comprehensive and involved appointment of a special rapporteur. Canada was among 29 nations supporting it. The subject of Chile, also put forward by Mexico, was much more controversial. The United States opposed continuation of the work of the special rapporteur on Chile. Canada objected to the Mexican draft as unbalanced and inaccurate, maintaining that the commission should encourage Chile's co-operation rather than simply denouncing it, and supported major West German amendments. The Western amendments narrowly failed, and Canada abstained on the Mexican text. While Canada stated that it supported extension of the special rapporteur's mandate, it indicated concern "at the disproportionate attention being directed for political, rather than human rights motives, to the situation of human rights in Chile."[36]

During the 37th session, the Canadian delegation was engaged as well with several African situations. Canada sponsored a resolution on Uganda and co-sponsored a resolution on the Central African Republic to provide advisory services and assistance to these countries in reconstructing respect for and observance of human rights following decisive changes in government. Canada sponsored a resolution on a plan of action for the restoration of human rights in Equatorial Guinea. Of ten resolutions dealing with specific situations of violation, Canada introduced five.

Some 17 situations were reviewed confidentially at the 37th session. Those in Argentina and Uruguay, both military dictatorships at the time, were among them. Despite considerable evidence submitted by NGOs and relatives and friends of victims, as well as documentation provided by the Working Group on Involuntary Disappearances, no initiative was undertaken to bring either country into public review.

The 1981 session provides a glimpse of Canada's participation in the commission. The delegation was sizeable, energetic, and well led and undertook a number of positive actions. Some general observations might be ventured. First, the Canadian government was strongly committed to the forum. Canada maintained a large delegation, appointed a vocal and colourful head of delegation, and twice sought re-election. Second, Canada sought strengthening of the Commission's resources and capabilities and related staff. In the debate on the plan of work for the commission presented to the 37th session, the Canadian delegation stressed the need to staff adequately the Division of Human Rights and to improve UN capacity to respond to urgent situations. This advocacy built on the approach of Flora MacDonald, who had urged, while external affairs secretary, UN appointment of an international ombudsman or high commissioner for human rights, with powers to intervene in urgent situations – at the very least, upgrading of the director to under-secretary-general for human rights.[37]

Third, the delegation participated in sessional working groups, development of drafts, sponsorship, and vote-seeking, advancing several of the commission's normative projects. Fourth, Canada helped establish such new instruments as the Working Group on Involuntary Disappearances and used relatively new instruments, like special rapporteurs, to accomplish its own priority objectives, like the project on mass exodus.

From a political point of view, Yvon Beaulne took satisfaction from Canada's re-election to the commission with Third World rather than eastern or western European support and expressed shock at the aggressive misbehaviour of American delegation head Michael Novak (1981, 1982). However, the Chilean case displayed Canada in a role much closer to the United States than to its closest Latin American counterpart, Mexico. While Canada engaged in a project on Guatemala that no other Western power seemed willing to initiate, the approach was so cautious and moderate as to be of questionable worth. Indeed, the resolution's relative weakness, the history of Guatemalan non-co-operation, and the obvious and sustained extent of violations make the action taken by Canada, the Netherlands, and others in the Western group look inadequate as well as belated. In a forum where the US approach was so politicized as to provoke recoil by its Western allies, Canada played the moderate and perhaps moderating member of the somewhat alienated allies.[38]

External Affairs and NGOs

Canada had been a member of the commission for several years in 1979 when External Affairs invited several NGO representatives to a consultation with members of the Canadian delegation. Consultations with human rights NGOs have now become an annual event, with wider participation, more extensive agendas, and more sophisticated exchanges.

Held in January, prior to the commission session, the consultations include a review of the normative and situational aspects of the agenda, departmental reports on past activity, and evaluative comments by non-governmental representatives. Participation has been at the invitation of the department, with sessions organized by its human rights personnel. The sessions, originally in a small conference room, now include 60 to 80 participants and occasion an address by the secretary of state for external affairs or the minister for external relations. A flotilla of departmental staff attends, including members of the commission delegation, Canadian expert members/alternates of the sub-commission, staff from the permanent mission in New York (including, on one recent occasion, Ambassador Stephen Lewis), and representatives from the human rights staff at Secretary of State. NGO representation has expanded from church and religious groups, labour, and Amnesty International (Canada) to include scholarly, indigenous, handicapped, and parliamentary spousal groups.

Canadian organizations using international fact-finding and research offices, like Amnesty, have used the meeting primarily to highlight priorities set by the international organization. Other groups, like the Canadian Labour Congress and, particularly, the inter-church coalitions on Latin America and on Asia, have presented detailed briefs on country situations of priority and on normative problems, such as disappeared persons or summary executions.

From time to time both partners to the meeting have expressed concern that it was simply a dialogue of the deaf, citing NGOs' unreasonable expectations or derogatory asides by uninterested departmental officials. NGOs have complained that while they presented detailed evaluations of situations of gross and systematic violations, government spokespeople gave only verbal summaries, with undocumented conclusions. NGOs have also pressed for closer consultation throughout the annual cycle and for inclusion of NGO representatives on the official delegation in Geneva.[39] Criticism was particularly virulent following Canada's undistinguished performance at the 41st session (1984).[40]

In preparing for the 42nd session, several fresh initiatives were taken. For the first time in the history of the consultations, the NGOs gathered to compare notes and ascertain common priorities. At the invitation of the Human Rights Centre of the University of Ottawa, more than a dozen NGOs participated in a two-day educational and evaluative session, discussing the value of the commission and of other multilateral instruments. The NGOs developed a short list of requests for External Affairs. The consultation began with circulation of a departmental "green book," including short country-by-country briefing notes,[41] a response to a persistent NGO request. Pressure from NGOs to have the government give the commission greater priority was met by appointing Gordon Fairweather, Canadian human rights commissioner, as delegation head. While no NGO representative was invited to join the delegation, departmental human rights officials did pledge close co-operation between the delegation and Canadian Amnesty and church observers at the session. The church observer, Bill Fairbairn, later reported frequent consultations with the delegation and "a high degree of co-operation and openness," in rather stark contrast to the situation at the 41st session.[42]

Nevertheless, it should not be presumed that NGOs regard these changes in the consultative process as sufficient. A number of them presented briefs to the Special Joint Committee on Canada's International Relations, recommending further procedural and substantive changes in Canadian human rights policy and execution. Several urged annual parliamentary review of the effectiveness of human rights policy in Canada's foreign relations, a recommendation endorsed by the committee.[43] Several favoured setting up of a regular human rights advisory body to the foreign minister, as has been done in several states, including France and the Netherlands. Church coalitions continued to stress substantive weaknesses in the department's human rights evaluations not only of certain country situations, like Chile's, but also of persistent factors like militarism, which contribute to gross and systematic violations.[44]

For some NGOs, the annual consultation is only one step in a constant interchange over human rights, which may include meetings with or presentations to minister(s) and departmental bureau staff, fact-finding reports and correspondence directed at departmental bureaux, and telephone consultation. A number of NGOs are part of international bodies that monitor, and seek to influence, the human rights process within the UN system. Amnesty, the International Commission of Jurists, the International Confederation of Free Trade Unions, and the World Council of Churches all maintain international personnel with this mandate. In addition, various groups have sent observers to the commission: churches (on six occasions), native groups – the World Council of Indigenous Peoples and the Innu and Naskapi-Montagnais of Labrador – (several times), and Amnesty International (Canada) and the Group for the Defence of Civil Rights in Argentina (once each). The Inter-Church Committee on Human Rights in Latin America has also sent representatives to New York to address commission rapporteurs, to meet with Canadian diplomats, and to attend meetings of the Third Committee of the general assembly when such matters as the commission's report or resolutions on country situations come before that body.[45]

The impact of this NGO pressure on Canadian participation in the UN human rights process is not easy to judge. While some leading officials repeatedly thank NGOs for their detailed analyses and continued commitment to human rights, others ignore or play down the NGOs' evidence. Yvon Beaulne and other departmental officials repeatedly lamented lack of public interest in human rights and minuscule media coverage of the commission and related events. Occasional floods of letters and telegrams to the ambassador and the minister from church networks led to expressions of exasperation from officials and appeals to "turn off the tap" of correspondence so that day-to-day work could be accomplished.[46] This background fire of letters and petitions – regarding Central America, Argentina's disappeared, Uruguay's political prisoners, South Korea, and the Philippines – probably ensured that Canada's position on some situations and its interventions in debate were more considered and perhaps more advanced than they might otherwise have been. The significant and growing constituency for international human rights has inspired those departmental human rights officials who wish to be involved. Some officials have been caught between the desire to increase the profile of issues in their portfolio and the desire for a simpler life, without NGO interference.[47]

The UN process and related consultations have provided an occasion for the NGO community to exert pressure on and to review and evaluate the government's performance. Together with pressure on parliamentary committees and on the minister, this has helped establish human rights as a recognized and significant, if ambiguous, strand in Canadian interests and foreign policy.

Canada as Observer

When Canada concluded its term on the UN Commission on Human Rights in 1984 without seeking re-election, NGOs, particularly church coalitions, pressed the government to seek re-election as soon as possible.[48] Following Canada's first session (the 41st, 1985), as an observer, controversy broke out regarding the approach of the delegation. A former senior government adviser on human rights, Philippe LeBlanc, attended the 41st session and assessed the Canadian performance as "characterized by hypocrisy and diplomatic maneuvering. The delegation was silent or kept a low profile on major human rights issues and its statements were low-key and non-committal, reflecting diplomatic niceties rather than a strong commitment to human rights."

LeBlanc cited the delegation's lack of critical evaluation of the much-criticized special rapporteur's report on Guatemala, its apparent accommodation to US objections to the wording of the Guatemala resolution, its "double policy" on apartheid, and its treatment of visiting cabinet member Walter McLean. He also noted the lack of serious treatment of NGO recommendations at the annual consultation. As one of the Canadian church observers, I had monitored the Guatemalan case closely and been in touch with colleagues in Canada who were pressing Ottawa for a more forthright position, and I would support this criticism. Leblanc's fundamental concern was that the delegation was engaged primarily in a diplomatic game rather than in applying or seeking implementation of human rights standards in urgent situations.[49]

LeBlanc's charges were answered in a speech given on 29 March 1985 by David Kilgour, parliamentary secretary to the minister for external relations. He described Canada's delegation as "very active" and "able to accomplish a great deal." He mentioned Canada's co-sponsorship of 12 resolutions and its negotiation of texts, particularly that on the rights of individuals to promote human rights. He termed the resolutions on Guatemala and El Salvador "significantly improved."[50] However, co-sponsorship of resolutions is a questionable measure of effectiveness. The lengthy lists of co-sponsors and interruptions of proceedings to declare adherence to this or that resolution have, in van Boven's opinion, effectively turned "the business of co-sponsoring into nonsense. It simply adds to the inefficiency and complexity of the proceedings."[51]

On the more substantive issues, while Canada did support the right to advocate human rights, debate over the Guatemalan resolution indicated weaknesses in its overall position. The telling issue over Guatemala was the question of arms. Clause 12 of the draft resolution circulated to the commission specifically called on governments "to refrain from supplying arms and other military assistance to all parties in conflict in Guatemala, in order to contribute to the improvement of the human rights situation in that country."[52] The US delegation pressed for removal of the reference and insertion of much more general and ambiguous language. The Irish, among others, pressed for retention. When the Western group adopted the American position (without significant Canadian objection), the Irish withdrew from co-sponsorship, arguing a direct connection between arms and militarization and the continued violation of human rights, an insight lacking in Canadian interventions. What Kilgour regarded as an "improvement" LeBlanc saw as a strategic weakening of the international position. The Irish delegation and Guatemalan and Canadian human rights organizations agreed.

Guatemala illustrates a further criticism made by LeBlanc: Canada's failure to adopt an independent position based on the merits of each case. He and other human rights advocates argue that the guiding factor ought to be objective assessment of the evidence regarding human rights abuses, together with recognition of causes, such as military control or militarization, underlying gross and systematic violation. Pressures – superpowers' desire to weaken resolutions critical of friends, efforts of the countries in question – against strong positions are considerable. The Canadian delegation's performance at the 41st session suggested that the Mulroney government had succumbed to them. However, the criticism led to a small but unusual spurt of press interest in Canada's role in the commission – and a defence in reply by a government spokesperson – and may have provoked Canada's changed approach in the following session.

At the commission in 1986 External Affairs appeared to have a strategy. It sought re-election at the May meeting of ECOSOC. It appointed a high-profile head, Gordon Fairweather, and several new and energetic delegation members; took a more studied and positive approach to NGO submissions, even publishing assessments of country situations in a briefing book; and dealt interactively and relatively openly with NGO observers during the commission's session.

CONCLUSION:
THE COMMISSION IN QUESTION

The 42nd session (1986) closed amid disturbing rumours of the "drastic implications" for the UN Centre for Human Rights resulting from proposals made by Assistant Secretary-General for Human Rights Herndl.

Proposed cuts included administrative reductions, such as halting human rights publications for the remainder of 1986 and ending short-term contract staff, cutting one of the three meetings of the Human Rights Committee, and eliminating the annual session of the Sub-Commission of Experts on Human Rights. Meetings of the three working groups of the sub-commission – on indigenous populations, on slavery, and on communications – were also threatened. As one former chair of the commission commented: "These cuts mean that the forty to fifty thousand communications and appeals that come each year will not be considered; they do what the Russians and others never succeeded in doing."[53]

Reductions in staff and contract staff had already led to charges of low morale and reduced treatment of urgent appeals and assistance to bodies like the working group on disappearances. With new cuts planned for mid-1986, a situation of questionable morale was turning into one of stark concern for survival.[54] Cuts to the sub-commission and other expert and working groups were termed by one experienced academic observer "a serious blow to the hopes and expectations of vulnerable groups."[55] Niall MacDermot, chair of the group of international NGOs related to the commission, called them "a serious threat to the activities of one of the most productive and innovative sources of human rights action in the U.N. system and a serious blow to the cause of human rights."[56] Since recommended implementation of a 10 per cent across-the-board cut in the UN budget left commission items like seminars and conferences untouched, while cutting expert bodies, it appeared "short-sighted," reflecting "distorted priorities" and liable to have a "negative impact far greater than the relatively modest level of reductions might suggest."[57] The sub-commission's functions were profoundly threatened, as a way for NGOs to influence the UN human rights agenda, as a method by which experts could consider evidence and make recommendations, and as an instrument for innovative and pioneering work in such fields as the rights of children and the disabled.

A number of Canadian human rights officials and diplomats opposed the proposed cuts.[58] Canadian NGOs and churches protested to Joe Clark and to Canada's UN ambassador, Stephen Lewis. External Affairs expressed concern but indicated commitment to the overall package for reductions presented by the secretary-general, "a delicately crafted document."[59] However, Stephen Lewis stated, on 30 April 1986: "My Government wishes with all its heart and soul ... to restore the 1986 convening of the Human Rights Sub-Commission ... and with it the Working Group on Indigenous Populations. Canadians are profoundly concerned that we should sacrifice so important a human rights meeting. We only bowed to it in the interests of preserving the package. If the package is fully reopened, we shall want to negotiate strongly to rescue the Sub-Commission."[60] In correspondence, Lewis shared the concerns of non-governmental critics of the cutbacks: "The Sub-Commission should never have been removed in the first place: it says some very sad things about the quality of Secretariat leadership."[61]

The implications of the cuts remain. As the Canadian church observer at the 42nd session reported, some serious situations on which action ought to be prepared for the 43rd session will not be addressed because of the sub-commission's temporary elimination. "Within the context of increasing attacks by the Reagan administration against the United Nations, the crisis is more political than it is financial."[62] Delaying consideration of serious situations, such as those in Guatemala, or long-standing concerns, like East Timor or Paraguay, plays into the hands of violator governments and their allies.

Restoration of the sub-commission and its working groups remains a priority for Canadian and international NGOs and, it seems, for Canada's UN ambassador and the government he represents. Whether the morale and effectiveness of the UN Centre can be rebuilt, and the system of communications, expert consideration, initiative, and innovation restored, remains in doubt. Commission and sub-commission must be made more efficient and effective and gain resources to meet more frequently or to operate through their bureaux or executives between meetings.[63] Whether or not the present leadership of these bodies can display the necessary will and recognizable commitment to human rights may be crucial for a favourable outcome. There is a continuing challenge to Canadian and like-minded governments to respond effectively to this urgent crisis.

CHAPTER SIX

The Human Rights Committee

CATHAL J. NOLAN

THE COMMITTEE

Canada's promotion of human rights through the UN system involves it in a constellation of organizations and agencies. Canada regards the Human Rights Committee[1] as second in importance only to the UN Commission on Human Rights.[2] The committee acquires this central standing from the importance of its three major responsibilities.

First, it is the body principally concerned with the International Covenant on Civil and Political Rights, which is the more immediate, and arguably cardinal, of the two international covenants.[3] The committee offers international legal interpretation of the rights outlined in it.

Second, the committee reviews reports prepared by countries party to the covenant, describing measures taken to facilitate implementation and highlighting shortcomings. Reports are the only formal device available to determine whether countries have complied. The procedure, though flawed, is a useful source of information about those few states that take this responsibility seriously. At best, preparing a report on implementation for an international body can improve laws and practice. At the least, reports demonstrate the distance between rhetoric and performance. In human rights promotion, knowing the depth of a state's hypocrisy can be useful.

Third, the committee seeks to protect individual victims of abuse. Until very recently it was the only UN-affiliated human rights body to which an individual could make direct appeal.[4] However, only people from countries that have ratified the Optional Protocol to the covenant may communicate with the committee. Jurisdiction in individual complaints is thus limited to a few states (37 as of April 1986). Complaints to the committee have on occasion led to changes in legislation that affected large groups of people and broad categories of rights; see note 24, below. This procedure makes available constructive international remedies for situations not otherwise successfully addressed.

In summary, the committee is concerned with a wide range of important rights, with state reports on implementation, and with individuals who seek redress for abuses. These responsibilities place the Human Rights Committee near the centre of UN efforts to promote and protect human rights. This was not always the case, however, as a review of the committee's origins will demonstrate.

Origins

The International Covenant on Civil and Political Rights was adopted – along with the Covenant on Economic, Social and Cultural Rights – by the UN general assembly (UNGA) in December 1966. It did not enter into force until March 1976.[5] The covenant established the Human Rights Committee, which was authorized to consider and make "general comments" on state reports on implementation. It was also commissioned to receive petitions from citizens of those countries, much fewer in number, that had agreed to the Optional Protocol. The committee was to be composed of 18 "expert" members serving four-year terms and meeting three times each year. It first met in March and April 1977.[6]

Members were to be "persons of high moral character and recognized competence in the field of human rights," who would serve "in their personal capacity," but consideration was to "be given to equitable geographical distribution of membership and to the representation of the different forms of civilization and of the principal legal systems." However, committee members have not always acted independently of their sponsoring states. It is an exceptional country that respects the concept of an independent expert. Moreover, even for those who want to act more independently, the inability of the UN Human Rights Centre to provide adequate support services has frequently forced members to fall back on their national missions.[7] Of course, the committee has been highly successful in meeting geographical and ideological criteria: from its inception, it has included members from all major political blocs and from most regions of the world.[8] As a result, the committee has had two main sources of internal conflict. First, there exists a constant danger of procedural and substantive inertia caused by bloc confrontation. Second, the committee's make-up at times creates an anomalous situation wherein nationals from countries that have not ratified the protocol sit in review of cases from countries that have. The committee's form as proposed under the draft covenant of 1954 differed greatly from how it was finally constituted. As originally conceived, implementation of the covenant would have been overseen by a committee with broad monitoring powers. For example, every signatory would have had the right to lodge complaints of non-compliance against any other signatory. Moreover, the committee would have had the quasi-judicial power to refer cases for advisory opinions to the compulsory jurisdiction of the International Court of Justice.[9] But when the UN Third Committee debated the proposed covenant, in 1966, a majority of countries opposed permitting other states to lodge complaints. Indeed, there was considerable opposition to the establishment of a committee in any form.

Soviet-bloc countries were wholly opposed to creating a committee that would monitor implementation – thereby undercutting propaganda gains from merely rhetorical involvement with human rights. Some African and Asian states wanted monitoring functions severed from mandatory judicial procedures.[10] Western countries argued for full monitoring power, because the human rights record of the Economic and Social Council (ECOSOC) had not been impressive, because ECOSOC was overburdened in any case, and because only a special body could provide the fact-finding and "good offices" called for in the covenant.[11] Although Soviet opposition remained unabated, Western and Third World countries worked out a compromise formula that so weakened the committee's proposed powers that even the Soviets ultimately acquiesced in its establishment. Provision for state-to-state complaints was made optional,[12] and all quasi-judicial functions were removed, along with authority to assess whether a matter involved a breach of the covenant and to comment on such transgressions. In short, the committee was limited to private reading of state reports. It could not inquire into the truthfulness of these reports or comment publicly on them.

Clearly, the committee would merely serve the interests of most states in appearing to support international supervision and promotion of civil and political rights. In practice, it was going to be as weak and ineffective as its opponents – the majority of signatories – could make it. It was not permitted to refer to a violating state even in its private communications. Instead, it was required to express its "views" in general terms, even though no provision was made for communicating these views to other countries and no consideration given to general publicity. It was allowed to send its general comments only to the state involved and to ECOSOC.

However, the possibility of inquiry into conditions within states was not entirely eliminated. For example, the committee retained pale beginnings of a fact-finding role, in that states had to submit reports. At one point it had been thought the committee might play a role as conciliator in disputes between states over rights questions. Provision was therefore made for an ad hoc and voluntary commission to help resolve interstate disputes.[13] The right of individuals to communicate (or petition) was added, but under an optional protocol. Assessing the merits of individual cases became one of the committee's duties.

The Human Rights Committee was not designed to serve as an enforcement agency, or even as a monitor of the covenant. Because sovereignty remains the constitutive principle and central fact of the modern international system, the task of guaranteeing rights is reserved to individual states. At best, the committee could offer good offices to states already disposed to fulfil their obligations as signatories. Any assessment of the committee's performance must take account of these in-built limitations, which reflect the persistent international political realities under which the committee continues to operate.

State Reports

When a country ratifies the civil and political covenant, it assumes a treaty obligation to other signatories to report on its implementation of the rights described therein. This report is supposed to be presented within a year of the covenant coming into force for a country. The majority of states have met this commitment, regardless of how poorly they treat the rights of their citizens, but the quality of most reports has left much to be desired. In 1979 Canada submitted by far the largest and most comprehensive report of any nation to date.[14] But some reports have been nothing more than general affirmations, filling as little as a single page. Others have been paeans of self-praise, assertions of complete compliance with the covenant, or both. Czechoslovakia, for example reported: "The rights contained ... in the Covenant are guaranteed in the Czechoslovak Socialist Republic by the constitution ... and by other constitutional acts and laws which frequently protect the civil and political rights of citizens to a greater extent than that required by the Covenant ... These laws are consistently observed in legal and political practice, which itself is in full conformity with the Covenant, and, in certain cases is more advantageous than as anticipated by the Covenant."[15]

Such wilful obfuscation is probably helpful only in evaluating the seriousness with which a government approaches its treaty obligations and the cynicism with which it regards international promotion of human rights. Nonetheless, in international politics a state's trustworthiness regarding treaty obligations is a useful thing to know.

Despite the committee's lack of authority to question reports, a few delegations have engaged in lively defence of their country's record. Through procedural reform and the efforts of outstanding members the committee has started to break down resistance to outside scrutiny, even though most countries continue to deny legitimacy to the monitoring process and block attempts to probe their rights abuses. Western countries, and some others, have supported procedures that would go beyond commenting on formal legal rights to allow review of actual conditions. For example, in 1981 the committee began to formulate "general comments" designed to draw attention to insufficiencies in reports. These comments have moved to interpretation of the rights outlined in the covenant. Once again, however, political limits to even procedural reform emerged quickly. Opposition – principally Soviet – to comments addressed directly to states has blocked further movement.[16] The committee's reservation of a right "to proceed further on individual reports at a later stage" is thus an admission of failure.

The committee has cited sources of information about abuses other than state reports, despite lack of provision for this procedure in the covenant. Members have cited information published by UN human rights bodies or provided by non-governmental organizations (NGOs).[17] Further widening of this procedural crack is a prerequisite to monitoring compliance. NGOs have been negligent in not pressing more forcefully for official standing with the committee. Canadian NGOs, in particular, do not seem to understand the committee's role or to have helped it develop its potential ability to scrutinize the records of violator states.[18]

In summary, there continues to be strong resistance to having the committee monitor compliance with the covenant. Many countries continue to insist that it has no authority to question the content of their reports and refuse to participate in any such examination.[19] Others have engaged in debate with committee members, while maintaining that the procedure is invalid. A few countries, Canada among them, have cooperated fully with the committee and supported procedural reforms to expand the committee's powers.

Guaranteeing rights set out in international arrangements is the obligation essentially of individual states, owing to the persistent reality of sovereignty. Outside bodies, even other states, can act only to facilitate respect for individual rights. The Human Rights Committee clearly understands its role as primarily one of providing "good offices." As one observer has said, for this reason it places most emphasis "on questions like the direct applicability of the covenant in national legal systems, the right directly to invoke the covenant before the courts, and the extent to which State Parties have actually adopted legislative or other measures to give effect to the rights recognized in the Covenant."[20] Although its rules of procedure allow the committee to decide issues by majority vote, it has made all decisions by consensus.[21] Proceeding by consensus can threaten immobility at times but appears also to have helped build constructive working relations with several countries. This non-confrontational atmosphere may encourage some states to ratify the covenant. However, given the ideologically charged nature of human rights issues, it is more doubtful that they will be convinced that opening domestic records to outside monitoring will not expose them to politically motivated assaults.

To avoid cynicism about the committee's usefulness, it is important to realize that it has a more limited purpose than bodies such as the UN Commission on Human Rights. As Louis Sohn has pointed out, the committee was considered less likely to involve itself with gross violations of human rights but would "deal primarily with the difficulties caused by the imperfect introduction of international human rights provisions into domestic legal systems."[22] It would thus be unfair to criticize the committee for not censuring gross and persistent violators. These extreme situations are more appropriately dealt with elsewhere, even outside the UN system altogether. Further, the quiet task of assisting better-disposed states to implement the covenant is not trivial. Evolution of committee procedures may yet prove an imaginative example of constructive international human rights promotion.

The Optional Protocol

As of April 1986, 37 of the more than 80 states party to the covenant had also ratified its Optional Protocol. Although countries from all power blocs and geographical regions acceded to the covenant, not one eastern European, Arab, or Asian state has accepted the protocol.[23] However, in addition to Western states, 9 African and 14 Latin American and Caribbean nations have accepted the protocol. The committee has received over 200 individual "communications" – a relatively small number that does not meet early expectations (or fears!). Proceeding by consensus has helped break down the reluctance of some countries to discuss violations. A number of countries have responded to critical comments regarding a single complaint by altering their domestic legislation or practice.[24]

In general, the committee has taken a liberal view of the protocol. For instance, when a state claims that domestic remedies have not been exhausted, the committee has gone beyond even the European Convention in supporting individual petitioners. It has placed the burden of proof about exhaustion of remedies on the country complained against and has required "specific details of domestic remedies which it claims to have been available to the alleged victim, together with evidence that there would be a reasonable prospect that such remedies would be effective."[25] This practice at least assures individuals that a petition will not be rejected merely owing to the unsupported denials of a government.

Moreover, as early as its first decision the committee indicated that it would seek to protect the protocol process against governmental obstruction. Under the protocol, countries petitioned against are obliged within six months to "submit to the committee written explanations or statements clarifying the matter and the remedy, if any, that may have been taken by that State." When this obligation goes unfulfilled, and the evidence supports the petitioner, the committee has found by default in the complainant's favour. As one analyst has said, this decision "established that the mere passivity of a State Party concerned authorizes the committee to take as proved the well attested allegations of facts."[26] A majority on the committee intended to place its responsibilities to victims of abuse as far as possible ahead of the privileges of states.

The committee relies mainly on the minor pressure that can be brought to bear on an offender through expression of critical views. The effort of some states to remove even this minor sanction by making protocol matters confidential thus threatened to strangle effectiveness at birth. A small group of members moved to circumvent this difficulty by – without formal sanction – publicizing critical findings along with the reply of the country concerned.[27] Also, "Final Views" began to inquire what a state would do by way of redress when it was found to have violated the covenant.[28] These new developments may yet lead to a significant monitoring role for the committee, particularly if interested states, such as Canada, and NGOs generate more publicity.

CANADA AND THE COMMITTEE

Early Involvement

Canada was not among the first countries to ratify the Covenant on Civil and Political Rights. Constitutional complications arising from divisions of domestic jurisdiction between federal and provincial governments were the main cause of delay. Ratification required prior assurances from the provinces that they would take the necessary legislative steps to ensure compliance. Following years of negotiation, Canada ratified within a few months of the covenant becoming operative in 1976. Canada also acceded to the Optional Protocol, despite reluctance by parts of the federal bureaucracy. Officials in the Department of Justice questioned the ability of the country's legal system to absorb demands made by protocol cases.[29] Early apprehensiveness was eventually overcome, however, and any lingering reluctance dissolved as officials became more experienced with the procedure. Since then, Canada has co-operated fully and enthusiastically with the committee, as shown by its record of participation in committee activities and in appraisals by international observers. A senior official at the UN Centre for Human Rights praised Canada's efforts as "first class, supportive and active." Another described Canada as playing "a leading role in setting an example of cooperation with the reporting procedure and even more so with the optional protocol."[30]

Once Canada had ratified the covenant it became eager to participate in its international elaboration. It therefore made a concerted effort to place a national on the committee, succeeding when Walter Tarnopolsky was elected one of the first members. Where membership would be drawn from a cross-section of states, it was prudent to have a national in position to help clarify peculiarities in Canada's laws and practice. Additionally, although Tarnopolsky served as one of the few truly independent experts, his presence indirectly promoted Canadian interest in maintaining a high UN profile. Canada hoped that he would help develop workable rules of procedure and worthwhile general operations.[31] These hopes were not unfounded: as part of a group of independent members, Tarnopolsky helped push for expansion of the committee's powers and duties. This group saw to it that proceedings were publicized and "views" circulated. Owing to continuous representation by capable people throughout the period of early development,[32] Canada influenced the committee's evolution.

In part because of Canada's active UN role on human rights over the past 20 years, of late no Canadian nominee has been elected to the committee.[33] Moreover, as international human rights efforts begin to concentrate on implementation, broad international opposition to Canadian positions and participation may increase. This problem is compounded by the lack of formal regional allocation of membership. Every two years 9 of the 18 members face electoral challenge. Elections are usually well contested, and candidates are selected irrespective of region. There is therefore little chance of Western nations to rotate nominations so as to assure each country periodic representation.[34]

Implementing the Covenant

Canada is not called upon to play a special or specific role on the committee. Nonetheless, it has emerged as a leader by setting an example of co-operation with reporting procedures and by responding positively and comprehensively to protocol complaints. Even a cursory examination of Canadian participation makes clear that considerable bureaucratic resources are expended to explain the country's domestic circumstances. The 1979 Canadian report, for example, was by far the longest and most comprehensive prepared by any state. This pattern continued with preparation of an extensive follow-up report in 1983. Canada endeavours to outline existing short-comings in domestic practice; its reports signify profound seriousness about covenant obligations. In 1979 Canada became one of a handful of states to make a voluntary declaration, granting the committee the right to consider state-to-state communications about its domestic practice. No country has yet invoked this procedure, mostly because the states that have made this declaration have the most exemplary internal records. Nonetheless, this procedure remains a potential avenue for interested countries to direct international attention to human rights abuses. Canadian co-operation is clearly part of a broad policy to improve the ability of international bodies to inquire into the records of other, less pliant states.

Canada's response to complaints has also been co-operative and positive. First, the Department of the Secretary of State has sought to inform Canadians of their right to seek international redress for alleged violations. That partly explains why Canada ranks second only to Uruguay in number of complaints lodged against. Indeed, several committee members once objected that inclusion of a list of communications in the annual report would give an inaccurate impression of the country's domestic performance.[35] Second, Canada answers complaints with care. As one UN official has said: "It is obvious that Canada spends a great deal of time and effort not only to reply *pro forma* to [protocol] complaints, unlike the useless replies of some states, but in explaining all aspects of domestic circumstances to the Committee."[36]

Canadian response to a complaint always involves three departments: External Affairs, Justice, and Secretary of State. It frequently involves also other federal departments and provincial governments. In the process, Canada prepares extensive legal arguments for presentation to the committee. Seriousness about defending itself also contributes to international legal interpretation of the covenant.[37] However, Canada's response to criticism has sometimes been ambivalent. For example, when the committee was hearing a case on Canadian parole legislation in 1981, the federal solicitor general, Robert Kaplan, gave vent to his frustration at international interference. He angrily announced that because Canada was an independent and sovereign nation the government would not consider itself bound by a committee finding that federal parole legislation violated the covenant.[38] However, most frequently Canadian governments have responded to committee criticism by admitting shortcomings and introducing legislative or administrative remedies. Reflecting this fact, UN officials single out Canadian examples as prime illustrations of what is hoped for from states under the protocol procedure.[39]

Close attention to the covenant and committee participation have had some effect on Canada's domestic life. The bureaucratic, legal, and political negotiations that envelop these processes may have heightened public and governmental knowledge about Canadians' rights and privileges. This is only part of a larger social and political phenomenon under way in Canada since at least the mid-1970s, perhaps reaching its zenith in 1982 with inclusion in the constitution of a Charter of Rights and Freedoms. Yet the possible impact of the international covenants on Canada's internal political and social debate should not be ignored. As Secretary of State for External Affairs Don Jamieson said in 1978:

International actions have directly affected domestic developments in the human rights field. Consultations related to Canada signing and ratifying the important human rights covenant ... had a catalytic effect on the evolution of human rights legislation in Canada. It encouraged, as well, the establishment of statutory human rights agencies at the federal and provincial levels. The international obligations we have assumed by ratifying the covenants ensure a continuing review of domestic performance judged against the covenants' standards.[40]

Promoting human rights in international bodies is part of a general foreign policy effort to extend liberal values, especially reliance on law, into the international arena. Precisely because these values are central to Canada's national life, international activity on their behalf has had an important, though almost certainly unforeseen, impact at home.

Advancing Political Interests

Canadian co-operation with the committee goes beyond self-interest in defending the country's domestic record, which is enviable by international standards. In addition to having a humanitarian concern to see rights respected in other countries, Canada has several important political interests at stake in international human rights bodies. First, all Western nations have a special interest in seeing the rights of the civil and political covenant accorded high priority. Emphasis by states on one covenant (civil and political) or the other (economic and social) in their rhetoric and policy reflects larger ideological divides in world politics. Canada finds itself in conflict with states that would prefer to dilute or otherwise undermine the concept of civil and political rights as part of a broader propaganda offensive against the West. Canada and other Western democracies seek to forestall decisions that could diminish that tradition and thereby assault wider Western interests.

As a middle power Canada has an essential interest in strengthening respect for international law and institutions, even in the exceptionally weak form these take regarding human rights. Canada also gains diplomatic prestige from membership in international bodies. But most important, support for the UN system as a potential guarantor of security has been a central priority in Canadian policy since 1945. This has created tension between the country's strong security interest in "functional" international organizations and its less pronounced promotion of liberal democratic values.

Questions of human rights tend to be ideologically charged and to disrupt international co-operation; pursuing them therefore sometimes harms other national interests. In recent years, however, participation in international human rights bodies has grown more attractive for Canada. Canadian officials have seen that support of international bodies furthers national security interests in preserving a working system of international organization. This belief in a connection between security and human rights was illustrated in remarks by Canada's ambassador to the United Nations: "Destruction of our carefully constructed mechanisms for the promotion and protection of human rights would further erode public support for this Organization in numerous member states. We cannot afford, and will not tolerate, a drift towards institutional paralysis in the human rights field."[41] This perception has grown in tandem with apparent default – financial and political – of US leadership in the United Nations. Canada's support for international human rights promotion is determined as much by national security interest as by concern for human rights.

Looking Ahead

What can be reasonably expected of Canada in the committee? First, Canada ought to – and almost certainly will – continue to encourage international scrutiny of its domestic performance. It is in Canada's interest to speak out when the committee oversteps its mandate by adopting politically motivated resolutions with no bearing on rights. For example, in 1984 the committee adopted a resolution that "production, testing, possession, deployment and use of nuclear weapons should be prohibited and recognized as crimes against humanity."[42] The effect – and usually the calculated design – of resolutions such as this are to diminish the value of the concept of human rights. There is provision in the covenant for Canada to respond to committee views. If such clear politicization is repeated, Canada might make more use of this provision. Further, in annual statements in the UNGA, Canada can make known its views on committee activities and express ideas it would like to see pursued. Such statements are closely examined by the committee[43] and could provide an avenue of influence even when no Canadian is a member. ECOSOC and the Third Committee might also provide venues for comment and debate.

Canada also can actively promote civil and political rights internationally. The need for human rights advisory assistance is growing. Canada might easily – and relatively cheaply – make available to other countries its experts experienced in international human rights procedures and law.[44] It could also provide in-country training or organize and support regional and country-specific seminars on civil and political rights. Advisory assistance already exists within the UN Centre for Human Rights. However, the centre's seminars have rarely been relevant to problems of a given country. Regional programs have proved more effective but also have been too diffuse in focus and have been undermined by certain states.[45] Canada should continue to press for more efficient and less politicized use of UN human rights facilities, but fresh advisory services are probably best urged bilaterally.[46]

CONCLUSIONS

A member of the committee has written that it gains authority from "inner qualities of impartiality, objectiveness and soberness."[47] This appraisal is clearly much too sanguine – not to mention self-serving. It ignores fundamental conflicts of interest and ideology that lie at the heart of interstate disputes concerning human rights. Nonetheless, consensus decision-making probably gives the committee some influence. For a majority of countries, opinions expressed by international bodies are important. However, "gross and persistent" violators will not respect even "legally binding" decisions by international bodies.

What about the committee's future? Because few additional countries are likely to sign the Optional Protocol soon, examining reports will be the committee's only means to evaluate compliance by most states. The prohibition against assessing other than merely legal and constitutional adherence will continue to hamper monitoring of the covenant. The committee has obtained and used outside information but faces sustained recalcitrance on the part of most states.

Proceeding by consensus has led to constructive dialogue between the committee and a number of states. In several cases this has helped gain redress for individuals and contributed to alterations in legislation and practice. These positive effects thus go beyond correction of the original abuse. The committee has chosen a middle way between confrontational demands and too ready concession to the self-interest of states. The committee has given what support it could to victims of abuse. Generally, its influence will remain limited to states committed to the rights listed in the covenant. Yet, even among these countries, the committee's sway will rest mostly on their unwillingness to appear to deny human rights.

Recognition that the committee's influence is limited and extends to few states – not including the most egregious violators – should not lead to despair. Advancing rights in even a few countries is important to advancing these rights everywhere. Elevating minimum standards for the treatment of individuals in democratic societies historically has tended to raise the level of popular political demands in other, more repressive societies. Despots of both left and right increasingly have had to claim to be practising "true democracy" or promise democratic rule in the future. Therefore, if the committee can assist even a few countries its work will be worthwhile. It remains to be proved that sanctions against violators work better than conciliation and quiet diplomacy. Indeed, available evidence concerning sanctions suggests much the opposite. Setting an example of civilized domestic practice may thus in the long run have the greatest impact on abuses outside one's borders.

Canadian policy toward the committee reflects a principled commitment to civil and political rights. Canada's record of openness to international review enhances its credibility when it speaks on violations elsewhere. This is not insignificant, insofar as persuasion and encouragement, rather than censure and condemnation, are likely to remain the main tools of effective human rights promotion in cases of less than "gross and persistent" abuse. More broadly, Canada supports international rights bodies out of its essential interest as a smaller power in development of a working system of international organization and law and out of its sense of a pressing need for Western leadership in the United Nations. Ultimately, however, the success of international organizations will require renewed US participation. It is therefore in Canada's interest – as part of a policy of broad support for human rights and the United Nations – to encourage American involvement, especially in bodies concerned with civil and political rights.

Canada should not uncritically support UN-sponsored human rights activities. It may not be necessary, and certainly it is not sufficient, to promote civil and political rights within the UN system. Useful UN efforts should of course be maintained; but there should be less hesitation to criticize or even abandon unsuccessful initiatives. Canada's first instinct is to refrain from criticism of the United Nations. Secretary of State for External Affairs Joe Clark recently told the UNGA: "We believe this institution is essential to the safety of the world, and we defend it even when its actions are foolish or infuriating or wrong."[48]

It is one thing to pursue Canada's interest in international organization as a general principle, another to maintain an exaggerated reluctance to criticize. There should be less hesitation to rebuke if the committee begins to elaborate positions that undermine the concept of civil and political rights. If this occurs, Canada would be blameworthy to keep silent. Canada should not permit its general interest in a functioning system of international organizations to cause acquiescence in manoeuvres that diminish the concept of human rights and fundamental freedoms.

Further improvement in the committee's monitoring role would be welcome support for bilateral efforts to advance protection of rights and freedom internationally. To this end, Canada and like-minded countries ought to continue to participate in non-confrontational measures that encourage states to accept international oversight of respect for human rights. New bilateral advisory assistance in civil and political rights could reinforce a quiet, pragmatic approach at the multilateral level. Although need for censure and condemnation will arise in a world of seemingly endless violations, there is surely room as well for policies that highlight conciliation, constructive criticism, and practical assistance. Quiet diplomacy, mediation by bodies such as the Human Rights Committee, and positive incentives for change in the form of advisory services may well provide the best long-term hope for real redress.

CHAPTER SEVEN

The International Labour Organization

KALMEN KAPLANSKY

THE ORGANIZATION

Role

The promotion and protection of social and economic rights around the world have been the main mission of the International Labour Organization (ILO) since its inception in 1919. The attainment of "social justice" has been the goal not only of its standard-setting activities but also of its research, promotional, and operational programs. From the ILO's perspective, meaningful discussion of human rights must refer to their social and economic components. Thus the manner in which Canada, a founding member, has carried out its obligations and relations to the ILO has reflected the Canadian response to human rights in foreign policy.

The ILO has been a pioneer in developing and monitoring binding international instruments. Its influence on national law and practice stems from its thrust and structure. For close to 70 years its standards – international conventions and recommendations – have been essential instruments and models for promoting social and economic equity. All member states were to participate, regardless of when they joined, their level of development, or the nature of their economic and political systems. All members have a common responsibility to work for the attainment of the organization's goals.[1]

The ILO is unique among international intergovernmental organizations in its long life and the institutionalized participation, on a basis of near-equality with governments, of workers' and employers' representatives in all of the organization's work. Occupational groups directly affected by ILO activities participate fully in the formulation and implementation of both standards and operations. Some think that tripartitism is closely tied to the "functional" concept of international organizations: experts representing vital social and economic interests are more likely to reach agreement on substantive policy than government representatives, preoccupied with preserving and protecting sovereignty.[2]

The establishment of international labour standards, in the form of conventions and recommendations, was one of the principal objectives assigned to the ILO by its constitution. It is a continuing task, a standing item on the agenda of its annual conferences. By 1985, conventions had been the subject of close to 5,200 ratifications, with an average ratification per member state of 34. The average for western European states is 60, for eastern European states 50, for the Americas 38, for Africa 26, and for Asia and the Pacific 20. Canada has ratified 26 ILO conventions. However, most ratifications have been for the main ILO instruments, dealing with freedom of association, the abolition of forced labour, and equality in employment, generally referred to as human rights conventions.

Ratification is not the only measure of the effect of ILO standards on national law and practice. There is ample evidence, based on individual country studies, that unratified conventions as well as recommendations have influenced adoption of national legislation and its implementation.

ILO Standards and UN Instruments

Although the ILO pioneered in the definition and proclamation of international concepts of social and economic rights, its work received powerful impetus from the UN general assembly's adoption of the Universal Declaration of Human Rights in 1948. The declaration, while not an international legal standard subject to national ratification, is an effective educational and hortatory instrument. Some believe its most innovative thrust is its emphasis on social, economic, and cultural rights. It translates traditional basic freedoms and constitutional rights into the language of present-day industrial society and emphasizes a wide range of social and economic rights relevant to ILO conventions and recommendations.

ILO instruments have a direct link with the rights spelled out in the declaration: the Convention concerning the Organization of the Employment Service (no. 88) of 1948 lays down certain principles regarding the right to employment mentioned in article 23(1) of the declaration; the Convention concerning Employment Policy (no. 122) of 1964 relates to the right to employment and protection against unemployment; the Convention concerning the Abolition of Forced Labour (no. 105) of 1957 relates to the free choice of employment; the Convention concerning Discrimination in Respect of Employment and Occupation (no. 111) of

1958 spells out the principles laid down in articles 20 and 23 of the declaration; and the Convention concerning Equal Remuneration for Men and Women Workers for Work of Equal Value (no. 100) of 1951 relates to articles 12 and 23 of the declaration.[3]

Further, the two international covenants based on the declaration and adopted by the UN general assembly in 1966, on economic, social and cultural rights and on civil and political rights, give added international authority to the concept of social and economic rights. Both covenants "recognize" in their preambles that "in accordance with the Universal Declaration of Human Rights, the ideal of free human beings enjoying ... freedom from fear and want can only be achieved if conditions are created whereby everyone may enjoy his economic, social and cultural rights, as well as his civil and political rights." Article 6 of the Economic and Social Covenant recognizes the right to freely chosen employment, article 7 to fair wages and equal remuneration, "a decent living," safe and healthy working conditions, rest, leisure, "reasonable limitation of working hours," and paid holidays. Article 8 obligates states party to the covenant to "ensure" the right to form trade unions and the right to strike as well as to observe the ILO 1948 convention concerning freedom of association and protection of the right to organize; article 9 recognizes "the right of everyone to social security," including social insurance; article 12 refers to the duty of ratifying states to create conditions that "would assure to all medical service and medical attention in the event of sickness;" article 13 recognizes "the right of everyone to education." Canada has ratified the two covenants.

A number of supervisory mechanisms have been established under UN instruments, providing for varying degrees of ILO involvement. The Covenant on Economic, Social and Cultural Rights provides in article 18 for arrangements between the Economic and Social Council (ECOSOC) and the specialized agencies for reporting by the latter on the observance of covenant provisions within the scope of their activities; ECOSOC, by special resolution adopted in May 1976, called upon the agencies to submit such reports. A close relationship has since been established between the ILO and relevant UN organs in complaints-receiving mechanisms as well as in formulation of new standards that straddle the jurisdictional boundaries of UN organizations.

Implementing ILO standards

In contrast to UN conventions and to regional instruments, which tend to have individual and distinct supervisory mechanisms, the ILO's pioneering supervisory machinery applies uniformly to all states and generally to all ILO standards. The ILO constitution of 1919 established an obligation for member governments to submit an annual report on the application of ratified conventions, and in 1927, two special bodies were established to examine these reports.

The Committee of Experts on Application of Conventions and Recommendations now consists of 18 international legal experts drawn from all parts of the world and appointed in their individual capacities. Its reports are submitted for examination to a Standing Tripartite Committee of the annual ILO conference. The latter committee also examines reports on unratified conventions and recommendations, specially requested each year from member states by the ILO governing body.[4]

Through a system of "direct contact" with governments, the ILO has developed an effective system of consultation (including missions by ILO officials) to advise member states on resolving difficulties in applying ratified conventions and in complying with constitutional obligations. The ILO constitution provides also for representations or complaints. Under article 24 a representation may be made by any employers' or workers' organization, and under article 26 the complaints procedure may be initiated by another state that has ratified the convention concerned or by the governing body on its own initiative or on a complaint by a delegate to the ILO conference. These procedures have been used rather sparingly, mainly on account of the effectiveness of the Committee of Experts and the Tripartite Committee, but also because of the work of another unique complaints-receiving instrument, namely, the Governing Body Committee on Freedom of Association.

Following the adoption of conventions relating to freedom of association and the right to organize and to collective bargaining in 1948, the ILO governing body decided to form mechanisms to examine complaints of violation of trade union rights. Thus its Committee on Freedom of Association was established in agreement with the United Nations; ECOSOC decided in 1953 that allegations of infringements of trade union rights received by the United Nations that relate to ILO member states should be forwarded for consideration to the ILO governing body. Alleged violations submitted to the committee (about 30 each year) continue to be far greater than the infrequent representations and complaints concerning non-observance of ratified conventions. Obviously the ILO's Committee on Freedom of Association, which meets three or four times annually, is better adapted to respond to complainants' needs than the annual meeting of the ILO's general supervisory bodies. Also, this committee's facilities may be used even where relevant conventions have not been ratified. The committee thus retains the main responsibility for dealing with complaints relating to freedom of association.

This committee's decisions have also acquired a normative influence, having established a broad range of principles that point out the practical implications of the concepts and standards relating to freedom of association laid down in the ILO constitution, conventions, and recommendations. In addition, the procedural simplicity of filing a complaint has contributed to the committee's popularity with many trade union activists in countries where the principles and practices of freedom of association and the right to organize are open to public debate and scrutiny.

Canada's ILO membership, its ratification of several key ILO conventions generally regarded as human rights instruments as well as the use of ILO standards and machinery by government and non-governmental organizations (NGOs) in Canada should not be ignored in assessing the link between human rights and Canada's foreign policy.

CANADA AND THE ILO

History

The founding of the ILO in 1919 as a result of the provisions of the Treaty of Versailles coincided with a substantial advance in Canada's claim to national sovereignty.[5] Canada's move to dominion status and ultimately to full sovereignty became linked in 1919 to the creation of this intergovernmental organization.

While membership in the League of Nations and in the ILO hastened Canadian sovereignty and independence, it also imposed certain obligations on Canada that had important constitutional implications affecting basic internal policies. The League covenant and the ILO constitution provided two key features of the international protection of human rights: a commitment to strive for "social justice" as a means of achieving universal and lasting peace and the means of implementing that commitment through multilateral treaties, creating uniform obligations for all parties to the agreement. Allan Gotlieb has commented:

It is ironic that the Treaty of Versailles should have provided the legal basis both for Canadian participation in the international community and for the initiation of a type of international obligation which was to raise basic constitutional issues and cause difficulties for Canada in the years to come. The question of Canada's adherence to treaties on human rights was to give rise, over the years, to arguments for and against centralized solutions and for and against decentralized solutions, for novel methods of ratification and for abstention from ratification, for establishing federal legislative ascendancy and for recognizing the provinces as international persons, for delegation of powers and against such delegation, for constitutional reform and against such reform. In fact, the constitutional aspects of the protection of human rights have sometimes seemed, in Canada, to eclipse the practical aspects of the matter, and to have served as more of a debating subject for jurists than as a part of a search for effective legal methods for social action.[6]

Canada emerged from the First World War as a sovereign member of the international community. It faced, however, its new international capacities and responsibilities without constitutional provisions regarding the treaty-making and treaty-implementing powers that its new international status entailed. Moreover, Canada had not acquired sovereign status in 1867 when it became a self-governing dominion within the British empire. The imperial government continued to be responsible for Canada's external relations, and the British North America (BNA) Act, 1867, did not provide for treaty-making powers, except in section 132, which deals with implementation of international obligations contracted by Britain, insofar as such obligations were binding on Canada. Moreover, Canada was a federal state, in which jurisdiction over many of the activities of concern to the ILO lay with the provinces. Thus, in 1919, when Canada began to participate in the ILO's standard-setting activities, it faced problems with the ratification and implementation of ILO conventions.

Under the constitutions of some countries, international treaties, including ILO conventions, automatically acquire the force of internal law by virtue of the act of ratification. Not so in Canada. Under British constitutional practice, ratification and implementation were separate. In most federal systems, including those of the United States, Australia, and India, the power to implement all kinds of treaties, even those affecting the jurisdictions of the constituent parts, is allocated to the central legislative branch. Canada followed a different route, however, separating the treaty-making and treaty-implementation powers in relation to subjects of provincial competence.[7] This created considerable difficulties for Canada.

The judgment of the Judicial Committee of the Imperial Privy Council in the *Labour Conventions case* of 1937 brought this constitutional issue into sharp focus and continues to inhibit ratification of international conventions. That case arose out of an attempt in 1935 by Prime Minister R.B. Bennett to introduce in Canada a "new deal" in labour relations through ratification of three ILO conventions.[8] Their subject matter was partly within federal, but primarily within provincial, jurisdiction under section 92(13) of the BNA Act, namely, Property and Civil Rights in the Province.

The validity of this legislation was challenged in court by Ontario, New Brunswick, and British Columbia. The case eventually reached the Judicial Committee of the Privy Council, and a decision rendered on 28 January 1937 declared the federal statutes implementing these three conventions ultra vires of Parliament. The decision affects to this day ratification and implementation not only of ILO conventions but of international treaties in general. The judgment stressed the federal executive's power to make treaties and to assume international obligations. However, if such obligations affected subjects within provincial jurisdiction (section 92) implementation was within the competence of the provincial legislatures only. "The Dominion cannot merely by making promises to foreign countries, clothe itself with legislative authority inconsistent with the Constitution which gave it birth." Regarding ILO conventions falling within both federal and provincial jurisdictions, Canada needed to consult and co-operate with the provinces in order to fulfil its international obligations.

The decision was a blow to the federal government. It was interpreted to mean that the federal government was able to ratify only ILO conventions whose subject matter was within exclusive federal jurisdiction and could not ratify ILO conventions whose subject matter was within both federal and provincial jurisdiction, because it lacked the constitutional power to implement them at the provincial level. In fact, the decision did not affect the validity of ratification of the conventions concerned. Only the implementing federal legislation was declared null and void as being ultra vires.

Nonetheless, for almost three decades ratification of ILO conventions on matters partly within federal and partly within provincial jurisdiction was not pursued. Between 1935 and 1959, Canada did ratify several ILO conventions dealing with subjects within exclusive federal jurisdiction. These conventions laid down standards for the protection of dock workers and seafarers, such as safety measures at work, wages and hours of work, quality of catering services, medical examinations, and certification of cooks and able seamen.[9]

Then in 1958, the federal government considered ratification of a convention thought by the Department of Justice to fall within both federal and provincial jurisdiction: Convention 105, Abolition of Forced Labour, adopted in 1957. Justice took the position that there was no forced labour in Canada and consequently, no need for implementing legislation. Following this advice, the federal government ratified the convention in 1959. The general feeling at the time was that Canada could not "afford" to ignore this convention, banning activities abhorrent to the Canadian people; moreover, forced labour was a much discussed international issue, particularly in the context of the Cold War and revelations of its existence in the Soviet Union.

At about the same time, the Legislation Branch of Labour Canada reviewed the decision in the *Labour Conventions case* and concluded that the judgment did not preclude ratification of conventions partly within federal and partly within provincial jurisdiction. What was needed was close consultation and co-operation with the provinces before ratification, to make provincial governments aware that once a convention had been ratified fulfilment of Canada's obligations would depend on continuous conformity of provincial and federal legislation. Consultation was essential: provincial concurrence ("consent") to ratification does not restrict in any way power of provincial legislatures to enact laws that might contravene ratified conventions. Under the doctrine of parliamentary supremacy, the sovereignty of Parliament and of legislatures within their respective fields of power is not affected by ratification. Parliament and legislatures may place the government of Canada in default of Canada's international obligations by enacting laws that encroach on provisions of ratified conventions. Such legislation would be valid: under present Canadian constitutional practice, the courts are not called upon to enforce ratified international treaties, including ILO conventions, but only to enforce Canadian laws. They act under the assumption that international conventions ratified by Canada do not acquire the force of domestic laws. Labour Canada pursued this path in the spirit of "cooperative federalism," and, in consequence, Canada was able to ratify several ILO conventions on matters within both federal and provincial jurisdiction: basic rights conventions dealing with employment policy, discrimination in employment, equal remuneration for women workers, and freedom of association and the right to organize.[10]

Those Canadians who have worked for many years in human rights may feel bedevilled by the lack of clarity of the federal powers to ratify and implement international social and economic instruments in cases of divided jurisdiction. Seeking unanimous provincial consent before ratification is helpful, but provincial governments have enacted legislation contrary to the spirit and content of international instruments that they had authorized the federal government to ratify. They claimed that they were within their constitutional rights. At best, therefore, ratification is an expression of national consensus to act in accordance with the provisions of the ratified instrument. Commitment by Canada after unanimous provincial support, exemplified by the ratification of ILO conventions dealing with freedom of association and the right to organize and to bargain collectively, has failed to provide legal redress when domestic law was silent or ambiguous on these issues. Department of Justice officials and in many cases the judiciary have concluded that, in cases of conflict between international and national standards, national legislation prevails. Courts have called on international obligations as a means of interpreting laws, on the assumption that Parliament did not intend to act in breach of its international obligations. But where there is head-on conflict, domestic law will prevail.[11]

Complaints to the ILO

As there is at present no clear indication of the effectiveness of international covenants in influencing the decision of the Canadian judiciary, the Canadian Labour Congress (CLC) has made increasing use of the ILO complaints-receiving machinery to advance claims about violations of trade union rights in Canada. Decisions of ILO supervisory bodies have often had a salutary effect on the capricious behaviour of governments and served as a reminder that membership in international intergovernmental organizations as well as ratification of international standards should not be taken lightly. The mere ventilation of the complaints of Canadian organizations in international forums attracts public attention at home, thus presumably influencing political decision-making. CLC complaints have alleged infringements by Canada of two ILO conventions, namely no. 87 (Freedom of Association and Protection of the Right to Organize), adopted in 1948, and no. 98 (The Right to Organize and Collective Bargaining), adopted in 1949. In 1978, the ILO adopted convention 151 – Labour Relations (Public Service) – and special machinery may be extended to complaints alleging infringements of that convention, though many and perhaps most governments will likely oppose any such innovation.

The complaints are processed and resolved by the Committee on Freedom of Association. It is composed of nine regular members and nine substitute members drawn from the governments and employers' and workers' groups of the governing body. Considering the quasi-judicial nature of its work, members of the committee participate in a personal capacity, not as representatives of governments or organizations. Committee sessions are private.

Complaints must be submitted either by governments or by organizations of employers or workers of recognized national or international standing. Complaints may be presented against a government whether or not it has ratified the freedom of association conventions. When a complaint is received by the committee, it is communicated to the government concerned for its observations. The complaining organization is allowed to supply further information in support of its complaint, which likewise is communicated to the government. The committee may communicate to the complaining organization observations received from the government for comment. If comments are made, the government is given the opportunity to reply.

The committee may recommend that the complaint be referred for further investigation to the Fact-Finding and Conciliation Commission. This rarely used procedure requires the consent of the government concerned, except in the cases covered by article 26 of the ILO constitution, which gives the ILO governing body discretion to proceed without consent. Alternatively, the committee may recommend to the governing body that the attention of the government concerned be drawn to situations contravening freedom of association conventions and indicate remedial steps. The committee may also inform the governing body that the complaint was unfounded and no breach of conventions took place.

The committee's report, if approved by the governing body, is communicated to government and complainant. When the findings confirm a breach of a ratified convention, the report is also communicated to the Committee of Experts on Application of Conventions and Recommendations for further action. Reports are published in the ILO's *Official Bulletin*. Committee findings are thus widely disseminated and may prove embarrassing to the offending government.

Since it was set up in 1951, the committee has dealt with over 1,000 cases, covering most aspects of freedom of association and the protection of trade union rights. Often, when examining a complaint, the committee refers to its previous decisions, creating continuity in criteria applied in reaching decisions.

The first complaint filed by the CLC resulted from a bitter loggers' strike in Newfoundland.[12] It was submitted in a communication by the congress dated 2 November 1959, alleging infringement of trade union rights by the government of Newfoundland. It was directed against the government of Canada, because Canada, not the province, is the ILO member. The complaint referred in particular to legislation decertifying the International Woodworkers of America locals and providing for dissolution of unions and for the confiscation of their funds where "it appears" that certain circumstances obtain. The complaint was supported by the International Confederation of Free Trade Unions in a letter dated 23 December 1959. Interim reports by the Committee on Freedom of Association were adopted in 1960 and 1961. The committee issued its final conclusions at a meeting held in Geneva on 4 and 5 November 1963, following Newfoundland's repeal of the contested legislation in 1963. It was generally recognized at the time that the processing of the complaints and the ILO reports contributed to repeal.

In 1967 the CLC filed a complaint alleging that legislation in Saskatchewan (the Essential Services Emergency Act) and in Newfoundland (the Hospital Employees Employment Act, 1966–7) infringed on trade union rights. Again the complainants could claim success. The ILO committee settled both cases following repeal of the contested legislation. It settled the Saskatchewan matter in 1968; on Newfoundland it issued an interim report in 1968 and a final report in 1969. These complaints were followed by other CLC submissions, some still pending. The large number of complaints emanating from Canada reflects not restrictive Canadian legislation but the trade unions' decision to use international machinery to seek redress for grievances.

In 1985, the CLC submitted complaints to the ILO on behalf of its affiliates against Newfoundland, Ontario, Alberta, and British Columbia centred on public-sector labour legislation introduced 1982–5 allegedly in violation of convention 87. Pressed by the CLC and with the consent of the federal government, the ILO, for the first time, sent a study and information mission from its Geneva headquarters to Canada. The mission, headed by Sir John Wood, a professor at the University of Sheffield and a member of the Committee of Experts on Application of Conventions and Recommendations, met with government and union delegations in Newfoundland, Ontario, and Alberta from 11 to 25 September 1985.

The mission submitted its report to the Freedom of Association Committee on 1 November 1985, supporting many of the CLC's allegations. The major theme was that Newfoundland and Alberta, as well as the previous government of Ontario (Conservative, to June 1985), restricted the bargaining rights of provincial workers without prior consultation with them. This gave "ample opportunity for confusion, misunderstanding and a serious breakdown in internal relationships." Hence, it was up to the provincial governments to "re-establish the normal industrial relations process – consultation, conciliation and mutual understanding."

Based on the report, the Freedom of Association Committee developed recommendations adopted by the ILO governing body on 14 November 1985. One recommendation stated that restrictions on the right to strike of a broad range of Alberta's public-sector workers "go beyond acceptable limits which are recognized in Convention No. 87." The ILO also made substantive recommendations regarding desirable changes in labour legislation in Alberta, Newfoundland, and Ontario. It expressed disappointment that the mission was not able to visit British Columbia; the BC government had "simply manipulated the ILO complaints procedure to avoid being formally asked by the ILO to permit the mission to come to their province," by withholding their response to the second CLC complaint "until after the Freedom of Association Committee met in June 1985."[13]

The ILO's Influence on Canada

Long-time practitioners in Canadian labour law and administration name the work of the ILO as a key influence on labour legislation, despite the difficulties and unresolved issues that prevent full implementation of ILO standards.

The ILO has influenced Canadian law and practice. ILO standards and decisions have profoundly influenced not only labour relations in most countries, but also social and economic policies. This, of course, includes Canada. The ILO spurred government action on social security, protection during old age, unemployment and sickness, hours of work, and industrial health and safety. The very concept of "equal pay for work of equal value" for women, and Canadian provincial and federal legislation based on that formula, originated in 1951 with ILO convention 100; Canadian ratification was urged by the Royal Commission on the Status of Women. Protection of the young and children as well as of indigenous peoples is the subject of ILO standards and ILO research and publications; these, too, have influenced Canadian law and practice. The use of ILO complaints-receiving machinery has affected Canadian policy. As one seasoned practitioner observed: "It is a source of pride that Canadian governments have supplied full information and co-operated generally in the ILO procedures. They have often changed their laws or practices when these were determined to be not fully in accord with ILO recommendations. In other cases, the union complaints have been found to have little justification, and this too has had an educative effect on all parties."[14]

Nevertheless, the system of universally applicable international conventions is still the cornerstone of the ILO. Formal ratification and full implementation remain an important measure of a member's commitment. Unfortunately, Canada's attitude to international intergovernmental organizations (the ILO being the most visible example) has been profoundly affected by internal considerations, absent from most other countries. Having failed to ratify basic ILO conventions, Canadian decision-makers sought refuge behind a cloak of false complacency, thinking that the nation's labour laws and practices are superior to the international norms, "so why get involved in the laborious process of ratification?" As Mainwaring noted: "The problem for Canada in the 1920s, although nobody wanted to admit it, was that each of the ILO conventions was ahead of current Canadian practice, and even thinking. Canada was not ready for the eight-hour day, for maternity protection, for the abolition of night work for women and young persons, for a minimum age of 14, or even for the moderate government measures against unemployment set out in Convention 2 ... Prime Minister King, in speaking to a Dominion-provincial conference on unemployment in 1922, was to urge delegates to encourage 'traditional Anglo-Saxon reliance upon self-help in preference to governmental action.'"[15]

When the Department of Labour began in 1966 to look seriously into the possibility of ratifying certain ILO human rights conventions, it finally laid to rest this myth. It discovered that none of the provinces or the federal jurisdiction was in full compliance with many of the provisions of international labour standards. However, constitutional difficulties and long-ingrained negative assessments of the value to Canada of international instruments influenced Canadian attitudes to the formulation of new international human rights standards. Consequently, Canadian representatives have by and large opted for less binding instruments, like recommendations and resolutions, or, even less threatening, research and education.

More seriously, international instruments ratified by Canada lack the standing of domestic laws. Why do Canadians make such a fuss over ratification, claiming to take this process seriously in contrast to "irresponsible" governments, when these acts are of doubtful legal value domestically? A number of these unresolved constitutional issues remain on the agenda of the human rights constituency in Canada. Some may soon reach the Supreme Court of Canada, as that body decides on the judicial effect on domestic law of international obligations assumed by Canada, as well as the extent of federal powers to assume obligations in matters of divided federal and provincial jurisdiction. Until such time it will be difficult to assess the ILO's full impact on human rights in Canada.

Perhaps Canadians should have a closer look at attitudes that inhibit inclusion in the Canadian Charter of Rights and Freedoms of social and economic rights, proclaimed in such instruments ratified by Canada as the International Covenant on Economic, Social and Cultural Rights, the ILO Convention on Discrimination in Employment and Occupation, the ILO Equal Remuneration Convention, and the ILO Freedom of Association and Protection of the Right to Organize Convention. Some Canadian authorities still share the North American view that somehow these rights are not really fundamental and, although subject to legislative measures, should not be entrenched. As one noted authority recently stated:

In Canada there exist universal legislative programs for public education, unemployment insurance, medical treatment and hospitalization, old-age pensions, family allowances and others. These were all achieved through political and legislative rather than judicial processes and, perhaps as a result, Canadians tend not to speak of them in terms of "human rights." They are not included in the *Canadian Charter of Rights and Freedoms*. This may be viewed as ironical in light of Canada's ratification of the *International Covenant on Economic, Social and Cultural Rights* as well as several Conventions of the International Labour Organization.

... This category (Economic, Social and Cultural Rights) has received virtually no entrenched constitutional recognition as an essential component of basic human rights. However, a historical and current survey of the relevant areas, indicates a high level of both public expectation and of governmental response through legislation. Since this category essentially involves the obligation of a State to its inhabitants, it is through direct government programs and legislation that these rights are most likely to be achieved. Nevertheless, public recognition and government commitment are moving towards a time when this category might well find express recognition in the *Canadian Charter of Rights and Freedoms*.[16]

THE ILO'S INFLUENCE: LIMITS AND OPPORTUNITIES

In assessing the historical importance of the ILO, one should reflect on the limits in using this UN agency to encourage respect for human rights everywhere.

Like all international intergovernmental agencies, the ILO operates in a world environment where the concept of national sovereignty has hardly been dented. Despite "one world" rhetoric and numerous efforts to foster internationally binding standards and supranational institutions, no country is prepared to give up its ultimate claim to national sovereignty. Structurally, the ILO also finds itself constantly buffeted between two often mutually exclusive concepts – universality of membership and tripartism. While aiming to follow the UN founding principle of being the voice of all the peoples of the world, the ILO is on occasion confronted with the jagged, uneven, and often hostile approaches to basic rights taken by many of its member states.

It has been obvious, practically from the beginning of the ILO's existence, that international labour legislation could not eliminate international trade competition based on poor working conditions and exploitation of labour. Several major founding states, first the United Kingdom, refused to ratify and implement the hours-of-work convention; other members failed either to ratify or to implement other standards. Toward the end of the Second World War, when a new network of international economic institutions was being planned, the ILO attempted unsuccessfully to carve out a decision role in planning and implementing international economic and trade policy. New organizations, like ECOSOC, the General Agreement on Tariffs and Trade (GATT), the world financial institutions, the Organization for Economic Co-operation and Development (OECD), and the European Community, have acquired much more power and influence than the ILO, thus restricting its initiatives and minimizing its influence.

The ILO's experience in dealing with the always delicate issue of censuring the behaviour of member states, or offering advice for structural changes, was often disappointing. In a world dominated by superpower conflict, it is difficult to maintain an objective approach not only to international standard-setting, but also to research, promotion, and practical activities. Many smaller states, now the majority in the UN system, use international forums for their own, often narrow, political purposes, with unfortunate consequences for the specialized or technical agencies, like the ILO, raising the spectre of "politicization." ILO staff, technical experts in particular, have on many occasions alienated a big financial contributor or incurred the wrath of a government complained about, either of which can limit their activities or ignore their advice and efforts. However, the ILO's traditional thrust still offers important, albeit limited opportunities to promote and advance fundamental rights. Perhaps its most important long-term contribution is its recognition of nongovernmental groups under international law within the tripartite fabric of the ILO.[17]

Mindful of the difficulties inherent in its traditional approaches, the ILO, under its long-serving director-general, David Morse, embarked during the early 1950s on a comprehensive program of "practical activities," aimed at providing technical advice and assistance to industrially less developed countries as a means of promoting social justice. During the past 40 years the ILO has conceived, promoted, and administered many projects in the Third World in consumers' and producers' co-operatives, small-scale industry, vocational training, management training, tourism, and worker and management education. These projects are financed largely by the UN Development Program (UNDP); some countries have provided direct financial backing for ILO projects.

On its 50th anniversary in 1969, the ILO launched its World Employment Program, placing on the international agenda the immense problems arising from the lack of remunerative work for the ever-growing populations of the Third World. The ILO maintains that about 1.5 billion jobs must be created in the world between now and 2025.[18] It predicts that the world's active population will reach 2.75 billion by 2000 and 3.65 billion by 2025.

Spearheaded by Director-General Francis Blanchard, the ILO has drawn the world's attention to the plight of "the unprotected majority" – the more than 1 billion underemployed or unemployed. In his annual report to the June 1986 session of the International Labour Conference,[19] Blanchard emphasized the recurring ILO theme of the need to link worthwhile social objectives to economic development because about three out of five in the world's labour force face economic and social insecurity. He pointed out the ominous trend toward long-term joblessness which can be reversed only by sustained growth in both North and South. This problem, while slowly being recognized, has not been addressed by sufficiently extensive or concerted efforts in trade, aid, and monetary policies.

Blanchard has warned of the consequences of the stringent rules imposed on debtor nations by the International Monetary Fund, which have harmed already weak groups in these countries, often precipitating mass violence and political upheavals. The twelfth conference of American states members of the ILO (Montreal, 18–26 March 1986), attended by delegates from 30 countries including 22 labour ministers, resolved to "invite" the international financial agencies to consider, in close consultation with the ILO "the social and political dimensions of the policies they advocate to countries needing their help, and that these agencies be aware of the key part that the expansion of employment and the protection of income must have on any strategy to promote stable economic and social development."[20] The 72nd session of the International Labour Conference (Geneva, June 1986) voted 318–11 (with 32 abstentions) to authorize the ILO governing body to "prepare and convene" a high-level meeting to examine, in the light of the ILO's social objectives, the world economic situation and, in particular, the effect of international trade and financial and monetary policies on employment and poverty. The governing body was asked to communicate the meeting's conclusions and recommendations to member states, to employers' and workers' organizations, and to relevant international agencies. [21]

With these new initiatives, emphasizing the social objectives of economic development as well as the awesome implications of unemployment, the ILO is attempting to put new vigour in its original mission of seeking "social justice," affording yet another opportunity to its member states to promote universal social and economic rights.

CANADA'S IMPACT ON THE ILO

As a founding ILO member, Canada has remained loyal to the organization and enjoys universal respect and recognition for consistent support of its basic thrust. Canadian governments have fulfilled their budgetary obligations, based on criteria similar to those of the United Nations, and have complied with the constitutional obligations of membership. Canadians have been elected to the highest positions in ILO conferences and in the governing body. For over 60 years, Canada sat on the governing body. Moreover, Canada is one of the few countries with tripartite representation in the government body. Canadians have been consistently elected as members of the employers' and workers' groups of that key ILO organ.

During critical periods in the life of the organization, when its very existence was threatened, Canada has lent crucial support. The ILO found refuge during the Second World War at McGill University in Montreal, when it could no longer function safely and effectively in Geneva. Similarly, in the period between US notice of withdrawal (1975) and departure (1977), Canada attempted to prevent the break. It helped to bring the United States back to the organization in 1980.

Canada consented in 1985 to receive the ILO mission to investigate labour practices in several Canadian provinces and extended every facility to it. Canadian governments have gone to considerable expense and administrative trouble to provide information and to comply with ILO official procedures and requests. Federal and provincial governments have changed laws and practices found to be in conflict with ILO standards.

Canadian trade unions have always regarded the organization as a forum to promote freedom of association, collective bargaining, and the right to organize. Moreover, they have made ample use of the ILO's complaints-receiving machinery to seek support for changes in labour laws and practices. Union representatives from Canada to International Labour Conferences and in the ILO governing body have, often with representatives of other countries' union organizations, initiated, promoted, and helped structure ILO human rights instruments. A Canadian union official was spokesman for the workers' group in the 1957, 1958, and 1960 ILO conferences and later in the governing body, during drafting and implementation of one of the most-ratified ILO conventions, Discrimination in Employment and Occupation. Canadian trade union representatives were also prominent in ILO efforts against apartheid, chairing the ILO Conference Committee on Apartheid.

Canadian employer representatives have served on ILO executive bodies and have attended regularly ILO international, regional, and special conferences, defending the interests of their group as well as the integrity of the ILO system. Their position, like that of counterparts in countries similar to Canada, is basically "defensive." They have been sceptical about the ILO's ability to improve labour conditions in other countries and have expressed reservations about Canada's competitive ability to improve its own labour standards. Canadian employers have generally favoured ILO technical co-operation and the work of its industrial committee meetings, emphasizing the advantages of sharing information and experience.[22]

While Canada has not displayed much enthusiasm for structuring new ILO human rights standards, because of constitutional constraints and, perhaps, lack of appreciation of the fundamental nature of economic and social rights, government representatives have sought to protect and preserve the organization's monitoring and supervisory machinery. This support has been particularly evident during the last several years, when the ILO supervisory system came under attack from the Soviet Union and its allies, stung by a series of critical findings and reports from the Committee on Freedom of Association and the Committee of Experts on the Application of Conventions and Recommendations.

The Canadian government delegate defended the ILO system at the 1984 conference, noting that "these supervisory procedures stand second to none in the United Nations family." Dealing with "interference in internal affairs," he continued: "How the Committee of Experts can do otherwise than call attention to objective facts is difficult to see. The importance of monitoring the extent to which member States comply with the requirements of Conventions they have ratified is recognised in the Constitution of the ILO and the Standing Orders of the Conference. These monitoring functions cannot be construed as interference in the internal affairs of member States. The monitoring functions are essential to the practical implementation of the aspirations that led to the founding of the ILO." While praising the "positive contribution" of "a comprehensive set of labour standards which serve as targets for social progress" and noting "the positive contribution these standards have made to the development of labour legislation in all countries," he defended the objectives of the ILO system: "In the first place, it is fundamental that the integrity of the Committee on the Application of Standards be maintained. This Committee has been described as the conscience of the ILO. It is concerned primarily with the obligations a Government assumes when it ratifies an ILO Convention. Its work, along with the work of the Committee of Experts, the Committee on Freedom of Association and ad hoc bodies on complaints and representations, is crucial to the success of the system of ILO standards."[23]

Canada has also co-operated with the ILO Declaration concerning the Policy of Apartheid in South Africa, reporting on 5 November 1985 what it had done to implement the declaration.

This positive approach contrasts, however, with the attitude of succeeding Canadian government to the ILO's directly financed (as distinct from UNDP-financed) initiatives and programs that aim to reduce poverty, create remunerative jobs, and promote the social objectives of economic development in Third World countries. Canadian government spokesmen have not challenged the ILO's basic findings, criticizing instead its "competence" to pursue these activities. When Canada's minister of labour was elected president of the 12th conference of American states members of the ILO, he regretted, cautiously, that "the relationship between economic and adjustment policies on the one hand, and the social impact that these policies have on the other, has not received much in depth attention in the past." The Canadian delegation did not object to the conference's urging the international financial agencies to take fully into account "the social and political dimension" of their policies. [24]

Likewise, when the 1986 International Labour Conference debated a resolution concerning the link between economic development, foreign debt, and the ILO's social objectives, the Canadian spokesman cited Canada's announcement at the UN Special Session on Africa of the terms of a Canadian moratorium on repayments of development assistance loans from sub-Sahara Africa. He stated that Canada "believes that it is legitimate for the International Labour Organisation to concern itself with an issue which, like the international debt crisis, has major implications for the objectives of social justice and social progress, which are so fundamental to the purposes of this organisation." However, while supporting the legitimacy of the ILO's "concern," he questioned its competence to deal with this and similar issues, as "the actions which it is asked to undertake must be consistent with its mandate and with its specific functions and areas of competence." Canada, therefore, joined a number of Industrialized Market Economy Countries (a group that Canada chairs) in expressing reservations about the action-oriented conclusions of the resolution. Finally, jointly with the Canadian employers' delegate, Canada abstained in the plenary vote, while the Canadian workers' delegate voted for the resolution. Still, Canada did not join France, Japan, the United Kingdom, the United States, and West Germany, which cast negative votes.[25]

Canada's lukewarm attitude toward ILO initiatives in this area stems, perhaps, from its rather rigid but consistent approach to multilateral aid. Canadian representatives in UN forums have always supported a centralized approach to aid and development projects administered with funds provided by the UNDP. As a long-standing contributor to the World Bank and the International Monetary Fund (IMF), Canada has also protected their jurisdiction. Canadian representatives have voted for ILO research and publications activities, as well as hortatory declarations of the ILO on such innovative and challenging policies as the World Employment Program, the Basic Needs Program, and popular participation in development. But Canada is extremely hesitant to allow any significant role for the ILO in matters that are the responsibility of the international financial institutions. It fears proliferation of institutions with overlapping jurisdictions and prefers the weighted distribution of voting power in institutions such as the IMF, the World Bank, and regional development banks.

Canada has also usually refused to join donor states like Denmark, Norway, Sweden, and West Germany that directly finance ILO technical assistance projects that fail to obtain UNDP funding. These people-oriented endeavours, such as employment creation pilot projects, workers' education efforts, co-operative projects in poor rural areas, and specialized vocational training for women and the handicapped, generally enjoy low priority among decision-makers in many recipient countries and consequently are not approved by the UNDP. This direct form of financing, referred to as "multi-bi" aid, forms a rather substantial portion of the overall ILO budget assigned to "practical" activities.

There are indications, though, of Canada's growing awareness of the link between social objectives and economic development in poor countries and, accordingly, of the need to restructure Canadian aid to fit this approach. There is also evidence of growing appreciation of social and economic rights and their intimate link to traditional political and civil rights. The June 1986 report of the Special Joint Committee of the Senate and the House of Commons on Canada's International Relations[26] supports this view. It quotes approvingly the Canadian Council of Churches: "Basic needs – food, water, shelter – (are also) inviolable rights, without which it is impossible for human beings to sustain life." Questioning economists' traditional assumption that economic growth would automatically promote social and political development, the committee echoes the finding of the ILO World Employment and Basic Needs programs that mere growth of the gross national product is not by itself an adequate or just goal of development. There is some logic to the ILO's argument that growth of remunerative and freely chosen employment, access to fresh water, adequate food consumption, basic educational facilities and environmental protection should become separate and distinct objectives of economic development. Should this approach be adopted by Canadian decision-makers, they ought to have another close look at the opportunities offered by the ILO as one of the forums to promote human rights and human dignity, both in Canada and abroad.

CHAPTER EIGHT

The Helsinki Process

H. GORDON SKILLING

A conference on human rights in Ottawa in 1985 indicated the importance assigned to this subject since adoption of the Helsinki Final Act at the Conference on Security and Co-operation in Europe (CSCE) in 1975. When the diplomats were drafting the text in Dipoli and Geneva (1972–5) and when, at Helsinki, their heads of government, with appropriate pomp, were signing the product of their labours, no one dreamed that a decade or so later a conference devoted exclusively to human rights would take place under CSCE auspices. Pierre Trudeau's government would have been astonished that one of its successors would propose such a conference and another would be the host for the first CSCE meeting in North America. The growing significance of human rights in the Helsinki process, and Canada's deepening engagement in this subject, were parts of a gradual and unanticipated transformation of the CSCE into an institutionalized web of meetings, including regular follow-ups in Belgrade (1977–8), Madrid (1980–3), and Vienna (from 1986) and experts' meetings and other forums, of which the gathering in Ottawa was but one.

During the years of slow advance toward a conference on European security, it was at first not even certain that Canada (or the United States) would be invited to participate, nor was it known what the agenda would include.[1] When the USSR first pressed for such a conference in 1965, it had envisaged an exclusively European one that would deal largely, if not solely, with European security and would recognize the territorial status quo in central and eastern Europe, including the division of Germany into two states. By 1969 Moscow had accepted the idea of North American participation and had formulated several principles, such as national sovereignty, territorial integrity, the inviolability of frontiers, and the non-use of force, to buttress its main objective. Among Western countries there was no consensus as to subject matter.

The Soviet principles were acceptable only if they did not recognize existing frontiers, or irrevocably confirm the partition of Germany, and did not confirm the Brezhnev Doctrine, enunciated after the Soviet invasion of Czechoslovakia (which, it was believed, was a fundamental contradiction of the very principles proclaimed by the Soviet Union). By 1969 the Western countries, including Canada, had proposed, to counter-balance the Soviet emphasis on military security and the territorial status quo, the idea of freer movement of peoples, ideas, and information. Human rights in a broader sense played no part in negotiations on the conference agenda during the 1960s and 1970s.

HELSINKI: THE FINAL ACT

It was only at the multilateral preliminary talks in Dipoli, a suburb of Helsinki, between November 1972 and June 1973, which Canada attended as a full participant, that human rights entered the picture.[2] They were introduced not in the discussion of the recommendations relating to human contacts and freer movement (basket III, as it came to be called), but in the earlier section relating to security (basket I), in particular in the "principles" that were to guide the relations of the participating states and promote peace and security in Europe. As a result of a proposal by the representative of the Holy See, principle VII, referring to "respect for human rights and fundamental freedoms, including freedom of thought, conscience, religion or belief," was one of the ten principles eventually agreed upon.[3] Canada, however, seemed to have had little or nothing to do with inclusion of this principle in the talks. Its overriding preoccupation was with the provisions of basket III concerning human contacts, particularly relating to family reunification. Humanitarian affairs were regarded by Canada as "the single most important item on the conference agenda."[4]

The Final Act emerged, at least in skeletal form, in the recommendations adopted at Dipoli.[5] Like all subsequent CSCE negotiations, these talks had been an "exercise in consensual diplomacy,"[6] requiring unanimous agreement for every phrase, every word, every punctuation mark. Two more years of long and tedious discussions in Geneva were necessary before these tentative provisions were embodied, in revised form, in the Final Act. The principle of consensus created a kind of dynamics in the diplomacy of the Geneva stage (1973–5),[7] as each side (East and West) sought to make its agreement to the demands of the other side dependent on satisfaction of its own proposals. The Western countries, for example, delayed acceptance of the revised version of the ten principles, especially those most cherished by the Soviet delegation, until they were sure that they would be able to attain the more specific goals of basket III. Similarly, within the ten principles, there was a process of balancing between the Soviet emphasis on territorial integrity, sovereignty, and non-interference in domestic affairs and the Western stress on modifications of these principles and on human rights.

During the Geneva talks Canada continued to emphasize human contacts. Mitchell Sharp, secretary of state for external affairs, in his opening address on 4 July 1973 said that "freer movement of people" was of "the highest importance" and that family reunification would be "the touchstone of the Conference." In discussing the ten principles he made no mention of human rights.[8] The next day the Canadian delegation submitted a proposal on measures to encourage travel and family reunification.[9] As a result the Canadians took over responsibility for these matters on behalf of the Western alliance and, according to one observer, played a "brilliant role," successfully pressing the draft agreed upon by the NATO caucus to ultimate acceptance, despite stubborn resistance by the Soviet Union and the German Democratic Republic.[10]

Although human rights per se were not high on the Canadian list of priorities, Canada's representative, Gaby Warren, worked out a consensus on the ten principles, acting, however, as mediator and co-ordinator, not initiator. Discussion of the principles consumed 337 sessions and thousands of hours of talks over a period of two years. In the final reading, however, agreement was achieved in three days, with Warren playing a crucial role in reconciling conflicting positions. Principle VII, as finally adopted, embodied genuine consensus.[11]

Agreement on the text of principle VII was difficult and time-consuming, requiring 56 sittings over three months, but the final result reflected Western conceptions.[12] Eight paragraphs in all, it was the longest of the principles, and "the most innovative."[13] At the outset the Soviet Union had hoped to embody this principle in one sentence, which was to be a mere restatement of the title heading of the Helsinki final recommendations. When it became clear that French and Yugoslav proposals, and other Western amendments, would greatly expand the text, the Soviet delegation sought to give prominence, in paragraph 1, to the international human rights covenants, which they had recently ratified. Western delegations were reluctant to take this as the starting point: some governments, notably the United States, had not ratified the covenants, and a number of "escape clauses" weakened their effectiveness. In the end they succeeded in relegating reference to the covenants to the final paragraph, clearly subordinate to those mentioned earlier – the United Nations charter and the Universal Declaration of Human Rights approved by almost every state in the world and containing unqualified commitments.[14]

Each of the eight paragraphs of principle VII was initiated by individual countries and ultimately reconciled with those of the others.[15] Many provisions restated or amplified principles embodied in other international treaties, conventions, or declarations and in some cases might therefore be regarded as legally binding, though the Final Act as a whole was not so considered. Negotiators were influenced greatly by the recently concluded UN Declaration on the Principles of International Law concerning Friendly Relations and Co-operation among States (1970) but went far beyond that document in human rights. The final text, with some repetition and some ambiguities, declared "freedom of thought, conscience, religion or belief"; "civil, political, economic, social, cultural and other rights and freedoms"; the rights of persons belonging to national minorities; the "universal significance of human rights and fundamental freedoms," which was said to be essential for peace and friendly relations; and the "right of the individual to know and act upon his rights and duties." It also stated the commitments of signatories to act in conformity with the UN charter and the Universal Declaration and to fulfil their obligations under other declarations and agreements, such as the international covenants.

Entirely novel was the provision asserting the "right of the individual to know and act upon his rights and duties." This developed from a British proposal concerning the citizen's right to participate in efforts to promote human rights and to have information on these matters.[16] Canada, at one point, firmly stated the importance attached by the West to the rights of the individual.[17] When the Soviet delegation added the term "duties" to "rights," Western governments modified the text by adding the phrase "in this field," so as to bar only actions that would impede the rights of others and exclude duties that overrode rights.[18] This emphasis on the role of the individual, although strongly opposed by the Soviet Union, was ultimately accepted in the general bargaining that led to agreement. It was reinforced by principle IX, on co-operation among states, which confirmed that "governments, institutions, organizations and persons have a relevant and positive role to play" in promoting co-operation. The impact of these modest sentences was not anticipated by initiators or opponents and not fully grasped by commentators.[19] Within a year or two, however, these provisions led to formation of groups, such as the Helsinki monitors in the Soviet Union, to check on their governments' implementation of the Final Act and of human rights organizations in Poland and of Charter 77 in Czechoslovakia. Repression of such activities by Soviet and eastern European governments became a crucial issue at later CSCE meetings.

The potential of principle VII as a whole was not fully appreciated at the time. Most signatories, including Canada, regarded such abstract principles as less important than the specific provisions of basket III, on matters such as reunification of families, rights of foreign journalists, exchange of information, and co-operation in culture, education, and science. These provisions were thought of as "applying," concretely and comprehensively, the broad intent of principle VII and as dealing with human needs important to many Canadian citizens and therefore to their government. A Canadian legal specialist, Walter Tarnopolsky, later pointed out, however, that the specific items listed, although significant, were marginal aspects of human freedom and would cease to have much importance if the guiding principles of human rights were fully implemented.[20] While basket III provisions dealt with only "the human element of the relations among states," he wrote, principle VII referred to "the position of human beings in their own community" – to relations of citizens and their governments, including freedom of thought, conscience, religion and belief – and, in its reference to the Universal Declaration and the international covenants, to the whole range of human rights and fundamental freedoms. This approach struck at the very essence of the eastern European political systems and their legitimacy. Canadian official policy initially paid the greatest attention to specific problems of divided families, journalistic opportunities, availability of foreign newspapers, and international exchanges and presupposed that their satisfactory resolution would promote incremental change in the communist systems. More and more, however, attention shifted to the principles of human rights in general. Public opinion, too, transferred its concern from basket III, often wrongly regarded as the human rights basket, to principle VII, particularly rights of citizens and their denial by the Soviet Union and its partners.

The full significance of other provisions of the ten principles was also revealed only much later. For instance, the statement that all ten were of "primary significance" and would "equally and unreservedly be applied, each of them being interpreted taking into account the others," was taken by the Soviet authorities to mean that the principles of sovereignty (I) and non-intervention in international affairs (VI) overrode principle VII, at least in excluding criticism of human rights practices. Western countries pointed out that the relationship of the several principles was reciprocal, so that commitments to rights limited sovereignty and justified criticism of violations. Participating states were bound, under principle X, "in exercising their sovereign rights, including the right to determine their laws and regulations," to "conform with their legal obligations under international law" and "pay due regard to and implement the provisions in the Final Act."

Canada's official view of the Final Act and of its future was stated in terms of modest realism, although not without ambiguity, by Prime Minister Trudeau in his address to the concluding session in Helsinki on 31 July 1975. Paying tribute to the achievement of consensus through long and patient negotiations, Trudeau stated that this accord recognized that change was inevitable in international relations, but that there should be no use of force in the process. Frontiers were declared to be inviolable but were not immutable. Apart from these brief references, he made no mention of the ten principles as a basis of peace and security and spoke not a word about human rights. Security and co-operation could not be the product of state activity alone, he went on, and harmony could not be achieved without intercourse among people, the promise of family reunification, and an interchange of ideas and opinions. Trudeau stressed the importance of stability in Europe, not only for Canada but for the world at large, and emphasized the need also to assist developing lands and limit the use of nuclear weapons.[21]

BELGRADE (1977–8)

It was only at the two follow-up meetings, at Belgrade[22] and Madrid, that the significance of principle VII became fully evident. At Belgrade human rights "occupied front stage," because of the prominence given this theme by the Carter administration in the United States, the crusading spirit of the chief American delegate, Arthur Goldberg, and the growth of human rights movements in the Soviet Union and eastern Europe and their harsh repression.[23] As a result, Belgrade set the precedent for the Helsinki process of a wide-ranging review of shortcomings in fulfilment of commitments, including human rights violations. Although the Americans were the most militant in criticizing Soviet malpractice and "named names," most other Western delegations, including some neutral and non-aligned (NNA), joined in the censure, though sometimes more moderately and without naming countries or individuals. Canada, aiming to be "objective and dispassionate" and critical of the "confrontational" US approach, did mention specific cases and severely criticized treatment of religious believers and human rights monitors in Eastern states. A consensus emerged among Western delegations and most NNAs that rights violations were matters of legitimate concern and that their discussion was not precluded by the principle of non-intervention. Whatever recognition the Final Act had given to the territorial status quo (and this remained a matter of dispute), it had not endorsed the political status quo, at least in the denial of human rights.

Moreover, several NATO group proposals would have strengthened the carrying out of principle VII and substantially changed operation of the communist systems. One would have reaffirmed the role of institutions, organizations, and persons in implementation of the Final Act. Soviet opposition denied these proposals the unanimity required for adoption. Nor was consensus reached on some 60 others, so that Belgrade closed with a communique almost empty of content.

Canada assumed an active and prominent role at Belgrade and gave increasingly higher priority to human rights in its broader meaning. In his opening statement, Klaus Goldschlag, representing the secretary of state for external affairs, emphasized the "human dimension" of the Final Act and interpreted this as respect for rights by all signatories and recognition of the right of the individual citizen to be concerned with these matters. Human rights had become "a central preoccupation" of his government. In major speeches Canadian delegates stressed principles VII and IX and co-sponsored the two major human rights proposals of the NATO group. Canada had not abandoned its interest in human contacts, which remained, said Goldschlag, a "special concern," and family reunification continued to be given "priority"; Canada co-sponsored and helped draft several humanitarian proposals, including three on family reunification.[24]

In spite of the prominence of human rights at Belgrade, little was accomplished in advancing respect for these values. Soviet behaviour did not improve during the conference, nor did its bloc partners change their attitude to human rights or to their own citizens' movements to defend these rights. In fact a major trial of Czechoslovak dissidents was held during the meeting. Had Canada associated itself with a cause that was already lost?

MADRID (1980-3)

The only positive outcome of Belgrade had been decisions to continue the Helsinki process with several experts' meetings and with another follow-up at Madrid in two years' time. Would this be another Belgrade? Or would it be more productive in promoting respect for human rights?

The Madrid meeting lasted much longer – almost three years – and was even more wracked with controversy than its predecessor.[25] The Soviet invasion of Afghanistan prior to its opening, and the beginning of the crisis in Poland during the preparatory meeting, threatened to prevent the holding of a meeting at all, and the declaration of martial law in Poland in December 1981 seemed likely to block its continuance. The human rights situation in the Soviet Union seriously worsened, as evidenced by harsh repression – indeed virtual liquidation – of the Helsinki monitoring groups. Severe measures were taken against Charter 77 in Czechoslovakia, and even stricter persecution occurred in Poland after December 1981. Only during the Solidarity period in Poland had there been a marked improvement in human rights, indeed a veritable flowering of freedom, clearly the product of domestic forces, perhaps influenced in some degree by the CSCE process.

The Madrid talks were also dominated by human rights as a result of increasing public pressure, manifested by a "counter-conference" in Madrid convened by human rights organizations and exiled dissidents.

Madrid saw a kind of reprise of Belgrade, especially in a wide-ranging review debate on implementation of all parts of the Final Act, particularly the principles, including, of course, number VII.[26] Once again the Soviet Union, later Poland, and to a lesser degree Czechoslovakia received severe condemnation. Although the forum was largely superpower confrontation, the debate was joined, on the Western side, by almost all democratic states, neutral or aligned, including Canada. Once again, over violent Soviet protests, the legitimacy of international concern over human rights violations was vindicated. In spite of increasing international conflict, Madrid, unlike Belgrade, produced, after long and laborious negotiations, a substantial concluding document based on consensus.[27] To achieve its primary goal in the security sphere, the Soviet Union agreed, after persistent strong opposition, to a series of 15 paragraphs devoted to human rights. Many were restatements of provisions of principle VII, but others represented small advances in their application. For instance, in reaffirming the "right of the individual to know and act upon his rights and duties" in this field, the governments stated that they "will take the necessary action in their respective countries to effectively ensure this right." A new provision was intended to ensure the right of workers freely to establish and join trade unions. In spite of continued repression at home, the Soviet delegation gave verbal approval to greater emphasis on rights and reaffirmation of the role of the individual.

Canada's part at Madrid was similar to Belgrade. Its delegation joined in the general debate in the same spirit as its Western partners, co-sponsored proposals, and negotiated final adoption. Most striking was the Canadian initiative in the opening general debate. The new secretary of state for external affairs, Mark MacGuigan, perhaps to the surprise even of his own delegation, suggested a CSCE experts' meeting, or even a high-level meeting, to discuss "the protection of the principles of human rights and fundamental freedoms ... in principle VII ... and the application of these rights in Basket III dealing particularly with the question of freer movement of people among the participating states."[28] This double-barrelled proposal was eventually divided into two parts – a human rights experts' meeting, proposed by Canada and co-sponsored by Spain and the United States (and eventually approved by the NATO group), and an experts' meeting on family reunification, sponsored by the United States, with the support of the entire NATO group.[29] The Canadian delegation, acting under instructions from its government, made the former proposal its own special concern and more than once warned the Soviet representatives that Canada would not accept a concluding document that did not include such a paragraph.[30] The Western group was united in refusing consent to the Soviet-proposed security conference without experts' meetings on rights and contacts.[31] Eventual Soviet acceptance of the concluding document, with its greatly extended human rights provision, was undoubtedly due to the trade-off embodied in the final text. A follow-up in Vienna in 1986 was also agreed upon.

HUMAN RIGHTS: OTTAWA 1985

The Human Rights Experts Meeting took place in Ottawa from 7 May to 17 June 1985.[32] It was to be a conference devoted exclusively to human rights – something which the Western negotiators of the Final Act could not have foreseen in their most pleasant dreams, or Soviet diplomats in their worst nightmares. The form of the meeting was not defined in the Madrid concluding document, but the Canadian delegation had already worked out, in some detail, an agenda and modalities, attached as an annex to a revised proposal to be included in a statement by the chairman. This would have provided for an undefined period for opening statements, followed by 14 days, spread over three weeks, devoted to discussion of (a) the nature of human rights and their role in the development of friendly relations and co-operation, (b) international human rights obligations and national sovereignty, (c) enhancement of the role of governments, institutions, organizations, and individuals in implementation of such obligations, and (d) examination of implementation of human rights obligations by the participating states. The formal opening and closing of the conference, and the opening and closing statements by delegates, would take place in open plenary meetings.

Canada's proposed agenda proved unwelcome to some of its NATO partners (although all had endorsed the idea of a meeting) and was described as too detailed by Austria. In any case, as one of several proposals introduced after the Polish crisis in 1981–2, it was not acceptable to the Soviet Union and could not be used even as a basis for negotiations. This was made clear in the round of visits by Harry Jay, head of the Canadian delegation, to signatory countries prior to the Ottawa conference. As a result, when the preliminary meeting opened in Ottawa on 23 April 1985, no procedures had yet been worked out, and all the thorny questions involved had to be solved before formal convening on 7 May. The meagre and somewhat ambiguous provisions of the Madrid document provided for a meeting of experts "on questions concerning respect, in their States, for human rights and fundamental freedoms, in all their aspects, as embodied in the Final Act." This would "draw up conclusions and recommendations to be submitted to the governments of all participating States."

One important decision had been made in advance in Madrid, or in later negotiations, or simply as a matter taken for granted. The meeting would consist not of experts (specialists acting independently as experts) but of diplomats acting under instructions. It is not known whether an alternative procedure, on the model of the CSCE scientific forum in Hamburg (or the later cultural forum in Budapest), was considered, or why the initial Canadian proposal, of a meeting of experts consisting of "representatives of government and of private groups concerned with implementation of the Final Act," was dropped. It was agreed at Madrid that Canada would host and prepare the meeting, in particular ensuring security of delegates and arranging access by the media and others. The Canadian government, in agreement with the other participants, assigned these tasks to Louis Rogers, who, as Canada's chief delegate at Madrid, had been central in securing approval for the conference.

Preparatory Meeting

Elaborating the agenda, timetable, and procedure of the conference proved difficult and time-consuming. Right up until Tuesday 7 May, no agreement had been reached, and there was doubt whether the meeting would take place. During the final hectic weekend, the clock was stopped: the "Friday" meeting continued until early Monday morning. Plenary sessions were frequently adjourned for long "coffee breaks" – devoted to private negotiations and endless meetings of group caucuses and inter-caucus "contact groups." Only on 8 May, after the formal opening, was a compromise reached.

The opposing positions of East and West were set forth in two major draft proposals, one by the NATO group, the other by the Warsaw Treaty Organization (WTO) group, with a third, the Romanian, resembling the latter.[33] The deadlock related to the number of sessions to be open to the press and the time to be devoted to general discussion of human rights, to measures to improve respect for human rights, and to conclusions and recommendations.

The dispute over the first issue was described by the media as a battle as to whether the conference should be open or closed. In fact the delegates were all agreed that most sessions would be in camera: they differed only on how many sessions would be open at the beginning and at the end. The Soviet Union wanted only one – the formal opening ceremony, at which the Canadian external affairs secretary would welcome the delegates. Western delegates wished several, for initial and concluding statements by all delegations. The Romanian draft proposed that only the first and last sittings should be open. The ultimate compromise provided for one open session at the outset and another at the end. In practice, the proceedings were more porous: many delegates distributed texts of speeches given in closed sessions, the US delegate briefed the press after each session (and other delegates did so less regularly), delegations gave occasional press conferences, and texts of proposals submitted during the second phase became unofficially available.[34]

The second issue was also more controversial in form than in substance. The Western powers wanted three full weeks of general debate – ample opportunity for a full review of implementation. The Soviet bloc wanted less, assuming correctly that it would be used for severe criticism of their policies. Their proposal suggested a day or two dedicated to the 40trh anniversary of the victory over Nazism and fascism, did not mention opening statements, and allowed two weeks for general debate. This would leave about three weeks for consideration of conclusions and recommendations; the Western plan allowed one week to discuss measures to improve human rights and another to draw up conclusions and recommendations and make concluding statements. The Romanian draft reduced still further time for general debate. In the end consensus was reached on a day for commemorating the 40th anniversary, a little more than two weeks for debate, a week for discussing new measures, and some ten days for drafting conclusions and recommendations. This represented a fair compromise of opposing views.

Debate

The conference itself lasted almost six weeks (7 May–17 June 1985). Almost three weeks, including days set aside for opening and concluding speeches, were devoted to review of implementation of the human rights provisions of the Helsinki Final Act.[35]

At the outset the Soviet delegation envisaged merely a mutual exchange of experiences, with each country reporting on its own performance and listening without criticism to the reports of others. According to their initial agenda proposal, the debate would take place with strict respect for the "principle of non-intervention in internal affairs" and for "the rights inherent in the sovereignty of participating states, including the laws and regulations of each country." Although these limitations were not included in the agenda eventually adopted, the Soviet delegation continued to argue that criticism of other states constituted interference.

Western delegations, neutral as well as NATO, made clear from the beginning that they regarded the Soviet viewpoint as outdated by postwar human rights agreements and contrary to the precedents established at Belgrade and Madrid. They reiterated their long-held view that a critical review of the record was legitimate and systematically criticized Soviet behaviour. The American chief delegate, Richard Schifter, adopted a militant style, sharply attacking Soviet-bloc violations and appending long lists of the names of victims. Other delegates, including some NATO members, were more moderate, Canada, for instance, criticizing unnamed (although easily identifiable) states and only occasionally naming victims.

In contrast to Belgrade and Madrid, the attitude of Soviet representatives underwent a subtle evolution and became somewhat contradictory. They responded increasingly to Western censure with a *tu quoque* reply, condemning "massive" breaches of human rights in the West generally, or in the United States or other countries, citing unemployment, homelessness, poverty, racial discrimination, and lack of equality for women, free health care, and education. They also began to respond to specific criticisms of their own laws and practices, defending, for instance, treatment of religious believers or imprisonment of dissidents. All of this tended to undermine their argument that such criticism was illegitimate interference in domestic affairs.

The debate, as a result, was not the frank and open dialogue that Western delegates professed to desire, but a polemical confrontation. It was marked, however, by participation of neutral and non-aligned states, which, while not committed on matters of high policy, shared the values and many of the ideals of the NATO countries. As a result, the sessions became a philosophical debate between democratic and communist states and focused on the relation of the state and its citizens, the classic theme of political theory and of political controversy for centuries.

Speeches mirrored democratic or Marxist-Leninist positions but also reflected the view of national governments. Delegates often explained in detail their own human rights record and sharply criticized that of others. As though by common consent, however, international questions (for instance, Afghanistan and Nicaragua) were avoided, presumably as not related to human rights "in their states" (in the wording of the Madrid mandate). Nonetheless the debate revealed clearly the almost unbridgeable chasm between democratic and communist doctrine – and the wide gap between theory and practice of the latter.

The debate was not, however, an impartial and balanced discussion of human rights in all participating states. The Soviet Union was placed in the dock; Poland, Romania, and Czechoslovakia were also condemned, but less frequently; Hungary and even East Germany (the target of sharp West German attacks at Madrid) were spared criticism altogether. The Western powers also avoided censure of allies such as Turkey, or neutrals such as Yugoslavia and Malta, whose records merited rebuke.

Proposals

The other main item on the conference's agenda, as decided at the preparatory meeting, was "consideration of proposals for recommendations" and "adoption of conclusions and recommendations." The Western draft agenda had spoken of "measures to improve respect for human rights." The conference was in fact deluged with 45 proposals.[36] Their content, like the review debate, indicated a great diversity of ideas and the absence of common ground between East and West. Not one achieved the consensus necessary for adoption. Nor did the efforts of the NATO, WTO, and NNA groups to combine these many suggestions in a single concluding document succeed. In the end, in the absence of agreement, each bloc tabled a composite document amalgamating its own proposals in a "manifesto" of human rights.[37]

The NATO manifesto emphasized civil and political rights, including such subjects as the "right to know," monitoring, information, the role of individuals and organizations, freedom of thought and conscience, religious freedom (taken over from the Holy See's draft), trade union rights, equality for women, freedom from torture and terrorism, access to courts and prisons, protection against psychiatric practices violating human rights, and regular meetings to discuss human rights. There were no recommendations concerning economic and social rights (other than to form trade unions), although these were discussed in plenary debate.

The Soviet manifesto referred to human rights in very general terms and warned that they should not be used to aggravate the international situation or imperil détente or to justify intervention in domestic affairs. It also included measures to prevent the revival of Nazism and fascism. The manifesto stated that it was essential to promote both civil and political and economic, social and cultural rights and desirable that all states should ratify the international human rights covenants and other conventions, such as those on racial discrimination and genocide. The main thrust was, however, economic and social, including equality for women, the right to work and to free education and health care, measures to deal with poverty, hunger, and homelessness, the right of workers to participate, and the rights of young people and of migrant workers. The Soviet manifesto called for an end to torture and made no reference to terrorism; it urged elimination of racial and religious discrimination (but omitted an earlier reference to the abuse of medicine).[38] It placed emphasis on the need to avoid war and to end the arms race but did not declare the "right to life" to be the "supreme right," as in one of its original proposals.

As at Belgrade and Madrid, the NNA group made strenuous efforts to bring together the view of East and West. Finland took the lead, presenting informally a long compromise draft that included not only many general statements and some specific proposals of the Soviet draft, such as the right to work, but also many Western formulations, including the right to establish trade unions. It recommended adherence to the international covenants, but also to the Optional Protocol, which the Soviet Union had not ratified. It asserted the individual's right to know and to act on his or her rights, but without specific reference to monitoring. It proposed another experts' meeting on human rights and also restated Finland's own proposal of bilateral round-table meetings on human rights. This gallant effort was not fully acceptable to the West but was doomed by Soviet rejection of some of its essential points.

Final Deadlock

By the weekend prior to closing, scheduled for Monday 17 June, the delegates found themselves in complete deadlock, with no possibility of an agreement on a document on Finnish lines. On the 14th, the NATO draft, somewhat revised, was tabled by the Italian delegation and a final version of the Soviet-bloc manifesto was tabled by Czechoslovakia. Would delegates be able to reach a consensus on a briefer document or terminate the proceedings without any agreed statement? A Swiss proposal – little more than a Belgrade-type communiqué, recommending only that the possibility of convening another "experts' meeting" be considered at the Vienna follow-up – made no headway and had to be dropped. Austria, in the name of the NNA group (including Yugoslavia, but without Switzerland), made a last effort at compromise, submitting a draft slightly more substantial than the Swiss, which referred to concern over "serious violations of human rights and fundamental freedoms" and described the Ottawa discussions as "useful" and "consistent with all the principles of the Final Act." It recommended that at Vienna the delegates consider "the possibility of convening another meeting of experts" concerning human rights. A Czechoslovak draft in response omitted references to "violations" and to the "consistency" of the debate with the Final Act. The draft mentioned that "a question of another meeting" had been raised and that views had been expressed that "such questions might be subject for consideration" at Vienna.[39]

There ensued, as in the days prior to the conference, a long hectic weekend: the clock was once more stopped, plenary sessions were repeatedly adjourned after a few minutes, and during hour-long coffee breaks a nine-member contact group, representing NATO, WTO, and NNA, desperately sought a consensus. Western delegations were ready to support the neutral draft, *faute de mieux,* but the Soviet Union insisted on "amendments," embodied in document 50. France still hoped for a compromise. Most Western delegations had concluded by Monday that no document was better than an emasculated, Soviet-style one, papering over serious conflicts, misleading the public, and containing no serious reference to a future experts' meeting. At the final pre-closing plenary, weary delegates reluctantly decided that, for the first time, a CSCE meeting would end without a concluding document.

Canada's Role

As a country with costly experience in two great European wars and close ties with Britain, France, and other European states, Canada has had a deep interest in the CSCE, both in its goals of security and in its promotion of freer movement of peoples and goods. In view of human rights' "high priority" in Canada and "important place" in Canadian foreign policy, Canada had considerable[40] interest in the human rights component of the CSCE, and that interest had grown since Helsinki. The country's ethnic make-up intensified its interest in Europe, in expanded rights of emigration, in national minorities, and in human rights in countries of origin of many of its people. As initiator and host of the 1985 meeting, the Canadian government was determined on a successful outcome. Its policy was, as usual at CSCE meetings, to avoid open confrontation and to abstain, where possible, from naming names, but to criticize frankly violations of rights. Some observers saw this as speaking too "softly"; others thought it likely to be more effective than stridency and more in line with the Canadian tradition of quiet diplomacy.

Chief responsibility for expounding Canada's position at the meeting was assigned to retired diplomat R. Harry Jay, former deputy permanent representative to NATO and former ambassador and permanent representative to the United Nations in Geneva. The small delegation included officers from three federal departments: five from External Affairs, one from Justice, and one from Secretary of State. Jay worked closely also with members of other government departments. Politically he was responsible to the external affairs secretary and to the government as a whole and received his instructions from the former. A number of parliamentarians, representing the three political parties, and drawn from the Sub-committee on Human Rights in Eastern Europe of the House of Commons Committee on External Affairs and National Defence and the Senate Foreign Affairs Committee, were appointed as observers. The sub-committee, chaired by Reginald Stackhouse of Toronto, had held hearings on 30 April and 1 May to receive evidence from interested Canadian groups.[41] There was some dissatisfaction, voiced in both houses, that selection of parliamentary observers was not completed until the very opening of the conference. Their participation in the daily work of the delegation was limited, but some did attend caucus meetings and plenary sessions, and they served as a useful link with Parliament and public.

The role of non-governmental organizations (NGOs) was controversial. The Eastern bloc denied them any significant status and had liquidated monitoring organizations in their countries. The United States provided NGOs with much information and easy personal access to its delegation through staff members of the Washington Commission on Security and Cooperation in Europe. Canada, like most Western states, did not include ethnic groups and human rights organizations in its delegation but gave them as much information as possible, without jeopardizing the code of privacy generally accepted at CSCE meetings. With government approval, the delegation professed an open-door policy for NGOs and held two formal briefings, before and after the meeting, at both of which Secretary of State for External Affairs Joe Clark and other officials spoke on Canada's aims and tactics.

In opening the meeting, Clark stressed the importance of human rights in the search for peace and firmly stated that progress in respect for human rights was a matter of natural concern for government and individual citizens. In the session devoted to the 40th anniversary of the defeat of fascism and the end of the war, Harry Jay, a veteran and former prisoner of war, speaking briefly and extemporaneously, was overcome with emotion at the end of his speech and was applauded, a tribute rare in diplomatic gatherings. The Soviet spokesmen, having paid homage to the Western contribution to victory, singled out for special mention the "bravery of Canadians" and the loss of 5,000 in the "tragedy of Dieppe," remarks in Russian which were not made known to the media, for which no English translation was made available.

In his opening statement on 13 May, Jay, without referring to specific countries, admitted frankly the little progress in human rights since Helsinki and added that the situation was, if anything, worse. He spoke of rights denied: the right to emigrate, "to know and act" on one's "rights and duties," and to form free trade unions and the rights of minorities and religious groups. He argued that these abuses had nothing to do with political systems as such but stemmed from bureaucratic rigidities, ethnic chauvinism, or religious intolerance.

In the first of four substantive addresses (17 May), Jay addressed the "right of the individual to know and act upon his rights and duties" – the "bedrock" on which all other rights must rest. He described at length Canada's efforts in this area, referring to the Charter of Rights and Freedoms and ratification of the international covenants and to provincial human rights codes and commissioners. Federal, provincial, and municipal governments encouraged public discussion of human rights, and extensive reports were prepared on implementation. Jay spoke of Canada's acceptance of the Optional Protocol, which gave the individual "the right to bring the Canadian government before the bar of international scrutiny" and of Canada's efforts since 1980 to promote the rights of the individual in the UN Commission on Human Rights. He expressed concern about the systematic frustration of individuals and groups in acting on these rights, citing Anatoly Scharansky, Mart Niklus, and Andrei Sakharov as illustrations from the Soviet Union and Charter 77 in Czechoslovakia. Why, he asked, were individuals, acting on their rights of free thought and free speech, penalized for suggesting that all was not perfect in their home countries? As noted above, Canada co-sponsored three proposals confirming the rights of individuals and groups – (1) supporting international co-operation, (2) protecting the right to monitor fulfilment, and (3) encouraging publications about human rights.

In a second major statement (21 May), Jay dealt with freedom of religion or belief. Citing a recent decision of the Supreme Court of Canada which declared invalid legislation requiring commercial establishments to remain closed on Sundays, Jay concluded that freedom of religion meant not only the "freedom to practice a chosen faith" but also the "absence of coercion or constraint" on religious grounds. Certain states represented at Ottawa, Jay noted, while professing freedom of religion, exacted a price for citizens who practised their religion, thus contravening provisions of the Helsinki and Madrid documents. The Soviet state sought to promote atheism but forbade propagation of religious faith, circumscribed teaching of religion, and discouraged people from professing their faith by various forms of discrimination. States must do everything possible to assure freedom of belief and to engender tolerance. "The efforts of governments must be aimed at eliminating intolerance – not at eliminating religion," he concluded.

In a third speech (24 May), Jay dealt with the "explosive" question of national minorities and their rights, in which Canada was vitally interested because of its multi-ethnic composition and the close ties of many Canadians with the victims of national discrimination in Europe. Canada, he said, by virtue of its Charter of Rights and its multicultural policy, sought to safeguard the rights of national minorities but admitted that there were still failings to be corrected. The obligations of the international covenant, the Helsinki Final Act, and the Madrid concluding document were not fulfilled when a state denied that a minority existed, or set out forcibly to disperse or assimilate it, or restricted the use of its mother tongue. Expressing Canada's grave concern, he referred to Soviet Jews and in careful diplomatic language expressed the widely held belief that "their cultural identity may be at risk." Later, in general discussion, Canada joined with the United States and the United Kingdom in criticizing the Bulgarian denial of rights to its Turkish minority, but it refrained from any censure of Turkey's policy toward its Kurdish minority.

In Canada's fourth statement (28 May), Jay broke new ground and advanced substantial and original arguments in support of the interrelationship of the two sets of rights – civil and political; economic, social, and cultural – which was enunciated by a number of other delegations (including the Soviet bloc). The two sets were indeed "intertwined," Jay contended, "nourishing one another in any worthwhile society." Although he did not deny the importance of economic and social rights for assuring civil and political rights (the Soviet argument), he stated the reverse proposition: the only assurance that economic and social interests are recognized and satisfied is that citizens should have the right "to voice their views fully and freely."

There *was* a difference between the two sets of rights, he admitted, echoing views expressed by other delegates. Civil and political rights "lend themselves to legal definition involving the individual, are readily justiciable and tend to be thought of as absolute, inalienable and easily realizable." Economic and social rights could only be "achieved over time." "These two aspects of human rights are neither mutually exclusive nor incompatible, but are in fact mutually supportive." The right to work, for instance, was not synonymous with full employment, although governments had an obligation to generate employment for all those seeking to work. But of equal importance was "the right of the individual to choose freely where, and in what conditions, he or she is prepared to work. We impose no obligation to work. Nor can a worker be dismissed for any cause unrelated to performance on the job." Economic and social rights included guarantees to ensure the right of workers freely to establish and join trade unions and the right of unions freely to exercise their activities and other rights free from state control, as stated in the Madrid concluding document.

A Balance Sheet

The Human Rights Experts Meeting in Ottawa was but one small step in a long historical march toward expanded human rights, and a link in the more recent chain of documents embodying human rights as a concern of international diplomacy. It was a direct consequence of the application – at Helsinki, Belgrade, and Madrid – of similar ideas to Europe and was the first meeting in the Helsinki process dealing exclusively with human rights.

The meeting broke up in stalemate. Had Ottawa been a fiasco, as some newspaper headlines suggested? Delegates were almost unanimous in declaring the meeting "useful."[42] In Western eyes, the three-week review of implementation reconfirmed the legitimacy of international concern for human rights violations and the irrelevance of the "domestic jurisdiction" argument. Yet the emphasis had been one-sided, neglecting violations in some Western, NNA, and Eastern-bloc nations. A more balanced review would examine the record of all states, as in UN human rights bodies. The failure to reach an accord reflected the gap between East and West and was preferable to papering over these differences. Even failure to recommend another meeting of "human rights experts" did not prevent a decision in Vienna to hold such a gathering at the Vienna follow-up. Ottawa had also demonstrated the unanimity attained by the NATO group on a manifesto of human rights, which had won the support of many neutral and non-aligned states and would serve as a guideline for future CSCE meetings.

Despite limitations, the meeting had put the spotlight on human rights as a proper subject of international diplomacy. The Soviet Union found itself forced onto the defensive and isolated, enjoying support only from its allies, and was subjected to constant pressure, not only in formal sessions but also in the corridors and lounges, by other delegations, and by the media and Western NGOs. As at Madrid, NGOs and exiled dissidents, through press conferences and demonstrations, publicized the denial of human rights in their homelands and the plight of dissidents and other victims of repression. At Ottawa, Mrs Scharansky demonstrated outside the Soviet embassy, and a Hungarian went on hunger strike outside the conference centre. Relatives of Andrei Sakharov held a press conference and were received by Joe Clark and Harry Jay; they pressed their case personally inside the conference centre with most of the delegations, including even the Soviet one

Soviet representatives termed the conference a success, in spite of Western interference in the domestic affairs of the socialist countries, and emphasized the useful exchange of experiences that had taken place.[43] They believed that their own proposals had made a "weighty contribution" to the dialogue and had directed attention to the "supreme right" – to live in peace and freedom. They were confident that they had had an effect on world opinion by exposing Western violations and "double standards."

BUDAPEST AND BERNE

After Ottawa, two other CSCE parleys took place: the Cultural Forum in Budapest (1985) and the Human Contacts Experts Meeting in Berne (1986), both ending without an agreed final document. Each dealt with a specific part of basket III of the Final Act, on humanitarian co-operation. Although the Helsinki provisions related only to certain limited international aspects of these matters, not to human rights as such, the two meetings broadened deliberations to include cultural freedom and freedom of movement in general, thus continuing the work begun at Ottawa.

The Cultural Forum, held in Budapest (October–November 1985), was the first CSCE gathering to occur in a communist country and to include as delegates prominent cultural figures from each country, some 600 in all.[44] The latter participated in subsidiary working bodies, which, although frustrating to non-diplomats, provided a rare opportunity for direct exchange of views across boundaries and ideologies. Individual participants, except from the Soviet bloc, were free to express opinions independently, without government instructions, and to submit their own recommendations. The result was some 200 proposals, official and non-official – too many to include in a single concluding document. The Canadian delegation, headed by J.E.G. Hardy and including eight cultural figures, officially co-sponsored seven proposals, dealing with such matters as cultural rights, unhindered access to broadcasts, and the rights of national minorities and of religious groups.

The general debate revealed an unbridgeable gulf between West and East. The West emphasized individual creative freedom and independence and sought removal of obstacles to international contacts and exchanges. The East stressed so-called dialogue and co-operation and the obligation of culture to support peace and security and to resist the arms race and the nuclear danger. The Soviet delegation refused even to discuss the composite Western concluding draft and presented its own. The NNA countries submitted, in vain, a compromise draft, which included in an appendix all the proposals made. This document was acceptable to the Western delegations but not to the Soviet bloc, which advanced 66 amendments.

The final breakdown was the result not of East-West conflict but of the deep clash between Hungary and Romania over the latter's treatment of its Hungarian minority in Transylvania. During the sessions Hungary avoided associating itself with extreme Soviet positions but was unusually frank in criticizing Romania's nationality policy. Romania was almost silent, in spite of censure by Hungary and several Western delegations. At the last minute Hungary, as the host country, tried to save the situation by submitting an anodyne concluding document of the Belgrade type, which did, however, suggest that all proposals should be referred to the Vienna follow-up. Romania refused the necessary consensus, and the conference ended without even a communiqué.

A simultaneous unofficial forum, sponsored by the International Helsinki Federation for Human Rights, was attended by Hungarian dissidents, such as Laszlo Rajk, several Czech exiles (Jirí Gruša et al), some Western cultural personalities (such as Susan Sontag and Per Wastberg), and even a few Western diplomats. The theme was "Writers and Their Integrity," and papers were read or distributed on topics such as European cultural unity and its present crisis, censorship and self-censorship, and the conditions of Hungarian writers in Transylvania. Participants had to crowd into several private apartments, since Hungarian officials refused to permit the use of a hotel as planned, a fact deplored in speeches in the official forum and in private talks among diplomats.[45]

The Human Contacts Experts Meeting in Berne (April–May 1986) focused on meetings of divided families, family reunification and marriages, travel, and tourism, all of special interest to Canada, which has one million citizens who speak eastern European languages and has a tradition of welcoming immigrants from this area, including many political refugees. The chief Canadian delegate, William Bauer, repeatedly made the point that if all CSCE countries lived up to the International Covenant on Civil and Political Rights by allowing citizens to leave their country and return without hindrance – Canada's practice – most problems of human contacts referred to in the Final Act would be removed.[46]

In the general debate, the Canadians, like other Western delegates, focused on Eastern-bloc practices, particularly Soviet, which hampered family meetings and reunification and travel in general. Of the 20 Western proposals, Canada submitted four (CSCE BME 9, 10, 11, 12), to permit family members to decide two things – with whom and where to be reunified, to remove travel restrictions on families that included "illegal" emigrants (who had left without official permission or illegally), and to encourage visits by whole families (without "hostages" left behind). Canada also sought to remove obstacles to foreign travel by persons belonging to national minorities and regional cultures, as well as barriers to tourism in general. Canada supported other Western propositions, in particular the radical one by France for abolition of exit visas (which would have eliminated most obstacles to family visits and reunification). Canadian delegates conferred with eastern Europeans about specific cases of reunification, but the Soviet Union, for the first time in CSCE history, refused even to discuss such cases with Canada.

The Soviet Union showed no willingness to relax its exit policies and thus bore the brunt of Western criticism. It refused to accept most of the major Western proposals or introduced amendments that made them meaningless. Romania aligned itself with the Soviet Union more than usually and was equally adamant in rejecting Western resolutions. Most Soviet-bloc proposals were mere restatements of the Final Act. The East-

West gap was so great that the Soviet delegation walked out of the final negotiations on a concluding document. Although Western delegations sometimes found themselves in disagreement, they usually managed to achieve consensus, and their ways parted only during the final days of crisis.

As usual, the NNAs sought to bridge East and West, although they themselves were often divided. In the final, climactic hours, the Swiss and Austrians introduced a compromise draft that omitted or watered down most of the major Western proposals. In Canada's view the draft had "marginal utility" and was "only just acceptable."[47] In his penultimate speech (21 May) William Bauer expressed doubts that delegates could agree on more than "a piece of paper without meaningful substance."[48] Some Western countries were ready to accept even a weak compromise: West Germany was anxious not to jeopardize emigration of tens of thousands of Germans from the east. The Soviet bloc, including Romania, was ready to accept the Swiss-Austrian draft. At the last minute, without consultation with its partners, the United States announced its unwillingness to accept a document that contained "loopholes damaging to compliance."[49] The breakdown of Western unity was due to serious differences over the Swiss-Austrian document and to snags in communication with Washington during the Memorial Day weekend. The Soviet delegation had a week or so earlier indicated willingness to settle some 200 reunification cases but apparently did not use this as a chip in the last-minute bargaining, and the Americans did not secure clearance to accept the list. As a result, the Soviet Union scored a double triumph, blaming failure on the United States and, after the conference, announcing its readiness to settle the 200 cases. Canada did not "mourn" the absence of a concluding document; "just another paper was not enough."[50]

VIENNA (1986–)

The third Helsinki follow-up opened in Vienna in November 1986. It faced the task of reviewing Ottawa, Berne, and Budapest, each of which had failed to achieve a consensus or to broaden the scope of Final Act commitments. The CSCE Stockholm conference had been more successful and had substantially expanded the scope of confidence-building measures (CSBMs) in the military field. The Vienna conclave had to decide whether to hold new conferences in these fields and to evaluate progress, or lack of it, in economic, industrial, and technological cooperation (basket II) and information and education (basket III). The delegates had the opportunity once again to review implementation of human rights and to criticize violations and had to discuss some 150 new proposals.

At Vienna the West proposed two separate sets of negotiations on security matters – one, to consider CSBMs going beyond Stockholm, and the other, outside the regular CSCE framework, on "conventional stability," to discuss conventional troop reductions among the 23 nations directly concerned (excluding, of course, the NNAs). The Soviet bloc proposed a single successor to Stockholm, under the CSCE umbrella, which would deal with CSBMs but would move on to a "second stage" of general European disarmament.

On the human side, the West made proposals for a mechanism to monitor human rights observance, an experts' meeting to decide on a subsequent Conference on the Human Dimension, and a special meeting on human rights to be held at the request of any one CSCE member. The Soviet Union suggested discussions on economic and social rights and a meeting on "humanitarian issues," including human rights, to be held in Moscow.

During four sessions in 1986 and 1987 delegates debated at length rival conceptions of security and human rights. The West continued to press for safeguards of freedom of thought, conscience, religion and belief, and movement. Canada laid great emphasis on the rights of national minorities, the Soviet Union stressed security questions and assigned priority to economic and social rights. As always, the West sought to balance security and human rights and to reach a compromise over rival conceptions in both spheres. In spite of NNA efforts to draft a document that would reconcile conflicting and mutual interests, East and West remained far apart. There seemed to be no early prospect of consensus when the fifth session opened in January 1988.

HELSINKI PROSPECTS

It was damaging to the image of the CSCE and its future that successive conferences had been deadlocked and had produced no fundamental changes in Soviet attitude and behaviour on human rights in the general sense and only minor progress in concrete provisions of the three baskets. This raised doubts in the West about continuing time-consuming conferences in which both sides proclaimed high ideals but few concrete changes in Soviet-bloc practice occurred. Some Soviet exiles concluded that the CSCE should be scrapped and replaced by a policy of linkage that would demand improvements in humanitarian policies in return for concessions in trade and technology.[51] Western governments and human rights organizations, however, as well as Polish and Czechoslovak dissidents, believed that the CSCE process was worthwhile and should continue.[52] This view was encouraged by unquestioned improvements, under Gorbachev's policy of perestroika and glasnost, including the release of some political prisoners, increased emigration of Jews and Germans, reduction in control over official media and over culture and scholarship, and a proliferation of independent groups and journals. Western delegates expressed keen disappointment, however, that the "new thinking" advocated by Gorbachev was not reflected in the behaviour of Soviet delegates at Vienna.

Canada's goal, and its continuing hope, were that sustained criticism, within and outside the Helsinki process, would encourage Moscow and its allies to modify further the repressive features of their systems and rectify continued glaring violations of human rights. It was recognized that such a secular transformation, if it took place, would be the product of domestic forces more than of outside pressures. The CSCE conferences meanwhile provided useful forums for holding high the standards of human rights in a world context and for giving moral support and encouragement to those in the Soviet bloc who were taking great risks and suffering much in their defence of Helsinki ideals and who might well contribute to more fundamental change in their own societies in the long run.

CHAPTER NINE

International Financial Institutions

RENATE PRATT

The Canadian government has affirmed on a number of occasions that the promotion and protection of internationally recognized human rights are major objectives of its foreign policy. Nevertheless it has not sought to have this concern reflected in the decisions of international financial institutions (IFIs). Canada has declined, with only a single exception, to instruct its executive directors in the International Monetary Fund (IMF), the World Bank, and the regional development banks to consider gross and systematic violations of basic rights when deciding on credit or loan applications made to these institutions. Nor has Canada proposed that the staff of these institutions include such criteria in its assessment of credit and loan applications.

In this chapter I will examine the reasons given by government officials for these decisions and review the position taken by Canadian executive directors on a number of projects. I will test the consistency with which the government has adhered to its stated policy and assess the appropriateness of that policy. The analysis that follows reflects the judgment that it is both desirable and feasible for IFIs to insist that basic rights be respected in countries that receive financial assistance and that Canada ought therefore to work toward that end.

THE INSTITUTIONS

Structures and Policies

The decision to establish the IMF and the World Bank was taken in July 1944 by the UN Monetary and Financial Conference at Bretton Woods. The IMF was to promote international monetary co-operation and to facilitate balanced growth in international trade by, among other things, making its resources temporarily available to members under adequate safeguards, thus allowing them to adjust their balance of payments, without resorting to measures destructive of national or international prosperity. In recent years and in response to the growing financial crisis of the developing countries, the IMF has emerged "as an important co-ordinator and organizer of joint official/private financial 'rescue' operations. Its seal of approval for domestic stabilization and adjustment programs has become more important than ever – the very centrepiece of the international debt restructuring and adjustment process."[1]

Subscriptions to the IMF come from member countries. Loan decisions reflect the voting power of IMF members, which is weighted in proportion to each country's share ownership. The United States holds the largest single block, roughly 20 per cent, of IMF shares. On the executive board France, Japan, Saudi Arabia, the United Kingdom, the United States, and West Germany each have an executive director. Other member-countries are grouped in geographical clusters, and each cluster is represented by one executive director elected by them. Canada's executive director also represents Antigua and Barbuda, Bahamas, Barbados, Belize, Dominica, Grenada, Ireland, Jamaica, St Christopher and Nevis, St Lucia, and St Vincent and the Grenadines, with a total voting power in 1986 of 3.27 per cent.[2]

The World Bank, which now includes its subsequently established affiliates, the International Development Association (IDA) and the International Finance Corporation (IFC), was originally charged with assisting the reconstruction of post-war Europe, hence its original and official name, the International Bank for Reconstruction and Development (IBRD). Since the early 1960s it has increasingly concentrated on Third World development assistance. World Bank loans are financed with money borrowed from the private capital market. Its concessional low-interest and long-term loans – administered by the IDA – are funded by grants from member donor countries. These grants are negotiated every three years. Voting procedures and representation in the World Bank are very similar to those of the IMF. The United States again holds roughly 20 per cent of shares; Canada's executive director represents the almost identical cluster of countries, with voting power in 1986 of 4.15 per cent.

An official vote is practically never taken in either the IMF or the World Bank. Executive board members are typically canvassed about upcoming decisions to facilitate a "consensus" approach. Traditionally, the managing director of the IMF is a European, the president of the World Bank a US citizen. Canada's minister of finance is the Canadian governor of both the IMF and the World Bank. His department is responsible for formulation and co-ordination of policies with regard to the two international institutions.

Canada is also a member of the four regional development banks established in the 1960s. These banks are modelled on the World Bank, with emphasis on development projects and programs particular to the regions. Canada appoints its own executive director to the Inter-American Development Bank (IDB) and to the Caribbean Development Bank (CDB), in which it exercises 4.38 and 12.0 per cent of the vote respectively (1986 figures). The IDB's executive vice-president, the bank's chief administrative officer, is traditionally a US citizen appointed by his government. The United States holds 34.5 per cent of IDB votes. In the African Development Bank (AfDB) and the Asian Development Bank (AsDB), Canada's executive directors represent member-countries with votes respectively of 7.32 and 9.7 per cent (1986 figures).

The Canadian International Development Agency (CIDA) formulates and co-ordinates Canada's policy in the regional banks. Regular consultations take place with the Department of Finance and occasionally with other departments on instructions issued to the Canadian executive directors. The Canadian governor for the regional development banks is the secretary of state for external affairs. In 1985-6 the World Bank and the regional development banks received 19 per cent of Canada's total official development assistance, the largest single block of aid after bilateral assistance of 36 per cent.[3]

Despite a fair body of opinion that human rights criteria should be integral to decision-making on loan disbursements from the IFIs, their management and governors have held that such practice would constitute political interference and would conflict with the charters of these institutions. As Sir Joseph Gold, former legal counsel to the IMF, said in 1983: "Domestic policies are 'social' and 'political' if they do not fall within the scope of the purposes of the Fund as set forth in Article 1, and the Fund may not base its decisions on political considerations of this character. Members have decided to retain sovereignty over domestic social and political policies."[4]

In 1978 Earl Drake, then Canada's executive director of the World Bank, elaborated: "The constitutions of the World Bank and other IFI's state that only economic and financial criteria can be applied to projects and only unconditional contributions can be accepted from governments. IFI managers dislike the human rights issue because it is politically divisive within their boards and because their staff has no legal authority or training to deal with the subject."[5]

Protecting Human Rights

A significant accumulation of ideas, writings, policies, and legislation has emerged over the last decade that witnesses to a growing concern that the IFIs should be more responsive to human rights observance.

Various executive directors in the IFIs have from time to time registered their opposition to specific disbursements on the grounds that applicants were engaged in gross and systematic violations of human rights.

During the Carter administration, for example, US executive directors of the World Bank and of the regional development banks opposed 118 loans for human rights reasons. These negative votes were almost evenly divided between "leftist" (34 per cent) and "rightist" (31 per cent) governments.[6]

The Harkin Amendments. From 1975 on, major action in the US Congress led to a number of human rights amendments that became known as "the Harkin Amendments,"[7] after Representative – now Senator – Tom Harkin, a Democrat from Iowa. Thus, an early amendment to the International Development and Food Assistance Act specified that no economic assistance be provided to any government that engages in a "consistent pattern of gross violations of internationally recognized human rights."[8] Congress also turned its attention to executive branch decision-making in the World Bank and the regional development banks. Here Harkin and his colleagues, mindful that almost one-third of US foreign aid was channelled through multilateral agencies, sought to introduce human rights criteria that would be binding on the US executive directors of these banks.

The first Harkin amendment became law in 1977. Under section 701 of the International Financial Institutions Act, aid through multilateral institutions was prohibited to countries with a pattern of gross and consistent violations of internationally recognized human rights unless the aid satisfied basic needs. Controversy ensued over the term "consistent." This terminology gave the US executive branch discretion to disburse funds to a human rights violator by claiming that improvements had taken place and that the pattern of violations was therefore no longer "consistent." A final sub-amendment to the Harkin amendment, removing the word "consistent," was adopted only in 1983. Also under section 701, executive directors of the World Bank and the regional development banks are obliged to advance by voice and vote the cause of human rights. They are authorized and instructed to oppose any loan, any extension of financial assistance, or any technical assistance to any gross violator unless such assistance serves basic needs.

The Harkin amendments also gave congressional committees responsibilities to receive quarterly reports from and to consult with the US executive branch about prospective changes in policy toward countries with poor human rights records.[9] A further Harkin initiative in 1978, which sought to extend to the IMF human rights criteria in US decisions, passed the House of Representatives but failed in the Senate.[10]

These congressional efforts were counteracted, however, by the reluctance of successive US administrations to apply human rights criteria consistently and to extend them to bilateral aid disbursement. Nevertheless, they constitute the most important effort to date by any country to direct its executive directors in these institutions to be responsive in their voting to human rights observances.

The World Bank. In 1972, in an important contribution to the debate about basic rights, Robert McNamara, then president of the World Bank, placed the plight of the world's poorest on the bank's agenda. He told the governors: "The most pervasive, and the most persistent poverty of all ... is the poverty of the low-income strata ... roughly 40% of the total population in all developing countries. It is they who – despite their country's gross economic growth – remain entrapped in conditions of deprivation which fall below any rational definition of human decency."

McNamara promised World Bank financing for projects that would reach the poor who were not served by major infrastructural projects and greater priority for programs to reduce "the skewedness of the income distribution" in order "to achieve development's most fundamental goal: ending the inhuman deprivation." He pledged support for establishment of growth targets "in terms of essential human needs; in terms of nutrition, housing, health, literacy, and employment."[11] This affirmation, many World Bank officials notwithstanding, placed human rights criteria firmly into the bank's decision-making; each of these goals represents aspects of the social and cultural rights outlined in the Universal Declaration of Human Rights and is integral to basic rights.

Of similar importance were World Bank policies initiated in the mid-1970s with regard to projects that affect the socio-cultural rights of tribal peoples and the establishment of the Environment, Science and Technology Unit, charged with advising and assisting regional staff on environmental aspects of World Bank projects. The World Bank recognized that, unless protective measures were adopted, tribal people would be harmed by development projects: "The Bank will not assist development projects that knowingly involve encroachment on traditional territories being used or occupied by tribal people, unless adequate safeguards are provided. ... The Bank will assist projects *only* when satisfied that the borrower or relevant government agency supports and can implement measures that will effectively safeguard the integrity and well-being of the tribal people."[12]

With regard to "human suffering and hardship caused by involuntary resettlement" of tribal peoples, the bank instructs its staff at the time of identification and appraisal of a project "to determine whether people must be displaced, and, if displacement is unavoidable, to reduce it to a minimum compatible with the purpose of the project. The costs of resettlement should be included in the project and taken into account in the rate of return analysis."[13]

The Operational Manual Statement on "Environmental Aspects of Bank Work" states: "Since 1970 the Bank has steadily increased its attention to the environmental opportunities and risks introduced by the development process." The Environment, Science and Technology Unit, identified as the bank's oversight and enforcement arm for the bank's adherence to environmental standards, also "is the Bank's designated focal point" for relations with the UN Environment Program.[14]

It is clear from these policies that the World Bank considers factors that go beyond the strictly technical and economic. Although protection of the rights of tribal peoples and of the environment clearly entails technical considerations and economic costs, these considerations are qualitatively different in their intent from the bank's usual technical criteria. Thus it is inconsistent for the bank to claim that it would be "political" and therefore beyond its mandate to consider human rights criteria in its disbursement decisions. Environmental concerns and socio-cultural rights of tribal peoples are no less "political" than human rights violations.[15]

The IMF. In 1983 US legislators imposed restrictions on IMF credits to South Africa. IMF and World Bank lending to South Africa had created tensions between the UN community and the two IFIs for two decades. In 1967 the World Bank had refused to implement a 1966 general assembly resolution calling on it to cease loans to South Africa and to Portugal because of their apartheid and colonial policies. That same year the bank advanced $10 million to Portugal and $20 million to South Africa. It ceased making such loans subsequently, not in response to any UN instructions but because of its own decision to concentrate on less developed countries. The IMF, however, continued to disburse credits to South Africa.

In 1976, the year of the Soweto uprisings, the general assembly adopted a resolution against giving IMF credits to South Africa. Ignoring the resolution, the fund approved three credits to South Africa for a total of $464 million. Of this total, $371 million was advanced after the uprisings and South Africa's harsh response to them. According to research undertaken by the Center for International Policy, objections were raised by the executive directors representing 17 black African member-states during discussions of these credits at the IMF board meeting. Their argument presaged the one eventually adopted by the US Congress in 1983. Antoine Yameogo of Upper Volta pointed out that apartheid created structural economic inefficiencies and that the IMF, with its mandate to insist on correction of such inefficiencies, was making an unusual exemption in the case of South Africa. Revealingly non-technical language was used by the British executive director, who, in approving the first $93 million, commented that the loan would give the South African authorities "some additional room for manoeuver and some feeling of international support, which they deserve."[6]

In November 1982, the IMF approved a $1.07-billion credit for South Africa, the largest-ever single credit for that government. The issue aroused vigorous debate internationally. It resulted in a year-long wrangle in the US Congress, where the black caucus led a tenacious fight for a bill to prevent the US executive director in the IMF from supporting any future South African application for funds. The act as finally approved was a compromise, but a major departure from previous exclusion of congressional oversight of specific, as opposed to general, IMF allocations.

Although the act's provisions are couched in required IMF terminology, its political meaning is inescapable: "The Congress hereby finds that the practice of apartheid results in severe constraints on labor and capital mobility and other highly inefficient labor and capital supply rigidities which contribute to balance of payment deficits in direct contradiction of the goals of the International Monetary Fund."[17] The law requires that the United States oppose IMF loans to South Africa unless the secretary of the treasury certifies in person and documents in writing before relevant congressional committees, at least 21 days before any vote on IMF drawings, that the loan would reduce the severe constraints on labour and capital mobility, increase access to education for black South Africans, benefit economically the majority of people living under apartheid, and reduce racially based restrictions on the geographical mobility of labour, and that South Africa could not raise the funds from private-sector sources.[18]

More recently, the adverse impact of IMF-imposed economic adjustment policies on the poorest sectors of Third World debtor countries has led to increased support for the view that these policies should not ignore social and human development. Third World governments that strive to protect the most vulnerable in their societies and/or fear destabilization of their democratic structures have joined development agencies and economists in their disagreement with IMF policy and practices. They accept that the IMF should negotiate conditions for credits but request that the fund consider the effect of its conditions on the poor.

Referring to measures currently advocated by the IMF, Richard Jolly of the Society for International Development comments: "There are alternatives. It would be possible consciously to recognize that the human consequence of adjustment should not be left as an inevitable and unfortunate by-product – but treated as an essential concern. The protection of minimum levels of nutritional status and other basic human needs could be monitored and made as much a part of the objectives of adjustment as the balance of payments, inflation and economic growth."[19]

James Grant, executive director of the United Nations Children's Fund (UNICEF), appealed to governments to protect the most vulnerable when determining policies: "The time has arrived when we need to apply the same human concerns that emerge in response to natural disasters to the man-made consequences of adjustment ... We must not merely provide warning but actually avert the human disasters which we know can follow, albeit unintentionally, from these government actions."[20]

During opening debates in the general assembly in September 1985, several Third World heads of state raised similar concerns. Julius Nyerere, then president of Tanzania, asked: "Must we starve our children to pay our debt?"; Alan Garcia Perez, president of Peru, stated bluntly: "The choice is dramatic: debt or democracy"; and President José Sarney of Brazil described his country and its neighbours as crushed by foreign debt and warned that policies aimed solely at generating trade surpluses to pay interest were intolerable.

All these appeals agree that the IMF should, as a matter of principle and as resources permit, combine promotion of economic objectives with protection of the basic right to subsistence. Conklin and Davidson argue that the IMF is in fact obliged to do this: to meet its legal obligation under the Universal Declaration and the covenants, the IMF should alleviate the negative economic, social, and political effects of its stand-by credits.[21] The fund is obligated to consider the inequitable impact of its stabilization programs under article 1(ii) of its articles of agreement, which pledges "to facilitate the expansion and balanced growth of international trade, and to contribute thereby to the promotion and maintenance of *high levels of employment and real income* and to the development of the productive resources of all members as primary objectives of economic policy" (emphasis added).

Canadian Initiatives. Despite debates in the United States and elsewhere, there has been scant discussion in Canada about IFI responsiveness to human rights. Nor, until very recently, have parliamentarians talked about considering human rights criteria in Canada's voting decisions in the IFIs. Parliamentary debate has revolved mainly about applying human rights criteria to Canadian bilateral aid.[22] Discussion of IFI decisions has been left to scholars and non-governmental organizations. For example, one scholarly article, published in 1985, argued: "A minimal compliance in regard to basic human rights should be one of the conditions attached to any IMF credit beyond the first tranche. This same requirement should, by extension, apply to the loan and credit programs of the other international financial institutions such as the World Bank and the regional development banks. The major international institutions should be pressed to do what they can to ensure that the global system consolidates and entrenches that recognition of the centrality of basic human rights, which is now so widely, if not formally, acknowledged."[23]

Member churches of the Taskforce on the Churches and Corporate Responsibility (TCCR) have questioned ministers and public servants about decisions taken by Canadian executive directors in a number of IFIs on disbursements to violator régimes. The taskforce has submitted general proposals for including rights criteria in IFI operations. One such proposal was made in June 1983 for possible incorporation in legislation being prepared for the November augmentation of Canada's IMF quota under the Bretton Woods Agreements Act. The churches requested "that Canada oppose an application to the International Monetary Fund (IMF) from any government that is engaged in or condones consistent and gross violations of basic human rights, for drawing and standby credits in excess of its gold [reserve] tranche."[24] This proposal was rejected by the minister of finance on the grounds that such a position would contravene the IMF's apolitical stance.

When the Bretton Woods Agreements Act was to be amended early in 1985, the taskforce participated in public hearings held by the House of Commons Standing Committee on Finance, Trade and Economic Affairs. It proposed that the committee recommend establishment of human rights criteria in IFI voting decisions, social criteria for IMF stabilization measures for debtor countries, basic needs criteria for World Bank loans for violator countries, and annual reviews by Parliament of human rights observance in countries with which Canada has significant relations.[25] The standing committee did not accept any of these proposals.

The public inquiry by the Special Joint Committee of the Senate and the House of Commons, eliciting the views of Canadians on Canada's international relations, resulted in 1986 in a major report, *Independence and Internationalism*. The report contains two sets of comments and recommendations directly relevant to our theme. With regard to severe economic stabilization and adjustment measures, the parliamentarians write: "We are concerned that the often tough measures imposed on many debtor countries in order to manage the debt problem cannot continue without resulting in a major crisis. The economic difficulties facing a number of developing countries place intolerable strains on their people and on democratic governments. We perceive an urgent need for measures designed to promote economic recovery and development in the debtor countries."[26] Concerning human rights criteria in the IFIs, the report recommends that "this would be a departure from the established IFI principle, defended repeatedly by Canada, of judging applications solely on their technical or developmental merits. The committee is acutely conscious of the dangers of further politicizing the IFIs in the name of promoting human rights. Nevertheless, we recognize that the most extreme violations of human rights destroy the possibility of economic and social development. Accordingly, we recommend that Canada use its voice and vote at meetings of international financial institutions to protest systematic, gross and continuous violations of human rights."[27]

Politicization

Parallel to the movement seeking to protect human rights there has also been de facto politicization of the IFIs. The most revealing evidence of this is found in a study by the US Treasury Department dated February 1982. It illustrates that American political and strategic objectives are advanced by participation in the multilateral development banks (MDBs): "The fact that actual country allocations of MDB lending [are] generally compatible with current US foreign policy preferences means that friendly governments are receiving development assistance far greater than the US alone could supply."[28] Policies and programs of the World Bank and the Asian Development Bank are particularly consistent with US interests: "The international character of the World Bank, its corporate structure, the strength of the management team, and the Bank's weighted voting structure have ensured broad consistency between its policies and practices and the long term economic and political objectives of the United States." Satisfaction is expressed with the frequent and effective co-ordination with major donor countries such as Canada, France, Japan, the United Kingdom, and West Germany on World Bank issues important to the United States.[29]

High-level political influence, involving at different times the president, Treasury, State, or a combination of these, is credited inter alia with termination of lending from the World Bank and the Inter-American Development Bank (IDB) to Chile during the Allende years and with the resumption in 1977 of concessional lending from the World Bank to Indonesia, Thailand, and the Philippines.[30] With regard to the IDB, however, the study records some frustration:

Although the United States has greater individual voting strength [in the IDB] than it does in any of the other banks, it has proved more difficult to pursue US interests in the IDB because the combined voting strength of the donor countries is relatively weak. The Bank is dominated by Latin-American members who, despite relatively small hard currency contributions, hold the majority voting power and who tend to present a united front ... Management also tends to be more responsive to borrower concerns than the World Bank. The US has sometimes been able to make its views prevail in the IDB, particularly when supported by other developed donor members, but not without expending considerable effort and incurring political cost."[31]

Policy-makers are advised that such situations may require heavy expenditure of political capital and possibly the exercise of financial leverage.[32] In 1986, for example, the US delegation to the IDB's annual convention made its support for a capital increase conditional on a shift by the bank from its traditional project loans to program lending with tough economic policy conditions and on a change in executive board voting rules on loan decisions from a simple to a 65-per-cent majority. As the United States holds 34.5 per cent of IDB shares, this change would provide it with an effective veto.[33]

How determined the United States is to achieve its political objectives despite opposition from other member states has been vividly demonstrated by its attempts to prevent Nicaragua from receiving IDB assistance. In 1982, Nicaragua applied for an agricultural development loan of $59.4 million.[34] By November 1984 the application had passed through the various technical processes. Bank staff had judged it to have met all the economic and technical criteria and had recommended adoption of the loan request by the executive board.[35] However, the proposal never reached the board, which had been scheduled to vote on it in early 1985. The US executive director had already indicated his opposition, and when the Central American and northern European representatives insisted on a decision and it became clear that the United States would be out-voted, its representative threatened to walk out of the meeting. IDB rules require a quorum of executive directors representing three-quarters of the bank's voting shares; a decision cannot be made without the presence of the American executive director.

Annoyed by these manoeuvres, the Latin American and Caribbean countries insisted on a decision, and at this point the US administration intervened directly. To prevent the loan proposal from reaching the executive board, the secretary of state took the unusual step on 30 January 1985 of writing directly to Antonio Ortiz Mena, president of the IDB, summarily overruling the economic and technical advice of IDB management. George Shultz declared Nicaragua to be non-creditworthy for macro-economic reasons. Bluntly stating his political objective, he added: "As you are aware, money is fungible; monies received from the Bank would ... free up other monies that could be used to help consolidate the Marxist regime and finance Nicaragua's aggression against its neighbors, who are members in good standing." Exercising financial leverage, Shultz warned: "There is little doubt that Executive Board approval of the proposed agricultural credit loan for Nicaragua would make our efforts [to secure appropriations] even more difficult."

This American political interference was noted internationally, although it did not result in public objections from those states that often stress the need to protect the non-political character of the IFIs. This is evident from a letter by Kevin O'Sullivan, then executive assistant to the executive director for northern European member states. Writing to H.J. Arbuthnott, British under secretary, International Division, Overseas Development Administration, on 8 February 1985, O'Sullivan described these events in the following terms:

The project has not been submitted to the Board because of a series of highly questionable actions taken by Management, presumably under American pressure. These include deliberately misleading statements to the Board, the unauthorized removal of items from the agenda of various Management committees, suppression of information and the disappearance of documents and files. The matter is an open scandal ... Against this background the Nicaraguans have continued to make repayment on their existing loans ...

At the same time external sources are financing the sabotage of the economic infrastructure of Nicaragua, including the destruction of food crops and export crops. The same sources have sponsored the destruction of oil supplies which Nicaraguan authorities have to import at the cost of convertible currency. ... The last IDB loan to Nicaragua was the Fishing Industry Rehabilitation Programme (PR-1144). Discussion of this project, again after interminable delays, took place in the Board in September 1983. On that occasion the U.S Director attacked the loan in every conceivable direction ... But what mystified the Board, after acrimonious exchanges, was the final insistence of the U.S. Chair on including in the Operating Regulations (whose approval is a condition of the first disbursement) an obligation on the borrower to guarantee adequate provision of fuel for the boats. You will find no precedent for such a fuel clause in any previous IDB fisheries loan. The following week saboteurs blew up the fuel depot in the port of Corinto, their single most effective blow to the Nicaraguan economy (and its capacity to service external debt).

O'Sullivan's indignation was not shared by the British Foreign Office. An earlier internal memo of 12 October 1984 from J.W. Watt, a senior official of the Mexico and Central American Division, stated candidly: "We continue to oppose proposals for Nicaragua by finding technical reasons for doing so ... The problem of explaining it in public will, however, persist and we shall need to stick to our present line of claiming that our position is based on technical grounds." Someone had scrawled below this entry, "if we can find them."[36]

CANADIAN POLICY

"Non-Political"

The Canadian government has opposed the consideration of basic rights in the operations of the IFIs. This position has not been inadvertent or accidental; it has been deliberately adopted and is persuasively advocated. Central to this is the assumption that human rights are political matters and therefore have no place in the decision-making of these agencies, which should be concerned exclusively with economic and technical considerations. The most careful exposition of this policy is offered by Marc Lalonde, when minister of finance, in correspondence concerning the Inter-American Development Bank (IDB):

In choosing not to consider explicitly the social and human rights performances of the [IDB] recipient countries, we are confronted with an extremely difficult problem. However, we have decided that in order to preserve the independence of institutions like the [IDB], to the maximum extent possible, issues outside the realm of economic and technical factors should not be brought into play, no matter how worthwhile or valid. Currently, in the [IDB], the Executive Director representing Central America is from El Salvador, his alternate from Guatemala, his assistant is from Nicaragua. They are able to work together because the objectives of the Bank are kept narrowly defined. As an example of what can happen when other issues (including bilateral views) are brought into play, I can cite the position taken by the USA over the last five years. During the term of President Carter, the [IDB] was placed under considerable pressure to reduce programs in Chile and Haiti in response to human rights considerations. Currently, for quite different reasons, the USA Administration is seeking to restrict loans to Nicaragua and Guyana. We and other member countries have resisted these efforts by the USA to make the [IDB] an instrument of bilateral policy ... The original motivation for bringing the outside factor into play may have been very laudable, but the end result may be the destruction or weakening of a valuable institution.[37]

Ministers and public servants involved in policy-making regarding the IFIs argue that Canada discharges its obligation for promotion and protection of human rights through participation in the UN Commission on Human Rights and other UN organs and through bilateral diplomatic channels. Canadian officials in the IFIs as well as their colleagues in Ottawa continue to affirm that the Canadian executive directors see their role as non-political bankers whose task is to examine loan applications exclusively for their development potential and technical viability. Unless specifically instructed, they base their assessment on these criteria.

Canada's position in the IDB with respect to Nicaragua exemplifies this policy. American opposition to all IFI disbursements to Nicaragua had been formally adopted as a policy in 1981. When the United States vetoed completion of a road begun in 1978 from the US-controlled "soft-loan" fund for Special Operations, Canada's executive director expressed impatience: "Whatever the macro-economic policies of Nicaragua may be, it seems to us that in this particular case the benefits of the completion of the road project are certainly commensurate with the costs and the macro-economic policies of the country would seem to bear little relation to the completion of the project."[38]

Canada has continued to resist US pressure. It extends bilateral assistance to Nicaragua and, at the time of the American-imposed trade boycott in 1985, facilitated establishment of a Nicaraguan trade office in Toronto. On the political interference over the Nicaraguan agricultural loan, Canada's executive director has played a muted role, insisting that Canada would judge the project on its economic and technical merits if and when it came before the board. His senior staff told the author that the matter was political and therefore handled more appropriately during an IDB annual meeting, where political issues were aired.[39]

At two annual conventions of the IDB, in Vienna in 1985 and in San José, Costa Rica, in 1986, Canada's representative supported the entreaties made by other member states: "We must continue to resist the excessive pursuit of those rigid bilateral interests which impede institutions such as this one in the carrying out of their responsibilities."[40] That Canada meant the rigid bilateral interests in American policy toward Nicaragua was made clear in a letter from the external affairs secretary to the TCCR, which had initiated this discussion with him.[41]

While with regard to Nicaragua Canada has consistently steered an independent course on IDB loans (and other policies) and has sought to implement its basic "non-political" approach, the cases that follow illustrate that Canada has not always pursued a non-political path. Its responses to loan and credit applications from major human rights violator régimes have at times clearly been influenced by political factors and have contradicted its own bilateral aid policy and its official judgment about the régimes in question. Indeed, a submission in 1986 by the Canadian International Development Agency (CIDA) to the Standing Senate Committee on Foreign Affairs articulates the political and economic advantages to Canada of participating in the regional development banks: "Over the past twenty years or so, the regional banks have become increasingly important vehicles for the promotion of Canada's foreign policy and broad economic interests as well as development assistance channels."[42] That Canada has also sought such political objectives in the IMF and the World Bank will be demonstrated.

"Technical Considerations"

Guatemala and the IDB. On 21 December 1982 Canada supported an $18-million credit from the IDB to the Guatemalan régime of General Rios Montt for a rural telephone system. Eleven days earlier Canada had co-sponsored in the UN general assembly a resolution drawing attention to the widespread repression, massacres, and displacements experienced by Guatemala's rural indigenous population at the hands of their military rulers. Already in September, when the member churches of the TCCR had first learned of Guatemala's credit application, they had sought to convince Canada's minister of finance to oppose the credit on the grounds that telephones in rural Guatemala would only strengthen the military and would have no development content. In his reply, the minister noted that CIDA had withdrawn its project aid from Guatemala "because of the political and social environment" there, but he nevertheless stressed that this IDB loan would "meet the needs of the poor."[43] He did not elaborate on how the installation of telephones would serve the needs of rural Indians who had been decimated and driven from their homes by the military.

In this case, Canada at a multilateral level contradicted CIDA's assessment that its bilateral development projects could not be implemented under prevailing conditions. At the IDB, Canada also found itself at odds with one of its co-sponsors of the general assembly resolution. Sweden, on behalf of the Nordic states, opposed the telephone credit on human rights grounds.[44] Canada supported the United States, which had disregarded the ruling of the appropriate congressional sub-committee that credit should be opposed because it would not meet the basic needs criteria applicable to violator countries. Canada's decision to back the United States clearly compromised its allegedly non-political approach.

El Salvador and the IDB. Canada has shifted its position with regard to El Salvador. In 1980 its executive director joined Denmark, Mexico, and West Germany in withholding support from an agrarian project. In 1981 he joined western European and Scandinavian representatives in abstaining in a decision for construction of a rural road project in Chaletenango. In each case he cited technical reasons for Canada's position: in view of the civil war, conditions in the conflict area were not sufficiently stable to guarantee implementation.[45]

With increasing American support for El Salvador, Canada's technical considerations in the IDB for El Salvador projects lost their force. In 1983, at the same time as Canada supported a general assembly resolution that condemned El Salvador for gross and systematic violations of human rights, it gave unreserved support for an IDB credit to reconstruct the San Marcos bridge over the River Lempa, destroyed by El Salvadorean insurgents. Unlike the previous one, the new bridge was to be built to military specifications. Clearly, this IDB project would be as endangered by the civil conflict as the road project of two years before. Yet correspondence between the TCCR and Marc Lalonde, then minister of finance, show that Canada no longer raised such technical objections.[46] There was yet another contradiction, for at the same time CIDA project assistance had been withdrawn from El Salvador because of the level of violence there!

El Salvador and the IMF. In July 1981, the IMF executive board considered a request from El Salvador for a $36-million credit from the IMF's Compensatory Finance Facility. This type of credit is normally advanced only if the technical staff recommends its adoption, and the IMF staff had concluded that in this case it could not make such a recommendation. The American executive director nevertheless argued successfully for approval of the credit before the board. Thus, the technical rules normally applied by the IMF were broken. During the debate, executive directors from Belgium, Britain, France, the Netherlands, the Nordic states, and West Germany protested US pressure for adoption under the circumstances and withheld approval. Canada, however, supported the American position. The Canadian representative took issue with the unfavourable staff report and argued that the benefit of the doubt lay in favour of the request.

In 1983, a mid-term staff review of El Salvador's economic performance preceding the release of further funds again cautioned that, contrary to program expectations, the economic situation had worsened and that no recovery could be predicted for the immediate future. Canada again supported the disbursement.[47] Although "concerned about El Salvador's economic performance," Canada continued to give it "the benefit of doubt."[48]

In the case of these three Central American credits, Canadian political neutrality and exclusive adherence to economic and technical considerations were abandoned in favour of supporting the US position.

Canada and Corporate Pressure. In December 1983 Canada's credibility as a non-political actor in the IDB was further strained when the Canadian executive director failed to support a $268-million credit to Chile to improve the efficiency of that country's copper industry. The abstention was caused not by Canada's desire to reflect the support it had given to a general assembly resolution calling for re-establishment of human rights in Chile but by an intervention of the Canadian Department of Energy, Mines and Resources.

That department, joined by Finance, had acted in response to pressure from the chairman of the subcommittee for mineral resources of the Canadian Business-Industry Advisory Council. Interviewed by *Le Devoir*, M.W. Deeks, a senior executive of Noranda Mines, itself a major copper producer, explained the concern of Canadian industry: "When we addressed the Canadian government, we said that Canada ought to think of the production of its own [copper] industry." Explaining Canada's opposition to the Chilean credit at the IDB, Canada's executive director read from a text carefully prepared to contain only an oblique reference to the interests of Canada's copper producers: "There is a real risk that an augmentation of Chile's production will result in losses elsewhere. I am not only thinking of the copper production in industrial countries like Canada, but also of that in developing countries."[49] In this instance, Canadian corporate interests clearly had the advantage over human rights: while the Canadian government regarded the defence of human rights in the IFIs as improper political interference, it did not hesitate to act when Canadian corporate interests were at stake.

South Africa and the IMF. In early October 1982, when it became known that South Africa had applied for a $1.07-billion credit from the IMF, member churches of the TCCR wrote to the secretary of state for external affairs and to the minister of finance. They requested that the profound infringements of human rights inherent in apartheid be considered a major impediment to unconditional approval of the credit and pointed out that the funds requested were almost equal to South Africa's increases in military spending in fiscal 1981–2.[50]

In explaining why he could not accept the churches' request, the minister of finance wrote: "The IMF must be careful ... not to be accused of meddling in the internal affairs of sovereign states." This was a puzzling reply, given the IMF's insistence on substantial economic adjustment measures in most countries as a condition for credit disbursements after the initial tranche. The external affairs secretary did not reply until April 1983: "So long as South Africa adheres to the articles of agreement of the IMF, and the loan meets normally applied criteria, Canada would not oppose the loan requested."[51]

On 3 November 1982 the executive board met, disregarding the request by nine directors representing Third World states for a postponement of the discussion. Anticipating the support of the industrial countries in the weighted voting system, Jacques Larosière, the fund's managing director, had declared a consensus to move ahead as scheduled. Opposition to the credit was led by Saudi Arabia and India, whose representatives argued that South Africa did not meet normally applied criteria, since apartheid conflicted with the free-labour-market concept of the IMF.

Others said that South Africa's continued ability to borrow from the private sector rendered its drain on IMF resources unnecessary. It was also noted that South Africa's fiscal imbalance was due in large measure to its increasing military spending.[52] Canada did not contribute to the discussions. Overriding the objections of Ireland and Jamaica, two members represented by Canada, Canada's executive director provided the crucial 4.19 per cent to grant the credit by a 52-per-cent majority.[53]

Only subsequent to this hastily arranged credit was an IMF staff team dispatched on a country mission to South Africa, a sharp deviation from usual IMF practice. Its report documented that the "labour market regulations in South Africa are clearly not consistent with the realization of the country's full growth potential." It noted "the impediments to the geographic mobility of black workers" and "the system of short term migrant labour contracts whereby black workers have to be returned to their point of recruitment on the expiration of their contract." This regulatory system, the report said, "is based on noneconomic considerations," and it recommended as "essential that the impediments and restrictions in the labour market be eased" to avoid "serious imbalance in the country." Similar technical and economic impediments were attributed to South Africa's unequal and underfinanced black education system, said to be "detrimental to the maximum utilization of South Africa's manpower resources."[54]

The IMF routinely insists that precisely these kinds of economic inefficiencies due to state interference in the market economy be corrected. Canada chose not to raise these economic and technical questions and favoured the political decision to support South Africa's request.

Canada's secretary of state for external affairs assured the Association of South-East Asian Nations (ASEAN) in 1983 that: "Canada will not support in either its bilateral programmes or through multilateral institutions the provisions of economic assistance to Vietnam which would have the effect of subsidizing or rewarding Hanoi's continued military occupation of Cambodia."[55] On these grounds South Africa deserved the same forthright admonition for its continued military occupation of Namibia in defiance of the ruling of the International Court of Justice and UN Security Council resolutions which Canada had accepted. Canada was willing to apply this obvious political criterion when considering IFI loans to Vietnam but failed to do so with regard to South Africa.

World Bank Project Modification. In June 1983 Canada supported a World Bank proposal, drawn up by the Chilean government, the World Bank, and Chile's commercial creditors, to modify a planned road-sector development project by increasing its funding to $300 million, of which the bank would act as guarantor for $150 million. This proposal was circulated by the president of the World Bank on 6 June 1985 for consideration of the executive board on 20 June. It was designed to provide Chile with immediate new money for its commercial debt obligations and to reassure the commercial creditor banks as they prepared for major debt rescheduling.[56]

Member churches of the TCCR protested to the Canadian government that development projects should not be transformed into a financial rescue operation for the Chilean government and its commercial creditors. The minister of finance responded that Canada's executive director had paid particular attention to this proposal "because of the general policy implications for the Bank as well as the economic and *political* situation in Chile" (emphasis added). However, on reflection, Canada had decided to "go along with the consensus" in not opposing the proposal. "The financing and guarantee to be provided by the World Bank was considered vital to the success of a much larger financial package being put together by the IMF for Chile." Nevertheless, in contradiction to this point and in response to the churches' request that Chile's human rights violations be taken into account, the minister also reiterated Canada's position that it had "resisted the introduction of factors which are beyond the strict economic and technical aspects of financing proposals."[57]

There had in fact not been a consensus on the executive board when the proposal was approved. The executive director for the five Nordic countries had opposed it on human rights grounds. The executive directors for Italy (representing as well Greece, Malta, and Portugal) and for Belgium (representing as well Austria, Luxembourg, Hungary, and Turkey) had opposed the proposal on technical grounds, an important fact given Canada's emphasis on the technical aspects of loan proposals.[58]

A Change of Heart?

A first tentative departure from Canadian policy that decisions in the IFIs be determined by technical and economic decisions alone occurred in late 1986. In the World Bank and in the IDB, Canada, together with a number of other member states, recorded abstentions on Chilean loan proposals and made it clear that its decisions had been motivated by human rights considerations.

On 20 November the World Bank approved a $250-million structural adjustment loan (SAL) for Chile. Canada's executive director, representing the bloc vote for his constituency members (Ireland and the English-speaking Caribbean), abstained on the SAL vote. He was joined by Belgium and the Netherlands, each representing its respective bloc votes. Significantly also, because its bloc vote included a large number of Latin

American states, Venezuela withheld its support, representing Costa Rica, El Salvador, Guatemala, Honduras, Mexico, Nicaragua, Panama, and Suriname, as well as Spain. France and the United States abstained. The Nordic states and Italy's executive director, the latter representing Greece, Malta and Portugal, actively opposed the Chilean SAL. An unusually high percentage of the total weighted votes (42.52 per cent) failed to support the loan, while 7.27 per cent registered opposition. The loan was approved by a slim majority of 87 votes, including the bulk of Third World countries, Japan, the United Kingdom, and West Germany.

On 2 December 1986 the IDB approved a $319.3-million loan for Chile's Pehuenche hydroelectric plant. Here as well, Canada joined the US position. The combined voting power of the two states brought abstentions on the Chilean loan to nearly 40 per cent of the total vote. In contrast to the World Bank, where abstentions are not counted, the IDB considers an abstention to be a vote against a loan application.[59] In terms of Canadian policy, therefore, Canada's abstention on the Chile project in the IDB had greater significance than its abstention on Chile's SAL in the World Bank.

That human rights considerations had indeed been the reason for Canada's abstentions was confirmed by the minister of finance in a letter to the TCCR. He at once cautioned that these had been exceptional cases and that Canada would continue to apply only economic and technical criteria. Two House of Commons standing committees were still to advise on whether Canada should use human rights criteria in its decisions in the IFIs: "The abstentions were exceptional actions, designed to express our concern in company with others over the human rights situation in Chile. Pending the outcome of our in-depth examination of how we might further human rights interests in the multilateral development banks without impairing their effectiveness, the government will continue to judge each loan proposal solely in terms of its contribution to development."[60]

The minister offered no explanation as to why, in the absence of a change of official policy, Canada withheld support from these Chilean loans because of that government's human rights violations. These violations had been the subject of international outrage since the military dictatorship seized power in 1973, yet never before have they determined Canada's vote and may perhaps not ever do so again.

In December 1986, Secretary of State for External Affairs Joe Clark published the government's response to the Report of the Special Joint Committee on Canada's International Relations. This response addressed, among others, the recommendation that Canada use its voice and vote in international financial institutions to protest systematic, gross, and continuous violations of human rights.[61] Clark guardedly acknowledged the importance of the issue. While granting that these institutions "must be sensitive to the impact of human rights situations," he advised against "further politicization which might seriously impair the effectiveness of these institutions in their critical task of bringing about needed development and adjustment in developing countries." Clark asked that this issue be examined in detail by the Standing Committee on External Affairs and International Trade as well as by the Standing Committee on Human Rights.[62]

In due course the Standing Committee on External Affairs and International Trade issued its comprehensive review of Canadian aid policies.[63] This report recommends "that Canada work for changes to allow human rights concerns to be put openly on the agenda of the international financial institutions and, in addition, examine very critically multilateral loans to countries deemed 'human rights negative' or 'human rights watch.'"[64]

The response of the government deals with this recommendation with remarkable blandness. It uses the present tense, as if reporting an established and well-accepted practice: "Canada endeavors to ensure that human rights issues are given due consideration in the activities of the international financial institutions."[65] This can be made a truthful statement only by interpreting due consideration to mean little or none. But then, though formally truthful, it would also be deliberately misleading.

Third World Debt and Human Rights

During the 1970s, governments of developing countries judged creditworthy had been able to borrow heavily from private international banks. But most of the Third World, certainly the poorest and least developed countries, did not have access to commercial loans. For them the IMF had been virtually the only source of funding when they faced balance-of-payments difficulties. The severe global recession in early 1980 brought about an extreme liquidity and foreign exchange crisis in these countries. At the same time, the major newly industrializing countries (NICs) that had borrowed substantial sums from the private banks were also forced to turn to the IMF as they faced soaring interest rates along with a sharp decline in their foreign earnings. Since that time, these deeply indebted NICs have been competing with the least developed countries for the same IMF resources.

Third World debt thus became a significant part of this generalized foreign exchange crisis, particularly as default by one or two of the few very major debtors could endanger the whole international financial system. Because the IMF imposes economic adjustment policies as a condition for assistance, it has assumed a central role in the response to this crisis. For countries such as Argentina, Brazil, and Mexico, which have incurred major private debts, acceptance of an IMF policy prescription has become a precondition of any rescheduling of this debt. In establishing policy conditions, the IMF not only consults the debtor countries but also seeks the concurrence of the commercial creditor banks and their governments.

The IMF's assessment of a country's international debt management and its structural adjustment policies has increasingly come to dominate funding decisions by the World Bank and regional development banks and even lending policies of the major national development agencies, including CIDA. In her evidence before the Senate Committee on Foreign Affairs in 1986, CIDA's president, Margaret Catley-Carlson, spoke about the "Baker Plan," an American initiative to deal with Third World debt which Canada had endorsed: "This has affected all development programs [in that] there is more of a tendency to look at programming in developing countries, taking into account the debt situation, the balance of payment situation and the overall management of that particular country ... Our programs are very much keyed to ... discussions with the IMF and the World Bank."[66]

We have seen that international social development agencies, development economists, and Third World leaders have confirmed that the IMF's assessments disregard the impact of its economic adjustment policies on the most vulnerable sectors of a debtor country's population. On occasion, the IMF has responded sympathetically to a debtor state's request to ease the rigour of its demands. This has tended to occur with established or recently re-established democracies. Their governments must balance the sacrifices they can impose on their populations without endangering their democratic institutions and, if possible, without abandoning their own national development goals and the degree to which they can satisfy the demands of the IMF and their private creditors. However, IMF forbearance with this dilemma is by no means the rule. Senegal's minister of planning and co-operation has articulated the dilemma and discontent of the Third World: "Many heads of state, driven by necessity and anxious to avoid defaulting on the debt, have had to accept adjustment policies in order to show good faith. But the truth is that power has been transferred; the rules are now dictated from outside the country, by purely financial considerations, instead of evolving from the country's own development needs ... Both the underlying thinking and the consequences are punitive. And the brunt is borne by the poorest sectors of society."[67]

The problem of satisfying the basic right to subsistence is aggravated for those with governments insensitive to the plight of the poor. Military dictatorships, for example, increase repression when they meet with popular resistance to austerity programs. They do not request and are not offered measures that would ease the social cost for the most vulnerable: "Military regimes seem to find rigorous stabilization packages congenial. The preference does not stem from a firm belief in automatic market adjustments. Military instincts are interventionist. But military leaders can conveniently rationalize political repression in the name of needed price and wage flexibility. The objective is not adaptation to a given economic structure but radical reconstruction of civil society. Falling real income then becomes a symbol of policy success because it shows the determination to stay on course until the underlying economic model is applicable."[68] In such instances, the IMF tacitly accepts the policies of a repressive régime opposed to reduced inequalities,[69] exacerbating the violation of the rights to subsistence and to security of person.

That Canada manifests little concern for the validity of these considerations can be gleaned from the remarks of Marcel Massé, Canada's executive director of the IMF, to the Senate Committee on Foreign Affairs. Massé explained the central role played by the IMF in developing an integrated model of the global economy to assess and make coherent the economic policies of Western industrialized states and to prescribe policies for the developing countries. He made very clear that the IMF was assuming leadership in knitting together its own global policy objectives and those of the World Bank and the regional development banks: "International institutions must have a role in advising individual countries on the policies that would make sense from the point of view of the total world economic community."

When using the word "advising," Massé had a decidedly stronger message in mind. When states facing a foreign exchange crisis seek IMF support, the fund expects its recommendations to be implemented. In Massé's words: "The Fund ... of course will make these recommendations a condition of its lending."[70] One searches in vain in Massé's testimony for any concern about the impact of IMF conditionality on the basic right to subsistence. He did not address the possible socio-political cost faced by a government with little choice but to accept the IMF conditions, nor did he contemplate the effects of IMF demands on people already suffering under a repressive régime. When asked, for example, about the relation between IMF and private creditor banks and the latters' reliance on the fund to impose economic adjustment measures before rescheduling their own unpaid loans, Massé's response was disheartening: "If the banks believe that the IMF is too soft, they will talk to their contacts in the IMF and say "Come on, our people have been doing a study on this," and there will be some negotiation there about whether there is a need to reinforce a target."[71]

Catley-Carlson did concede in the Senate hearings that IMF economic adjustment measures may entail social destabilization in a Third World country and endanger the survival of vulnerable population groups. She noted, with regard to an IMF agreement with Ghana, that CIDA, working closely with the IMF and the World Bank, told the Ghanaians: "We know that if you take on this program of reform it will cost you. Your food prices are going to shoot up, and in the urban areas that is going to be very destabilizing. So we will put in some food aid and help you out over this very difficult period." Such supplementary CIDA aid is offered to countries if they "put their house in order," if they "put together a program of economic stabilization and better policy measures."[72] These remarks indicate CIDA's willingness to dovetail its programs with IMF austerity measures.

When, in December 1986, the external affairs secretary responded to recommendations made in June by the special joint committee, he dealt with its concern that austerity measures may "place intolerable strains on their people and on democratic governments."[73] Clark's reply was evasive and platitudinous: "We must continue to seek effective measures which take into account the fragile political and economic fabric in many countries ... [the] pursuit of sound economic policies by these countries to restore credit worthiness and attract and retain needed investment and capital; promotion of trade ... and sufficient financial resources to tide these countries through the adjustment period ... The government believes that recent progress in increased and more flexible lending to support debtor country efforts ... must be continued. Canada will strengthen its active pursuit of these objectives multilaterally and bilaterally."[74]

Little in this response suggests that the government intended to address the serious issue raised in the committee's report: the difficulties confronting Third World debtor states as they face an enormous foreign exchange crisis and severe debt management demands while their poorest people are at risk and their democratic institutions are increasingly threatened.

CONCLUSIONS

Despite assertions that protection and promotion of international human rights constitute an integral and important element in foreign policy, Canadian governments, both Liberal and Conservative, have remained untouched by international and, more recently, national discussions about promoting basic rights through the IFIs. When questioned, Canadian ministers and officials expressed unfaltering faith in the non-political character of the IFIs, which excludes, according to their definition, the introduction of human rights into decisions on applications for funds.

Canada has not examined factors that have led other states to consider the status of human rights observance when voting on loan applications. Canada has not reviewed the compelling arguments that led US legislators to debate and to make recommendations about the implications for human rights of decisions in the World Bank and in the regional development banks. No Canadian parliamentary committee routinely reviews decisions by Canadian executive directors of the IFIs, let alone their human rights dimensions. Thus, until very recently, debate about participation in the IFIs as an element of foreign policy and the potential role and significance of IFIs in human rights promotion has been muted. The work of the Special Joint Committee on Canada's International Relations provided the first break in this pattern.

In recent years, particularly since the election of President Reagan, American concern for human rights has eroded. This is of pivotal importance within the IFIs because their weighted voting procedures give American executive directors a major influence in loan decisions. As this influence has shifted from active promotion of rights and social development to promotion of American geopolitical objectives, there is much to recommend in Canada's position that one ought to guard against political interference in the IFIs and to ensure that decisions are made solely according to economic and technical criteria. It is therefore all the more important to discern political objectives disguised by "economic and technical" language. While Canada has resisted blatant political interference by the US administration over Nicaragua, in other instances it has itself certainly temporized with its adherence to exclusively economic and technical considerations.

Insistence that the IFIs are non-political and that protection and promotion of international human rights are political matters has facilitated the tight compartmentalization of human rights concerns in Canadian foreign policy. The appropriate forums for these pursuits, the government long argued, are the UN organs established for these purposes and bilateral diplomatic channels. Hence, Canada perceived no contradiction in condemning a government for gross and systematic violations of rights in the political arena of the United Nations while approving that same government's application for funds in the economic arena of the IFIs.

It is an untenable argument. Political and economic policies cannot be separated surgically; they are intractably intertwined. It is inappropriate to equate the pursuit of international human rights with "political interference." Application of political criteria implies that judgments about IFI disbursements are influenced by the ideological positions of governments. Such a practice should be resisted, as it violates the charters of the IFIs. Promotion and protection of basic rights are a preoccupation of a quite different order.

International institutions, particularly those within the UN system, ought to further the consolidation and enforcement of those basic rights that are now universally acknowledged. Because of the increasing use of non-political language for political ends in the IFIs, the pursuit of human rights must be clearly distinguished from "political" and "economic and technical" considerations. Promotion and protection of international human rights should be an objective that stands on its own. Because the IFIs are among the most powerful international instruments, observance of basic rights should be a co-determinant in decisions on credit and loan applications.

This clearly was the view of the all-party Special Joint Committee on Canada's International Relations, which unanimously recommended that Canada use human rights criteria in its voting decisions in the IFIs. This position was recommended again by the House Committee on External Affairs and International Trade. In response, the government has announced, albeit unenthusiastically, that Canada endeavours to ensure that human rights are given due consideration in IFI activities. It remains to be seen whether and to what extent Canada's resolve will be manifested in the IFIs. Long-standing resistance by politicians and bureaucrats to this proposition, and the almost indiscernible way in which the policy change was announced, suggest that this latest development may yet prove part of a longer-term strategy to resist full and systematic implementation of this policy.

A final postscript: As this volume went to press the pessimistic predictions in the above paragraph appeared only too justified. On 5 May 1988, the minister of finance, responding to a request from the TCCR that Canada initiate in the World Bank a formal process for applying human rights criteria, wrote: "I believe that the introduction of human rights criteria would politicize the World Bank's decision-making with negative consequences for its activities." This statement must be the last word on the quest for a Canadian policy to consider human rights in the IFIs. It makes clear the Newspeak character of the government's response to the Winegard report. It demonstrates beyond doubt that the significant recommendations that had been made by two broadly based parliamentary inquiries and that the government claimed to have accepted have not in the slightest modified the government's position since the issue was first raised in the early 1980s.

PART THREE

Bilateral Diplomacy

CHAPTER TEN

Development Assistance

T.A. KEENLEYSIDE

It seems appropriate in any analysis of the role of human rights in the conduct of Canada's bilateral relations to examine its place in Canadian development assistance policy. First, many of the globe's worst human rights offenders are developing countries; while Canada may have little influence on their behaviour, its aid programme – as one of the most important dimensions of Canada's relations with these states – is at least a potential instrument for that purpose. Second, aid (unlike withdrawal of commercial services, trade sanctions, and so on) is flexible; it need not be confined to disciplinary use to punish gross violators (by the cessation of aid, for example) but can, with sensitivity and imagination in project selection, advance observance. Third, and most important, as Bernard Wood, director of the North-South Institute, said recently: "All aid is or should be about human rights," since "it is supposedly an instrument for the promotion of economic and social rights and the basic standards of a minimum decent existence for those who do not have access to them."[1]

In their more enlightened moments, officials of the Canadian government have acknowledged this intrinsic relation between development in the Third World and human rights: they have sometimes perceived development as advancement of the whole person, embracing his or her economic, social, and, indeed, political well-being. In an eloquent statement in 1976, for instance, Paul Gérin-Lajoie, then president of the Canadian International Development Agency (CIDA), wrote: "There ... remains a single central objective ... which has first claim on our attention. It is an objective which supposes on the part of governments and individuals a concrete will to have as the focus of their activities the human person ... This central objective is the total liberation of man." Liberation meant meeting basic needs by freeing human beings from hunger, disease, illiteracy, unemployment, and chronic underemployment. At the same time, however, if deprivations in these areas prevented the enjoyment of fundamental rights, "the same must also be said of the use of force to silence dissenters, systematic recourse to political imprisonment, and the torture of prisoners."[2] It is, then, appropriate in examining the role of human rights in Canadian bilateral relations to focus on Canadian development assistance: it is a policy instrument aimed, rhetorically at least, at improving the human condition in all its aspects.

Taking human rights into consideration in the making of Canadian aid decisions emerged as a matter of discussion in the mid-1970s, prompted, in part, by the US Carter administration's severing of assistance to several gross violators. Parliament was one of the earliest loci of the debate. In March 1977, and again in March 1978, a private member's bill was introduced to prohibit aid, Export Development Corporation (EDC) credits, or tariff concessions to any consistent and gross violator of human rights.[3] Later, in 1982, the parliamentary Sub-Committee on Canada's Relations with Latin America and the Caribbean recommended in its final report that "Canadian development assistance be substantially reduced, terminated, or not commenced in cases where gross and systematic violations of human rights make it impossible to promote the central objective of helping the poor." In June 1986, this position was reaffirmed in the report of the Special Joint Committee of Parliament on Canada's International Relations. Finally, in May 1987, the report of the House of Commons Standing Committee on External Affairs and International Trade on aid policies and programs proposed the adoption by CIDA of a four-tier country classification grid for Canadian aid recipients that would "provide incentives for good behaviour as well as penalties for poor human rights performance."[4]

A number of Canadian experts in international relations and development have, since the late 1970s, supported linking aid to rights observance.[5] A 1983 study commissioned by CIDA from Martin Rudner of Carleton University was also significant. After carefully examining the issue of linkage, Rudner proposed "explicitly, coherently and functionally " integrating human rights "within the broader framework of foreign policy," including development assistance.[6] Certain interest groups and/or those writing under their imprimatur, including the North-South Institute, Energy Probe, and various church groups, have also called for greater attention to human rights in aid decisions.[7] Finally, in the press there has been support recently for tying aid to observance, with the *Globe and Mail*, in particular, frequently appealing for "more boldness in External Affairs and CIDA" on this subject.[8]

Since the late 1970s, then, pressure has been mounting from a variety of sectors for attaching higher priority to human rights in development assistance policy.

Nominally at least, human rights have had a place in government aid policy for some time. In the Trudeau government's 1970 review, social justice was adopted as one of the six basic themes of Canadian foreign policy, committing Canada to advance human welfare globally both by supporting economic development in the Third World and by encouraging respect for basic rights. These two sub-themes seemed linked in the review: development assistance was to be concentrated in countries with governments that pursued external and internal policies broadly consistent with Canadian values and attitudes.[9] However, until the late 1970s, Ottawa generally reacted negatively to suggestions that provision of aid be made conditional on satisfactory observance of rights, as reflected in Trudeau's 1977 statement in Parliament that Canada had "not made it a condition of our assistance to starving people in the third world that their governments be above reproach."[10] Nevertheless, increased parliamentary preoccupation with this issue in the 1970s led the government to set out a somewhat different position.

In October 1978, Secretary of State for External Affairs Don Jamieson reiterated that Canadian aid is "designed to help meet the basic human needs of the poorest people in the poorest countries" (and by inference should not normally be affected by human rights criteria). He declared, however, that "human-rights considerations are, nonetheless, a factor in determining levels of aid and the orientation of programs ... On a few occasions when the human-rights situation in a country has deteriorated to a stage where the effective implementation of the aid program is made extremely difficult, Canadian assistance has been suspended or not renewed."[11] During the Clark government, a similar position was outlined in a brief review of foreign aid policy undertaken by CIDA, and countries were cited where aid had either been suspended or not renewed because of problems of implementation, namely Equatorial Guinea, Kampuchea, Uganda, and Vietnam.[12] With the return of the Liberals to power in 1980, this policy was maintained, with aid curtailed to El Salvador and Guatemala as well, because "gross violations of human rights or conditions of conflict" made "the provision of an aid program impossible."[13] A new element was soon added. Speaking in the House of Commons on 16 June 1981, Secretary of State for External Affairs Mark MacGuigan stated: "We believe that it would be inappropriate for our foreign policy to reward adventurism and interference. Countries of the Third World face desperate and formidable challenges. It is for this reason that we have withdrawn aid programs from those countries whose scarce resources are diverted to war and conquest." The following month he said that aid had earlier been withdrawn from Vietnam and Cuba because of their "imperialist adventures."[14]

Under the Mulroney government the central thrust of policy has remained the same – action only in extreme cases, principally (although not all statements have been explicit on this point) when breakdown in order renders an aid program ineffectual.[15] There have been only vague references to other criteria: "Canada does ... take account of broad human rights considerations when we determine to which countries Canadian aid will be directed," and "the nature and extent of our programme" is affected by "the human rights records of development partners."[16]

This chapter first examines the advantages and disadvantages of linking development assistance to human rights observance; second, taking these arguments into account, it proposes a strategy for the future; and third, it explores and analyses the history of Canadian linked action, evaluating its appropriateness in the context of both stated government policy and the suggested strategy.

LINKAGE: PROS AND CONS

One of the principal arguments proffered in favour of linking aid and human rights is the one advanced in a wider context in chapter 1. All states are responsible for ensuring global respect for human rights: "Today there is near universal international agreement, at least in theory, although often not in practice, that certain things simply cannot legitimately be done to human beings,"[17] including torture, arbitrary arrest and detention, summary execution, and wilful imposition of malnutrition or starvation. Application of rights criteria to aid then becomes appropriate for donor countries because it demonstrates that they recognize a responsibility to enhance respect for universally cherished rights without which no individual is able to lead a life of dignity and worth.[18]

A second, more pragmatic argument is that aid provided to states that abuse basic rights – economic, social, and political – is unlikely to be effective, because meaningful development depends on respect for the individual and his or her basic rights. This point of view is well expressed by Robert Carty and Virginia Smith:

> Human rights must be a central criterion for selecting aid partners and determining aid effectiveness because they are an integral part of the development process ... The abuse of civil and political rights is not only a direct violation of the integrity of the person but an additional impediment to integral development, because the political participation of individuals and groups in society is restricted. In the same way, the abuse of economic, social and cultural rights makes the full realization of political and civil rights impossible because the economic and social participation of different social classes is grossly unequal.[19]

Even well-intentioned and appropriate aid is unlikely to reach the needy if régimes are not committed to rights; it is likely to be diverted to perpetuate the status of existing élites and to facilitate their repression of the impoverished majority. Attaching conditions to aid may help to ensure that assistance promotes equitable, non-discriminatory development that benefits the least privileged; the net effect may be to strengthen developing countries' "resolve to make progress in the implementation of human rights."[20]

A third argument is that it is in Canada's enlightened national interest to take rights into account in development assistance, because repression often leads to civil unrest and revolution that may be damaging to global security and, hence, to Canadian strategic interests, especially if "friendly" but authoritarian régimes are overthrown. Further, stable Third World states with relatively egalitarian development will in the long run make better trade and investment partners for Canada than countries where persisting violations perpetuate underdevelopment, inequality, and political uncertainty.[21]

The fourth and final argument is that taking human rights into account in aid policy is in accord with the concerns of the Canadian public. In his report for CIDA, Rudner reminded the agency that "those groups in Canadian society that are most pronounced in their support for international development co-operation are also those which place high value on human rights."[22] Regard for human rights may, therefore, help to preserve a constituency supportive of the agency's endeavours. Others have asserted that basic rights reflect values central to the Canadian community which, if neglected in foreign policy, may atrophy internally.[23]

A wider range of arguments has been proffered in opposition to linking aid to human rights, but it is the contention of this chapter that, while many of them have merit, collectively they constitute a case not so much for discounting rights in aid policy as for acting cautiously – for formulating a carefully considered strategy that emphasizes positive rather than punitive initiatives.

First, state sovereignty and non-intervention in the internal affairs of other countries are a central ordering principle of the international system; some argue that linking aid to human rights performance violates that concept. Since the editors address this subject in chapter 15, it need be stated here only that donor states "can quite properly manage their economic relations as they see fit,"[24] deciding when, where, and how to expend their own aid funds without fairly being accused of intervention.

Second, a more vigorous stand may provoke reciprocal attacks by developing countries on rights violations in Canada, including charges of racism and ill treatment of certain groups, like native peoples and new immigrants. Rather than being an argument against linkage, however, this serves as a reminder that Canada must vigorously pursue human rights at home while giving this issue greater attention in its foreign policy. It also suggests the wisdom of confining punitive action (that is, cessation of aid) to extreme cases, where comparisons with the Canadian situation would be inapposite.

Third, the ability of Canada acting on its own to influence rights behaviour through its aid program is perhaps limited, because aid from Canada is rarely critical to the recipient. However, this argument merely points to the wisdom of acting in concert with other states wherever possible rather than being a justification for doing nothing.[25] Yet unilateral action should not be discounted, since carefully considered initiatives may induce like responses from other states or even achieve modest results on their own.

Fourth, Canada has a range of interests in its bilateral relations with developing countries, and thus to give attention to human rights in aid policy might well conflict with the realization of other interests, principally of a security and commercial nature.[26] While the centrality of strategic/security considerations must be recognized, Canada's interests in this respect are generally best served by promoting observance of political, economic, social, and cultural rights and, hence, stability in developing countries. Likewise Canadian commercial interests are best advanced by serious attention to rights and creation of conditions of equity and stability in the Third World. To argue in favour of taking rights into account is, then, not to discount Canada's acting on the basis of national interest, but rather to suggest that in most instances such an approach is likely to be in Canada's enlightened interest.

Fifth, there is potential for inconsistency in the application of the aid instrument, especially given that many developing countries violate human rights. For example, initiatives might be taken only where Canada has no significant interests at stake while grosser violations in other countries are ignored because of political/security or commercial interests.[27] The decision to act might also be heavily influenced by media attention to a country and related public attitudes rather than by the severity of violations. Further, there are problems in reaching a consensus on what constitute the most basic rights and on the meaning of "consistent pattern of gross violations," as well as in determining the reliability of evidence, all of which may lead to inconsistent application.[28] Finally, Canada's response probably *should* vary from state to state: countries are at different stages in their respect for human rights, and Canada's expectations may legitimately vary from country to country.[29] In general, for example, human rights observance is much higher in the Commonwealth Caribbean than in Central America. A realistic policy must take that into account and shape Canada's responses so as to reflect awareness of each country's past and its current stage of political and social evolution. These very real difficulties suggest a strategy which, to be consistent, does not ignore serious violations anywhere but is flexible enough to enable varying responses, depending on circumstances. A policy that merely stops aid in selected gross cases subject to media exposure and where no particular Canadian interests are involved would thus be insufficient.

Sixth, a related difficulty is the double standard if Canada uses aid to influence developing countries, where the presence of a program offers that option, but fails to take other forms of action with states – developed and developing alike – that are equally guilty but where the aid instrument is not available. Indeed, reliance exclusively on aid as a tool could be seen as a form of racial discrimination, with Canada treating violations more harshly in non-white, developing countries than elsewhere.[30] An appropriate strategy would thus have to embrace alternative measures for non-aid recipients equally guilty of violations.

Seventh, and the argument most emphasized by the government in opposing anything more than a limited rights orientation, is the effect of such an approach on Canada's ability to meet the needs of the poorest people in developing countries, the alleged focus of the aid program. To place strictures on aid going to those already suffering under repression may be to punish them a second time for the transgressions of their governments.[31] This argument suggests a strategy with initiatives other than termination of assistance, so long as Canadian aid is truly meeting basic needs of the poorest.

Eighth, in a recent article, Martin Rudner refers to increasing calls to use aid as a political instrument to achieve a range of policy goals, of which human rights observance is only one. "Such demands," he argues, "for a more politicized approach would treat development assistance expressly as an instrument for the promotion of politically determined objectives, and reinforce the movement away from the earlier poverty-focused strategy."[32] Linking aid and human rights as part of a general broadening of the acceptable objectives of Canadian aid is hardly compatible with the intentions of most human rights advocates. Again, this potential problem reinforces the notion that Canada's aid–human rights strategy should be "poverty focused." To the extent that aid directly helps the neediest, it fosters basic rights; under such circumstances, aid termination (as opposed to reshaping) is probably unwarranted, even if there are violations within a recipient country.

A FOUR-PART STRATEGY

Bearing these considerations in mind, the following strategy is proposed for the federal government to use in relating development assistance to human rights observance. It represents an ideal standard and a basis for evaluating actual performance.

(1) In instances of gross and persistent violations of subsistence and security rights, where repression is such that Canada cannot alleviate the suffering of the most disadvantaged through carefully selected aid instruments, Canada should undertake a phased withdrawal of aid. In countries with no aid program, other forms of public-sector involvement should be terminated: for example, Export Development Corporation credits and insurance, activities related to aid but with little relation to meeting basic needs in developing countries.

Subsistence and security rights are those "first-priority needs," "without which existence is either not possible or unbearable,"[33] and the related violations include arbitrary deprivation of life, whether by summary execution or deliberate denial of food and medical attention; torture or other forms of cruel, inhumane, and degrading treatment; forced migration; and arbitrary arrest and protracted detention without trial. Canadian policy should take account of violations of other human rights, but in those situations alternatives may be more appropriate. Further, the violations enumerated here cannot be countenanced under any circumstances. For example, under conditions of international or civil war, there may be grounds for abridging certain political and civil rights and freedoms, as even Canadian law allows, but not these rights (save perhaps to some degree for the last one enumerated). Thus a distinction between subsistence and security rights and other rights should legitimately find expression in Canadian aid policy.

The notion of phased withdrawal is advanced because graduated application of pressure provides time for a government to alter its behaviour, preserves Canadian leverage for a period, and allows for diplomatic persuasion in conjunction with withdrawal. The phases might include an initial warning of the intention to curtail aid, elimination of capital aid projects, suspension of other forms of government-to-government assistance, and finally elimination of humanitarian assistance via non-governmental organizations (NGOs).

(2) Where gross and persistent violations of subsistence and security rights exist, but there is some capacity to meet basic needs through provision of food, medical care, clothing, housing, and education, aid should be confined to these forms. In particular, capital aid projects, lines of credit, and such, where the neediest are not the direct targets, should be gradually eliminated; such aid gives legitimacy to the régime in power and is unlikely to help the masses under existing circumstances of repression. Thus only aid that helps to sustain the disadvantaged and may give them capacity to struggle against the government should be offered. It may be preferable to rely on NGOs and mission-administered funds (i.e. funds disbursed for small projects at the discretion of Can-

ada's posts abroad), through which it is often possible to bypass government channels and deliver aid directly to those most in need, including the most affected victims of repression.[34] In many cases of gross violations of rights, it will not be possible to provide meaningful aid even through such channels as these, but not to seize the opportunity, where it exists, would be incompatible with the responsibility of a government with a human rights–oriented aid program to meet basic economic needs.

(3) In all other countries where Canada has an aid program, all existing and new projects should, in effect, be put through a human rights filter with two purposes in mind. First, projects that have been contributing to or may in future foster human rights violations in the recipient country should be phased out or not initiated. In particular, this would include projects that are overtly discriminatory as part of a government design to advance the interests of certain sectors of society at the expense of others on such grounds as sex, religion, language, ethnicity, or tribe, and projects that harm segments of the population without their having participated in the decision-making leading to the project.[35] Second, projects should be identified that might assist human rights observance by, inter alia, encouraging equitable development for all groups within society,[36] stimulating democratic forms of political participation (without which benefits of economic and social development will be unevenly distributed and errors will be made in developmental policies even by well-intentioned régimes[37]), and by curbing physical abuses through provision, where feasible, of such forms of aid as judicial and police training and assistance in the establishment of human rights offices.

For reasons stated earlier, especially the need for consistency, Canada's strategy should not ignore serious violations anywhere or of any kind. Indeed, focus on only the worst abuses of security and subsistence rights might render Canada's efforts largely useless, since they would be concentrated on those states most impervious to external influence, while failing to help check abuses in other states before they become excessive. Further, such a restricted approach would ignore the interrelatedness of human rights and hence the need for simultaneous progress in security, subsistence, civil, political, economic, and social rights for those in any one area to be secure. Yet, given the varying degrees of abuses in developing countries, differing traditions of respect for rights, and the unpredictability of reaction to external pressure, a strategy should tailor Canadian action to the requisites of each situation and, in addition to entailing penalties, offer positive encouragement for reform.

(4) Canadian aid should be gradually shifted to concentrate on a smaller number of states that respect basic rights and that have a genuine commitment to improving the lot of their least privileged people – states with a "basic needs" strategy of development that involves the disad-

vantaged in decision-making.[38] Only then will Canadian aid contribute to equitable development and reflect concern for the realization of basic rights. Only with such a focus will Canada also advance its global security concerns through its aid program. Such a reorientation would require, however, that Canadian aid be confined to promoting Third World development, with particular emphasis on meeting basic needs. To reduce or terminate aid to some recipients because of gross violations of some rights, while still permitting non-development motivations – especially Canadian economic gain – to find a place in aid policy, will lead to charges of hypocrisy and inconsistency. The effect of Canadian aid will not be equitable, grassroots development but uneven economic growth – if growth at all – that perpetuates existing élites and thus obstructs the realization of economic, social, civil, and political rights. In sum, the extent to which Canadian aid is directed at genuine equitable development will test Canada's commitment to advancing rights in developing countries.

HISTORY

Punitive Action

Although there is some evidence of increased government attention to relating of development assistance to human rights performance, Canadian action has been both halting and inconsistent.[39] This has been so since the first apparent case of linkage – that of Indonesia. Starting in the 1964–5 fiscal year, Canadian food aid was terminated for a two-year period in response to Indonesia's confrontation with Malaysia. Further, no new capital projects or commodity shipments to Indonesia were undertaken in 1965–6.[40] Although Canada never explained the withdrawal, it was apparently due to Indonesia's unprovoked attacks against its neighbour in violation of territorial sovereignty and the self-determination of peoples and to parliamentary criticism over aid to a state diverting its resources from development to finance external aggression.[41]

This early incident is particularly revealing in light of subsequent policy toward Indonesia. Canadian aid to Indonesia in the 1960s had been extremely limited and confined largely to food. Indeed, relations in general had been insignificant; the Sukarno government's anti-Western orientation and chaotic management of the economy had rendered Indonesia neither politically nor commercially attractive to Canada and the West in general. However, following Sukarno's fall in 1965 and the gradual reorientation of Indonesia toward the West under President Suharto, the country took on new political and economic importance to Canada, reflected in the decision announced in 1970 "to concentrate more funds for development programmes" in Indonesia.[42] Since that time Indonesia has been a core recipient, with $367 million disbursed bilaterally between 1970-1 and 1985-6.[43] Based on country-to-country aid disbursements over the past three years, it currently ranks fourth as a Canadian aid recipient and, apart from Pakistan, is the largest one outside the Commonwealth.

Yet Indonesia's human rights record has remained bleak throughout this period. Thousands were arrested and detained without trial for many years for purported involvement in the 1965 coup, and as late as 1984 Amnesty International reported that approximately 200 of these people were still held, while those released under a program initiated in 1976 were subject to a variety of restraints.[44] Since 1965 thousands more have been arrested and detained on suspicion of belonging to groups opposed to the government, and there have been "persistent reports of the torture and ill-treatment" of these detainees as well as extrajudicial killings of ordinary criminal suspects.[45] More appalling still has been Indonesia's treatment of the former Portuguese colony of East Timor, which it invaded and occupied in 1975. Since then, it is estimated that 250,000 East Timorese, approximately one-third of the population, have perished as a result of starvation and indiscriminate killings by the occupying Indonesian army. Accordingly to Amnesty International, Indonesian forces "systematically tortured and killed people in East Timor" after the invasion. In 1983, there was a new wave of disappearances and death in custody as an operation was launched to eliminate supporters of FRETILIN, the organization that in 1975 had declared East Timor's independence from Portugal; there were even reported killings of prisoners who surrendered after being promised amnesty.[45]

From 1976 to 1980 Canada abstained on UN resolutions deploring the Indonesian invasion and calling on all states to respect the right of the East Timorese to self-determination, and it has cast negative votes on resolutions regarding East Timor since 1980. At the same time, it has maintained a major aid program entailing sizeable capital equipment purchases and support for large-scale infrastructural projects,[47] forms of aid inappropriate for a régime with a long history of political repression. The decision to maintain aid without strictures in the face of the invasion of East Timor is strikingly inconsistent with the posture adopted in the face of the far less destructive assault on Malaysia in the mid-1960s. It also makes a mockery of the government's assertion in 1981 about withdrawing "aid programs from those countries whose scarce resources are diverted to war and conquest."[48]

The reason for the inconsistency seems transparent. In the 1960s Indonesia counted for little in Canadian foreign policy. In the 1970s and 1980s, however, it has been deemed strategically important, especially since the fall of South Vietnam and the communist ascendancy throughout Indochina. Together with its fellow members of the Association of South East Asian Nations, it has been viewed by Canada as "the last bulwark against communism in this part of the world."[49] With its great wealth in natural resources, Indonesia also has "great potential as a locus for Canadian exports and investments," so that Canadian corporate interests have "certainly militated against withholding aid on a human rights basis."[50] The government, however, rationalizes the current high level of Canadian aid on the grounds of the régime's genuine commitment to development.[51] It resists using aid to induce the enhanced respect for human rights that is, in fact, necessary to establish a climate in which equitable development can occur and in which Canada's long-term strategic and commercial interests can be secured.

Canadian development assistance to the brutally repressive Pol Pot régime in Kampuchea – responsible for the deaths by torture, murder, and starvation of from one to three million people – was terminated in 1977. However, as in the Indonesian situation in the mid-1960s, aid had been minimal and the government never stated that its decision was a result of human rights violations.

In response to the Vietnamese invasion of Kampuchea, which led to the fall of Pol Pot, all new Canadian bilateral aid to Vietnam, including food assistance, was cut off, in accordance with the policy of not countenancing external aggression. The persecution of the ethnic Chinese in Vietnam was, according to officials, a secondary factor in cessation of this program, which once more had been limited. Vietnam was treated particularly harshly: in October 1979, Canada, together with the United States, requested at a meeting of the governing body of the World Food Program that WFP assistance to Vietnam be postponed. When the WFP failed to act, due to resistance from other members, Canada and the United States specified that their own WFP contributions not be sent to Vietnam.[52] Canadian policy in the Vietnam case hardly seems consistent with the approach taken toward Indonesian aggression in the 1970s. Nor is it consistent with maintenance of aid to meet the needs of the most disadvantaged even in cases of serious violations – a position that most officials claim to support and, indeed, many use to justify assistance to other violators where Canada is loath to take punitive action.

Finally, following the Soviet invasion of Afghanistan, Canada decided in January 1980 not to recognize the new puppet régime and to suspend all aid. In this decision, according to officials, political and security reasons were interwoven with human rights considerations.

In sum, in the Asian cases we can see inconsistency and lack of explicitness with respect to the role of human rights in the withdrawal decisions. In all instances where action was taken, the régimes were either communist or strongly anti-Western, aid was limited, and Canada had few vested interests at stake. By contrast, Ottawa seems loath to consider linkage in Asian states with long records of abuse if the countries are major aid recipients and have other important ties with Canada. These include – in addition to Indonesia – Bangladesh and Pakistan, the first- and second-ranking Canadian aid recipients worldwide, where violations are certainly of such an order as to require careful shaping of the Canadian programs to discourage abuses and make a constructive contribution to the achievement of social justice.

In Africa, the principal instance of action has been Uganda: "Virtually all CIDA projects ... were suspended in January 1973 due to a lack of commitment to development shown by the Amin régime." Only the scholarship program for training Ugandans in Canada was allowed to run its course, without renewal.[53] While the human rights situation was appalling and the Amin régime had been universally condemned, aid was suspended not specifically because of the human rights situation, but because the chaotic internal situation, together with lack of local personnel and other support services, had rendered aid ineffective and placed Canadian lives at risk.[54] The human rights argument was thus largely a post facto justification offered in the face of growing pressure in Canada for curtailment of aid to repressive régimes.[55]

Following the overthrow of Amin in April 1979 and restoration of Milton Obote to power the following year, there were grounds for hoping that human rights would improve. In December 1979, the UN general assembly asked the international community to contribute generously to rehabilitation and development, and Canada responded with bilateral aid for the purchase of spare parts and materials needed in reconstruction and with $2 million in emergency food aid.[56] By early 1981, however, Amnesty International had found evidence of arrests by the Ugandan army without legal authority, ill-treatment of prisoners, torture, disappearances, and murders, and the situation continued to deteriorate thereafter. Canadian aid was not again suspended, although it has remained limited and been designed largely to reach those most in need.

In Equatorial Guinea, a one-party state and absolute dictatorship was established in 1970 by Macias Nguena, who forced one-third of the population into exile and slaughtered some 35–50,000 political detainees during his 11-year rule.[57] In August 1979 he was overthrown in a bloodless coup and replaced by a military junta, which improved respect for human rights.[58] Throughout the period of repression, Canada offered no development assistance, but it has provided only nominal aid since that time, which suggests that relations were not constrained by the earlier human rights situation.

While it is difficult to quarrel with Canadian policy in these two African situations, action was not taken explicitly for reasons of violations and both countries had only limited development and commercial relations with Canada.

With regard to Latin America, the first instance of Canadian action was the quiet withdrawal of government-to-government aid to Chile following the 1973 coup that toppled the democratically elected Allende government, replacing it with the repressive Pinochet régime, which has since violated a wide range of security, political, and civil rights. However, yet again, no apparent effort was made to use this decision politically to encourage change. Indeed, the Canadian government seems to have acted reluctantly and only because of its perception of public opposition to aid to Chile. Thus a confidential cabinet document in 1974 asserted that "the attention which the churches and various Canadian groups have focused on the Chilean Government's use of repression against its opponents has led to an unfavourable reaction among the Canadian public – a reaction which will not permit any significant increase in Canadian aid to this country."[59]

In this situation, too, Canadian bilateral aid had been extremely limited, with disbursements varying between $740,000 and $2.4 million between 1970–1 and 1973–4. Had Canada wished to signal its displeasure at Chilean repression, other measures were called for, including termination of Export Development Corporation (EDC) activity. Yet no such action was taken. Indeed, EDC involvement in Chile increased, with Canadian concessional loans over the period 1974–86 amounting to $89.5 million and insurance to exporters to $109.3 million.[60] Further, EDC activity has arguably served to help sustain this universally condemned régime. For instance, the corporation extended a $5-million loan to Chile shortly after the overthrow of Allende to finance the purchase of Twin Otter aircraft; their short-take-off-and-landing capability makes them potentially useful for counter-insurgency.[61] In 1980, the EDC financed a $6.1-million sale of Buffalo aircraft and spare parts by de Havilland Aircraft of Canada to the Chilean air force. The Buffalo, a military support transport plane, can handle troops and equipment. Canadian action toward Chile has thus been inconsistent and hardly constitutes an effective response to persistent repression.

In 1978, CIDA's bilateral aid to Cuba, launched in 1975, was terminated. The ostensible reason was Cuba's military involvement in Angola, indicating that it had "no more need for Canadian aid, given its new priorities,"[62] but this was probably a post facto rationalization designed "to make political mileage" in the face of Canadian parliamentary "criticism of Cuba's military involvement in Africa"; in fact, the aid program had probably "run its course without Cuba's request for renewal."[63]

Whatever the reason, action on aid was not supplemented with strictures in other areas, for EDC support for exports to Cuba continued, with, for example, $128.3 million of EDC insurance made available between 1978 and 1986. Certainly, Canada has not communicated a consistent signal to the Castro régime.

It would be possible, officials acknowledge, to identify viable projects in Cuba that would have a real development impact. In accordance with the strategy outlined earlier, Cuba (like Vietnam) remains a legitimate target for carefully structured aid directed at basic economic needs, but Ottawa is unwilling to consider such a program. Indeed, Canada does not even offer mission-administered funds to Cuba, although such a program exists even in South Africa, the most widely reviled human rights violator.[64] The reason seems to be, as stated by one official, that "the regime is hard-Marxist-Leninist, worse than some Eastern European states" and remains heavily committed to overseas military expenditures. Cuba and Vietnam, contrasted with Indonesia, thus suggest that Canada has a different view of "foreign adventurism" depending on whether a régime is communist or pro-Western.

Two of the most widely publicized Canadian punitive actions were the decisions taken in March 1981 to suspend planning for new bilateral projects in El Salvador and to allow the program in Guatemala, begun following the 1976 earthquake, to run out.[65] Although these were later sometimes characterized by the government as motivated by human rights offences, the administrative impossibility of carrying out the program and the risks to Canadian personnel were the key factors. The CIDA annual report of 1981–2 stated: "Political turmoil and civil strife, with an inability of governments to guarantee the protection of development workers led to the suspension of CIDA bilateral programs in El Salvador and Guatemala."[66]

That human rights was not the motivating factor is apparent also in that in both instances Canada had been providing assistance for some time despite evidence of escalating repression. In El Salvador, from the election of General Carlos Humberto Romero as president in 1977, "the power of the military could no longer be realistically challenged by peaceful legislative, administrative, or judicial means" and "political repression had become institutionalized,"[67] yet Canadian aid roughly doubled each fiscal year between 1977–8 and 1980–1 and then almost tripled in 1981–2, before the suspension came into effect. Once again, suspension did not entail a clear message about human rights.[68]

On 3 December 1984, Joe Clark announced resumption of direct assistance to El Salvador, initially in the form of an $8-million line of credit for purchase of agricultural-sector products. Out of the counterpart funds generated by the line of credit, Canada intended to establish "basic needs" projects, including aid to those displaced by civil war, to be administered largely by NGOs. It justified the reversal of policy by the improved situation in El Salvador, including contraction of human rights abuses.[69]

Resumption of aid to El Salvador has been controversial. America's Watch reported an improved rights situation in 1984: death squad killings and disappearances dropped sharply; but they increased again in 1985, leading the organization to state that there has been no general improvement in the human rights situation, which remains "terrible."[70] Further, there are serious doubts about the Duarte government's will and capacity to surmount the entrenched military and economic establishment and introduce the reforms necessary to ensure that Canadian aid will, in fact, help the long-suffering peasantry. Unfortunately, a line of credit, in effect balance-of-payments support for the government, implies approval of the régime itself. Also, the government controls the use of counterpart funds generated by the line of credit, giving it the potential at least to use them to advance its political goals.[71]

Ottawa's view of Guatemala prior to 1987, when bilateral aid recommenced, was that "the terrifying human rights situation" continued "to rule out any consideration of a resumption of Canadian government-to-government assistance"[72] (although other forms of aid were made available). Despite this firm position (bilateral aid in any event was always limited), Canada offered confused signals, not curbing EDC activity, with loans and insurance amounting to $45.9 million between 1981 and 1986. One observer remarked: "Canadian-Guatemalan relations have been almost humorously Byzantine in the desire to balance commercial and human rights issues."[73]

In 1983, Canada terminated a very small program in Suriname because of the repression that followed the 1982 coup, leading to liquidation of much of the political opposition. In this instance, human rights violations seem to have been the principal motivation, although aid was so limited that this initiative constituted merely a symbolic gesture.

By contrast with Canadian measures with respect to these Latin American states, the government has not curtailed aid to Honduras, the largest recipient of Canadian aid to Central America over the last three years. Yet many observers have noted significant deterioration in human rights observance there and have called for limitations on assistance.[74] Honduras has served as a base for the covert war against Nicaragua waged by the anti-Sandinista contras, yet, inconsistent with its position regarding Cuba, Vietnam, and Indonesia in the 1960s, Ottawa has not seen fit to sanction Honduras for its foreign intervention.[75]

In sum, then, in instances in Asia, Africa, and Latin America where Canada has taken punitive action, aid and other relationships were limited (and no significant Canadian interests were jeopardized),[76] the role of rights violations was ambiguous, and Ottawa was inconsistent in treating different states. In the words of Bernard Wood: "If you try to chart the scales of violations against the scales of sanctions in our past policies, it is not possible to find any systematic pattern."[77]

Selective Action

With regard to filtering out harmful projects in countries where abuses have been marked, but less gross or persistent, only two clear instances have been identified. In November 1980, the government removed newsprint from the list of commodities eligible for purchase under a line of credit to Guyana when it became clear that newsprint was not reaching the opposition press.[78] In 1985, Canada placed on indefinite hold its contribution to Sri Lanka's massive Mahaweli River dam and irrigation scheme, the world's largest foreign aid project. Saudi Arabia had withdrawn from its portion of the scheme (due to Sri Lanka's increasing relationship with Israel), thus affecting the project's financial viability. However, Ottawa also made clear its unhappiness with racial discrimination in Sri Lanka's resettlement plans for the affected area. It would provide no further funding beyond current commitments until financing had been resolved and until it was clear that Tamils as well as Sinhalese would benefit significantly from the project.

The Sri Lankan government apparently intended to resettle some 1.5 million Sinhalese in the 250,000 acres of scrub forest that would be turned into arable land by the project, thus diluting the concentration of Tamils in the Eastern province and concomitantly weakening the Tamil secessionist movement that had evolved into a violent guerrilla campaign in the north and east. This is an interesting first instance of the application of human rights criteria to aid a major recipient. In the Canadian government's view, given Sri Lanka's generally good human rights record until the recent ethnic conflict, termination of assistance was not called for, but rather insistence that Canadian aid be channelled impartially to both communities. However, given the absence of project proposals related to Tamil areas, aid to Sri Lanka was declining significantly by 1985–6.[79]

Creative Action

In terms of positive shaping of aid to support equitable development of all groups, CIDA has made the most significant progress in the area of women in development. The agency has established an Integration of Women in Development section, and every CIDA project is reportedly now monitored from its inception to ensure that it encompasses women as well as men and that both sexes benefit. CIDA has also exposed its officer staff to a short course to sensitize them to the vital role played by women in the development process.[80] The Women in Development approach could be applied by CIDA more generally to ensure that broad-based human rights criteria are taken into account in establishing and evaluating all Canadian programs and projects.

Other creative endeavours to encourage rights observance have included use of mission-administered funds to provide legal materials for the Supreme Court library in Guyana and for the Guyana Human Rights Commission. Recently, the Canadian government indicated its willingness to assist Third World countries in developing institutions necessary to achieve effective observance of human rights, through such means as providing legal assistance and assisting in development of procedures for democratic elections and in establishment of human rights ombudsmen. Ottawa is exploring the mechanics of establishing an institute, separate from CIDA, to administer initiatives of this nature.

There has been only limited Canadian involvement in police and military training, essentially in the Commonwealth Caribbean. In 1984, for example, Ottawa began to assist restructuring of Grenada's police force, entailing provision of equipment as well as an advisory service for police training and curriculum planning.[81] Aid of this nature must, of course, be approached with extreme caution. It is unlikely to be welcome where it is most needed, and it might be used for unintended purposes and aid a state's application of repression. Nevertheless, Canadian police forces have well-established programs for disciplined, apolitical training of personnel in procedures of arrest, interrogation, and detention, and the Canadian armed forces have an exemplary record in peacekeeping abroad, which requires restraint, tact, and sensitivity, often under intense provocation. Canada may, therefore, be well suited to assist certain developing countries in achieving conditions of law and order, thereby helping them to establish just environments in which economic, social, and political development can take place.

In sum, action by Canada relating to human rights has been largely punitive in nature and directed at "worst-case" situations. Only now is some support emerging for applying human rights criteria more broadly to all country programs and reshaping them so as to avoid projects that detract from observance and support those that can enhance it. Officers sensitive to human rights may be subjecting projects to a form of human rights filter, but there is no institutionalized project-by-project assessment, applying a broad range of criteria, including political participation. Thus the human rights dimension, beyond perhaps women in development, tends, in the words of one officer, to get "lost" as other traditional criteria are applied in evaluating projects.

Meeting Basic Needs

Finally, an analysis of Canadian aid from a human rights perspective requires a brief assessment of its efficacy in meeting the basic economic and social needs of the most underprivileged. The proportion of Canada's assistance directed to the least developed countries, as classified by the United Nations, has increased substantially since the early 1970s. Measured in terms of country-to-country disbursements, it stood at 26 to 28 per cent of the total over the years 1983-4 to 1985-6. However, of the top 20 Canadian aid recipients since 1983-4, only 5 (Bangladesh, Ethiopia, Niger, Sudan, and Tanzania) are among the 36 least developed countries.[82] Further, Canada has concentrated more aid on some relatively prosperous developing countries as it has sought commercial gains from its development assistance program in an intensely competitive international trading environment. Thus, of the top 20 aid recipients 1983-6, 2 countries, Jamaica and Peru, have per capita GNPs of roughly $1,000, while 4 (Cameroon, Indonesia, Thailand, and Zimbabwe) have figures over $500. Increased Canadian aid has focused on "the higher-growth low-income countries, some of which qualify as 'middle income' by World Bank standards, countries in which the incidence of poverty, economic performance and commercial opportunities seem to come together especially propitiously."[83]

In part because of this growing interest in developing countries with commercial promise, and more obviously because of the resistance for reasons of diplomacy to eliminating countries from the aid program (especially francophone and Commonwealth partners), Canada continues to disburse aid to an inordinately large number of countries. In the 1985-6 fiscal year, for example, at least 120 states received aid from Canada. Apart from reducing aid for the neediest states, this policy harms Canada's development effort. CIDA's capacity to select carefully appropriate development projects, to evaluate effectiveness of implementation, and to ensure that local administration is honest and efficient and that recipient régimes are committed to egalitarian development is seriously hampered by a cumbersome aid program dispersed over so many countries. More specifically, CIDA cannot familiarize itself adequately with the situation in each country and so cannot assess the human rights implications of each project. It would thus be highly desirable to focus on a much smaller number of needy states seriously committed to grassroots, economically redistributive development.[84]

The problem of dispersion is compounded by tight strictures on CIDA's administrative costs, which have resulted in inadequate numbers of trained agency personnel, especially in the field. This situation also hampers project identification, implementation, and evaluation and leads to selection of schemes where large sums of money can be disbursed with minimal overhead costs, for small-scale "basic needs" projects tend to require substantial administrative resources.[85]

If the focus is to be assisting the poorest, there must be significant "untying" of Canadian aid. With 80 per cent of bilateral assistance tied to the provision of Canadian goods and services, Canada operates the second most tightly controlled program among countries of the Organization for Economic Co-operation and Development, with numerous harmful consequences. Because of generally higher Canadian costs, tied aid reduces the value of Canadian assistance by roughly 20 per cent. As a result of complex procurement procedures, tied aid also increases administrative costs and retards disbursements. Still more seriously, tied aid distorts the development priorities of recipient countries toward projects for which Canada can furnish goods and services and leads to reliance on imported rather than local inputs or those from other developing countries.[86]

Finally, tied aid is incompatible with giving priority to the needs of the rural disadvantaged for increased agricultural output, health care, education, and so on. Such projects need untied funds for largely local purchases rather than requiring Canadian equipment and services. Tying, therefore, means that "much foreign aid is finding its way 'to rich people in poor countries,'"[87] so that despite CIDA's intention, as set out in its 1975–80 strategy – and reaffirmed in 1981 – to focus more attention on the neediest in developing countries,[88] there has been no dramatic reorientation; rather, many traditional forms of infrastructural aid, such as electrical power generation and distribution and transport, have been simply reclassified as aid to the agricultural and rural sectors.[89]

Of particular concern has been the tendency in the 1980s to place still higher priority on potential commercial benefits to Canada. In 1978, for instance, an Industrial Cooperation Program was established, enabling CIDA to finance feasibility and starter studies by Canadian investors in the Third World. At about the same time, CIDA also initiated parallel financing: developing countries receive two separate credits for a project – a loan from the EDC and a low-interest loan or grant from CIDA.[90] The resulting attractive financial package induces the developing country to purchase goods from Canada rather than a competitor country. According to a study published in 1987, "Since 1978, CIDA and the EDC have engaged in associated financing for twenty-three projects, which had a total value of $1.5 billion in procurements of Canadian goods and services."[91] Such co-financing increases the emphasis on developing countries with commercial promise for Canada, at the expense of the neediest, and on capital as opposed to "basic needs" projects.[92]

In light of this growing preoccupation with commercial spin-offs, it is particularly discouraging that no significant constituency within the government appears to recognize that meeting basic economic and social needs is central to the program's sensitivity to human rights. The foreign policy establishment seems generally to believe that aid is and should be a broad policy instrument to promote not only development but also the government's political and commercial goals.[93] There is, indeed, a naïve faith that Canadian interests in the latter areas can be met without sacrificing the developmental quality of Canadian aid. Thus at least until recently there has not been much evidence of support for major reforms to allow aid to contribute significantly to the realization of global social justice.

CONCLUSION

In the last few years there has been increasing attention in Canada on human rights considerations in the context of official development assistance. There are, however, both positive and potentially negative factors to be borne in mind in linking aid disbursements to human rights observance. It is important, therefore, that Canada carefully construct a framework for action flexible enough to fit the circumstances of each case and encompassing not just punitive measures but – especially in cases of serious but not extreme abuses – creative initiatives that will encourage improved respect for human rights.

To date, Canadian action has been largely punitive and has focused on perceived extreme cases. In the most publicized instances, aid was suspended only when violations hindered implementation of programs and placed Canadian personnel in jeopardy. Such action did not deliver a message to offending régimes to alter their behaviour. In other, less well-known instances, there has usually been ambiguity about the role of human rights in precipitating Canadian action. Further, with this essentially negative approach, involving suspension of non-renewal, Canada has confined itself to only a few cases, lest the aid program be seriously disrupted. It has given little attention, apart from the specific area of women in development, to shaping the aid effort in all recipient countries so as to nurture respect for human rights in all their dimensions – security, political, civil, economic, and social. Further, action has been inconsistent and selective. States guilty of similar offences have been treated radically differently, and initiatives have been confined largely to countries where Canada's development and other relations have been minimal. Thus Canada has sustained assistance, unrestricted as to amount or form, to some repressive states on the dubious assumption that that fosters Canadian commercial and security interests.

Finally, the program's usefulness in helping bring about equitable development in countries seriously committed to social justice is in doubt because of the intrusion of political and, more particularly, commercial consideration into decision-making. In the final analysis, Canada's commitment to human rights in the aid program can be measured by the extent to which aid is directed at the basic needs of the world's most underprivileged. Government rhetoric to the contrary, only a modest proportion of assistance is so targeted.

For all these reasons, Canada is still a long way from fulfilling the goal, once so eloquently stated, of making the human condition the focus of its development activities and the liberation of humankind the central objective.

CHAPTER ELEVEN

Military Sales

ERNIE REGEHR

Canada's national objectives obviously include promotion of universal respect for human rights. However, this goal may and often does conflict with pursuit of Canada's other objectives, most notably domestic economic prosperity. Pursuit of prosperity is not necessarily incompatible with promotion of rights, but some of the means by which it is pursued may be so inimical to the promotion of human rights as to warrant their severe restriction or even prohibition. This dilemma is brought sharply into focus by Canada's military exports.

Canada is seeking to increase sales of military products to its allies in the North Atlantic Treaty Organization (NATO) as well as to Third World nations. While sales to the United States involve Canada indirectly in US projection of military power into the Third World, with obvious implications for human rights, sales to the Third World create problems directly regarding Canada's commitment to human rights. The militarization of political power, closely related to growth of political repression and violation of human rights, is increasing noticeably in Third World countries. This development is facilitated by international arms transfers. Ruth Leger Sivard, in her annual review of world military and social expenditures, reports that by 1986 50 per cent of Third World governments were controlled by the military, in contrast to 28 per cent of a much smaller number of independent states in 1960. Moreover, there was evidence of rights violations under all military régimes, and, in half, violation through official terrorism was frequent enough to seem institutionalized.[1] As Canada promotes the sale of military exports in the Third World the possibility increases that it will supply countries run by the military and subject to institutionalized violation of human rights.

The international arms trade in the mid-1980s has become a thoroughly commercial affair. Most countries, with the partial exception of the superpowers, have always sold arms for economic reasons, but most impose restrictions, owing to the special political implications of military equipment. Recently, however, competition for sales has increased, and the current global trend is to reduce such constraints, including those related to human rights. Thus, countries that impose restrictions are likely to find a host of less discriminating competitors ready and willing to take their place. In consequence, restrictive policies carry a real economic cost – inevitably understood as undermining the national pursuit of prosperity. This trend is reflected in Canadian policy. While human rights are considered in regulation of arms exports, Canadian policy does not always prohibit sales to serious and persistent violators. In the following pages I shall explore the extent to which economic objectives have undermined human rights as factors in regulation and control of Canadian military exports.

THE GLOBAL ARMS TRADE AND CANADA

From the mid-1970s to the early 1980s conventional arms transfers to the Third World more than doubled (as measured in constant dollars).[2] World-wide sales reached a peak in 1982 when the Third World collectively ordered US $45 billion worth. Since then, there has been a sharp decline, and Third World orders in the mid-1980s are running at about US $30 billion per year. World-wide recession and saturation of the Third World market contributed to the recent decline, and the record levels of the early 1980s are unlikely to return soon.

Accompanying this levelling off has been a major change in arms suppliers. Throughout the 1960s and 1970s the two superpowers dominated – almost monopolized – the arms trade. Together with Britain, France, Italy, and West Germany, they supplied 90 per cent of all arms to the Third World during the 1970s; other industrialized and Third World states, including Canada, the remaining 10 per cent. Early in the 1980s, however, the pattern shifted. Not only was US and Soviet dominance reduced as the western European four increased their share, but the superpowers' and the western Europeans' combined share dropped to 75 per cent.

The sharp increase in the market share of other suppliers presages much more competition. While the shift indicates the persistent and growing export trade of other industrialized producers (East and West), Third World producers are now arms merchants in their own right, even though their share of sales is still small. The leading Third World producers are India and Israel (one-half of all Third World production), South Africa, Brazil, Taiwan, the two Koreas, and Argentina; these eight together account for 90 per cent of Third World production.[3]

Direct Canadian military sales to the Third World currently account for less than one-half of one per cent of world arms sales to the Third World. These averaged about $150 million a year 1980–5 (compared with world-wide military sales to the Third World of $35–$50 billion). However, almost 80 per cent of Canadian military exports in the 1980s has gone to the United States; as about 10 per cent of US military production goes to the Third World, about 10 per cent of Canada's contribution to US production probably also reaches the Third World. Thus, in 1985, another $165 million in Canadian military exports also reached the Third World.

Other indirect sales occur through export of Canadian engines and components to aircraft industries in countries such as Brazil, Israel, Italy, and Switzerland (which in turn re-export them as part of their military exports). Most of these engines leave Canada classified as civilian, due to size and weight, but are used in military aircraft, such as the Israeli short take-off and landing aircraft (the ARAVA) or patrol and trainer aircraft of the Brazilian manufacturer Embraer. These sales add about $20–$30 million to Canada's military sales each year. During the 1980s, therefore, combined direct and indirect military transfers from Canada to the Third World have averaged over $300 million a year, approaching 1 per cent of the annual world total.

Promotion of Canadian military sales to the Third World has gradually become an objective of Canadian trade ministries. In the late 1950s and the 1960s such sales were largely to newly independent Commonwealth partners. In the 1970s, when sales to the United States declined in post-Vietnam economic restraint and political détente, Canada looked at the larger Third World market with greater interest. Direct sales in the 1970s ranged between $30 million and $164 million, in the 1980s between $98 million and $248 million (current dollars). Growth is erratic, and no "breakthrough" is apparent.[4]

Canada's military industry is geared to produce components for weapons designed and built elsewhere. Aside from military transport aircraft, Canada has traditionally produced few complete weapons systems. As a result, Third World countries have not seen Canada as a significant source and Canada has thus had to seek out countries already receiving major US systems that might need Canadian-built components. During the 1970s, for example, Iran, due to its enormous imports of US military equipment, was the object of major attention. The Defence Programs Bureau[5] had a direct representative in Tehran, and Iran purchased over $50 million worth of Canadian military commodities – making it Canada's largest Third World customer during that decade.

By the 1980s conditions were changing. Canadian industry produced military patrol and transport aircraft, military trucks and motorcycles, armoured vehicles, and communications equipment, allowing Canada to market complete systems. This added capability, however, coincided with the entry of other military producers into the market. Canada has therefore had to struggle (relying on publicly funded promotion) just to maintain export levels reached in the late 1970s.[6]

As with suppliers, a few states dominate the list of arms recipients. Half of all Third World military imports go to the Middle East. This region has been the major market since 1945, with other regions (Africa, Latin America, South Asia, and the Far East) fluctuating according to political and military conditions. In 1980–4, for example, just under half of arms imports went to those areas: Africa, 16.7 per cent; Latin America, 13.5 per cent; South Asia, 10.1 per cent; and the Far East, 8.9 per cent.[7]

Within the then steadily expanding arms trade, fluctuations in volumes and destinations of military goods reflected changes in the international strategic environment. The late 1950s and the 1960s saw weapons transfers based on strategic/military considerations. The superpowers enjoyed a virtual monopoly as arms suppliers and used weapons transfers, prominently through aid programs, to extend and consolidate their spheres of influence. Overall demand for weapons increased by an average of 7 per cent per year. In the 1970s arms transfers entered a more commercial period. Western Europeans became important suppliers, and the United States and the Soviet Union began to emphasize sales rather than aid. Demand increased by an average of 12 per cent per year, but the arms trade also expanded in four other ways: the number of recipient countries increased, advanced weapons systems proliferated throughout the Third World, arms production facilities increased in the semi-industrialized countries of the Third World and the sale of technology that can be used for repression increased.[8] This last development has particular implications for human rights.

Repression technology is military and paramilitary equipment designed for use against civilians and dissidents or insurgents. It ranges from artillery and aircraft for counter-insurgency campaigns to computers, electronic eavesdropping devices, small arms, and other equipment to intimidate, control, and even eliminate "hostile" individuals and groups. It is acquired not to defend the state against an external aggressor but to attack and control internal "enemies."

Repression technology reflects the political and economic interests of the supplier.[9] Through judicious supply of arms and repression technology, powers aid régimes that serve their interests. Major arms exporters seek political leverage by encouraging the recipient's dependence for spare parts, training, and maintenance of the weapons sold.

Acquisition of this military technology and equipment enhances the capacity of recipient military institutions to defend their country against external aggressors and to impose internal discipline. Implications for human rights vary according to the equipment. The Canadian government has held that only military commodities directly usable against civilians should be subject to human rights–related restrictions. However, military transfers are a unique expression of solidarity with the recipient state and thus provide political and moral support for its repressive practices. The former president of Tanzania, Julius Nyerere, has put it this way:

> The selling of arms is something which a country does only when it wants to support and strengthen the regime or the group to whom the sale is made. Whatever restrictions or limits are placed on that sale, the sale of any arms is a declaration of support – an implied alliance of a kind. You can trade with people you dislike; you can have diplomatic relations with a government you disapprove of; you can sit in conference with those nations whose policies you abhor. But you do not sell arms without saying in effect: 'In the light of the receiving country's known policies, friends, and enemies, we anticipate that, in the last resort, we will be on their side in the case of any conflict. We shall want them to defeat their enemies.'[10]

Those wanting to relax restrictions on military exports to human rights violators argue that military commodities that do not directly enhance repressive capacity do not increase a state's political capacity for repression and thus do not imply support for the recipient régime. Canadian military sales are not government to government, and even the role of the crown agency Canadian Commercial Corporation is not viewed by some policy-makers as altering this principle. Major sales, however, frequently require high-level political involvement in order to seal the deal; witness Joe Clark's visit to Saudi Arabia to promote Canada's efforts to sell armoured vehicles.[11] Officials acknowledge that such overt intervention implies political support.

However, the requirement for export permits is already acknowledgment that military trade is not like any other – it is not a purely commercial affair but a political/military transaction that requires direct government involvement. Sound business practice and principles are not sufficient to regulate commodities with such extraordinary political and moral implications. Normal business practice is not believed competent to determine matters that raise political and moral questions. A body able to discern and reflect the moral and political consensus of the broader community must decide. Therefore if permits do not represent political endorsation of the recipient, as Nyerere suggests, they at least define the boundaries of acceptable political and moral behaviour with regard to arms transfers. Granting of an export permit declares a sale to be acceptable behaviour.

To the extent that permission for a military sale is also an expression of solidarity, states have moral and legal obligations to withhold sales when human rights violations are involved. In the view of some Canadian churches, for example, international human rights instruments obligate all signatories to promote the interests of citizens of every state, even beyond encouraging respect for human rights: "In our view, signing the universal human rights declarations and codes obliges each state to restrain other states and their agents from violating the rights of their citizens."[12]

The obligations include taking certain initiatives. States must protect the rights of citizens but must also restrain the abuse of rights by other states. In arms sales, states must surely, at least, refrain from supplying governments that grossly and systematically abuse human rights.

Restraint of the arms trade requires full disclosure of sales. Secrecy about military exports downgrades human rights in foreign policy by denying the public an opportunity for the informed assessment on which international respect for rights ultimately depends. As standards are difficult to define – particularly the point where violations become gross and systematic – policy should depend on broad political assessments within a public arena rather than close technical decisions within a bureaucracy. Human rights standards can be universal, but application requires assessment of their political and cultural contexts. Political definition must be a public process and requires full disclosure of official practice.

US law requires reasonably full disclosure of military sales, but Canada has no such obligation. Canadian access-to-information legislation exempts disclosure on several grounds, including "commercial confidentiality," designed to protect private firms from the commercial disadvantages of disclosure – namely, loss of sales. Reduced sales, however, are precisely the point of regulation and disclosure. Greater regulation impedes the free flow of military goods and thus mitigates undesirable social and political effects. Disclosure is part of the process of restraint and is intended to inhibit the trade in weapons.

EXPORT PERMITS

Canadian military sales are regulated through the Export and Import Permits Act, which requires permits for the export of strategic goods and technologies, including military and military-related goods. All such goods on the Export Control List (ECL) require permits for export, except to the United States. The act requires permits for the shipment of all such goods, whether on the ECL or not, to countries on the Area Control List (ACL).[13] The strategic and military sections of the ECL are derived from controls defined by the Co-ordinating Committee for Multilateral Export Controls (COCOM), which is composed of NATO members and Japan. COCOM seeks to control shipment of military and strategic goods and technologies, and it determines proscribed countries as well as defining military and strategic good.

The Export and Import Permits Act addresses itself exclusively to security considerations, defining as its objectives, in article 3: "to ensure that arms, ammunition, implements or munitions of war, naval, army or air stores or any articles deemed capable of being converted thereinto or made useful in the production thereof or otherwise having a strategic nature or value will not be made available to any destination wherein their use might be detrimental to the security of Canada."

The act permits additional guide-lines to regulate the granting of permits. The current (as of 10 September 1986) guide-lines state:

Canada [will] closely control the export of military goods and technology to:
1. countries which pose a threat to Canada and its allies;
2. countries involved in or under imminent threat of hostilities; and
3. countries under United Nations Security Council sanctions; or
4. countries whose governments have a persistent record of serious violations of the human rights of their citizens, unless it can be demonstrated that there is no reasonable risk that the goods might be used against the civilian population.[14]

There are essentially three categories of permit applications for the export of military goods: to Warsaw Pact and ACL countries, which are automatically rejected; to Canada's NATO allies and other friendly countries such as Australia, New Zealand, and Japan, which are routinely, if not automatically, accepted; and to any other country, which are reviewed on a case-by-case basis.

Because permits are granted for specific destinations, the exporter must obtain assurances that the stated place is in fact the ultimate destination. The primary instruments for obtaining such assurances are import certificates or licences from the recipient's government, delivery verification certificates, and end-use certificates (commitments to the supplier's government). Members of COCOM have introduced a system of import certificates designed primarily to control the trans-shipment of restricted goods to Warsaw Pact countries, and other countries are being encouraged to adopt such certificates. Where an import certificate or licence is not provided, the exporter is required to obtain an end-use certificate from the importer, stating the ultimate destination of the commodity.[15]

Canadian authorities can require only that the exporter undertake to receive an end-use certificate in good faith and to complete the application form honestly. A fine can be levied on the exporter for submitting a false application, but there is no recourse in Canadian law if the importer fails to honour the end-use certificate. While an importer found to have provided a false certificate would risk not receiving further goods from the Canadian exporter, this may not be a major risk in a buyers' market. If an import certificate were not honoured, the importer would have to answer to its home government, which issued the certificate.

If a product is transformed in some way in the recipient country, the end-use provisions no longer apply. The end-use certificate is intended to certify that the commodity will be used for the purpose indicated in the destination indicated. In case of components, however, the purpose indicated is manufacturing, and there are no restrictions on the re-export of the transformed product. Given that much of Canada's military production is components, many of its military exports travel beyond their initial destination.

A wide range of circumstances, over and above, and often more important than, those noted in the published guide-lines, affect ultimate approval or rejection of an application to export. They include national security, political affairs, defence relations, intelligence, and trade relations.

For many years Canada's policy has been described by officials as "restrictive." The Notice to Exporters issued by External Affairs says: "Exporters of military, military related and strategic equipment are advised that Canadian policy with respect to the export of such goods is a restrictive one."[16] Joe Clark put the case more strongly in 1985: "Canada maintains one of the most restrictive policies of any Western nation concerning exports of military goods."[17]

"Restrictive" is widely used internationally in arms transfer policy but means rather less than it implies. The Stockholm International Peace Research Institute (SIPRI) describes the primary criterion for restrictiveness as forbidding supply to a party to a conflict.[18] While the restrictive policies of some states contain other criteria, this one is common to all. The political principle embodied is non-involvement in conflicts. Some states make this a legal requirement, others, such as Canada, simply a policy directive. A restrictive policy – non-involvement in a conflict – is perhaps best understood as being in contrast to a directed policy – selective involvement, or support for a particular party to a conflict.

Thus a restrictive policy need not include prohibitions on arms sales to repressive régimes.

Canada appears to have a "restrictive" policy. Military equipment should not be supplied "to countries involved in hostilities or where there is an imminent threat of hostilities."[19] Joe Clark states it categorically: "In order to prevent the escalation of regional disputes, the Government does not issue permits for the export of military goods to countries that are engaged in or under imminent threat of hostilities."[20]

Canadian practice does not bear this out, however. Department officials themselves immediately qualify the assertion in official guide-lines. Neither policy nor implementation follows even the relatively narrow international interpretation. Of the more than $8 billion in Canadian military exports 1980–5, for example, about 90 per cent went to NATO members. Obviously, there was no interruption of exports to Britain during the Falklands/Malvinas war (although permits to sell to Argentina were not granted) or to the United States during the Vietnam War or more recent, smaller conflicts. Thus Canadian policy is more properly described as "directed" rather than "restrictive."

Further, even where the guide-lines are considered relevant (in exports to the Third World), they are not requirements but merely points to be considered. Indonesia's involvement in hostilities in East Timor has not disqualified it as a recipient of Canadian military and military-related equipment. Saudi Arabia's formal state of war with Israel and its active support of the Palestine Liberation Organization (which would seem to make it a party to hostilities, real or imminent) has not disqualified it. Indeed, both nations are objects of special sales efforts.

Thus a variety of considerations overrule the guide-lines. Publication of formal guide-lines implies their high priority, but the act does not require compliance. The law says that exporters must have permits, and the guide-lines merely point to some factors that the government will consider in deciding on a permit.

External Affairs does not have an operational definition of conflict or imminent conflict. In general, internal conflicts or civil war are included, so that a country involved in actions against insurgent forces would be unlikely to qualify. But there, too, there are mitigating circumstances. For example, the government argues that it may not be clear whether the "conflict" is an attempt to control criminal elements (as officials have suggested may be the case in Peru or the Philippines) or genuine civil war. A country's relations with Canada and the nature of the equipment to be exported also affect decisions. If Canada has strong, friendly relations with a country, including significant economic ties, it would be much more reluctant to refuse military commodities. If the equipment does not have a clear combat role, a permit would also be much more readily available.

SALES TO VIOLATORS

It is difficult to assess the extent to which the military export guidelines prevent sale of Canadian military commodities to known human rights violators. The federal government does not disclose information on the recipients of export permits or detailed sales data. However, it is possible to put together a partial picture from other sources.[21]

According to Project Ploughshares, 45 Third World countries were eligible for military commodities during the period 1980–4. Of these, 60 per cent had been cited by Amnesty International and other groups as regular ("unexceptional") violators. Using the more restricted definition of the UN Commission on Human Rights, 40 per cent were violators. Half of the latter states had received Canadian military commodities, including Argentina, Chile, Guatemala, Pakistan, Paraguay, the Philippines, and South Korea. Chile, Indonesia, Pakistan, and Syria received Canadian military supplies during 1986.[22]

Clearly Canada does not seek to avoid military exports to human rights violators. Not all countries cited are "persistent" violators; not all material that Canada sold or was willing to sell was repression technology. Nevertheless, the evidence does not suggest scrupulous avoidance.

On 1 March 1984 an amendment to the Notice to Exporters eliminated the guide-line emphasizing human rights questions in the issuing of permits. Previously, "military and military related and strategic goods" destined for "military end-users" were not to "be supplied to regimes considered to be wholly repugnant to Canadian values especially where such equipment could be used against civilians." Joe Clark and other officials in External Affairs have argued that removal of that guide-line did not change departmental practice. They were probably right. The guide-line was ambiguous. It implied prohibition of certain kinds of equipment – repression technology – but was not interpreted that way. Rather it was taken to mean that such equipment should not be exported to places where it was "likely to be" used against civilians (not merely *could* be used). Official statements indicated a requirement to demonstrate the probability of such use before a permit would be denied. In January 1984 an official had explained that "application for permits to export defence equipment that might possibly be used against civilians are carefully scrutinized and would be rejected *if it appeared that such a use were probable.*"[23]

The phrase "wholly repugnant to Canadian values" is not easily defined and was never invoked. Noting that "it has not been necessary to designate any country with this characterization," a departmental letter explained that Chile had not been designated and that Canada was "prepared to continue normal relations" with that country. The issue was not "normal relations" but provision of military goods. Apparently one could invoke a guide-line directed at military exports only if one were prepared to interrupt overall relations – prohibiting military exports required forbidding all exports. The point of the guide-line was, of course, that while one may be able to justify trade with a country that has values wholly repugnant to one's own, there can be no justification in providing military equipment. The latter carries a political message – of support.

Despite removal of the guide-line, Joe Clark insisted in 1985 that its principle still applied: "When permit applications for military exports to countries with poor human rights records are being reviewed, the principle issue is whether there is a risk that the goods will be used against the civilian population."[25] Following an internal departmental review, a new guide-line was set in September 1986: no permits for countries "whose governments have a persistent record of serious violations of the human rights of their citizens, unless it can be demonstrated that there is no reasonable risk that the goods might be used against the civilian populations." Application, however, is not straightforward.

Canada does not maintain a list of human rights violators to which military sales are automatically prohibited. On the basis of recent interpretations, sales to violators seem acceptable in many circumstances. There is, for example, an assumed right to self-defence for *all* countries. A permit to export surveillance equipment to Chile in 1984 was justified by the "need, indeed the right, of the recognized government of Chile to protect its borders and coastal waters from illegal penetration."[26] It was argued that such equipment was not related to repressive practices.

The type of equipment involved also makes a difference. Where weapons have been used against civilians, it is considered acceptable and within the guide-lines to sell equipment that clearly could not be used against civilians. For example, one could sell sonabuoys to the Chilean navy. But "the issuance of a permit to export military rifle and howitzer repair parts to the Chilean army was refused in 1983 on the grounds that these goods could be used against the civilian population."[27] Repression technology does appear more closely controlled, even though there, too, the principle is narrowly applied. "Body armour and flak suits" for bomb disposal units would assist the Chilean military, not only in legitimate national defence but also against insurgents and political dissidents. The department's interpretation, however, was that these were protective items that did not threaten civilians. This is, of course, technically correct, but to an adversary a shield is offensive: it permits the wearer to enter the fray more aggressively.

CONCLUSIONS

The Canadian government does not view military exports as an instrument to encourage greater recognition of and respect for basic rights in the international community. Military exports are used, instead, to enhance domestic prosperity. The control system was developed as a watchdog to minimize the extent to which commercial pursuits undermine concerns about human rights. As a result, military exports are regulated through a negative power (a system of vetos) rather than as positive initiatives on behalf of human rights. Military sales are a positive initiative intended to advance domestic prosperity.

The confluence of political forces in Canada tends to encourage bold initiatives in support of economic objectives and to discourage anything that might inhibit economic objectives. These tendencies are reflected in Canada's regulation of military exports, revealing gradual movement toward less stringent guide-lines and use of discretionary power to increase exports and reduce political impediments to them.

In general, then, export guide-lines seem ineffective in limiting Canadian military exports. Canadian materiel goes directly and regularly to human rights violators and/or countries involved in hostilities. The most effective constraints are probably the Third World recession and the relatively limited range of military wares available from Canada.

CHAPTER TWELVE

"America's Backyard": Central America

FRANCES ARBOUR

Unlike the Caribbean, with which Canada has long-standing commercial, financial, and historical ties, Canada's interests in Central America are of recent origin. Only in the last few decades has Canada forged links with that region through trade, investment, and aid. Nonetheless, Central America has now eclipsed the Caribbean in terms of foreign policy concern, largely because of its human rights situation, with violations among the most brutal and extensive in the world.

In 1982, a Canadian parliamentary sub-committee recommended that Central America be designated a "priority region" in foreign policy and that human rights criteria be accorded greater weight in relations with the area.[1] Similar conclusions were drawn in the June 1986 report of the Special Joint Committee (of the Senate and the House of Commons) on Canada's International Relations; the committee received more submissions on Central America than on any other single subject and was impressed by the growth of public support for a human rights dimension in Canadian foreign policy.[2] These reviews recognized that the economic, social, and political crises of Central America threaten the peace and stability of North and South America and therefore Canada's own security interests; human rights criteria had become essential in a foreign policy that seeks to promote socioeconomic development and peace, and violations of rights and extreme inequality seemed at the root of the potential revolutions next door.

The other neighbour next door – the United States – is the geopolitical reality that links Canada and Central America. American historian Walter LaFeber has documented how "as the dominant power in the area for a century, the United States bears considerable responsibility for the conditions that burst into revolution."[3] Every US intervention in the hemisphere in the twentieth century has occurred in the Central American/Caribbean region. Each has been justified as necessary to protect and advance US commercial and strategic interests. The interests of Latin American sovereignty, peace, and justice have never been foremost. The Reagan administration seems bent on recycling America's interventionist history. The president has repeatedly said that he views Central America as a front line in the East-West conflict: other dominoes, other Cubas, could topple and send a tidal wave of refugees across the Rio Grande to swamp the United States. The administration feels that the battle lines must be drawn there – by invading Grenada, by militarizing the isthmus, by orchestrating attacks on Nicaragua, and by supporting the counter-insurgency war in El Salvador.

The United States does have legitimate security interests in Central America, as Canadian governments, both Liberal and Conservative, have recognized. On occasion Canada has opposed US policy – in its relations with Cuba since the early 1960s and, more recently, with Nicaragua. In other situations, however, Canadian political leaders and bureaucrats have not differed from their American counterparts in their analysis of regional conflicts. Whether because of direct or indirect American influence, a coincidence of strategic thinking about the region, or other factors, Canada's policy takes into account the policies, practices, and pressures of its foremost ally and commercial partner. How Canada deals with them – the degree to which its policy reflects its own unique interests and values and distinguishes between legitimate and illegitimate US interests in the region – is a measure of the autonomy of its foreign policy and of its ability to ensure that human rights inform that policy.

The Canadian response is also one measure of the efficacy of Canadian policy. If it is to promote distinct interests and values, Canadian foreign policy should become more independent of US policies. There is a difference between real US interests in Central America and those perceived by the current administration. The Reagan administration has reinforced forces responsible for most human rights violations, has created obstacles to authentic development and justice, and has thus jeopardized peace. The region and its people require a major social transformation to satisfy basic needs and to achieve respect for fundamental rights. Such a transformation requires more than mere electoral or leadership change; it must include the participation of all people through popular organizations (trade unions, co-operatives, professional associations, community organizations, churches); it requires dismantling of the apparatus of repression. Only such a transformation can provide effective guarantees for human rights and promote justice and authentic development, the basis for peace and security. This should be the analytical foundation for Canadian policy in Central America.

THE HUMAN RIGHTS CONTEXT

For the past decade, human rights have been grossly and systematically violated in Central America as the region experienced an unprecedented escalation of political conflict. Since 1978, some two million people have been made refugees – including one-fifth of the population of El Salvador – and approximately 200,000 have lost their lives; many more have been wounded and maimed.[4] Of the five nations of Central America, only Costa Rica has largely escaped political killings, although it too is experiencing growing polarization and militarization as it is drawn into the regional conflict. Elsewhere, state security forces, paramilitary units, and élite-or state-related death squads have violated basic rights – access to life and security of the person – through kidnappings, disappearances, extra-judicial executions, massacres, torture, detention without trial, and exile. There has also been a general deterioration of civil, political, social, and economic rights. In the current economic crisis, a great many citizens have no guarantee to the right of subsistence. In 1980, 41.8 per cent of the regional population (or over 8.5 million people) could not satisfy "biological-nutritional requirements." Military conflicts have worsened the economic crisis, leading to severe capital flight. According to the UN Economic Commission for Latin America and the Caribbean (ECLAC/CEPAL), the per capita product descended in 1986 for the eighth year in a row; this signified a 26 per cent contraction with reference to 1978.[5]

The pattern of rights violations is rooted in post-colonial social structures. These nations have vulnerable, agro-export economies dominated by a few élite families ("oligarchies") whose control of land and wealth has grown through most of this century. The peasantry and indigenous peoples have increasingly been deprived of land and converted into a landless labour force for export agricultural production or for urban industries. State structures, which serve the oligarchies' interests, have long been headed by dictators, or fraudulently elected civilians, and have often been dominated by powerful military and police forces which ensured labour discipline and political stability through physical coercion. Recent elections in several countries have not significantly diminished the power of these forces, the extent of their repressive activity, and the degree to which they operate with impunity, irrespective of civilian authorities. These nations depend on US markets, capital, and protection of local élite and US interests. US "gunboat diplomacy," common from 1900 to 1930, has been replaced by financial and technical support for police and military. Such assistance, which expanded notably after the Cuban revolution, has reinforced the traditional military/police structures.[6]

Nonetheless, the region has a deep history of popular rebellion. But in this century most such movements have been brutally crushed by local forces (El Salvador's "matanza" of 1932, in which 30,000 peasants were slaughtered), by US-backed counter-insurgencies (Somoza's campaign against Sandino), or by a US-organized coup d'état (the 1954 overthrow of Arbenz in Guatemala). Despite economic expansion after 1945, increasing concentration of land ownership and continuing maldistribution of the benefits of economic growth led in the 1950s and 1960s to formation of reformist parties, unions, peasant associations, and church organizations demanding social, political, and economic transformation. Local oligarchies, supported by US administrations and capital interests, responded with violent repression. State intransigence in the face of demands for democratization drove a widening spectrum of opposition forces into armed struggle. The internal wars that erupted – all of them of a "non-international" character – led to further erosion of basic rights as military and police forces pursued counter-insurgency strategies and allowed full rein to death squads.

The 1979 Nicaraguan revolution was a historic departure. The Somoza dynasty's corruption and brutality fomented an extremely broad-based coalition, led by the Sandinista National Liberation Front (the Frente Sandinista de Liberacion Nacional – FSLN), which overthrew the dictatorship. The pattern of systematic violation of rights was reversed by a popularly supported government. The prestigious human rights organization Americas Watch, six years after the revolution, noted evidence of problems, but "these do not compare in scope or violent character with those common in the years of the Somoza dynasty or those committed by existing governments in neighboring Guatemala and El Salvador."[7] In 1985, it noted growing evidence of abuses by US-backed Contras, whose forces routinely attack civilian populations, forcibly recruit refugees, and kidnap, torture, rape, and murder health workers, teachers, and other government employees.[8]

El Salvador, ruled by the military since 1931, experienced a coup by reform-minded officers in October 1979. Since then, an estimated 60,000 persons (mostly civilians) have died in civil conflict, most killed by military and security forces. The initial civilian-military junta failed to control the armed forces and to implement promised reforms.[9] Some civilians in the government resigned to form the Frente Democratico Revolucionario (FDR), which later entered into alliance with the Frente Farabundo Marti de Liberacion Nacional (FMLN). José Napoleon Duarte, a veteran Christian Democrat politician, joined the junta in December 1980 and became the nation's president, offering a civilian face during 1980–1 when rights violations were at their height. In January 1981 alone, the legal aid office of the Roman Catholic archdiocese of San

Salvador counted some 2,644 murders of civilian non-combatants by armed forces and allied paramilitary groups. For 1981, 13,000 such killings were registered, an extreme of brutality used by some to blunt the impact of more recent statistics.[10]

Elections for the constituent assembly in 1982 failed to improve the situation significantly: the armed forces remained in control; torture, kidnapping, and murder continued. Violations appeared to diminish slightly during local elections and when US aid to El Salvador was under debate in Washington, only to increase thereafter. However, a change in the nature of abuses did occur. While in El Salvador in December 1983, US Vice President George Bush warned political and military leaders that the US Congress would not approve economic and military aid unless they acted to restrain death squad killings. From that time on, the number of such murders did decline; the human rights monitoring office of San Salvador archdiocese recorded 239 death squad killings in the last four months of 1983, compared with 160 killings in the first four months of 1984, which coincided with the presidential election campaign. However, reduction in such killings, often cited by US administration officials, is not an accurate indicator of the level of abuses. Both before and after Bush's warning, most non-combatant deaths were caused not by death squads but by military and police forces.[11] And, in any case, killings and disappearances have remained extremely high by global standards.

Elected in 1984, Duarte has been tolerated by El Salvador's military and right and by the Reagan administration because he has been a legitimate conduit for aid to continue the war against the rebels.[12] As long as military defeat of the rebels was the primary goal of the Salvadoran military and the Reagan administration, the military was able to increase its autonomy, power and privilege, as it was strengthened by massive US aid. Duarte could not bring it under civilian control. "This in turn limited efforts to control human rights abuses, democratize political institutions, or pursue reform."[13] After Duarte's election, US aid and military assistance increased significantly, and military strategy changed. To deprive the FMLN of a population from which to obtain support, the army, bolstered by US military advisers, started extensive aerial bombardment and counter-insurgency in areas controlled or dominated by the guerrillas. A UN study says that these operations "have resulted in numerous civilian victims," although local human rights monitors admit that they have great difficulty conducting research in many areas of the country where abuses occur during military operations.[14]

Meanwhile, Duarte was not able to dismantle the death squads or to improve a situation in which, according to both local and international human rights organizations, 90 per cent of rights violations are committed by military and security forces ostensibly controlled by a civilian government. In 1985 there were 136 death squad killings, 108 assassinations by groups affiliated with the armed forces, 81 disappearances attributed to military or paramilitary forces, 3,721 indiscriminate killings by the army, and another 1,045 people killed by the army in military operations, most believed to be civilians, although rights organizations were unable to conduct on-site investigations.[15] As of mid-1986, Duarte had little control over the army; aerial bombardments against civilians continued; a state of siege was in its sixth year; torture, disappearance, extra-judicial killings, and death squad activity appeared to be on the rise, human rights monitors had once again been persecuted, with nine members of the non-governmental human rights commission abducted, tortured, and detained; and the judiciary had not convicted even one officer for rights abuses.[16]

In Guatemala, political terror is the principal means of governance. Widespread repression aimed ostensibly at a small guerrilla opposition in the 1960s was turned in the 1970s into a pattern of ruthless killing of opposition politicians, unionists, peasant leaders, religious, and professionals. By the late 1970s, centrist politicians and reformers became murder targets. When a guerilla opposition reorganized, military forces went on a rampage in the countryside. Most of the victims were indigenous people. The terror was unimaginable: entire villages razed, their inhabitants slaughtered; children beheaded, babies impaled on bayonets, pregnant women raped and disembowelled.

Despite a death toll exceeding El Salvador's and even the Nicaraguan insurrection, repression in Guatemala has received less international attention, perhaps because the status quo, albeit brutal, has not changed for three decades; perhaps because so much of the legal and revolutionary opposition has been wiped out; perhaps because so many victims were indigenous peoples; perhaps because there has been little direct US involvement.

After 1982, political killings were curtailed in the capital city while the government mounted a "merciless struggle" in the countryside. Military sweeps through rural villages destroyed the real or imagined network of guerrilla support – the model for later operations in El Salvador. This scorched-earth policy substantially reduced the guerrilla threat – at a horrendous cost in human lives – and in early 1986 the military turned over the presidency to a civilian for the first time in 16 years. However, with the military still in control of much of the state apparatus and with élite economic groups opposed to any reform, it is difficult to see how President Vinicio Cerezo, with his current power base, can democratize institutions and restore human rights.

The extent of rights abuses in Honduras is not nearly as great as in El Salvador and Guatemala, but the pattern is similar. Many abuses are linked to land disputes and economic inequality in the country, the poorest in Central America. Violations of fundamental rights – disappearances, kidnappings, torture, extra-judicial executions – became much more serious after 1981, in spite of a transition to civilian rule. National and international rights monitors link the worsening situation to US militarization of the country.[17] Honduras seemed to be being prepared as the future home of the US military in the region. It is the site of virtually permanent US military manoeuvres, drafted into support of the Contra guerrilla war against Nicaragua and El Salvador's battle against its insurgents along the Honduras–El Salvador border. Rights violations are increasingly related to the military's response to internal criticism of its close US alliance, its deepening involvement in regional conflicts, and the militarization of the nation.[18] As the Committee for the Defence of Human Rights in Honduras (CODEH) notes: "There is in Honduras a real problem of institutionalized violence which results from the dominance of military power over civilian institutions."[19]

In summary, except in Nicaragua, there has not been substantial improvement in human rights in Central America in the past decade. The fundamental causes of abuses – deep social, economic, and political inequality and military dominance – have not changed, despite new civilian faces. Recent US policies have reinforced the power and increased the resources of local military and security forces, traditionally the agents responsible for gross human rights violations in Central America.

CANADIAN POLICY

Canadian policy toward Latin America has been characterized by surges of enthusiasm for trade and investment opportunities, tempered by Canadian policy-makers' awareness that, because of US dominance in the area, there is little to be gained by deep entanglements in either US initiatives or Latin problems. Canada's 1970 foreign policy review recognized that the United States screens Canada from Latin America.[20] It also showed that policy-makers believed that the United States and Canada had common interests in and responses to economic relations with Latin America. While differing from US administrations on some issues of hemispheric security, Canadian policy-makers shared US concerns about the potential of Central American revolutions to disturb North American interests.

Until the early 1980s, policy-makers showed a "reluctance to become embroiled in a region dominated by the United States."[21] Canadian commercial involvement in Central America dates back to the first decades of this century, but except for INCO's more recent and disastrous investment in Guatemalan nickel deposits, Canada's investment presence has not been highly visible, nor have trade levels been significant. Since the early 1970s, however, Ottawa has shown interest in expanding economic ties. Canada began development assistance financing for projects in Costa Rica, El Salvador, Guatemala, Honduras, and Nicaragua, and by the early 1980s this program was well established and growing. The first high-level Canadian trade and investment mission to Central America took place in 1979.[22]

But the region gained prominence in Canadian foreign policy only after the 1979 Nicaraguan revolution, as civil conflicts in El Salvador and Guatemala worsened and US military involvement expanded. Human rights concerns were highlighted in media coverage and brought forward to government by Canadian human rights groups and organized public pressure, especially after the assassination in El Salvador of the FDR leadership, Archbishop Romero, and four American church women and several exceptionally brutal massacres in Guatemala in the early 1980s. Public awareness was also generated by the arrival in Canada of several thousand Salvadoran and Guatemalan refugees, bringing many Canadians into direct contact with victims of persecution. Central American conflicts became the focus of mass demonstrations on Parliament Hill and the subject of much attention by a parliamentary sub-committee. Concern for human rights in the region became, according to one secretary of state for external affairs, "a fundamental element in our foreign policy."[23]

Still, a Canadian prime minister has never visited the region, and Canada has only two ambassadors there – in Guatemala (covering Honduras as well) and in Costa Rica (covering Nicaragua, Panama, and El Salvador) – far less than the five embassies maintained by Britain, which would seem to have far less interest in the region and in hemispheric security. Canada is not a member of the Organization of American States (OAS) or of the Inter-American Treaty of Reciprocal Assistance, although it has observer status in both. As a result, Canada does not participate in the OAS's Inter-American Commission on Human Rights; instead, Ottawa's primary multilateral channel for expressing human rights concerns is the UN Commission on Human Rights.

In this context – widening civil conflict, rapidly expanding US military involvement, growing concern among the Canadian public and in Parliament, and limited Canadian diplomatic presence and experience – how has Canada responded, and what rank and role have human rights enjoyed within that policy? I will look first and most thoroughly at El Salvador. It suffers gross human rights abuses and is the object of concerted US policy engagement; human rights assessments are a crucial factor in judging the government's legitimacy and in justifying armed struggle as a response to tyranny. I will then look briefly at Nicaragua, Honduras, and Guatemala.

El Salvador: A Case Study

Although Canadian business involvement in El Salvador dates back to the 1920s and trade and aid links were expanded in the 1970s, Canadian public awareness and government consideration intensified only after 1979.[24] The visit of the president of Mexico to Canada in 1980 significantly raised the profile of El Salvador within the Canadian government and the Department of External Affairs. A joint declaration by Prime Minister Trudeau and President Lopez Portillo[25] set the framework for Canada's approach to El Salvador and the region. The leaders "noted with concern the increasing socio-economic instability in some countries. They expressed the hope that these problems can soon be overcome through the free expression of the will of the people and without foreign interference." The statement clearly recognized "internal" causes for the conflicts, implicitly rejecting "external" explanations – a position soon to become important with the change of US administrations. The Trudeau–Lopez Portillo meeting revealed a new willingness in Ottawa to consider an important Latin American nation's analysis of regional conflicts. Afterward, Canadian officials appeared more open to exploring the positions of the Salvadoran opposition. In July 1980, senior officials from External Affairs held a series of meetings with representatives of the FDR/FMLN, and six months later the minister, Mark MacGuigan, met personally with the organization's leaders.[26]

While Canadian policy had now recognized the socioeconomic roots of violence in El Salvador, it was far less clear about the nation's power structure and, hence, about where to assign responsibility for rights violations. One analysis was brought forward to government by the Inter-Church Committee on Human Rights in Latin America (ICCHRLA), a Canadian group representing the major churches and reflecting the views of an extensive church and human rights network in Latin America. In a major brief in early 1980, the ICCHRLA argued that El Salvador's military and security forces were responsible for the vast majority of rights abuses under the "civilian-military" government. This view was supported by the earlier conclusions of the fact-finding mission of the Inter-American Commission on Human Rights.[27]

In contrast, the Carter administration continued to argue – long after most reformists had resigned – that El Salvador's government was moderate, centrist, and reformist, under attack from extremists on both left and right who were equally responsible for the violence.[28] That perspective was shared by a source that might have been expected to provide the beginning of a "Canadian" analysis – Canada's San José–based regional ambassador, R. Douglas Sirrs. Four months after most reform-minded civilians had left the junta, two months after the assassination of Archbishop Romero, and with repression escalating, Sirrs criticized Canadian rights groups for focusing on violence and blaming the government: "Sometimes they draw the wrong conclusions. There is an inclination perhaps that decides that the junta is responsible for all this when in fact to the best of my knowledge it isn't ... You've got violence being precipitated from the extreme right and the extreme left and they are in the middle of it all, and they are being improperly blamed for it by some groups in Canada."[28] Sirrs would later be uncharacteristically criticized by Canadian parliamentarians for trying to arrange a one-sided, anti-Sandinista agenda for a visit by MPs to Nicaragua. A departmental official later explained Sirrs's insensitivity to human rights: "Our diplomatic representation in Central America was essentially a trade promotion."[30]

In Ottawa, analyses by the Canadian ambassador and the Carter administration must have seemed mutually reinforcing. Throughout 1980, Mark MacGuigan continued to defend US military aid to El Salvador: "The American authorities have assured us that this assistance includes no offensive weapons and is intended to help the Salvadoran government to maintain civil order, in the face of threats from both left and right, with a minimum of lethal force."[31] Canadian rights groups pointed out that MacGuigan's defence of US aid appeared inconsistent with the Mexico-Canada declaration about the socioeconomic roots of the violence and the hopes for a solution without foreign interference. For the Canadian churches, the distinction between offensive weapons and aid to protect civil order was irrelevant in the midst of a civil war: "It may be quite true that the United States does not provide heavy equipment which could be used in an attack against Guatemala or Honduras, but they certainly do give more than enough weapons for the Salvadoran military and para-military to massacre many thousands of defenseless peasants."[32]

While the Canadian government would not publicly criticize growing US military involvement, it expressed its concern for the deteriorating situation. In late November 1980, as FDR leaders were being murdered and mutilated in San Salvador, Ottawa announced suspension of bilateral aid. (Multilateral aid flows would continue.) Reasons for the cut-off were cited variously as rights violations, political instability, and the government's inability to protect Canadian aid workers – Canada clearly did not want to put forward any single reason.[33] In December, Canada voted for a UN resolution condemning rights violations and opposing US military aid to El Salvador. But a few days later, the Canadian delegation dissociated itself from the clause opposing military aid. Correspondence with External Affairs showed that Ottawa was still disposed to accept US assurances that its aid was not "offensive."[34]

After Ronald Reagan's inauguration in January 1981, Canadian policies toward El Salvador entered a distinctive phase, shifting notably toward US government positions. The new administration had determined, in the words of Secretary of State Alexander Haig, to "draw the line" in El Salvador, although no mention had been made previously of this civil war as a crucial part of the East-West conflict.[35] At a meeting in February 1981, Haig presented to MacGuigan the now discredited US "white paper" purporting to show conclusive evidence of external communist subversion in El Salvador.[36] MacGuigan appeared convinced by the "evidence" and, thereafter, in even more direct contradiction of the Mexico-Canada declaration, seemed increasingly disposed to view the conflict as fundamentally an East-West one. He was now prepared to condone US shipment of offensive arms: "I would certainly not condemn any decision the United States takes to send offensive arms [to El Salvador] ... The United States can at least count on our quiet acquiescence."[37]

Throughout 1981, MacGuigan continued to express his concern for the "violence from both the left and the right," an analysis that lacked any objective sense of proportion. He defended US military assistance as balancing other outside involvement, although senior departmental officials would later admit that they had never seen any conclusive evidence of Nicaraguan or Cuban involvement.[38] However, the minister insisted on the accuracy of his own analysis, even launching a quickly aborted attempt to discredit Canadian, especially Catholic, church sources on Central America.[39] MacGuigan thought the Salvadoran government "the most feasible channel through which the people of El Salvador can realize democracy."[40] His speeches and correspondence gave only secondary or minor attention to human rights. They all but ignored continuing government-related rights abuses, highlighting instead confidence in the Duarte régime.[41] It was as if an East-West conflict somehow diminished the need for attention to human rights.

Canada's acceptance of the new US administration's analysis generated harsh criticism from opposition parties, churches, and the media and stimulated a flood of mail to External Affairs. Officials say that from this moment Central America became the greatest regional concern in mail to the government on foreign affairs.[42] Critics attacked both form and substance of Canadian policy, particularly its reluctance to criticize US policy. Whatever disagreements Ottawa may have had with Washington, McGuigan clearly preferred to convey them through quiet diplomacy: "I do not believe that it is Canada's role to mount a public protest against the United States but rather to continue to express its view in appropriate ways as before."[43] As a large demonstration converged on Parliament Hill during Reagan's visit to Ottawa, MacGuigan suggested that Canada mattered little to El Salvador and El Salvador little to Canada: "I don't think anyone should look to us for profound insights on what is happening in El Salvador or what should be done. It is not an area of vital interest to Canada, unlike the Commonwealth Caribbean ... It's not an area in which we feel any commitment to solve the problem."[44]

However, the government did appear to bow to parliamentary and public pressure in the spring of 1981, when it did not seek to block establishment of Canada's Relations with Latin America and the Caribbean, a sub-committee of the Standing Committee on External Affairs and National Defence. It seemed thereby to admit a role for Canada in Central America. The minister's statement to the sub-committee contained only a minimal expression of concern for human rights, but the group's first two reports established a high level of concern and insisted on an "internal causes" analysis of the conflicts in Central America.[45]

The limits of the government's willingness to incorporate human rights concerns in its El Salvador policy were seen also in international forums. In March 1981, at the Geneva meeting of the UN Commission on Human Rights, the Canadian delegation supported a resolution condemning rights violations and endorsing appointment of a special rapporteur for El Salvador. But, again, Canada would not endorse criticism of US positions. At the United Nations in December 1981, Canada abstained on a resolution condemning violations and US military assistance. Several months later, in March 1982, Canada once again abstained on a UN Commission on Human Rights resolution on El Salvador, noting with "deep regret" that it could not support a paragraph calling for "negotiations towards a comprehensive political solution." It was suggested by Canadian church observers that Canada had come under significant US pressure not to support this resolution.[46]

In other international forums, human rights were not considered. Canadian foreign policy had supported the traditional concept (debatable in principle as well as in practice) that technical criteria alone should be the basis for deciding on loans and programs within international financial institutions such as the World Bank, the Inter-American Development Bank, and the International Monetary Fund (IMF). But, in 1981, Canada supported the United States in approving credit for El Salvador from the IMF's Compensatory Finance Facility, despite the refusal of IMF staff to recommend approval. In overriding the staff's technical assessment, the two allies appeared to abandon political neutrality; most western European executive directors of the IMF issued a protest.[47]

Mark MacGuigan decided not to send observers to the March 1982 elections in El Salvador, apparently in response to public pressure and a recommendation from the sub-committee, which was concerned that sending observers would appear to grant respectability to a flawed process. Initially, MacGuigan was pleased with the electoral results: he mistakenly interpreted the victory of right-wing parties as likely to lead to reduction in military power – an illustration of his misconceptions regarding El Salvador's power structure.[48]

The strongly pro-American, anti-communist perspective of the MacGuigan era changed with the cabinet shuffle in the fall of 1982. The new secretary of state for external affairs, Allan MacEachen, was also unwilling to confront Washington on El Salvador, but his response to the sub-committee's final report indicated that he was more willing to criticize US policies toward Nicaragua.[49] The Canadian government implicitly recognized massive rights violations by establishing a special program for Salvadoran and Guatemalan refugees, which has since processed several thousand victims of repression. After three years of abstaining or voting against resolutions on El Salvador within UN bodies, Canada supported a December 1983 resolution in the general assembly albeit with reservations. It also supported subsequent resolutions condemning rights violations in El Salvador – the Liberal government at the UN Human Rights Commission in March 1984 and the Conservatives at the general assembly in December 1984 and 1985.

During MacEachen's tenure as minister, an approach was set for foreign policy in Central America that would continue under his successor, Joe Clark. It represents a fairly consistent expression of several principles: recognition of US security interests in the region; emphasis on the indigenous socioeconomic sources of the crises; support for diplomatic negotiations and political solutions and in particular, from mid-1983 onward, for the Contadora initiative; expressions of concern for human rights violations; and expressions of concern for continuing militarization.

In El Salvador, however, MacEachen, like his predecessor, continued an illusive search for a viable centre. He turned a blind eye to the irregularities of the 1982 electoral process – the inability of the left to participate for fear of assassination, the violent elimination of two newspapers critical of the government, the fraudulent 25 per cent inflation of the vote totals, and the decision of the armed forces and the US embassy to override the election results by installing as president someone who did not take part in the election. MacEachen's policy was based on the belief that the elections had established a legitimate régime: "The Government of El Salvador has its faults, but it is the legitimate government of that country ... It enjoys a broad degree of political support, as demonstrated by the 1982 elections."[50] While condemning rights violations at the United Nations, Canada continued to ignore the fact that elements of the Salvadoran state were primarily responsible for continuing and systematic murder, torture, and kidnapping.

Canada's hastily taken decision to observe the March 1984 presidential elections suffered from a similar myopic view of Salvadoran reality. Its observer team was to examine only technical aspects of the process. It did not ask its observers to examine the widespread civil war, all-pervasive rights violations, lack of participation by some major political groups, and active US involvement in the electoral campaign.[51] However, at the same time as Canada was announcing its decision to observe the election, MacEachen displayed Canada's displeasure with the situation in El Salvador by omitting the country from the itinerary for his April visit to the region. This decision was taken despite strong US pressure on him to balance his visit to Managua with one to San Salvador. MacEachen's visit marked the point of greatest Canadian dissension over US policy, especially concerning its mining of Nicaragua's harbours.[52]

However, after José Napoleon Duarte's election, External Affairs fell into step with Washington's assessment that human rights were significantly improving. Joe Clark, who had become minister in September 1984, pointed to "a much changed situation in El Salvador, including the democratic election of a new government committed to national reconciliation, to investigating human rights abuses and to reforming the judicial system, a decrease in the number of civilian deaths attributed to human rights violations."[53]

External Affairs maintained that it was still concerned about human rights but expressed its belief that the gap between intentions and achievements was narrowing. Clark argued that the "level" of violations was declining and that "in particular there has been a notable decline in right wing death-squad activity." Documents released under the access-to-information law reveal that the department believed that human rights had improved "in a radical way" under Duarte, that charges of civilian deaths resulting from government aerial bombardments were from the "extreme left" and without proof, and the US support and pressure had helped "to improve the military and political situation in a significant way."[54]

This kind of analysis justified the December 1984 announcement of Canada's intention (fulfilled in 1986) to resume bilateral aid to El Salvador. The US administration had encouraged its allies to resume aid. In Canada's case, domestic political factors were also important; right-wing members of Brian Mulroney's cabinet had demanded resumption of aid, arguing in support of the Duarte government and for a balance to Canadian aid to Nicaragua.

Nicaragua

Canada's foreign policy on Nicaragua is distinct from US policy in several respects. Canada recognizes the Sandinistas as a legitimate government and defends Nicaragua's right to self-determination and sovereignty; while the US government has cut off trade and aid, Canadian trade and aid have been maintained; and Canadian ministers have regularly stated their opposition to US military support for the anti-Sandinista guerrillas, although this criticism is usually "balanced" by an equal, though imprecise criticism of perceived outside involvement in El Salvador, an attempt at diplomatic symmetry not reflected in the respective US and Soviet involvement in the region.

Canada also recognizes the improvement in human rights since the overthrow of Somoza. Prime Minister Mulroney, in the context of criticizing outside interference in Central America, has faulted Nicaragua for "grave civil rights violations."[55] But External Affairs officials admit that the human rights situation is not serious; there are violations, but they are not gross or systematic. Canada has raised human rights in discussions with the Nicaraguan government – generally civil and political rights (for example, restrictions on the freedom of the press and policies toward the Miskito Indians) and church-state relations. However, Canada has been notably quiet on an issue of increasing concern to human rights bodies such as Amnesty International and Americas Watch: namely, gross and brutal abuses against the civilian population by the anti-Sandinista guerrillas, the Contras.

Honduras

In the case of Honduras, there is a significant contradiction in Canadian policy. While Canada upholds Nicaragua's right to self-determination and sovereignty in the face of Contra attacks, it has maintained substantial aid to Honduras, even though that country harbours forces that engage the state in acts of intervention against a neighbour. Honduras is violating the principle of non-intervention which, in other instances, has been grounds for suspending Canadian aid.

Human rights monitors in Honduras and groups in Canada and abroad believe that many abuses there are caused by militarization since 1981. Although Canada has criticized the militarization of Central America, it has refrained from direct criticism of the US military build-up in Honduras and of joint US-Honduran military exercises.

Guatemala

Repression in Guatemala has directly touched Canadian lives. A Canadian missionary, Raoul Léger, a lay member of the Foreign Mission Society of Quebec, was killed in violent and still unclarified circumstances in July 1981. In the aftermath, several Canadian diplomats and their families were recalled as efforts to investigate were met with Guatemalan-style threats to officials. All members of the Mission Society also had to leave. In December 1981, a group of Canadian religious sisters also left when they learned that their names were on an army list, presumably a death list.

Canadian officials have apparently raised concerns in bilateral talks more frequently and more energetically in Guatemala than elsewhere in the region. Canada cut aid in 1981 because of the "extreme circumstances" in human rights.[56] Canada has co-sponsored several resolutions in the UN Commission on Human Rights condemning abuses in Guatemala. And it expressed alarm and outrage at the deaths of leaders of the Group of Mutual Support and the murder of a Guatemalan woman on the eve of her departure for Canada in 1985.[57]

However, Canada's expressions of concern have been private. Human rights interest groups have complained that in the UN Commission on Human Rights Canadian officials have tended to weaken condemnations of abuses.[58] While bilateral aid was halted, the Canadian embassy's mission-administered funds grew during the 1980s, even as Canadian missionaries were killed or forced to leave. Canadian rights organizations have been very critical of a 1981 loan by the Export Development Corporation to Guatemala for purchase of Montreal-made locomotives; they have also criticized the granting of an export permit for the sale in 1983 of Twin Otter aircraft to a régime engaged in intensive counter-insurgency.

In 1987, Canada removed its ambassador, thus decreasing the number of Canadian diplomats in the region and diminishing its capacity to monitor politics and human rights at a critical period. On 16 November 1987, it announced resumption of bilateral aid, despite evaluations by international human rights bodies that systematic and gross violations continued, even if numbers had decreased from previously extreme levels. Militarization of rural areas remained intact, and death squad activity appeared to be on the rise.

CANADA'S INADEQUATE RESPONSE

Since 1980, when Central America became important in Canadian foreign policy, the government has often underestimated rights violations in the region, misunderstood human rights issues, and failed to appreciate the changing character of abuses.

More specifically, Canadian secretaries of state for external affairs and departmental officials have failed in four areas. (1) They have failed to recognize the primary responsibility of military and security forces for most violations. Senior officials now admit, with hindsight, that most abuses in El Salvador were caused by the right wing. But then, as now, they were reluctant to admit state complicity or to acknowledge that most violence is carried out by the military, not by the armed opposition.[59] (2) They have wrongly apportioned equal responsibility for violations to both left and right. (3) They have overlooked large numbers of civilians subject to abuses because of counter-insurgency warfare (in Guatemala), a US-funded guerrilla war against a legitimate government (in Nicaragua), and a US-financed and -orchestrated "low-intensity" war (in El Salvador). (4) They have not understood, above all, that civilian politicians cannot bring about reform as long as military and security forces, and the élite classes they represent, maintain their internal basis of political power and US support.

A change in any of these misperceptions would bring Canada into direct conflict with US policy. However, although Canadian perspectives have on occasion coincided with the US administration's, Canadian policy-makers do not think this way necessarily only because of US influence. Rather they identify – from their own political perspectives and reflecting the liberal and centrist character of Canadian society – with the "centre." This may account in part for the uncritical equation of abuses by the right with those by the left, for the belief that an apparently "centrist" government could not be responsible for atrocities, for the penchant to accept Duarte's promises of reform while overlooking lack of evidence of reform, and for failure to understand the power structure of Central American societies. Unfortunately, in Central America the "centre" is precarious and hard to define; democratic processes have rarely been the means for the transfer of power or for social transformation.

Canada's diplomatic personnel in the region seem untrained for human rights monitoring, do not give high priority to human rights, and in some cases are simply predisposed to accept US interpretations of events. Too often – both in the region and in Ottawa – they "go next door" and borrow a cup of information from the US embassy or the State Department. However, External Affairs officials and embassy personnel have not received the resources, systems, or mandate to make human rights monitoring more effective.

Attitudes and institutional shortcomings within the foreign policy process prevent a more clearly articulated and effective human rights policy toward Central America – as does US influence. Canadian policy is clearly distinct from US policy but at times US influence appears to have determined Canadian policy. The Reagan administration's East-West analysis of the Salvadoran conflict gained credibility with Mark MacGuigan, temporarily making Canadian human rights concerns and the traditional "internal causes" analysis subsidiary to American strategic perspectives. Canada's representatives gave questionable support to El Salvador in international financial institutions. A Canadian team was rushed to El Salvador to observe the elections within a very limited framework, and Canadian aid was restored. The Canadian government's responses elsewhere in the region can also be understood within the framework of US influence. There has been no direct criticism of the militarization of Honduras. Canada's relatively stronger stance on Guatemala is not seen as a direct criticism of the United States, whose involvement there is weaker than elsewhere. Only in Nicaragua has Canada directly confronted US policy – and even then with care.

Secretaries of state for external affairs and some departmental officials have regularly asserted that their policies are "Canadian," not dependent on the United States, not unduly influenced by Washington. However, other officials with experience in Central American policy-making admit privately that US opinion of what Canada does is always under consideration and thereby constitutes a significant pressure. It appears to be the only pressure, outside the government and the department, that constrains Canada from adopting a more independent foreign policy and a forthright human rights policy toward Central America. There appears to be very little business lobbying on Central American issues – there are few significant Canadian commercial interests in the region. Other sources of influence endorse a more prominent role for Canada and for human rights in the region; these include two all-party parliamentary reports, numerous briefs by leading human rights groups, and samples of Canadian public opinion.[60]

Political economist Stephen Clarkson has argued that Canada has taken pro-American positions on international issues in the hope of trading these good deeds for US concessions bilaterally. However, he notes, regarding the MacGuigan-Haig period: "There is little evidence that supporting the U.S. in El Salvador earned Canada diplomatic credits for application to bilateral questions."[61]

My examination of Canadian human rights policy in Central America suggests a corollary to Clarkson's analysis: Canadian policy too often succumbs to US points of view to avoid jeopardizing Canada's all-important bilateral relationship with that country. Allan MacEachen admitted that Canada would go only so far in criticizing US policy in Central America. MacEachen said that because US-Canadian relations are the first priority in Canadian foreign policy, there were limits on how boldly and aggressively Canada will criticize the United States: "Well, there's always a judgement as to what is the effectiveness of your views, whether you press them patiently and persistently, or whether you pound the table. But I don't think that it is appropriate for Canada, in the light of its overall interests, to escalate, beyond what we have done, our differences with the United States."[62]

Canadian foreign policy–makers say that they do not want to engage in "hollow gestures" in confronting the US administration, that Canada has clearly spelled out its differences, which have been communicated appropriately, usually in private discussion. This is the hallmark of Canadian "quiet diplomacy." As Joe Clark said on one occasion: "I am far from convinced that Canada's expressing views critical of American policy is going to change that policy." On another occasion he added: "You're going to have more influence on the Americans if you're seen not to be antagonistic."[63] And so many Canadian statements on Central America use phraseology which, rather than criticizing American policy, merely does not condone it. References to US policy are masked by allusions to "third party" intervention or the "interests of external powers," giving the illusion that both superpowers are equally at fault in the regional crisis.[64]

Quiet diplomacy has its merits in some situations. And Canada has repeatedly conveyed its criticism of US policy. However, in Central America, Canada's constant reliance on quiet diplomacy allows American policy-makers to assume that Canada, while not "on side," will not be a thorn in its side at this critical moment for the region. US policy should be recognized for what it is: hostile, aggressive, interventionist, and, in some instances, criminal. It seeks to overthrow a legitimate government in Nicaragua and elsewhere opposes forces favouring the social transformation that the region so badly needs. The character of US policy must be addressed with more than quiet diplomacy. A desperate situation demands a more forthright stance.

Canada can play a more active role in Central America. Central Americans view Canada as a friendly neighbour, a non-imperialist nation that does not share the United States's history of military intervention, political meddling, and economic exploitation. They hope that Canada, as a close friend of the United States, will use its good offices to act as a bridge and mediator. Such views are confirmed by the Contadora Group's warm attitude toward Canadian contributions to its process and by the wish of some of its members that Canada do more. As a leading Latin American diplomat at the United Nations put it: "You have money, bread, and the ear of the United States. Act for peace in Central America."[65]

A starting point for a more forthright human rights policy regarding Central America would be articulation of an autonomous appreciation of Canadian security interests in the hemisphere. Civil wars in the region could become protracted, with the risk of East-West confrontation. In this context, Central America is important to Canada's long-term security interests. Conflict in the region could lead to political instability, erode respect for international law (there and elsewhere), disrupt international commerce, jeopardize Canada's economic interests and the safety of its diplomatic personnel, entrepreneurs, and aid workers, and produce massive new flows of refugees – all of which represent enormous potential costs to Canada. The ICCHRLA has suggested that Canadian policy-makers should not assume that Canada's security interests are the same as those of the United States: "We would argue that long-term Canadian security interests do not coincide with the interventionist policies of the present U.S. administration ... Canadian foreign policy cannot neglect the issue of security – not the security of Latin American nations, not that of the United States, not our own. But Canada and these neighbours must place their hope in a common hemispheric security, in a mutuality of welfare and in an absence of injustice and fear throughout the Americas."[66]

ANALYSIS

This examination of the place of human rights in Canadian foreign policy toward Central America has identified five characteristics or tendencies, which we shall look at in detail.

First, in recent years human rights have gained a higher profile within foreign policy, particularly in relation to Central America, as a result of increased public and parliamentary pressure and greater media attention to grotesque and massive abuses. This higher profile compares favourably with official inattention at the time of the 1973 coup in Chile and the "dirty war" in Argentina.

Second, human rights concerns are susceptible to other political and economic considerations, including Canadian commercial interests, but perhaps the greater influence is that of the US government and its policies toward Central America. Canada's positions regarding causes of the crises, its search for non-military solutions, and its declared concern for human rights all can produce conflict with US foreign policy. To avoid this, Canadian policy has often been muted, and policy positions have not been fully pursued in practice. There has been undue concern that differences with the United States will harm bilateral relations on other matters. There is little evidence that Canadian support leads to diplomatic credits for application to bilateral questions. In fact, undue concern about offending the United States may be counter-productive. Lack of resolve not only compromises Canada's principles and its image abroad but looks like weakness, affecting negotiations in other areas. Nonetheless, the preoccupation continues, as shown in Brian Mulroney's reluctance to raise Canadian differences with American policy in Central America in his May 1986 visit to Washington, despite pressure from a wide range of Canadian public opinion and numerous editorial exhortations.

Canadian policy should address the policies of the US government, which, as the major external actor in Central America, is largely responsible for the region's crises and for undermining socioeconomic reform by supporting military solutions. Canadian policies, if they are to emphasize human rights, must address such policies as Washington's backing for the Nicaraguan Contras.

Consistency would allow Canada to formulate such a forthright policy with independence and integrity. As some officials and observers point out, Canada's consistent recognition of Cuba has protected Canada from undue US pressure; its policy has been accepted. Canada's relations with Central America – and with the United States concerning the latter's policies in that region – should be based on an autonomous assessment of Canada's security interests and should consistently stress human rights, sovereignty, non-intervention, and respect for political pluralism. Prime Minister Trudeau said in St Lucia in 1983: "In our view, states have the right to follow whatever ideological path their peoples decide. When a country chooses a socialist or even a Marxist path, it does not necessarily buy a 'package' which automatically injects it into the Soviet orbit. The internal systems adopted by countries of Latin America and the Caribbean, whatever these systems may be, do not in themselves pose a security threat to this hemisphere."[67]

Third, External Affairs seems unable to define and analyse observance of human rights and thus set priorities. It has stressed massive, systematic violations of basic rights, particularly the right to life, as in Guatemala and El Salvador. But even this analysis is flawed. Canada has underestimated the responsibility of military and security forces and has accused equally forces of left and right, despite massive documentation showing security forces to be the chief culprits. Its analysis has also failed to recognize serious military violations against civilians in contravention of the Geneva Convention of 1949 and the Optional Protocol of 1977. Policy-makers have misunderstood the power structure and the relationship between external aid and military/security forces, which resist reform and continue to exercise power by means of repression.

Where violations are more subtle and not often physically violent, as in Nicaragua (or in Cuba and Guyana in the Caribbean), Canadian policy demotes human rights and emphasizes non-intervention and quiet diplomacy, in deference to commercial and political interests. For this lower level of abuse – civil as opposed to human rights, according to one senior official – Canada has little apparent response. This does not, however, explain differences between Canada's approaches to Nicaragua and to Guyana, for instance, with respect to elections, freedom of the press, and church-state relations. A Canadian official admitted that violations in Nicaragua are not gross, but human rights concerns are raised there far more regularly than with Guyana.

Fourth, at External Affairs information systems and bureaucratic or institutional factors limit the capacity to monitor and analyse violations of human rights. Canada relies heavily on American and other governmental sources of information and analyses and does not take sufficient cognizance of non-governmental human rights bodies – both at home and in Central America.

Reliance on official US sources has exposed the department to manipulation, as in Mark MacGuigan's acceptance of Alexander Haig's now-discredited white paper on El Salvador. Canada has also relied unduly on other narrow criteria – the number of death squad killings and the staging of elections – which the United States promotes as indicators of improvement.[68] In interviews, officials have failed to reveal serious analysis of a broad range of human rights indicators such as torture, arbitrary detention, malfunctioning of the judicial system, and violations within the context of war.

There is not sufficient staff working on human rights concerns. External Affairs has a very small internal structure and a constantly changing staff for assessing human rights. Its mechanisms for gathering independent information on serious abuses, as in El Salvador and Guatemala, are very weak. Recently announced cutbacks in personnel in the embassy in Guatemala undermine the post's ability to gather and report essential data on human rights. There is no regular process for considering, setting priorities on, or even defining human rights concerns. Officials responsible for Central America and the Caribbean admit that they are still "on a learning curve" regarding election observation. Canadian observers have examined only the short-term context and technical aspects of voting and vote counting; it is essential to consider a much broader context, including democratic participation and accountability.

Human rights is a specialized field and requires training. Yet most departmental officers are generalists, and almost none has training in human rights. The specialized positions in the UN division are few, so that staff rotation provides limited experience in human rights. Nor is experience in human rights seen as being as important to career advancement as exposure to commercial and political areas or to aid and immigration.

External Affairs sends few specific reporting instructions to Canadian posts in Central America concerning human rights. This reflects the low priority of human rights and impedes the gathering of information for analysis of abuses. Because there is little or no consistent and systematic review of human rights concerns, some officials and observers note, individual officials can dramatically affect Canadian policy. The work of Ambassador Yvon Beaulne in the UN Commission on Human Rights was mentioned, as was (in a negative vein) the attitude of Ambassador Sirrs in Central America.

Without a structured and coherent human rights policy and mechanisms to introduce such concerns regularly into the process, human rights are left to the initiative of individuals. Pressures of the moment – from public opinion and Parliament – may result in higher or lower priority for human rights. Bureaucratic or institutional limitations within the Central American section lead to policy formulation based on official views and general impressions – often overly influenced by US sources, analyses, and perspectives – rather than on autonomous assessment of all available documentation, including information and analysis from human rights organizations.

Fifth, officials often state that Canada has limited influence and therefore limited ability to respond to human rights violations in Central America. This perception may account for vagueness on such issues. Some foreign policy-makers believe that deliberate vagueness enhances the perception abroad of Canada's limited influence and thus maintains the notion of Canada as mediator in international affairs. It may also explain Canada's tendency to express its human rights concerns and to concentrate its efforts in multilateral forums, such as the UN Commission on Human Rights and the general assembly, rather than using bilateral channels. However, Canada's multilateral efforts have also been hindered by its limited capacity to monitor violations. And its small influence relative to that of other powers does not excuse failure to take effective and appropriate action and to explore the full potential of its influence. The official perception of limited influence conflicts with declarations by the Contadora and other Latin American countries, which see Canada as a potential middle power ally that should use its influence with Washington to reduce regional tensions and to promote a more balanced view of complex regional problems.

RECOMMENDATIONS

Finally, this examination of Canadian human rights policy in Central America, particularly when compared to policy in the Caribbean, leads to several observations and recommendations. In comparing responses to the two areas, one senior diplomat noted that Canada tends to apply higher standards and expectations to the Commonwealth Caribbean because of familiarity with the institutional context: parliaments, a relatively independent judiciary, common language and legal systems. Guyana, for example, is viewed as a "treatable disease, an example of how the system we all know and love has broken down," whereas Central America is plagued by a "Latin disease" much less familiar to Canadian MPs and diplomats. However, this analysis does not take account of the rapid militarization of the Commonwealth Caribbean in the past two and a half years and the resulting changes in institutions and the practice of power. Militarization in Central America has demonstrated the intricate link between strengthening of military structures and increased violations of human rights.

In the Commonwealth Caribbean, Canadian foreign policy–makers can promote a preventive human rights policy rather than the fire-fighting type of policy necessitated by Central America's intractable and violent situation. For example, the recent call for a human rights treaty in the Caribbean Community and Common Market (CARICOM) enforced by a Caribbean judiciary, could benefit from Canadian funding and support. This plan would provide institutional support for human rights and reinforce an independent judiciary and expectations of justice – invaluable where people are increasingly cynical and therefore apathetic about ability to withstand external pressures and irrelevant foreign agendas. Such support would be consistent with Canada's promotion of regional mechanisms, such as the Contadora treaty, for resolving conflict. It would enhance Canada's image internationally as an independent, Western middle power, a country interested in protecting vulnerable Third World countries from the vagaries of superpower conflict and competition.

With respect to Central America, Canada could promote and co-ordinate support from European and Latin middle powers for negotiated solutions. It could encourage support for existing human rights institutions there, as well as in the Caribbean.

Promotion of respect for rights before violations occur should be a specific objective of Canadian policy. To this end, official development assistance should be used as a negative "stick" to admonish serious offenders and as a positive "carrot" to encourage preventive measures and support for regional institutions and organizations that defend these rights. Such "carrots" would include support for independent Central American human rights organizations such as the Salvadoran and Honduran human rights commissions (CDHES and CODEH respectively) and diplomatic and political support for individual human rights monitors, such as the representations made on behalf of jailed Salvadoran human rights workers in the spring of 1986. The urgent need for such international representations was underlined once more in October 1987, when the co-ordinating director of the CDHES, Herbert Anaya Sanabria, was shot dead in the streets of San Salvador by unidentified gunmen.

Human rights are still not a priority in Canadian foreign policy. They are a consideration, to be "factored in" along with other concerns, with no special status except in specific instances created by public pressure.

According to several officials and observers, pressure from churches and other groups has increased the attention paid to human rights in Central America in the past several years. This pressure must be continued and should be expanded beyond demands for official condemnation to include improvements in the "factoring" process and the structures of External Affairs. These demands must include the development of a preventive human rights policy instead of a merely responsive one.

Canada should place higher priority on human rights in the formulation of foreign policy toward Central America. There is obviously a need for human rights initiatives in the region. There is clear public and parliamentary support for a higher human rights profile. Recently, the Standing Committee on External Affairs and International Trade recommended establishment of mechanisms to condition aid more effectively on broadly defined human rights performance. It shows how human rights would be applied to Canadian foreign policy in a universal, consistent, and transparent manner in accord with international standards and on the basis of objective reporting.[69] Such initiatives would enhance Canada's status internationally. They would also support the security interests of Canada and all its hemispheric neighbours. But if it is to take human rights seriously in Central America, Canada must be prepared to condemn abuses immediately, directly, clearly, and publicly. Diplomatic and political initiatives and financial support must become clearer and stronger. More concerted action will send a clear Canadian message to those elements in Central America that increasingly see force and/or manipulation as viable means of protecting their minority interests. It is an urgent task. As ICCHRIA stated in a 1984 brief to the Canadian ambassador to the UN Commission on Human Rights: "The question is not one of having done something, but whether we have done enough, and whether what we have done has been done with sufficient 'directness' and 'dispatch'. Death squads do not wait for permission. Genocide cannot be stopped by resolutions alone."[70]

CHAPTER THIRTEEN

The Polish Case

STEFANIA SZLEK MILLER

Given the respective political systems and alliances of Poland and Canada, the latter's response to the declaration of a state of war in Poland on 13 December 1981 is entangled in broader East-West issues which include divergent interpretations of human rights. Although Canada and other Western countries can be accused of ulterior motives in focusing on alleged human rights violations in Poland while ignoring persistent and gross violations in other regions, the response to the Polish case was justified on principles fundamental to Canadian society. Certain social forces in Poland were defending these principles in opposition to their government. International pressure from countries such as Canada served to reinforce the efforts of reform groups and may have moderated the repressive measures with which the Polish authorities sought to suppress internal opposition. The Polish case, moreover, contributed to international recognition of what Canadians consider fundamental freedoms and of the review process of international organs concerned with human rights.

The first section of this paper will examine events leading to the imposition of martial law in Poland and the measures imposed under that and subsequent acts. The issue of the human rights involved will be addressed with reference to investigations and reports of the UN Commission on Human Rights and the International Labour Organization (ILO). The second section will focus on Canada's response to the situation and its position with respect to the United States and other countries of the North Atlantic Treaty Organization (NATO) and to the international investigations. The third will examine the Polish case in relation to broader issues, including the relationship of human rights to other strategic interests (and whether the former should take precedence over the latter in dealing with the Soviet bloc), the role of alliances in Canada's foreign policy, and the use of economic instruments in influencing foreign governments. In the concluding section, the concept of basic rights will be assessed in relation to human rights violations in the Soviet bloc.

THE POLISH SITUATION

Workers' strikes in August 1980 and subsequent recognition of the trade union Solidarity set in motion the possibility of peaceful revolutionary change of the Polish communist system.[1] At issue was the attempt to reconcile societal demands for civil liberties, including the right to form independent trade unions and other autonomous associations, with the communist ideological and constitutional provisions giving the Polish United Workers' Party (PUWP) a leading role in developing socialism. This type of provision constitutes one of the basic features of a communist system based on the Soviet model and justifies the communist party's de facto monopoly of the power to determine and, indirectly, to enforce socialist policy and order through state organs. Within this system, mass organizations such as trade unions are subsidiaries of the ruling party. The party also assumes direct responsibility for economic policies, and party-controlled state organs direct the operation of industrial enterprises.

The workers' demands for autonomous trade union organizations with the right to collective bargaining logically led to demands for civil liberties in general, that is, freedom of association, assembly, and the press and freedom of conscience and belief. The emphasis on the latter pair reflects widespread opposition to the official state ideology of Marxism-Leninism and the inherently discriminatory nature of its application in a predominantly Roman Catholic society. The strength of the Roman Catholic church in Poland is based on the fact that most Poles are Catholic, and church leaders, while urging caution and peaceful means, supported societal demands for state recognition of basic freedoms.[2] At its height, Solidarity could boast a membership of 10 million out of a labour force of 14 million, and pressure for reform infected all sectors of society, including the PUWP.[3]

Significantly, societal demands for civil liberties were justified by reference to international conventions and agreements pertaining to human rights, such as the ILO conventions concerning freedom of association and collective bargaining. International norms and agreements reinforced internal reform movements and their demands that the government respect principles that it had agreed to and defended in international forums.[4] The extensive external media coverage and support that Solidarity received exerted pressure on the Polish authorities to justify its position with reference to international standards. At the same time, the ruling party had to reconcile societal demands for human rights with its own power and ideological interests as well as those of its allies in the Warsaw Treaty Organization (WTO). Soviet-led intervention was a real possibility throughout the Solidarity period, as demonstrated by the Soviet bloc's hostile reaction to events in Poland and by the military manoeuvres of the WTO.

The inherent difficulty of resolving the internal and external pressures was aggravated by the country's grave economic situation and foreign debt commitments. Solidarity's First Congress Programme of October 1981 offered a plan for restructuring Polish social, economic, and political life, based on the principles of democracy, self-government, and the full range of human rights.[5] This program was unacceptable to the ruling party, and on 13 December 1981 martial law was imposed, trade union leaders were interned, and Solidarity was suspended.

The régime justified its emergency measures on the basis of state security and human rights. In the notification to the United Nations under article 4 of the International Covenant on Civil and Political Rights, the Polish government claimed that martial law was necessary "to divert the exceptionally serious danger threatening the nation and the state, as well as to create conditions for an effective protection of Poland's sovereignty and independence."[6] The government thus considered its actions to be justified, to avert civil war and possible external intervention. It suggested that the latter threat was from members of NATO, especially the United States, which wished to exploit the Polish situation for their own political interests and to destabilize East-West détente.[7] It also implied, however, that had it not imposed martial law its socialist allies, led by the Soviet Union, would have intervened, paralleling the suppression of Czechoslovak reform in 1968.

Polish officials also stressed the legality of the measures adopted. They insisted that the situation was within the domestic jurisdiction of the state and strongly opposed international investigations or inquiries into alleged human rights violations in Poland. In his address before the 37th session of the UN general assembly, the Polish foreign minister, Stefan Olszowski, maintained: "For the price of the provisional application of the extraordinary measures Poland avoided a civil war. We ourselves know how high a price it is but it is not the highest price, a mass scale loss of the basic human right – the right to live."[8]

The efficient manner in which the "state of war" was implemented indicates that plans for the emergency measures had been worked out well in advance of 13 December. Internment of potential resistance leaders, including most high-ranking Solidarity officials, and suspension of civil liberties, including freedom of association, as well as subsequent acts, such as the October 1982 trade union law, which outlawed Solidarity and set the basis for state-controlled trade unions,[9] reimposed the régime's interpretation of socialist order. By the end of 1982, certain emergency measures were lifted, and on 22 July 1983 martial law formally ended, and a general amnesty was granted to most of those interned.

Prior to the lifting of martial law, article 33 of the Polish constitution was amended on 20 July 1983 to include a "state of emergency" provision "if the internal security of the State is in jeopardy, or in cases of natural disaster." The Patriotic Movement for National Rebirth, established in the aftermath of martial law, was also included in the revised constitution. Its stated purpose was to unite citizens and associations, "irrespective of their world outlook, on issues concerning the functioning and strengthening of the socialist State" (article 1).[10] This provision was included to legitimize the government's claim of broad social input from Marxists and non-Marxists into the electoral and decision-making process. Constitutional provisions legitimizing the community party's monopoly of power remained unchanged, however, and the extension of emergency provisions to include threats to internal security provided additional legal justification for imposing harsh measures if deemed warranted by the ruling party.

Post–martial law legislative acts also affect human rights. On 28 July 1983 special legal regulations were approved by the Polish parliament (the Sejm) to restrict workers' ability to change employment and to enforce the constitutional provisions of a citizen's duty to work. Restrictions were imposed on academic freedom and the activities of professors and students. The penal code was also amended on 28 July to include up to three years' imprisonment for "whoever participates in a union of which the existence, structure or purpose remains secret from the state organs or which was dissolved or the legalization of which has been refused." In January 1984 a new law approved by the council of ministers defined the role of the press as that of "serving the society and the state."[11]

"Normalization" of the situation in Poland had thus entailed an attempt to re-establish the basic characteristics of the communist system. Aside from its claims pertaining to martial law, the Polish government also maintains that the socialist order since martial law is consistent with human rights as defined by international treaties such as the International Covenant on Civil and Political Rights and ILO conventions pertaining to freedom of association and the right to organize.[12]

Former Solidarity leaders, the underground opposition movement, and human rights activists, such as the Polish Helsinki Watch Committee, disputed, and continue to do so, the Polish government's claims. The government was accused of imposing martial law to reassert its dictatorial power over society. The measures imposed under that action were termed gross violations of human rights involving murder, torture, arbitrary mass arrests, and blackmail. Legislation prior to and after the formal lifting of martial law in 1983 was called illegitimate: it denies fundamental freedoms and civil liberties and violates principles of rule of law and democracy. The Soviet Union and its allies were accused of complicity and intimidation, if not direct intervention, in the repression of human rights in Poland.[13]

In publicizing their case, opponents of martial law appealed to the world to aid Poles in their struggle for human rights as defined internationally. Referring to the same documents, the Polish government argued that its actions were legitimate and safeguarded human rights. The Soviet Union and its allies supported the government's position and its insistence that the situation was within its domestic jurisdiction. The United States rejected these claims and took up the banner of Polish opponents to martial law. It denounced Polish and Soviet governments for violating the human rights of Polish citizens, imposed sanctions against both countries, and sought concerted action from its NATO allies.

Discussions in international bodies reflected similar political and ideological divisions. In the United Nations, Poland accused the United States and other NATO countries of aggression, subversion, and economic blackmail, in contravention of international agreements and the Helsinki accord.[14] The foreign minister, speaking before the general assembly, acknowledged assistance from Poland's allies, particularly the Soviet Union, and other friends: "We reciprocate the understanding and sympathy of the developing countries which can see in our situation a reflection of some of their own problems. In their attitude we can see the expression of reciprocity for numerous proofs of determined commitment of Poland on the side of the struggle against colonialism, neocolonialism and imperialism. We also give due credit to the stances of those western states which did not yield to the [US] pressure and continue normal relations with Poland."[15]

American officials in turn hailed the decision of the UN Commission on Human Rights in March 1982 to express concern over rights violations in Poland and to ask the secretary-general to undertake a study of the situation as "an historic event." "It was the first time in 38 years that the Commission on Human Rights had spoken out on human rights violations in an East European country. It demonstrated that Poland was not an East-West issue, but a matter of worldwide concern."[17] Richard Schifter, US delegate to the commission, explained his country's hope that the commission could exert moral suasion to improve the situation in Poland. He deplored the fact that progress in improving human rights in Poland had ended with imposition of martial law: "It is that giant step backward that caused such deep concern. It was a concern for the people of Poland, but it was also a wider concern; for in our view, open societies are the best guarantors of peace."[17]

The split vote on Poland in the commission (19–13–10; China not participating) indicates that the situation was an East-West issue and that concerns about rights were not universally recognized.[18] The resolution and resulting investigation at least partly balanced UN preoccupation with certain chronic cases, such as South Africa, and its emphasis on economic rights over civil and political ones.[19] The ILO's response to the formal complaint of human rights violations in Poland from workers' delegates from France and Norway is even more significant. Despite Poland's protest and threat to leave the ILO if it undertook the study, the ILO governing body on 27 May 1983 adopted a rarely used procedure to establish a formal commission of inquiry into the Polish case and to publish the commission's report.[20]

The respective 1984 reports of the UN Commission on Human Rights and the ILO present the most balanced, if not completely impartial, assessments of human rights in post-1981 Poland. The commission addressed violations during the 19-month period of martial law and reported that at least five Polish citizens died as a result of clashes. It reported significant progress in the release of political prisoners: as of 18 February 1984, 281 people were still detained, compared to 1,500 on 4 January 1983. It concluded that lifting of martial law and amnesty had "produced conditions favourable to a reconciliation between different sectors of Polish society." While expressing concern about the implications for human rights of laws approved during this period, the report stated that UN investigators were impressed with the "spirit of moderation" of Polish officials.[21]

The commission's figures on the number dead or still detained are said to be too low by sources such as the Polish Helsinki Watch Committee;[22] the ILO report concluded that the death of over 60 trade unionists could be attributed to security forces.[23] It nevertheless appears that restraint was used during the martial law period. It would be difficult to single out Poland, relative to other countries, as a gross and persistent violator of basic rights. The commission did, however, express concern about the measures that replaced martial law and stressed continuation of dialogue to ensure that rights would be respected.[24]

In its report, the ILO concluded that the dissolution of the Solidarity trade union on 8 October 1982 violated freedom of association respecting the right to organize and that the October 1982 trade union act unduly restricted workers' ability to exercise the right to collective bargaining, including the right to strike.[25] The ILO recommended "free and unprejudiced" exchanges of views between government and various workers' representatives (former Solidarity representatives were not specifically named) in order to restore the "harmony and agreement necessary for the resumption of trade union activity based on the standards of the ILO Conventions." Full restoration of civil liberties, as defined by the International Covenant on Civil and Political Rights and the Helsinki Final Act, was essential to economic recovery and "normalisation of the general conditions of life in the country."[26]

Poland's response to the ILO's findings was to give notice of its intent to leave that agency. The issues raised by the two reports appear unresolved. Other than by exerting moral suasion, neither the commission nor the ILO can force a state to rectify its record on human rights. Nor was concerted great-power pressure possible, given East-West division on the Polish case.

CANADA'S RESPONSE

During the reformist period preceding martial law, Canada supported the Polish government's attempts to reconcile societal demands for reforms based on civil liberties and fundamental freedoms and its efforts to deal with these demands and the difficult economic situation amid hostile and menacing signals from its Warsaw-bloc allies.[27] For example, Canada continued credit to finance grain shipments from Canada at a time when Poland was already encountering difficulties with its massive foreign debts (estimated at US $22 billion in 1981). At the request of the Polish government, Canada agreed in 1981 to defer repayments on official credits. Canada and other Western countries, at the NATO ministerial meeting in Brussels on 12 December 1980, expressed concern about possible external intervention in Polish affairs and warned the Soviet Union that such a development would seriously destabilize the international situation and compel NATO reaction. In response to Poles who did not wish to return home because of unstable conditions, Canada adopted special immigration provisions to allow them to remain.

Thus, even before martial law, Canada had anticipated worsening of events in Poland. Throughout this period, moreover, Prime Minister Pierre Trudeau cautioned against any Western actions that might provoke external intervention in Polish affairs. He emphasized consultation among Western allies to forge a united front on the Polish situation so as to avoid the NATO disunity shown in response to the 1979 Soviet invasion of Afghanistan.[28] The US tendency to assert a position on major international issues without prior consultation with allies – but premissed on their support – poses a constant problem for countries like Canada. This was the case with events in Poland.

The Afghan situation exemplified other problems relevant to Poland. Western sanctions against the Soviet Union had failed to change Soviet foreign policy and consequently did not improve human rights in Afghanistan. Canada's 1979 agreement not to take advantage of the American partial embargo on grain shipments to the Soviet Union, moreover, strained Canada's ailing economy and aggravated Canadian-US relations. The Canadian government saw the announcement in October 1980 of a US wheat sale to China as violating a US commitment – not to market surplus American grain in countries traditionally served by Canada and Australia – given in return for support for the US partial embargo against the Soviet Union. On 28 November 1980, Senator Hazen Argue, minister responsible for the Canadian Wheat Board, announced that Canada was not going to continue the Soviet embargo; in 1981, a new long-term grain agreement was signed with that country. Argue stated that both Canada and the Soviet Union had given assurances "that everything possible would be done to fulfil the contract."[29] As L. Cohen has concluded: "The experience with the 1980 grain suspension considerably increased Canadian-American rivalry in approaching economic relations with the USSR, and thereby lessened the potential for Canadian participation in any future cooperative ventures by Western nations to deal with aggressive Soviet international behaviour."[30]

The immediate concern following 13 December 1981 was that the Soviet Union would intervene militarily. Paralleling the position of government officials, the House of Commons on 14 December passed a motion calling on all nations to "refrain from any political or military actions that may in any way interfere with the internal affairs of Poland" and appealing "for peaceful negotiations between the Polish government and the people to end the crisis." The immigration minister, Lloyd Axworthy, announced continuation of special provisions for refugees from Poland and for Polish visitors in Canada who did not wish to return home. Secretary of State for External Affairs Mark MacGuigan informed the House that the government had no plans to impose economic sanctions on Poland. In response to a proposal to send more aid to the Polish people, MacGuigan stressed "that Canada had been one of the largest per capita donors of aid to Poland and that it was not practical to increase donations" until the situation was clarified and distribution of aid addressed.

The most controversial aspect of Canada's initial response was Prime Minister Trudeau's press statements. On 18 December, he repeated the government's concerns about the Polish situation and regretted imposition of martial law. He argued, however, that "if martial law is a way to avoid civil war and Soviet intervention then I cannot say that it is all bad." Trudeau also indicated that he saw no reason to break off Canada's friendship protocol of 1971 with the Soviet Union: such arrangements served "the interests of détente and of maintaining peace in Europe." A few days later, Trudeau expressed sympathy for the Polish government's inability to meet Solidarity's demands in view of the country's bankrupt economy. These views were strongly criticized in the press and at public rallies organized to protest martial law. They were perceived as legitimizing repressive measures and absolving the Soviet Union from its role while blaming the victims of oppression for demanding freedoms and rights that are fundamental to Canadian society.[31]

Canada's cautious initial response, including Trudeau's controversial analysis, was in sharp contrast to Ronald Reagan's strong condemnation of both Poland and the Soviet Union for alleged violations of human rights and his call for other governments to join the United States in imposing economic sanctions against both states. Canada's position paralleled that of other Western countries, most notably West Germany. Like Trudeau, Chancellor Helmut Schmidt was concerned about the destabilizing effect of the Polish crisis on East-West relations and feared that US initiatives might aggravate the situation in Poland. US allies were concerned that the American call for economic sanctions would damage Western economic relations with the Soviet bloc. American opposition to a natural gas pipeline to carry Soviet oil to western Europe was already a point of contention between the United States and its allies; it was to become a major issue in NATO discussion of the Polish crisis.[32]

The joint declaration issued at the meeting of NATO on 11 January 1982 was closer to Canada's position than to the American one. There was general agreement that imposition of martial law was a grave violation of human rights and in contravention of the Helsinki Final Act. Aside from calling on the Soviet Union to respect Poland's sovereignty, however, the NATO countries did not decide on any immediate sanctions. They agreed only to examine possible measures against the Soviet Union and to "consult each other about steps that might be taken to avoid undermining each other's efforts."[33]

The measures adopted against Poland were also restrained. They included suspension of high-level governmental visits and examination of other measures, such as reduction of scientific and technical exchanges or suspension of existing exchanges. The most important economic sanctions were suspension of negotiations on rescheduling Poland's 1982 foreign debt and of new official commercial credits (private banks were to retain liberty of action). Significantly, foodstuffs were excluded from suspension of new credits.[34] Their exclusion reflected humanitarian concerns, the problems over the Soviet grain embargo, and Canada's determination to maintain its trade agreements.

Measures aimed at assisting the people of Poland included: transmission into Poland of news to circumvent the government's curtailment and censorship of its own media; distribution of food, medicine, and other basic humanitarian aid through the Polish church and other non-governmental organizations; and establishment of further special immigration procedures to help Poles abroad who did not wish to return home, with priority for reunification of families.

The NATO declaration called on Polish authorities to lift martial law, free political prisoners, and resume dialogue with the church and Solidarity to resolve the crisis. The assistance measures cited above were to remain in force, subject to stabilization of the situation based on these three criteria. Other sanctions were to be examined in response to further violations of human rights.

Aside from supporting the NATO declaration, Canada adopted several bilateral measures. These included: suspension of Polish-Canadian academic exchanges, which affected merely three fellowships annually, and restrictions on the Polish airline, in order not to undermine US restrictions in American territory. Mark MacGuigan indicated that Canada would support UN initiatives to investigate rights violations in Poland. Canada did not, however, limit Poland's fishing in Canadian waters and was prepared to continue to supply credit for purchases of grain under an existing agreement with Poland. When that agreement expired at the end of 1982, it was not renewed, but for economic reasons: Poland owed more than $1 billion on grain credits received from Canada.[35]

Throughout this period, Canada did not disrupt trade with the Soviet bloc. It joined other Western countries in opposing both US efforts to impose more stringent sanctions against Poland and (in July 1982) extension of the initial US embargo on supplies and technology for construction of the natural gas pipeline to include supplies and technology from foreign subsidiaries of American companies and companies operating under US licences:

The Canadian government joined the European governments on 7 July in strongly protesting the extraterritorial extension of the embargo, calling it an unacceptable infringement of national sovereignty. Though Canada's position against the US policy was more a question of principle than of direct interest, Mr. Trudeau repeatedly warned that the gas pipeline sanctions might create a profound dissention [sic] within the Atlantic alliance, and he suggested that western European governments might now have a greater degree of sympathy and understanding about the purposes of Canada's Foreign Investment Review Agency.[36]

Canada's position was not altered by the October 1982 Polish decree outlawing Solidarity. US-allied tensions eased with Ronald Reagan's announcement on 10 November 1982 that the embargo against the pipeline was lifted. The release of Solidarity leader Lech Walesa from detention on 16 November 1982 evoked a positive response from Canada, in the expectation that his release would improve the situation in Poland. Martial law was formally lifted in July 1983, and a general amnesty was granted to political prisoners a year later. After the amnesty, Canada lifted its sanctions against Poland except on high-level official visits. It maintains that it continues to monitor human rights in Poland and that resumption of full normal relations "depends upon a positive evolution in the situation of human rights and fundamental freedoms in Poland."[37]

Canada (along with most NATO countries) has thus lifted most sanctions, even though the three conditions set out in 1982 have not been met, particularly the one calling for dialogue with the church and with Solidarity. By 1983 it was clear that the Polish government was not prepared to concede on this point. Negotiations with church leaders implied that the latter were not insisting on inclusion of Solidarity in the process of reconciliation.[38] Even underground dissidents were claiming that Western sanctions were not pressuring the government to improve human rights.[39]

From the Canadian government's perspective, no human rights purpose would be served by continuing sanctions. Moreover, the need to deal with Poland's debt to Western countries necessitated re-establishment of normal relations. Canada did not oppose Poland's admission to the International Monetary Fund (IMF); the United States acquiesced only at the end of 1984.[40]

Canada's decision to resume most normal relations was not opposed by domestic public opinion. In fact, from the beginning of the crisis, the Canadian Association of Slavists, the national organization of academics in Soviet and eastern European studies, had argued against cancelling official academic exchanges and had lobbied for reinstatement of exchanges with the Soviet Union. Following the lifting of martial law, the official organs of the large Polish-Canadian community also supported normal relations. In his report to the House of Commons Sub-Committee on Human Rights in Eastern Europe,[41] J. Kaszuba, president of the Canadian Polish Congress, agreed that normal contacts, such as the exchange of Polish and Canadian parliamentarians, should be resumed, "because they do help to get our ideas into Poland." Arguing that Poland is one of the "most advanced states of the so-called Eastern Bloc," Kaszuba noted Poland's extensive involvement in scientific, economic, and other fields of endeavour. He concluded: "We welcome these exchanges. Of course, during the time of imposition of martial law, this was one of the sanctions which, without doing harm to the Polish economy, was a sign that the west rejected this type of brute-force application." Kaszuba also approved resumption of normal economic relations with Poland and support for its application to join the IMF: "Poland ... owes about US $27 billion. This was due to the mismanagement of the funds obtained in the West. The admission of Poland into the International Monetary Fund would provide a certain amount of scrutiny of what Poland is going to do with the money. Had the admission of Poland into the International Monetary Fund happened some 10 years ago, it would probably have helped to provide better control over the funds which were spent in Poland."

Canada's decision to resume relations while continuing to monitor human rights is consistent with the conclusions and recommendations of the 1984 reports of the UN Commission on Human Rights and the ILO. The investigations of the latter revealed that restraint was used by the Polish government during martial law. Both reports expressed concern about post–martial law measures that restricted rights, including the 1982 trade union act. Both exhorted the Polish government to resolve these problems by constructive dialogue and reinstitution of civil liberties. While the ILO report focused on better relations between workers and government and re-establishment of genuine workers' organizations, it did not insist on Solidarity being re-established.

Canada had supported the decisions of the commission and the ILO to investigate the Polish situation and had urged Polish officials to cooperate. It urged Poland not to give notice of its intent to leave the ILO, arguing that all nations, including Canada, have been subject to international scrutiny over alleged violations.[42] As one of the few states that has ratified all the major international agreements on human rights, including the Optional Protocol of the Covenant on Civil and Political Rights, Canada was in a good position to offer such advice. Canada has consistently called for international standards and review processes in order to promote human rights.

HUMAN RIGHTS AND OTHER INTERESTS

In discussing the effects of the Polish case on the furtherance of human rights, several broader issues should be addressed. The first involves the argument that global peace and other national interests should take precedence over human rights. This position was expressed by Pierre Trudeau during the Polish crisis and was also reflected in analyses by some academics, such as Adam Bromke's discussion of the Polish crisis and its international implications.[43] For the purpose of analysis, Trudeau's position will be taken as a point of reference.

In opposing Ronald Reagan's adversarial approach to the Soviet Union and linkage of human rights to strategic interests, such as disarmament, Trudeau argued that maintenance of friendly relations (including economic ones) with the Soviet bloc is essential to national and global interests. In his 16 May 1982 address at Notre Dame University, at the height of US-allied disagreement over appropriate responses, the prime minister argued: "Since the major source of pressure exercised by the Soviets on the global balance of power derives from their military strength, the West should negotiate arms control and disarmament with single-minded determination. The Soviets threaten us militarily; not culturally, not politically and certainly not economically. Consequently, we should not seem to link non-military objectives with disarmament."[44] While stressing that other issues such as human rights are important, Trudeau argued that the primary concern is global peace and that this requires communication between the two superpowers and their allies. At a press conference on 10 June 1982, during a NATO summit meeting, he again emphasized his government's opposition to US "linkage" policies and maintained that "countries could use economic relations to influence other countries"[45] – in other words, economic incentives are more influential than sanctions.

That global peace should be a priority of Canada's foreign policy is obvious. Nevertheless, the assumption that one can isolate this priority from human rights considerations is unrealistic. The link is well established, whether one is referring to wartime allied agreements, the Cold War, or détente. After all, the Helsinki Final Act, with its security and human rights provisions, was signed at the height of détente. Soviet and eastern European leaders see peace as a human right that can be achieved in a world governed by communist values. The West in turn has its own perception of what constitutes a good society as a condition for global peace. As Cranford Pratt states: "Human rights have been caught in the propaganda and rhetoric of US:Soviet contention, with the US and its allies affirming the paramountcy of civil and political rights, which they feel are severely denied within the communist countries, and the Soviet Union and its allies championing economic and social rights which they in turn feel are seriously under-acknowledged in capitalist states." These divergent interpretations also carry the risk, as Pratt indicates, that human rights can be used "to demoralize and destabilize a régime for geopolitical and ideological reasons."[46] The most blatant expression of these objectives was Alexander Haig's account of White House meetings to discuss the Polish crisis.[47]

There is thus some validity to the Polish government's charges of moral hypocrisy and political expediency in Western states' avowed concerns about human rights violations in a Soviet-bloc country. The same charges, however, can be and are legitimately levelled at the motives of communist régimes in their concerns about human rights in NATO countries or their allies. The use of propaganda is part of East-West relations and also permeates the rhetoric and policies of Third World and non-aligned countries.

The use of human rights for propaganda purposes does not necessarily prevent furthering of those rights. Polemics place both powerful and weak states on the defensive. Global debate has helped establish international standards that the vast majority of states have agreed to, at least in principle. Further, important normative values are involved, and each state seeks to express, if not further, these values in its foreign policy.

Human rights must obviously be balanced with other important foreign policy objectives, in rhetoric and in practice. Trudeau's controversial statements of December 1981 neglected this rule, making his comments ultimately gratuitous. Poles do not need a Canadian prime minister or Western academics to remind them of geopolitical realities or that it was better to have hard-won liberties, which we in the West take for granted, suppressed by Polish troops than by the Soviet Union. Such efforts by Canada and other states to help prevent Soviet intervention were certainly important but could be distorted in the Soviet bloc as support for the Polish régime's crushing of the reform movement. Régimes with the military power to enforce their will on a population are not prone to be demoralized or destabilized by rhetoric. Victims of state oppression are.

As a member of the Western alliance, Canada cannot avoid becoming involved in matters pertaining to the Soviet bloc. In the Polish case, American initiatives served as a stimulant to address human rights violations; the reactions of allies, including Canada, constrained the bloc leader's attempts to formulate a stronger NATO response. The Polish case thus demonstrates that while alliances influence Canada's foreign policy, Canada also influences its allies. Analysts have argued that dissension within NATO caused more damage to the Western alliance than to the object of censure.[48] With the benefit of hindsight, this argument is difficult to sustain. Canada's position in urging restraint and in opposing American initiatives was shared by other allies; the joint NATO declaration reflected US acquiescence in that position and also affirmed the necessity for consultation within NATO, a practice that Canada has consistently advocated. Even though the United States imposed more stringent sanctions than its allies did, its rhetoric was much stronger than the measures adopted. The Polish crisis did not undermine NATO or harm East-West relations. Resumption of arms control talks reveals that other issues besides human rights impede a successful outcome. The decline in East-West trade during the 1980–5 period cannot be attributed solely to the Polish crisis; the Soviet Union "increased its imports, did not experience a decline in exports, and was able to increase its share of CMEA trade with the West by a substantial margin."[49]

Thus broader strategic and other national interests were involved in defining a Canadian response to Polish events. The use of military means was not considered, for obvious reasons. Even the diplomatic and economic sanctions adopted were restrained, designed to register protest while not aggravating the situation in Poland or imposing even greater hardships on its people.

From the beginning of the Polish crisis, in the summer of 1980, Canada joined other countries in warning the Soviet Union about the negative consequences of intervention. These persistent appeals may have deterred the Soviet Union. At a minimum, they removed the element of surprise so important in Soviet military intervention.[50] That the Soviet Union did not intervene militarily was undoubtedly in the interests of Poland and of East-West relations, and, from Canada's legalistic perspective, it also removed any justification for imposing sanctions against the Soviet Union – a position shared by other Western allies but at variance with initial US policy.

In addition, Western humanitarian aid eased the hardship of the Polish population and bolstered the position of the church. Between 1981 and 1983, Canada contributed about $2 million in humanitarian aid;[51] most was channelled for distribution through the church and other non-governmental agencies.

Canada's economic sanctions were not harsh, and the economic difficulties in eastern Europe were a result of other factors besides reaction to the human rights situation in Poland.[52] The decline in trade between Canada and Poland was a result of economic conditions in Poland and the "decrease in quality and quantity of Polish products,"[53] not sanctions. The 1982 grain agreement with Poland was also not renewed for economic rather than political reasons. The 1982 suspension of negotiations to reschedule Poland's foreign debts was not a sanction, given Poland's economic and political difficulties. Suspension of new credits was a sanction, but reflected the general loss of confidence in the credit reliability of all eastern European creditors.[54]

Canada's reluctance to impose stronger economic sanctions was consistent with the general reorientation of foreign policy initiated in the early 1980s to promote industrial development, trade, and markets. This focus was especially important 1980–2, when the economy was strained by recession. Domestic pressures focused on the economy, especially high unemployment and high interest rates. Thus, despite widespread sympathy for Solidarity and condemnation of martial law and violations of human rights, there is little evidence that Canadians were prepared to sacrifice their economic interests for the possible enhancement of human rights in Poland. Moreover, Canada's experience with economic sanctions over Afghanistan has been instructive, with the sanctions harming Canada's interests and dividing NATO allies while failing to alter Soviet policies. Sanctions can be easily circumvented unless universally applied. Poland was not universally censured for human rights violations, as discussions and voting in the UN Commission on Human Rights demonstrated. Moreover, Canada has economic relations with governments more universally recognized as gross violators.

It would be difficult to prove that stronger sanctions would have better promoted human rights in Poland. Trudeau's argument that the economic instrument is more effective as an incentive than as a sanction implies linkage of that instrument to other objectives. It also implies willingness to impose at least partial economic sanctions, should incentives prove ineffective. Sanctions did indeed place pressure on Polish authorities.

Polish officials maintain that Western economic restrictions considerably hurt the Polish economy. As of mid-1983, damage reportedly amounted to "several billion US dollars, or anywhere between ten and twenty per cent of [Poland's] annual national income."[55] Aside from the United States, Britain, France, and West Germany were singled out as having violated economic agreements with Poland; Canada was not mentioned. The most important restrictions identified were: prohibition of fishing by Poland in US waters; US suspension of most-favoured-nation status and consequent opposition to Poland's admission to the IMF and World Bank; and, most important, the credit blockade and stopping of technology transfers. Poland concluded from these restrictions that it had to increase "labour productivity and raw and intermediate material management" and intensify co-operation with "socialist states, first of all with the Soviet Union, switching over to more advanced and effective forms of socialist economic integration."[56] It also acknowledged, however, that it had to obtain co-operation from Western states to resolve its foreign-debt commitments. Its objective was to reschedule payment of debts "for anywhere between ten and twenty years, a certain grace period, preferential interest and facilitation of new credit operations."[57]

While these claims of damages resulting from sanctions are perhaps exaggerated in order to place the blame for Poland's problems on external factors rather than on the state's mismanagement of the economy and unresolved political problems, they demonstrate the leverage that Western states have in countries like Poland. Given the latter's national traditions and the post-1945 attempts to adapt communism to Polish conditions and values, a process dramatically demonstrated during the 1980–1 reform period,[58] resumption of normal relations with the West following the lifting of martial law was in that country's interest as well as the West's. It was in neither's interest for Poland to become more dependent on the Soviet Union. Resumption of debt negotiations and entry into the IMF serve mutual interests; they also provide the West with opportunities to influence Polish decision-makers.

Recognition by Polish officials that labour productivity and management have to be improved in order to resolve Poland's economic problems is linked to the issue of human rights. The ILO report stressed this linkage in arguing for re-establishment of freedom of association and other civil liberties. This was also the underlying premiss of Solidarity and continues to be the basis for resolving Poland's economic and political problems. As noted above, the Canadian Polish Congress has supported the Canadian government's decision to re-establish normal relations as a means of influencing Polish authorities to reinstitute civil liberties and to adopt a more productive approach to economic problems. Aside from continuing to monitor human rights in Poland and to use diplomatic and economic means to achieve that objective, no other measures that Canada could employ would be more effective.

BASIC RIGHTS AND THE SOVIET BLOC

In concluding that Canada's response to human rights violations in Poland was justified and that the means were appropriate to the intended objectives, I would like to take issue with the major focus of this volume, which is basic rights and the gross and persistent violators of them. In justifying the importance of basic rights and arguing for a Canadian foreign policy based on their furtherance, the editors conclude that continuing concern for other rights would still be legitimate but that priority should be given to basic rights.[59] A similar conclusion is enunciated in the June 1986 report of the Special Joint Committee on Canada's International Relations:

As witnesses testified before the committee, the international promotion of human rights is exposed to a multitude of dangers, not least of which are frivolousness and politicization. On one hand there is the urge to become the scolds of the world, on the other the temptation to pursue political or ideological goals in the guise of human rights. The first requirement in avoiding these dangers is to establish human rights standards.

The committee believes that a basic standard is available to trigger and guide Canadian human rights policy, namely the appearance of a pattern of systematic, gross and continuous violations of basic human rights.[60]

By this "standard" Poland has not been a gross and persistent violator of basic rights. Compared to other cases analysed in this volume,

Polish citizens were not exposed to the mass terror and deprivation inflicted on other societies. This conclusion, however, is based on hindsight. From the August 1980 strikes through the dramatic events that followed, developments in Poland could have precipitated a chain of events that would have resulted in massive loss of life and severe deprivations. The concern about possible direct Soviet intervention reflected this fear. It is the contention of this chapter that the responses of Canada and other countries to events in Poland helped to prevent this latter from happening, while affirming a conception of human rights that reflects what Canadians most value in their liberal-democratic system.

The West's emphasis on civil and political liberties does not exclude economic and social rights; it considers the former essential not only for individual liberty but also in defining the democratic means of deciding economic and social policies. This conception is thus not inconsistent with democratic socialist values, or necessarily just a product of affluent societies. The Soviet and eastern European systems are also relatively affluent compared to most of the world but do not allow for civil and political liberties, as suppression of Solidarity demonstrated in Poland.

In condemning the Polish government for violating rights, Canada also demonstrated its commitment to developing international norms and procedures for scrutinizing violations in international organizations such as the UN Commission on Human Rights and the ILO. The latter's use of a rarely used procedure to investigate the Polish situation and to publish its findings is a major step in developing international procedures for dealing with human rights violations.

That Poland reacted negatively to international censure and gave notice of its intent to leave the ILO does not mean that moral suasion is ineffective in human rights. As indicated, Solidarity and other reform groups referred to international standards, such as ILO conventions, in support of their demands for civil liberties, and critics and dissidents within Poland continue this practice. This pressure forces the Polish government to justify its position with reference to international standards and may continue to make it moderate its policies in order to deflect further international censure. Moral suasion cannot ultimately compel a state to comply, but it can undermine its efforts to win international and domestic legitimacy for actions that violate human rights.

The West can use its concern about human rights in Soviet-bloc countries for ideological or political purposes unrelated to human rights. This is, as noted, inherent in power rivalry between the superpowers and their respective allies. Even if Canada decided to focus on basic rights, as advocated by the editors and the 1986 report of the Special Joint Committee on Canada's International Relations, it would still be involved in this struggle, especially in situations such as the one analysed here.

Nevertheless, less powerful members of the NATO alliance can clearly influence the policies of the bloc leader on human rights. The use of rights issues for propaganda purposes, moreover, may still further genuine human rights, as demonstrated in the Polish case.

It is questionable that a focus on basic rights is less likely to be subject to politicization. Given East-West rivalries, the implied expectation of consensus on protecting basic rights may be as unrealistic as the expectation that the permanent members of the UN security council would agree to use UN provisions to stem aggression and threats to international peace. Relying on majority world opinion, as reflected in the general assembly, does not help to resolve conflicting interpretations of human rights or of gross and persistent violators. While many Canadians might or should press their government to adopt stronger sanctions against the South African régime, in terms advocated by the majority of UN members, would the same apply to the general assembly's position on Israel and the resolution equating Zionism with racism? As demonstrated in the United Nations, concern for human rights can lead to an anti-Western, anti-capitalist, or anti-Zionist stance, just as concern for civil and political rights can be used to fuel an anti-Soviet or anti-radical position. Third World countries have shown that they are no more virtuous than the superpowers and their allies in using human rights as a propaganda tool or in being highly selective in condemning certain violations while ignoring others.

Without denying the need to assist victims of mass terror or deprivation, I see real danger in setting priorities in human rights. The international covenants make human rights inalienable and indivisible. Canada's constitution stresses civil and political rights, in the expectation that they ensure individual liberty and provide the democratic means of defining policies congruent with liberty and a just society. Liberal democracies come closest to translating their ideals into practice in their respective domestic environments and remain open to further economic and social reforms by adhering to civil and political rights. The same conclusion cannot be drawn about the Soviet-style system, as demonstrated by the Polish case. As imperfect as Canada's system is, it is still better than the alternatives. To deny our conception of human rights in our foreign policy would be undesirable and unrealistic.

CHAPTER FOURTEEN

Black Africa and South Africa

RHODA E. HOWARD

In the current debate about Canada's foreign policy toward the South African apartheid régime, the question is often posed: why should Canadians be more concerned with human rights abuses in South Africa than in black Africa, where (it is assumed) the situation is just as bad, if not worse. This chapter will address the question by comparing South Africa with three independent black-ruled African countries, Nigeria, Tanzania, and Uganda. All three are Commonwealth countries with which Canada has close ties and that share with both Canada and South Africa a heritage of British colonial rule. Uganda is chosen because it is a "worst case" of human rights violations in black Africa; neither Nigeria nor Tanzania is a gross violator.

The chapter begins with examination of two propositions defending a greater concern with South African human rights violations than with black African ones: namely, that South Africa is a gross violator, and that Canada has a greater obligation to act on human rights abuses when inaction could leave it open to a charge of complicity. The third section reviews Canada's foreign policy toward Black Africa and South Africa, and the fourth analyses internal and external pressures pushing the Canadian government to a more concerned stance on abuses in South Africa.

GROSS VIOLATORS

In all spheres of human rights, South Africa is a gross and deliberate violator. Nevertheless, it is frequently assumed that non-whites suffer from abrogations of only their political rights and that, especially in economic terms, ethnic Africans are better off in South Africa than in independent black-ruled African countries. It is frequently forgotten that apartheid systematically violates basic aspects of human social life, such as the right to a family, which are generally preserved in black Africa.

With regard to economic rights, the available data do not suggest that blacks in South Africa are better off than Africans elsewhere. This is particularly true of Africans in the bantustans ("homelands"), for which allegedly independent areas the South African government conveniently does not keep statistics. Some basic health indicators tell the tale.

In 1985, the estimated infant mortality rate for blacks in South Africa was 80 per thousand (the rate for whites was 13), while in 1983, the rates in Nigeria, Tanzania, and Uganda were 113, 97, and 108 respectively.[1] However, the South African figures exclude the bantustans, where, by 1980, approximately 54 per cent of South Africa's black population lived on the 13.7 per cent of the nation's land reserved for them.[2] Estimates suggest that in some rural parts of South Africa, 30 to 50 per cent of children die by age five, whereas for Nigeria, Tanzania, and Uganda the figures up to age four were about 13 per cent, 11.5 per cent, and 13 per cent, respectively, in 1983.[3]

Another measure of the overall well-being of a population is numbers of patients per doctor. In 1981 in South Africa, the estimated figures were about 330:1 for whites, 730:1 for Indians, 12,000:1 for coloureds, and 91,000:1 for blacks. In the bantustans, ratios in 1975 ranged from a low of 6,200:1 in Swazi to a high of 213,661:1 in Transkei. By contrast, the figures in 1980 were 12,550:1 in Nigeria, 17,740:1 in Tanzania, and 26,810:1 in Uganda.[4]

Per capita income is also an indicator of economic rights. Per capita income is not necessarily higher for blacks in South Africa than for blacks elsewhere in Africa. In 1980 the South African Institute of Race Relations calculated that per capita income in the bantustans ranged from $154 per annum in Gazankulu to $403 per annum in Bophuthatswana. In 1979, per capita income was $670 in Nigeria, $260 in Tanzania, and $290 in Uganda. Moreover, in 1985 in South Africa, black households had between one-fifth and one-sixth the income of white households.[5]

Thus even a cursory summary of indicators of basic economic rights demonstrates that it is erroneous to assert that, whatever political discrimination they suffer, blacks are better off in South Africa than in independent black Africa. Moreover, South African blacks daily endure institutionalized assaults on their human dignity. South Africa is the only country in the world to have a legal system of racial discrimination (apartheid), which is directed against the approximately 85 per cent of its population that is not white. Blacks have been completely denied the vote, and nine million of them have been "de-citizenized" by expulsion to allegedly independent bantustans or "homelands."[6] To be considered a non-citizen, by virtue of one's race or for any other reason, is an assault on human dignity. But apartheid also denies to non-whites, especially blacks, the most fundamental and valued aspects of human social existence. Under a complex set of rules that have as their object to confine all non–wage-employed Africans to the bantustans, families do not have the right to live together. Minor children, unemployed wives, the aged, the ill, and the disabled are exiled to bantustans. Until very recently, all South Africans were deprived of freedom of choice in personal relations by laws prohibiting sexual relations or marriage among different "races."

Until 1986 free mobility in South Africa was denied to all blacks over the age of 16 by the pass laws, a system of labour regulation and "influx control" designed to keep white areas white. From 1948 to 1981, 12.5 million people were arrested or prosecuted for violations of pass laws; in 1984 alone, a further 238,000 were arrested.[7] Although the government abolished the pass laws in April 1986, it evidently intended to replace them with new forms of influx control based on migratory regulation of bantustan "citizens" combined with requirements that blacks show evidence of appropriate housing in white areas. In September 1987 the government announced that local white neighbourhoods would be allowed (but would certainly not be compelled) to choose to desegregate housing.[8]

How do such conditions compare with those in independent black-ruled states? Since 1971, conditions in Uganda have been extremely severe, as the country suffered, first, the very brutal rule of Idi Amin (1971–9) and, second, the continued civil war under Milton Obote (1980–5) and his successors. Perhaps 500,000 people out of 14 million died. Security of ordinary day-to-day life did not exist during either régime. In this sense, black Ugandans have had no more guarantee of basic human dignity than black South Africans. But Uganda suffered a civil war (which the government takeover by Yoweri Museveni in January 1986 appears to have ended[9]), whereas apartheid is a deliberate state policy imposed in peacetime; moreover, conditions in Uganda are not representative of conditions in black Africa as a whole.

In Nigeria and Tanzania, human dignity is not subject to constant, deliberate assault by the state. There is no institutionalized racial discrimination, there are no pass laws, and families are not routinely separated. The ordinary citizen of these two countries is free to come and go as he or she pleases and to establish a family with confidence that it will remain one. There is one exception to this generalization. In Tanzania, a massive population movement occurred in the mid-1970s, the object of which was to concentrate the rural population in villages. Perhaps 2.5 million people were moved by force.[10] This policy has now been ended. Moreover, it has resulted in better services for ordinary

Tanzanians – by 1980, 40 per cent of villages had running water and health dispensaries and 90 per cent had primary schools.[11] In South Africa, non-white populations are frequently removed from more prosperous to less prosperous areas. There is no attempt to provide adequate schools, clinics, and running water for blacks in the bantustans or in urban slums.

Blacks are still denied all political rights in South Africa, despite recent reforms establishing essentially powerless advisory councils of Indians and coloureds. There is no suffrage for blacks. Freedom of the press is increasingly limited. Some black trade unions have been permitted since the late 1970s, and industrial unrest is frequent, but union leaders are often harassed and arrested,[12] meetings are banned, and workers are charged with being illegal strikers and deported to their "homelands."[13] Any real participation in political activity endangers the individual. Even verbal criticism of apartheid is grounds for imprisonment under complex sabotage and anti-communism laws. The state is permitted to detain its prisoners indefinitely without counsel or any protections of due process. Torture is common, and at least 57 political detainees died in police custody from 1963 to 1983.[14]

Such a complete lack of civil and political rights is not typical of independent black Africa. Uganda is the exception: civil and political liberties were virtually non-existent from 1971 to 1986. The most grotesque and gratuitous physical tortures were commonplace under both the Amin and the second Obote régimes.[15] If a quantitative comparison could be made, it would probably show that Ugandans were worse off during this period than black South Africans. But abuses of political and civil rights arising from a state of civil war and severe disintegration of authority and order are different from those arising from deliberate state policy in peacetime. The question that remains and will now be examined is whether black African states in peacetime routinely deny the vast majority of their citizens the same range of civil and political rights denied blacks in South Africa.

In this connection, Tanzania is certainly vulnerable to criticism. Free trade unions have been banned since the 1960s.[16] The press is not completely state-controlled, but the range of debate permitted is quite narrow. There is universal adult suffrage, but only within a one-party system. Political dissidents can be, and are, imprisoned under a Preventive Detention Act, which, like South Africa's, provides for indefinite detention without trial. Torture, however, is not a feature of the Tanzanian prison system, and the number of political prisoners appears quite low.[17]

In Nigeria, citizens have enjoyed a surprising range of political and civil rights since independence, despite the civil war of 1967–70 and military rule since 1966 (save for a civilian interregnum 1979–83). Relatively free trade unions are permitted, as is a wide-ranging, actively critical press. Even under the military régimes, preventive detention and arbitrary arrest have been used quite sparingly. Nigeria, like Tanzania and unlike South Africa, does not routinely use torture or political murder to preserve the ruling régime.[18]

Thus this brief summary puts the lie to the allegation that whatever the deficiencies of apartheid, blacks are better off in South Africa than elsewhere in Africa. In any case, the comparison ought to be irrelevant. The relevant comparison is among different racial groups in South Africa. It is not normally an excuse for a country that, despite its human rights deficiencies, its citizens are better off than people elsewhere. For example, Western nations would not countenance arguments from the Soviet Union that its citizens are generally better off than people in poor capitalist countries such as Brazil.

That the comparison of South Africa with black Africa is countenanced has to do with more than simply the physical contiguity of the two areas. There is a long-standing racist perception in the Western world that blacks are simply inferior beings, incapable of caring for themselves. Like retarded adults, they are bound to remain perpetual wards of more competent whites, as in South Africa.

One should not assume that all Canadians believe that blacks in South Africa ought to have the entire range of human rights associated with liberal democracies. It is, however, no longer acceptable in Canadian public discourse to acknowledge outright racist views. Therefore spurious comparisons are made with the most disrupted African states to prove that Africans are incapable of governing themselves. Uganda is an example used frequently in the letters columns of Canada's daily newspapers. It is assumed that a majority-ruled South Africa is bound to deteriorate into another Uganda: "What does our government hope for? ... Does it want South Africa to come full circle like Uganda?"[19] Experts testifying in December 1985 before the Special Joint Committee on Canada's International Relations were asked whether Canada might not be practising a double standard. Patrick Crofton, Conservative member for Esquimalt-Saanich, said: "The great majority of governments in Africa are dictatorships ... There has been genocide practised by black Africans against black Africans, yet we do not hear a whole lot about that."[20]

A proper study of the whole continent suggests, however, that if hypothetical statements are to be made about the future of a majority-ruled South Africa, Nigeria is a much better country for comparison than Uganda. Like South Africa, it is rich in resources and has a fairly large class of educated people. Capitalism is relatively well developed. Despite a civil war and the continued existence of three distinct regions with competing economic, ethnic, and religious pressures, Nigeria has held together as a nation-state. In South Africa, ethnic differences among blacks are less salient than in Nigeria, because the process of proletarianization is far more advanced and all blacks are victims of a common régime. Nigeria has not turned into a brutalizing dictatorial country, routinely denying all economic, civil and political rights to its citizens. There is no reason to assume that a free South Africa would develop such a régime either.

Thus one reason for Canadians to focus on human rights abuses in South Africa rather than in black Africa is that South Africa is clearly a gross violator of basic rights. Nigeria and Tanzania are not. If Canada is to include human rights criteria in its foreign policy, then it ought to concentrate on improving rights in countries that are gross violators.

But from 1971 to 1985 gross violations took place in Uganda. What, then, made Uganda a less central target for a Canadian foreign policy influenced by human rights considerations than South Africa? The next section will argue that the difference lies in Canada's possible complicity in countenancing violations in the two countries.

CANADIAN OBLIGATIONS

In a world of almost unceasing human rights violations, the concerned Canadian citizen can easily be overwhelmed. She might well wish that her government would step in to save every life at risk everywhere in the world. Such an approach is, of course, not feasible. The criterion of gross violations of basic rights helps to set priorities. A further criterion is that of Canada's possible complicity in countenancing human rights abuses elsewhere. One should consider where, if anywhere, Canadian policy, by commission or omission, might implicitly condone violations of basic rights.

The philosopher Henry Shue suggests three levels of duties held both by citizens and by nation-states with regard to the safeguarding of others' basic rights. These are: "I. Duties to *avoid* depriving. II. Duties to *protect* from deprivation. III. Duties to *aid* the deprived."[21] This list is not derived from calculations of relative levels of need of those deprived of rights: by the criterion of need, it is obviously worthwhile to donate funds to victims of famine in Ethiopia, even though the famine was a consequence of natural and political events over which Canada had no influence. The list, rather, is derived from a notion of culpability. If Canada, in its foreign policy, is to be concerned with human rights, then at the minimum it should avoid complicity in depriving citizens of other states of their rights. If it can, through influence and pressure on foreign governments, go even further and protect foreign citizens from deprivations that might otherwise occur, so much the better. When all else fails, Canada can also aid those who have lost their rights. But to avoid the charge of hypocrisy, Canada's first obligation is to ensure that it does not itself implicitly condone violations of basic rights.

Canada is not responsible for the violation of human rights in South Africa; it did not initiate apartheid and does not support it. But a case can be made that Canada is "complicitous" insofar as it does not use all possible means at its command to pressure the South African government to reform. This complicity is rooted in Canada's moral and economic relations with South Africa.

Morally, Canada sent South Africa mixed messages until recently. Its criticisms of apartheid were tempered by an implicit acknowledgement of the cousinhood of white settler states with similar (if, in both instances, partial) roots in Britain. But it is precisely because of Canada's historic and communal ties with South Africa that its denunciations of apartheid are important. As Matthews and Pratt have noted: "Human experience reveals that meaningful obligations emerge between peoples that belong to a common community."[22] Words do have power: very few régimes are entirely immune to moral denunciations from their allies. The South African régime is dominated by white men who view themselves as Christians. Whatever the economic basis of apartheid, those who run it have a psychological need to view it as morally legitimate. Insofar as predominantly white and predominantly Christian Canada, then, has not persistently and strongly criticized apartheid since its inception, it bears some responsibility for legitimizing the system.

In a material sense, Canadian complicity with apartheid is reflected in its continuing (though diminishing) economic relations with South Africa. The South African racial hierarchy is based on the use of extremely cheap black labour, which is denied practically all normal wage and social security protections.[23] Many opponents of the régime call for punitive sanctions on the grounds that the most effective pressure is economic. It is argued that insofar as Canada is reluctant to deploy the full range of economic, as well as moral, weapons at its command to persuade South Africa to be more accommodating, it is, by omission if not commission, aiding in the perpetuation of apartheid.

The fact that Canadian corporations and banks are owned by private citizens, not by the government, is not necessarily an excuse to avoid Canada's obligations to South African blacks. Shue argues that "no individual or institution, including corporations, may ignore the universal duty to avoid depriving persons of their basic rights (or) ... thwart actions, including government actions, taken to fulfill any kind of duty correlative to a basic right."[24] From a moral point of view, the Canadian government may require its citizens to give up certain privileges (for example, profits from South African investments) that are obtained by depriving black South Africans of their basic economic rights. The Canadian government would not be requiring its citizens to give up their own rights or to give up valued goods merely to assist those unfortunately deprived of their rights by other people. It would rather be requiring Canadians to give up valued goods derived from complicity in deprivations of the rights of non-Canadians. Shue's view is similar to that adopted by the Canadian churches, which "contend that the actions of the private sector cannot be treated in isolation from government policies and interstate relations." They argue that "the government must resolve any ambivalence that exists between its stated policies – of eliminating apartheid, for example – and the behavior of Canada's domestic institutions abroad." [25]

Thus Canada has an obligation to make human rights violations in South Africa a central concern of its foreign policy in Africa, in order to avoid complicity with the South African government. But complicity is not an issue where black Africa is concerned. Although gross violations of rights occurred in Uganda from 1971 to 1985, these were caused by internal factors to which Canada did not, insofar as they were deliberate state policies, condone. Violations of human rights in Nigeria and Tanzania are not gross and are largely a consequence of historical underdevelopment and the difficulties of forging new nation-states.

The abuses in Uganda after Idi Amin's coup d'état in 1971 were horrendous. This can be seen, for example, not only in the reports of deaths and torture, but in Uganda's declining capacity to supply enough food for its own citizens. In 1982, Ugandan citizens consumed only about 78 per cent of required daily caloric intake, down from 91 per cent in 1977. Primary school enrolment declined from 67 per cent of the relevant age group in 1965 to only 60 per cent in 1982.[26] Any kind-hearted Canadian citizen would wish to see both political and economic rights restored to Uganda. But although Canada did not openly condemn the Amin régime until 1977 and did give some minimal aid to the post-1980 Obote régime, it is difficult to charge Canada with complicity in the gross violations that occurred from 1971 to 1985. The roots of the Ugandan catastrophe lie in the long-standing conflict between the old Buganda empire and other ethnic groups now contained in the new "nation"-state.[27] Neither Amin's nor Obote's régime was assisted by Canadian foreign investment or other economic relations.

Similarly, Canada is not responsible for violation of rights in Nigeria. The major violations have to do with distribution of the national (oil) wealth. By 1982, it was estimated that Nigerian per capita caloric intake was 104 per cent of the daily requirement. Primary school enrolment was up to 98 per cent of the relevant age group, as opposed to 32 per cent in 1965, while the infant mortality rate had declined from 152 in 1965 to 113 in 1983.[28] Despite this progress, Nigerians have not all benefited equally from the oil wealth, and it might well be feasible to arrange social investments differently so as to better use and distribute its profits. But whatever changes in social arrangements do occur will have to be the result of internal debate and pressure. In the absence of deliberate, direct, state-initiated and state-sanctioned policies to deprive the poor of their basic economic rights, as in South Africa, Canada would be ill advised to interfere in Nigerian affairs on a human rights pretext. Canada has no more expertise in how Nigeria – a new, underdeveloped multi-ethnic state – should run its economic affairs than do Nigerians themselves. Nigeria is not a gross violator of human rights.

It might be argued that in the case of Tanzania, Canada is partly responsible for the creation and perpetuation of unfortunate economic policies that have stemmed economic growth in the last 20 years. Between 1961 and 1980, Canada provided $208 million in bilateral aid to Tanzania.[29] Canada's ideological commitment to aiding Tanzania has been strong. Despite Tanzania's use of some internally repressive political measures, Canadians tended to regard it as a non-doctrinaire developing country of social-democratic leanings attractive to the welfare-democratic beliefs of many of Canada's politicians and activist citizens. Nevertheless, with hindsight, it is now well known that Tanzania has made many policy errors in its development programs, which have been heavily supported by foreign aid. Perhaps, then, Canada is responsible for violations of economic rights in Tanzania, insofar as its attempt to aid Tanzanian victims of underdevelopment and poverty may have been ill advised. Perhaps had Canada used a "stick" as well as a "carrot" – if it had, for instance, insisted as a condition of its aid that internal critics of Julius Nyerere's economic policies be given the right to speak out instead of being imprisoned – the policy errors could have been spotted and rectified earlier than they were.

But, as with Nigeria, Canada and Canadians are no more competent to devise appropriate development policies for Tanzania than are the Tanzanians themselves. Tanzania is not a gross violator of economic rights. Despite policy errors in planning and industrialization, substantial progress has been made. Per capita calorie supply in 1982 was 101 per cent of what was necessary; the increase in primary school enrolment was (coincidentally) exactly the same as Nigeria's, that is, from 32 per cent in 1965 to 98 per cent in 1982, and the infant mortality rate declined from 138 in 1965 to 97 in 1983.[30] In economic development, especially as reflected in absolute economic growth, Tanzania may indeed have made many policy errors, some with inadvertent Canadian help. In economic rights, it has made progress. In civil and political rights, despite aberrations from the ideal, it is also not a gross violator.

Insofar as Tanzania is a poor underdeveloped country and Canada has resources available for foreign aid, then Tanzania, like Nigeria and Uganda (now that it is again possible without serious threat to Canadian administrators), is a worthy recipient of that aid. Such aid may help remedy continued violations of human rights. But in relations with black African states, Canada is guided by Shue's third principle: assisting victims of others' (sometimes unintentional) violations of rights. In the case of South Africa, Canada has a stronger obligation to attempt to remedy intentional gross violations of human rights, in order to avoid complicity through its continued moral and economic links with the régime.

A REVIEW OF CANADIAN POLICY

Until very recently, black Africa was of marginal interest to Canada. "Our policies towards Africa were designed not so much to serve the needs of African states as the interests of Canada ... Our interests in Africa were, at least initially, derived in large part from our broader concern to maintain a strong and united alliance with the West ...; from a desire to foster the growth of the Commonwealth; from the necessity to search out markets ... and outlets for Canadian investment; and from a deeply felt need to sustain a favourable image of Canada as a non-racist and forward-looking state."[31] As Canada's foreign aid program grew in the 1960s and 1970s, so also did its interest in anglophone Africa. Under Pierre Trudeau, ties with anglophone Africa through the Commonwealth were increased as useful North-South links, cross-cutting the East-West barriers of the Cold War. At least in its rhetoric, Canada was also influenced by the 1974 UN call for a New International Economic Order that would redistribute some of the world's resources from the rich to the poor nations. Canada's image as a middle power with a benevolent, understanding attitude to the problems of emergent nation-states was strengthened by these Commonwealth links.

Foreign aid became a major tool of Canadian foreign policy in the 1960s.[32] It was used to stimulate Canadian trade with new markets, especially the export of particular goods that Canada specializes in producing, such as transportation and communications equipment. Debates about the appropriate purpose of aid (promoting trade v. "aiding" developing countries) produced a commitment in 1975 to concentrate Canadian aid, giving "priority to the poorest developing countries."[33] This moral commitment, however, was quickly eroded by the worsening economic situation of the mid- to late 1970s.

Foreign policy toward black Africa and elsewhere was not formulated or discussed in an explicit human rights framework in the 1960s and 1970s. Indeed, in response to a 1978 private member's bill to make respect for civil and political rights a condition of foreign aid, the government argued that to impose such conditionality would simply penalize the poor.[34] Economic development, not human rights, was to be the focus of aid. However, the International Covenant on Economic, Social and Cultural Rights (1966) clearly identifies the universal provision of basic needs such as food, shelter, and minimal health and education standards as human rights issues. Thus it could be argued that by focusing on development and especially, in principle, giving priority to the poorest, Canada had an implicit human rights bent in its foreign aid policy. Tanzania has especially benefited from this implicit focus on economic rights.

In contrast to South Africa, which was the object of specific human rights–oriented debate in Canada throughout this period, there were only two instances of public concern about the three countries of black Africa discussed in this chapter.

In 1968 some Canadians pressured the government to donate humanitarian assistance to secessionist Biafra, which was fighting a civil war against the federal forces in Nigeria. At the time, Africa was so marginal to Canadian interests that Trudeau's response to this pressure was reported to be "Where's Biafra?" Indeed, there was no diplomatic or national security reason for Canada to become involved in the Nigerian civil war. Moreover, there were strong reasons for Canada not to give any recognition to the Biafran secessionist régime; such recognition could have bolstered Quebec secessionism, the dominant political issue in Canada at the time.[35] Trudeau's choice was to favour preservation of sovereignty in Nigeria, despite the evidence of mass starvation presented by Biafra's advocates. Canada did not move to place Biafra on the UN agenda,[36] for it expected such a motion to be defeated. Canada did eventually send some aid to Nigeria, but carefully to both sides.[37]

After the coup by Idi Amin in Uganda in 1971, there was also human rights–inspired pressure on the Canadian government regarding its aid policy, but this time to cut off aid. According to one leading commentator, "Ottawa has traditionally been reluctant to cut off aid to repressive regimes, however repugnant their policies, as this could result in the victims being 'doubly penalized'"[38] – victims of political repression would suffer economically as well. In the case of Uganda, however, aid was withdrawn in 1973, when it became evident that political conditions rendered it impossible for Canadian advisers to carry on their work.[39] In 1977, Prime Minister Trudeau helped obtain Commonwealth condemnation of Uganda's human right violations.[40]

In not cutting off aid to Uganda until 1973, and not publicly condemning the Amin régime until 1977, Canada was perhaps weakly complicitous in the gross violations that occurred from 1971 to 1979. Moreover, it appears that Canada was overly sanguine in its support of Milton Obote when he returned to power in 1980. Canada had a representative on the Commonwealth Observers Group, which gave a relatively clean bill of health to the December 1980 elections, even though they were widely reported to have been rigged and violent.[41] Moreover, Canada provided some initial military aid to Uganda in an attempt to assist Obote to stabilize the country, though such aid appears to have been negligible, including a three-person medical team and some financing of medical costs.[42] By 1984, international human rights reports had made it clear that the scale of violations was still massive and gross, and in 1985 Obote was overthrown. Canadian "complicity," however, was largely the result of good will combined with unavoidable early ignorance of the real situation, as opposed to South Africa, where knowledge of the detrimental and gross consequences of apartheid has been available for many years.

In contrast to black Africa, South Africa was a major focus of human rights–oriented discussion in Canada throughout the 1970s and 1980s. Official policy since the early Trudeau years contained much rhetorical criticism of South Africa. The 1970 white paper on foreign policy included social justice in southern Africa as one of its major objectives.[43] However, Canada did not always vote for UN motions criticizing or condemning South Africa. For example, it opposed proposals for a conference on sanctions and for an oil embargo and abstained on proposals to end military and nuclear collaboration. The government contended that it was obliged to oppose or abstain on many such votes because of unacceptable language in them, such as concomitant denunciations of Zionism.[44] After Brian Mulroney became prime minister in 1984, Canada's condemnations of apartheid became much stronger.[45] In October 1985, Mulroney made a forceful speech in the United Nations denouncing apartheid: "Canada is ready, if there are no fundamental changes in South Africa, to invoke total sanctions against that country and its repressive régime ... If there is no progress in the dismantling of *apartheid*, relations with South Africa may have to be severed absolutely."[46]

However, until 1985 Canada took little concrete action. Measures taken during the 1970s were largely symbolic. When the South African government started to set up allegedly independent black "homelands," Canada refused to recognize them.[47] In 1977 it banned the entry of South African athletes into Canada.[48] In 1978 it introduced a voluntary code of conduct, covering such matters as trade union rights and racial equality, for Canadian corporations operating, or owning other corporations, in South Africa.[49] Also in 1978 Canada withdrew its official trade commissioners from South Africa.[50] At the same time, the government-owned Export Development Corporation (EDC) was ordered to cease using its government account to promote exports to South Africa.[51] Finally, the government adhered to the mandatory UN ban on arms trade with South Africa, imposed in 1977.[52]

Between 1977 and 1985 there was much public criticism of these policy initiatives for failing to adhere in practice to the principles enunciated.[53] The code of conduct came under special criticism for including no provision for compulsory reporting and no monitoring agency; for example, only one corporation wrote a report under its provisions in 1981–2. Although trade commissioners had been withdrawn, they were replaced by a South African employee of the Canadian embassy in Pretoria. The EDC continued to use its corporate account to promote trade with South Africa until 1982. Moreover, it was discovered that the Canadian government itself invested in South Africa through its partial or full ownership of Texas Gulf, Connaught Laboratories, and Massey-Ferguson. The latter manufactured equipment such as bulldozers, which could have been used by the South African military and police in their forced removals of blacks, coloureds, and Asians from residential areas that had been designated for whites only.

The Canadian government was also rather lax in enforcing the 1977 UN arms embargo. It was particularly lenient in permitting export of dual-purpose (civilian or military) items; for example, computers to a state-owned steel corporation in 1984. Canada was also criticized for its lack of alacrity in stopping illegal arms exports to South Africa by the Canadian- and American-owned Space Research Corporation in the late 1970s. It took no action against South African legislation that compelled Canadian investors to support the military; for example, Ford South Africa, a subsidiary of Ford of Canada, was obliged to supply military vehicles to the army, store weapons on its premises, and maintain all-white militia units. Finally, Canada approved a $1.07-billion loan application by South Africa to the International Monetary Fund in 1982.[54]

Between 1976 (the date of the Soweto uprisings) and 1985, internal and international pressures on the Canadian government changed. Largely in response to increased internal unrest in South Africa and the greater possibility of guerrilla warfare after the formerly white-ruled "buffer zones" of Angola, Mozambique, and Rhodesia became independent, many critics of apartheid began to call for complete withdrawal by the Western world from the South African economy. These critics included Canada's black African Commonwealth allies. In response to these changes, the Mulroney government introduced in 1985 and 1986 a series of incremental moves designed to reduce Canada's economic links with South Africa. Many of these changes answered the public demand of the preceding ten years that teeth be put into the symbolic measures of the late 1970s. None of these moves responded to calls from some sectors of the concerned Canadian community for a legislated end to Canadian bank loans to, or corporate investments in, South Africa.

In July 1985 the government made compulsory the previously voluntary reporting of Canadian companies' compliance with the 1978 code of conduct. It also made illegal any new contracts for Canada to process uranium from Namibia (a territory illegally occupied by South Africa), banned EDC insurance of exports to South Africa, and restricted exports of computers and electronic equipment. A voluntary ban on the import of the Krugerrand, a gold coin, was also urged. In September 1985 Canada placed an embargo on direct air traffic with South Africa and voluntary bans on new bank loans and crude oil shipments to it. On 12 June 1986, the government announced that it would no longer purchase any South African products and asked private Canadian groups such as the media and tourist agencies to stop promoting travel to South Africa.[55] Considerable public controversy was aroused that summer when External Affairs Secretary Joe Clark criticized Toronto's *Globe and Mail* for printing an advertisement by a South African travel agency promoting "fact-finding tours" for Canadians in South Africa.[56] Further, after the 1986 Commonwealth meeting on South Africa, the government announced a new round of limited sanctions. It banned South African steel and agricultural products and ordered the Canadian Wheat Board to cease selling grain to South Africa.[57]

But the latest round of sanctions was still symbolic and had little economic effect. The call for a voluntary ban on bank loans occurred several months after the banks stopped lending money to South Africa in reaction to political instability there – that is, for commercial reasons.[58] Likewise, the government's purchases from South Africa amounted to less than $1 million a year. The ban on steel satisfied the Canadian steel manufacturers' lobby, while the government continued to permit imports of metal ores – about one-quarter of Canada's imports from South Africa during the first six months of 1986. Indeed, Canadian imports from South Africa were reported to have risen almost 50 per cent from July 1985 to August 1986.[59]

Politically, the new round of sanctions sent a stronger signal to the South African government than previously that Canada would not continue to countenance apartheid. But this signal was weakened by failure to follow through. In December 1986, in reply to recommendations by a special joint committee of the Senate and the House of Commons, the government backtracked on Mulroney's 1985 threat to invoke total sanctions, stating that "a step-by-step approach to the imposition of limited sanctions ... will strike at apartheid without destroying the South African economy on which the blacks depend. It also provides time for concerted action with our allies."[60]

Aside from imposing sanctions against South Africa, the new round of measures of 1985-6 also contained some more positive steps to assist black South Africans. In June 1986, the government announced an additional $2 million to help finance education for young blacks, bringing the annual figure to $8.1 million.[61] It did not, however, provide direct aid to the liberation forces, especially the externally based African National Congress (ANC), perhaps remembering events in 1974. The Trudeau government had proposed humanitarian assistance to liberation forces in southern Africa, to be provided through non-governmental organizations in such a way as to avoid any direct government contact with the liberation movements.[62] But a storm of public protest arose: it was felt that Canadian assistance might free other funds, for example from the Soviet Union, to purchase arms.

It was in 1974, and continued to be in the 1980s, a fundamental principle of Canada's policy toward South Africa that Canada favours a peaceful solution; therefore the government could not and cannot risk accusations that it is financing a guerrilla struggle. Nor, by 1987, had the government recognized the ANC, which was engaging in guerrilla activities against the apartheid régime, as the legitimate representative of the South African people. But during a visit to Africa in January 1987, Brian Mulroney expressed understanding of the ANC's position regarding violence. In August 1987 Joe Clark visited Africa and consulted with ANC officials, and Oliver Tambo, its president, visited Canada. In its official statements to Tambo, the government continued to deplore violence. But in response to African Commonwealth leaders' discussions with Clark, it promised to consider direct "non-lethal" military aid to front-line states (including Mozambique as well as Commonwealth members) suffering from South African military and economic sabotage. This promise evoked public debate similar to that stirred up in 1974.[63]

The new policies of the Mulroney government did not appear to be a result of internal Canadian pressure on the government to show its disapproval of apartheid, though that pressure had certainly increased. Rather, they reflected the changing international situation, especially Canada's Commonwealth alliance with black African states, and a strong feeling that civil war was imminent in South Africa if international economic pressure could not induce substantial reform.

PRESSURES TO INCLUDE HUMAN RIGHTS IN FOREIGN POLICY

By 1987 Canada's human rights–based actions with regard to South Africa still fell far short of the complete economic and political sanctions advocated by activists in South Africa and by many critics in Canada. This could be considered surprising, given the minimal trade with South Africa. In 1985, Canadian imports from that country totalled only $228 million, or 0.02 per cent of total imports; similarly exports to South Africa amounted to $151 million, or 0.013 per cent of total exports. At the end of 1982, Canada had only $200 million worth of investments in South Africa, of which only $44 million was actually controlled in Canada.[64]

Canada's hesitance to invoke stronger economic sanctions reflected the overwhelming importance that generations of Canadian policy-makers have put on promotion of trade. Even if trade with South Africa is negligible, it is deemed important to maintain the principle of free trade and not to set a precedent.[65] Moreover, certain business sectors profit from trade with and investment in South Africa and would resent interference. The Canadian business class powerfully influences the nation's public policy.[66] The importance of the private sector and its heavy reliance on foreign trade make it extremely unlikely that the government will interfere with trade.

Given the government's reluctance to impose complete economic sanctions, despite considerable pressure, the role of Canadian public opinion in formulating policy toward Africa and in (possibly) injecting human rights into it must be considered. Cranford Pratt notes a counter-consensus emerging within the Canadian population that challenges prevailing business/government views of foreign relations. This new view is particularly concerned with issues such as "nuclear disarmament, human rights, international equity, and solidarity with oppressed peoples."[67] Many voluntary organizations, such as Oxfam (Canada) and the Canadian Council for International Cooperation, have joined some churches in pressuring the government for much stronger economic measures against South Africa. But this humanitarian counter-consensus appears to have little influence on the government. Corporate business groups, which maintain expensive, permanent lobbies in Ottawa and, more important, control a great deal of property and employment, have far greater access to government than less wealthy, and frequently less well organized, pressure groups such as churches and development organizations.

Moreover, the government is undoubtedly aware that the counter-consensus groups do not represent the vast majority of Canadians. There still appears to be a significant sector of the Canadian public that harbours racist views; for example, in a 1983 Gallup poll, 21 per cent of respondents said that they disapproved of black-white intermarriage; in a 1981 poll, 12 per cent said that they would cut off all non-white immigration, and 31 per cent would support organizations working to preserve Canada for whites only.[68] Within Canada's democratic framework, people holding racist views are as capable of making their views known to the government as is the counter-consensus group. Awareness of the racist views held by many private citizens permits the government to ignore pressure for sanctions against South Africa, should it so desire. In any case, the majority of Canadians appear unconcerned about South Africa. In a September 1985 Gallup poll, 34 per cent had no awareness of apartheid; of the other 66 per cent, 23 per cent advocated non-interference, 47 per cent supported maintaining relations while urging abandonment of apartheid, and only 26 per cent believed that Canada should sever relations.[69] Clearly the views of the majority of Canadians do not appear to be in accord with those of the counter-consensus on South Africa.

While South Africa is high on the agenda of Canadians interested in foreign policy, black Africa is decidedly less so. Even if one accepts a clear counter-consensus in Canadian society, that section of it interested in black Africa is very small, "too weak in numbers and resources to make a serious impact on the ignorance or apathy of a majority of comfortable Canadians."[70] Moreover, black Africans have no strong refugee or immigrant lobby in Canada, such as exists among eastern Europeans or Latin Americans, that might consistently raise issues of Canadian foreign policy. Mild changes in policy toward black Africa and relatively costless increases in aid can satisfy their weak lobbies.

The weakness of the lobby is not the only reason for far less pressure concerning black Africa than South Africa. The dominant class and the counter-consensus group agree on the broad outlines of foreign policy toward black Africa. Both want increased trade. The dominant class benefits from trade and recognizes the role of foreign aid in trade promotion. Counter-consensus groups want to increase trade and aid for human rights reasons, to provide a market for African goods in Canada and supply black Africa with the aid it needs for development. Eighty per cent of Canadian bilateral aid is "tied" – that is, 80 per cent of the money that Canada grants or lends to Third World countries must be spent in Canada. In the last 15 years, bilateral aid from Canada to East Africa, anglophone West Africa, and francophone West and Central Africa has equalled 77 per cent of the value of Canadian exports to those areas. Except in Nigeria, which purchased significant quantities of Canadian wheat, copper, and asbestos in the 1970s and 1980s without being an aid recipient, Canada would probably have little trade with black Africa without its foreign aid program.[71]

While the counter-consensus group and the business class will disagree over the purpose and conditions – such as tied aid – of trade promotion with black Africa, they both want economic and political links to be strengthened. The two groups disagree over South Africa, however. Any move to reduce political links or economic contact among Canadians and South African whites in order to pressure the South African government to reform or eliminate apartheid also threatens the good relations necessary for Canadian trade and investment. This fact and the relative unimportance of public opinion in determining foreign policy mean that we must explain the small steps against South Africa in the mid-1980s by factors other than public pressure. Among the strongest are Canada's long-standing bilateral and multilateral alliances.

Canada's actions toward South Africa are severely constrained by its links with the United States, which many critics argue is a key international actor perpetuating apartheid. Given Canada's military and economic dependence on the United States, probably no Canadian government would risk American displeasure by actively criticizing US policy toward South Africa. Alliance politics dictate Canadian prudence in any disagreement with the United States over South Africa, whether or not Canadian politicians agree that the Cape of Good Hope is strategic to Western interests or that a majority-ruled South Africa will drift into the Soviet sphere of influence.

With regard to sanctions, Canada has a further fear: divestment could open the door to US interference in Canadian affairs. If Canada were to exercise extraterritorial jurisdiction by legislating withdrawal of Canadian-owned or -registered firms from South Africa, it might become more vulnerable to US extraterritorial jurisdiction over US-owned corporations in Canada.[72] Thus Canadian officials argue that Canada must take care that its relations with the United States are not jeopardized, should Canada move to protect black South Africans from the deprivation of their rights which is made possible partly by US support of the South African government.

Offsetting Canada's fear of risking US displeasure over its actions against South Africa, however, is Canada's long-term interest in maintaining good relations with Commonwealth countries. Canada's trade with black Africa is still infinitesimal. In 1985, exports to Nigeria, Tanzania, and Uganda were $67.4 million, $17.2 million, and $0.6 million respectively; imports $230 million from Nigeria, $3.7 million from Tanzania, and $1.8 million from Uganda.[73] Nevertheless black Africa is valued as a potential long-term export market.

Moreover, Canadian policy-makers value strong Commonwealth ties, based on a shared colonial past and Canada's reputation as a sympathetic middle-level power. They wish particularly to have some influence in the world community separate from their southern ally. In June 1986, the Commonwealth Group of Eminent Persons, seven prominent emissaries to South Africa, advocated increased economic sanctions to force the government to make reforms that might forestall an otherwise inevitable civil war.[74] Black African Commonwealth members supported sanctions. These multilateral pressures, stemming especially from Canada's Commonwealth allies, but responding also to internal changes within South Africa, appear to have had more influence than domestic public opinion on Canada's tightening of the largely symbolic measures of the 1970s and its new sanctions.

Nevertheless Canada's bilateral ties should not be forgotten. Despite the increased calls for economic sanctions in June and July 1986, Margaret Thatcher continued resolutely to oppose them, even in the face of threats from countries such as Zambia that the Commonwealth might break up. In response to Thatcher's position, 32 Commonwealth countries boycotted the 1986 Commonwealth Games in Edinburgh, but Canada attended.[75] The United States, like Canada, very slowly increased pressure on South Africa. Thus Canada's future behaviour as regards South Africa cannot be predicted; its long-term interest in an alliance with the small Commonwealth states has to be balanced against its historic and extremely valuable ties with Britain and, especially, the United States. In 1987, Canada's aim at the Commonwealth Conference was to forestall a possible break-up over South African sanctions.[76]

Meanwhile, largely as a result of internal South African political unrest, divestment, while not an acceptable principle in the world business community, became de facto practice in the mid-1980s. After the upsurge of political activity in South Africa in the summer and fall of 1985, some banks called in unpaid loans to Pretoria ahead of schedule. Moreover, many businesses reduced their investment of their own accord. Five of 22 Canadian companies known to be active in South Africa ended their investments there between July 1985 and May 1986. The declaration of a state of emergency in mid-1986 furthered the trend to disinvestment.[77]

In such a situation, the Canadian government's largely symbolic sanctions lagged far behind action taken in the private sector, albeit for reasons of profit rather than principle. Nevertheless, investment could recommence should the South African government's crackdown on dissidents be successful. By 1987 South Africa had not yet marshalled its full armoury of repressive resources. Its future actions cannot be predicted. Indeed, as it sacrifices what limited international legitimacy it formerly had in the community of white states, it will have fewer moral restraints against large-scale, even more brutal political repression. Widespread political imprisonment could give way to widespread political murder, providing stability for Canadian and other investors through outright state terrorism. It remains to be seen whether, under such circumstances, Prime Minister Mulroney or his successor would act on his threat to invoke total sanctions.

CONCLUSIONS

This chapter has argued that in determining priorities for introducing human rights concerns into its foreign policy, Canada should focus on gross violators. Of the four African countries considered, neither Nigeria nor Tanzania is a gross violator, while both Uganda (until 1985) and South Africa are. Further, this chapter has argued that Canada has a particular obligation to take human rights into consideration in its foreign policy when it can be seen to be or to have been complicitous in gross violations of basic rights. Violations in Nigeria and Tanzania are largely the result of historical and contemporary economic conditions for which Canada is not responsible and which Canada has few, if any, tools to remedy. Similarly Canada is not at all, or at worst only very marginally and unintentionally, complicitous in abuses in Uganda.

By contract, Canada can be accused of complicity in South Africa's gross rights violations through its historic moral and economic links with the apartheid régime. Moreover, Canada can put pressure on the South African government to mend its ways. Canada's moral activities as an international actor and its participation in international economic sanctions could assist internal liberation forces in South Africa.

Human rights should be a central facet in all of Canada's foreign policy, despite the inevitable constraints of trade relations, non-intervention, and alliance politics; human rights should not be merely a residual consideration. Human rights attain a particular saliency in the case of relations with gross violators, especially when past Canadian complicity can be remedied by present actions. Recognizing this, the internal counter-consensus in Canada has focused on South Africa as the African country requiring Canadian attention from a human rights perspective. It remains to be seen whether Canada's actions in the late 1970s and mid-1980s, combined with increased international pressure on, and increased internal unrest in, South Africa will have any effect. Canada may be called on to take much more serious measures in the near future.

CHAPTER FIFTEEN

Conclusion: Questions and Prospects

ROBERT O. MATTHEWS and
CRANFORD PRATT

FURTHER QUESTIONS

The contributors to this volume share a deep concern for human rights and a desire that Canadian foreign policy should actively promote human rights internationally. Nevertheless, there are, as one would surely expect, some significant disagreements within our ranks on important issues. As well, as preparation of the volume proceeded it became clear that several broader issues of interpretation and emphasis not directly addressed by any contributor should be discussed in this volume. As its editors, we shall therefore first reflect in turn on four issues that either are identifiable points of disagreement between contributors or are suggested by previous chapters but not directly discussed therein. That done, we shall draw some conclusions about the place of human rights in Canada's foreign policy and about its future prospects.

How useful is the concept of basic rights?

In chapter 1 we introduced the concept of basic rights. Four rights were identified as basic: rights to subsistence, to freedom from arbitrary arrest and detention without trial, to freedom from torture, and to freedom from extra-judicial execution. These rights, we suggested, borrowing from Henry Shue, were basic: no other rights could be enjoyed if any one of these four was denied. However, we also acknowledged that Canadian foreign policy should promote internationally a broader range of rights than these four. Nevertheless, our introduction suggested by its emphasis, but did not defend in detail, greater stress on basic rights. Indeed, the identification of certain rights as basic implies that they should receive primary attention.

Although few contributors directly address this question, some implicitly disagree with this emphasis on basic rights. Gordon Skilling and

Stefania Miller, writing about human rights in the Soviet Union and eastern Europe, show that in these countries the primary issue is the complete denial of civil and political rights. Miller and Cathal Nolan both want Canadian foreign policy to emphasize civil and political rights, which are central to the Canadian political system and culture. Nolan indeed comments that perhaps they, rather than economic and social rights, are primary.

Canadian foreign policy certainly has been much influenced by Canada's commitment to civil and political rights. Canada understandably and correctly has been predisposed to cordial relations with countries that share this commitment. Canada is unlikely comfortably to have close relations with states which, while they substantially respect basic rights, are nevertheless politically repressive. And yet Canada's relations with a country will not necessarily suffer seriously if that state denies civil and political rights. In some instances, the Canadian government appears to have accepted that these rights may for the moment not be achievable or that their denial calls for no protest or comment. In other instances, other policy objectives have eroded any initial unease caused by civil and political repression, as in close relations with South Africa since 1948 despite apartheid and present relations with South Korea and Indonesia, to name but three examples. Nevertheless, at the least, political and civil repression in a country complicates its relations with Canada and can affect those relations. This is surely true of Canada's relations with communist states and with such oppressive right-wing régimes as Chile's. One suspects that severe political repression complicates otherwise close relations with a number of Commonwealth countries, such as Sri Lanka and Guyana.

The force of these various considerations can be seen by examining Canadian policies toward civil and political rights in the Soviet bloc. Most observers will probably agree that the Soviet Union and most, perhaps all, of the eastern European states are not gross and systematic abusers of basic rights. Nevertheless, their régimes, when consolidating their rule, were for a long period gross violators. They could become so again. Their denial of the whole range of civil and political liberties continues to be particularly severe. They and, at least as important, those whose rights they deny need to be reminded of the strength of Canada's concern about this. Moreover, substantial Canadian communities of immigrants from these countries and descendants of such immigrants remain painfully conscious of the earlier severe abuses and are deeply troubled by continuing total denial of civil and political rights. Moreover, if such structures as the UN Commission on Human Rights are to become more effective – an objective of Canadian foreign policy – then they must be pressed to concern themselves with human rights in those countries. Further, as Stanley Hoffmann has shrewdly argued,[1] in regard to a wide range of human rights, a nation's obligation and ability to influence are greater with states with which it is closely connected, for its motives will be less suspect, its tactical judgments better informed, and its claim to be listened to more easily established. All of this legitimates, indeed requires, a foreign policy toward those countries that goes beyond concern only for respect for basic rights. Canadian foreign policy thus is and should be concerned with a wide range of rights. Nevertheless, in our judgment, the distinction between basic and other rights remains important.

Canada can act with confidence internationally in regard to basic rights. Caution is required when one considers what Canada might do to promote, say, free elections, or equality for women, or adequate health care in other lands. One's judgment may be ethnocentric or take inadequate account of pressing exigencies. Can one be sure that it is reasonable to insist on immediate provision for these other rights? How does one act effectively? Moreover, in dealing with these other rights, Canada might contribute to efforts by foreign governments that use the language of rights to demoralize and destabilize a régime for geopolitical and ideological reasons.

The Special Joint Committee on Canada's International Relations has strongly endorsed the idea of basic rights. It wanted Canada to promote rights without becoming "the scolds of the world" or pursuing "political or ideological goals in the guise of human rights." "The first requirement in avoiding these dangers is to establish human rights standards. The committee believes that a basic standard is available to trigger and guide Canadian human rights policy, namely the appearance of a pattern of systematic gross and continuous violations of basic human rights."[2] The committee quoted a description of these rights very similar to the list we presented in chapter 1.

We conclude with an example that is not at all easy for the argument we are seeking to make but provides a good test. In recent years there has been increased recognition of the importance of political participation. Many people are less inclined now than 20 years ago to see political participation as a "second-generation" social value that will follow the achievement of economic progress by strong but authoritarian governments. People more likely feel that without effective popular participation the benefits of development will not be widely shared and basic rights will not be enjoyed with any security. Yet we hesitate to suggest that emphasis on political participation – particularly open and competitive elections – should be a paramount feature of Canadian foreign policy. In some countries cultural, social, and economic obstacles to meaningful elections are still great, and powerful interests are able to turn elections into a sham. In other countries new but fragile progressive régimes are genuinely threatened by internal forces in receipt of external help. In a few countries participatory techniques have evolved that do not fit Western perceptions but are nevertheless meaningful. In quite a few countries, not so much by deliberate design as because of the weakness of the central authority, there is much de facto local autonomy. Finally, in some parts of the world, in an era of East-West confrontation, emphasis on political liberties can easily feed into an anti-Soviet, international mobilization of opinion that may in fact have little to do with these liberties. We are not terribly comfortable with any of these counter arguments, though we think they have force. We would ourselves always incline to the argument that greater political participation would be beneficial. We would hope for imaginative policies to encourage more democracy in other countries. Nevertheless, we accept that championing freedom from torture, from extra-judicial execution, from detention without trial, and from starvation is far more straightforward than advocacy, say, of early elections or of greater freedom of association and of the press.

These considerations suggest to us a refinement to our argument about basic rights. The reality of politics in many contemporary societies and in many historical eras compels us to admit that the absence of the institutions of constitutional democracy or some alternative institutions of free political participation is not an abuse of human rights equivalent to gross violation of basic rights. Effective functioning institutions of political participation are a blessing and an achievement certainly, but they do seem to be the product of rather special, if hard to define, social, economic, and historical circumstances. However, many in Canada and elsewhere are beginning to regard peaceful and free communication about abuses of power in one's own country as an essential political right. When it is denied, as in eastern Europe, the Soviet Union, and South Africa, Canadians see a profound affront to the self-respect and dignity of those being oppressed. It is not a prerequisite of any other rights in the same immediate sense as are the four rights that we have identified as basic. However, it is clearly a human right of special importance and significance.

Is there a primary threat to human rights globally?

A major disagreement pervades much public discussion of human rights and Canadian foreign policy. It is not much in evidence in this volume, for no author had occasion directly to address it. However, it is so prevalent in public discussion that it should be identified and discussed.

There are two quite different current views of what is the primary threat to human rights in the world today. One view sees the major challenge to human rights globally as emanating from an expansionist international communism that scorns political and civil rights as bourgeois values and is determined to transform societies under its control in accordance with the dictates of its ideology. Communist movements are therefore, from this perspective, a triple threat to human rights. They will deny these rights if they can seize power; they will be sheltered by the Soviet Union, so that once in power their oppression will be very hard to reverse; and they will in turn nurture communist revolutionary régimes in neighbouring states and elsewhere.

The apparent alternative to this view sees as the primary threat to human rights the various socioeconomic and political disorders and inequities that breed intense tensions and repression. These tensions and this repression are multiple in character, and each is the product of different circumstances. Nevertheless, what they often have in common is the determination of an authoritarian régime to suppress profound and widespread popular discontent, sometimes over a denial of equality and adequate autonomy to linguistic, religious, or regional minorities, sometimes in response to enormous class differences embedded in land distribution, in control of the armed forces, and in the domination of capital.

It is easy to see why these two different underlying world views lead to such different perspectives about Canadian foreign policy and human rights. Those influenced by the first will be anxious that Canada's security alliances, determined as they are by a desire to contain Soviet expansionism, and Canadian promotion and protection of rights should be mutually re-enforcing. They will be cautious about criticizing the United States, as its power and leadership are central to the Western alliance. They will be likely to be tolerant of human rights abuses by régimes that at least stand firmly against the international spread of communist influence, and they will be unlikely to support liberation movements against such régimes. They will be at best ambivalent about situations where repression in undeniable but where the major opposition group has looked for Soviet support. They will be forthright in calling for strong Canadian positions in regard to human rights in countries within the Soviet orbit.

Those who operate from the second perspective will regard uncritical policies toward repressive but pro-US régimes as a serious obstacle to progressive change in those countries. They will be more concerned with the repression practiced internally by régimes than with their international stance in regard to US-Soviet rivalries. They will be quicker to criticize authoritarian régimes that sustain severely inequitable social systems and be less likely to be influenced by geopolitical counter-arguments. They will be more ready to accept that history and internal circumstances offer some countries no alternative to their present oppressive rulers save a left-wing, pro-Soviet movement. They will not regard the perpetuation of such régimes in power as preferable to a victory for such movements. They will hope for greater pluralism within the ranks of those régimes and movements that are broadly counted as within the Soviet orbit. Even were that not forthcoming, they would not automatically judge that such régimes ought to be primary targets of a Canadian human rights policy.

There is frequently antagonism between exponents of these two alternative views. They each tend to regard those holding the other view as at best seriously misguided, at worst cynically manipulating the language of human rights for other objectives. This division, moreover, is of major importance in Canadian public life, for exponents of each have powerful constituencies to which they can appeal. Those primarily concerned to contain communism can appeal to major communities of Canadians who are immigrants from, or are descendants of immigrants from, countries under Soviet rule. Those primarily concerned with the social injustices and the authoritarian rule that human rights abuses seem to perpetuate can appeal to the strong liberal and humanitarian components of Canadian political culture and to the institutions that sustain those components.

Some in each camp will be irreconcilable toward those in the other – anti-communists who fear any popular movement and radicals unable to criticize the Soviet Union and its allies. Yet in our judgment the division, though undoubtedly real, is surely artificial. Communist rule is highly repressive, and many highly unjust social systems are kept in place by oppressive right-wing régimes. Those concerned about apartheid in South Africa or about repression in Chile should not be critical of those primarily agitated about oppression in Poland or Cambodia. And similarly those concerned about communist oppression ought not to be impatient with those involved in the struggle for human rights in South Africa. Individuals and groups cannot be universally knowledgeable; their human rights commitments are bound to have particular foci. Our hope is that readers of this volume will be struck by the commonality of the concerns that unite the two views that we have here identified and that frequently are seen as mutually antagonistic.

Should respect for sovereignty constrain attempts to influence violator states?

The international system is decentralized: power and authority reside in its units, or states. These units have the right, though not always the capacity, to impose order, to carry out governmental functions within their territory, and to do so free from outside interference. They jealously guard that independence and actively promote their own interests. The sovereignty or autonomy of the actors in the system in theory precludes intervention in the domestic (or internal) affairs of another. Even the United Nations is prohibited from intervening in "matters which are essentially within the domestic jurisdiction of any state" (article 2[7]).

Nevertheless, many states have signed and ratified international accords on human rights, committing themselves to support human rights and to create supervisory machinery; as a result, one authority has claimed that international human rights law has "penetrated the veil of sovereignty." Despite such claims, the old order of state autonomy has not disappeared. The principle of sovereignty and its flipside, non-intervention, are incorporated in the UN charter and in all regional organizations, while in practice states remain anxious to maintain their autonomy. And there are good reasons why states continue to value sovereignty and non-intervention.[3] As sovereignty ascribes limits to the external behaviour of states in the domestic affairs of others, its observance will in the main reduce the likelihood of international conflict. To entertain the possibility of intervention in one instance may well undermine general adherence to the principle and thus increase the risk of other interventions, weakening the stability of the international system.

Kim Nossal suggests (chapter 3) that respect for sovereignty is particularly strongly felt by Canada's foreign policy-makers. We are similarly persuaded that this is a powerful factor in the Department of External Affairs and helps to explain the marginal consideration of human rights in many foreign policy issues – a theory highlighted by Frances Arbour (chapter 12), Vicky Berry and Allan McChesney (4), Terrence Keenleyside (10), Renate Pratt (9), and Ernie Regehr (11).

This respect for sovereignty need not, however, be an absolute principle. A few states claim that how they treat their own citizens is a matter of domestic jurisdiction and therefore charge that even "scrutiny and censure by other governments constitute intervention."[4] But such states are few and have, as one might expect, flagrantly violated the rights of their citizens. Most states have, since 1945, come to accept the legitimacy of international interest in human rights. This change in traditional state behaviour is reflected in the UN charter, the Universal Declaration of Human Rights, the two UN covenants, and other international conventions (regional and universal). Consequently, how a government treats its citizens – perhaps in commonsensical terms a domestic matter – has become partially internationalized. As one noted authority put it, "Virtually all states are now subject to some international law and obligations as regards at least some human rights of their inhabitants. To that extent their actions in regard to such human rights are, of course, not within their domestic jurisdiction."[5]

While domestic jurisdiction has increasingly been limited, the range of behaviour described as "intervention" has been narrowed. Certainly, no one would now condemn a state for expressing in public critical views about another state's treatment of its citizens. Nor could one label illegal steps that a state might take to modify its relations with other states that openly and consistently violate human rights. Such actions in our view do not constitute intervention but are instead legitimate attempts to influence the policies of other states. Where intervention ends and interference (of influence) begins is not entirely free from debate, but we are inclined to accept the view that intervention involves the "use or threat of force or substantially debilitating economic coercion."[6] And so, as Henkin persuasively argues, "It is not intervention or other improper interference for international organizations to monitor compliance with these (human rights) commitments; or for one party to an agreement to call another to account by peaceful diplomatic means for failure to abide by its commitments; or for one state, if it so desires, to take another's human rights record into account in determining the warmth of their relations, the level of friendliness, trade, aid, or other largesse."[7]

At least in law, then, there are very few options closed to a government that wishes, by an active human rights foreign policy, to influence the behaviour of other states toward their subjects. In certain clearly defined circumstances, a state may even legitimately resort to force or apply substantial economic coercion. And if the UN security council determines that a situation surrounding human rights violations constitutes a threat to international peace and security, it can impose sanctions on the offender. It has, of course, done that in only two instances – the partial (1966) and complete (1968) economic sanctions applied against the white minority régime in Rhodesia and, in 1977, the imposition of an embargo on the sale of arms to South Africa.

Declaratory support for human rights has not always been matched by compliance in practice. Even states with a good human rights record domestically, such as Canada, have been cautious and timid about expending resources and national goodwill to influence human rights policies of other states. We would not explain this caution primarily in terms of a defensible respect for the sovereignty of other states. The real obstacles to a more forceful human rights policy in our view are political and practical. Nothing perhaps makes this clearer than the undeniable evidence in this volume that Canada is much more forthright in condemning the human rights record of another country when that condemnation reinforces other foreign policy objectives. When economic, strategic, or political factors suggest moderation of criticism, Canadian initiatives and statements have been much more constrained.

Can we better explain the varying sensitivity to human rights in Canada's foreign policy?

The argument will be offered that understandably, indeed inevitably, human rights are weighted against other foreign policy considerations, such as security and economic interests. Decisions have to be taken, instance by instance, concerning the relative importance to be assigned to human rights as against other legitimate concerns. In the introduction we argued that Canadians demonstrate their attitude to human rights by how quickly or how reluctantly they stress rights over national advantages of one sort or another.

In many preceding chapters there was evidence of recurrent reluctance by External Affairs to give prominence to human rights. This was not true in every instance. In particular, reluctance could be overcome or moderated if the policy implications of human rights coincided with policies suggested by economic, security, or other factors. However, on balance there appears to have been a persistent bias against attaching much importance to human rights. This bias still needs to be explained.

An important clue is provided by Vicky Berry and Allan McChesney in chapter 4, on the policy-making process. They discerned from their interviews that three central presuppositions very often informed the judgments of foreign service officers: the importance of promoting economic growth, of Canada's role in the various Western security, political, and economic alliances, and of managing successfully US relations. Berry and McChesney suggest that these presuppositions, often unexamined, are deeply ingrained and shape Canadian foreign policy. The force of this observation is attested to in the chapters by Arbour (12), Foster (5), Howard (14), Keenleyside (10), Pratt (9), and Regehr (11).

We agree that ideology probably explains decision-makers' reluctance to attach more importance to human rights. To establish the reasonableness of this hypothesis, we draw on two important schools of analysis, neo-realist and dominant class, often regarded as antipathetic.[9]

Canada is a stable society: the hegemony of its capitalist class is not seriously challenged. No social democratic party has even shared political power in the federal government. There has been neither an alternation of parties in power with different class bases nor long periods in which governmental power has been shared by parties with political roots in different economic classes.[10] In societies such as Canada, with neither sharing nor alternation of power, structural and instrumentalist reasons explain why senior policy-makers will take as one of their primary responsibilities ensuring the health of capitalism in Canada. This is neither a radical nor an ideological proposition – it is almost self-evident. After all, Canadian prosperity and government revenues depend on that system, and the links between government and business are close, intimate, and continuous.

Parallel to this factor is a dynamic that operates in most foreign services. The international community is dominated by sovereign states. The Canadian foreign service sees its professional duty as advancing Canadian interests within an international system in which its counterparts are similarly championing the interests of their states.

Sensitivity to the interests of Canadian capitalism and preoccupation with expanding Canadian prestige, power, and influence internationally are the "natural," the most unquestioned characteristics of the ideology dominant among foreign policy decision-makers. This need not always mean preoccupation with economic and political objectives narrowly and immediately in Canada's interest. In some eras and in some policy issues it has meant championing international institutions that seem to offer effective arenas in which Canada can acquire influence and advance its interests. Nevertheless, these basic features, explained along the lines suggested, offer a persuasive hypothesis as to why proponents of human rights have found it difficult to influence Canadian foreign policy. A full analysis must make reference as well to other factors: pressure from major regional, linguistic, and ethnic communities; effective lobbying by special economic interests; and the input of the prime minister and the secretary of state for external affairs. However, the broad explanatory power of a combined use of dominant class and neo-realist approaches does seem to permit effective integration of much that has been detailed by individual contributors to this volume.

DISCERNIBLE TRENDS

Canada has recently shown in its foreign policy a genuine interest in human rights. This concern, however, is of recent origin. It was not until the mid-1970s that Canada was prepared to assign staff and resources to the task of promoting international respect for human rights. Until then the government had not spoken out with any force on human rights and had even expressed scepticism about including strong human rights provisions in the UN charter and about protection and promotion of specific rights.[11] Even in the case of South Africa, as Nossal points out (chapter 3), Canada only very slowly and grudgingly agreed to pursue the issue of apartheid beyond mere discussion.

Canada's low profile on human rights in the early post-war years can in part be attributed to the "conviction that there were too many honest and diverse national interpretations to permit much useful initiative by an international organ."[12] But, as Kaplansky (chapter 7) as well as Berry and McChesney (chapter 4) underscore, reluctance to speak out or to assume responsibility was related also to Canada's federal constitution. While casting Canada's vote in favour of the Universal Declaration of Human Rights, Lester B. Pearson made it clear that Canada did "not intend to invade ... the rights of the provinces under our federal constitution."[13] This concern continued to plague Canadian officials as they participated in the drafting of binding covenants on human rights.

Ironically, during federal-provincial negotiations on ratification of the two international covenants, Ottawa and, in particular, the Department of External Affairs became more committed to human rights. These internal discussions happily coincided with external developments that together gave human rights a more prominent place on the international agenda. The first was adoption of the Helsinki Final Act in 1975 and the first follow-up conference in Belgrade in 1978, where, as Gordon Skilling notes (chapter 8), review of human rights violations in member states became an "integral component of the Helsinki process." The Carter administration had already adopted a vigorous policy on human rights and thus given them greater visibility and respectability as a legitimate foreign policy goal. Finally, Canada's growing interest coincided with particularly gross and systematic violations of basic rights: the Khmer Rouge's reign of terror in Kampuchea, Idi Amin's rule in Uganda, and increasing repression by the racist régime in South Africa.

As a consequence of these events and persistent domestic pressure by churches and other non-governmental organizations, Canada became more concerned about human rights in the mid- to late 1970s. This shift was reflected in speeches by external affairs secretaries and, as Nossal demonstrates, in Canada's changing position on the meaning of domestic jurisdiction. How a state treated its own citizens could no longer be considered solely its own concern, as Canada had tended to argue. Canada began to concede that states had the right, even obligation, to promote and encourage respect for human rights in other countries. It thus gave a higher profile to human rights in its foreign policy from the mid-1970s on. However, this concern has been narrow in focus and largely subordinated to other foreign policy objectives.

The scope of Canadian human rights activities is limited, first, by the emphasis on political and civil rights. Given Canada's historical development and political culture, this should come as no surprise. Manzer demonstrates (chapter 2) that Canada's concept of human rights is rooted in its British constitutional heritage, a legacy that lends "primacy to political and civil rights" and erects "a formidable barrier to the adoption of a more inclusive concept of human rights that would embrace basic social rights." While Canadian officials have often argued that the two sets of rights are "intertwined" and of equal legal significance, they are usually quick to note a difference: whereas political and civil rights are easily defined in legal terms, "readily justiciable" and "absolute, inalienable and easily realizable," economic and social rights can be achieved only over time and through positive governmental action. Canada has argued on occasion that these different rights reinforce one another; yet officials usually emphasize that attainment of economic and social rights is dependent upon prior achievement of political and civil rights. The hard fact is, as Manzer and Kaplansky make clear, the Canadian government for decades did not much emphasize economic and social rights. The unfortunate consequence of the resulting bifurcation in Canada's doctrine of human rights has been failure to use the opportunities offered by such international institutions as the International Labour Organization to promote human rights and human dignity. As Manzer quite correctly judges, the split makes it very "difficult to develop a foreign policy that would give proper priority to basic social rights of subsistence and security."

Canada's approach to rights is limited also by its policy-makers' preference for international rather than bilateral measures. Compartmentalization is reflected as well in administrative structures and procedures of External Affairs. Berry and McChesney point out that the two offices with a specific mandate to deal with human rights are responsible for co-ordinating Canada's role within multilateral institutions; on bilateral questions their impact has tended to be sporadic and marginal.

Even more limiting is Canada's insistence on championing human rights through international institutions established for that purpose, such as the UN Commission on Human Rights, the UN Human Rights Committee, and the Helsinki forum. John Foster (chapter 5), Cathal Nolan (6), and Skilling (8) demonstrate that Canada has been a forthright and vigorous member of these structures and is trying to strengthen them and to augment their international prestige and authority. By contrast, as Renate Pratt points out (chapter 9), Canada long argued that human rights should not be the concern of international financial institutions.

Compartmentalization has had adverse consequences. First, the government neglects a whole range of instruments (bilateral, transnational, and even international) that might change the behaviour of rights violators. Keenleyside's study of Canada's development assistance (chapter 10) underscores how important that instrument could be, as so many of the worst offenders are developing countries; it also stresses how flexibly aid could be used if employed with sensitivity and imagination. Second, Canada's efforts at the UN Commission on Human Rights, for instance, are recurrently undermined by its unwillingness to ensure that human rights play an integral role in Canada's bilateral relations with other countries and in its voting decisions in international financial institutions. Arbour, for example, demonstrates (chapter 12) that Canada's critical stance on El Salvador and Guatemala at the Commission on Human Rights and the UN general assembly was weakened by its failure to act as forcefully in its bilateral relations with those countries and in the votes it cast in the Inter-American Development Bank and the International Monetary Fund (IMF). Renate Pratt provides chapter and verse for Canada's persistent reluctance to have international financial institutions (IFIs) take account of the human rights record of states seeking assistance and its failure to criticize the adjustment policies insisted upon by the IMF and the World Bank as the price for their assistance.

Canada's concern for human rights is not only narrow in scope but also subordinated to other foreign policy interests. Although claimed by the government to be a major principle of Canada's foreign policy, human rights has never been integrated into the decision-making process. When combatting of rights abuses conflicts with other concerns, such as promoting exports or maintaining the alliance with the United States, it has usually been discarded, or at least heavily discounted. This seems clearly to have been the case vis-à-vis South Africa, Indonesia after the fall of Sukarno, and Central America in recent years. Ernie Regehr (chapter 11) makes clear how limited as well were controls on military sales to grossly oppressive régimes. Canada pursues human rights actively only when that interest coincides or overlaps with other foreign policy goals, when its other interests are negligible, or when the public forces its hand.

Public opinion alone has not often changed human rights policies, unless the force of opinion coincides with other interests. The most recent such instance reveals how difficult such a change is to accomplish. Renate Pratt demonstrates how the government consistently opposed making human rights a determinant of loan and credit decisions by IFIs. Not until this viewpoint had been endorsed by a special joint committee and by the Standing Committee on External Affairs and International Trade did the government finally change its stance, and then it did so minimally and within months reverted to its old position.[14]

CONSTRAINTS AND COMPETING OBJECTIVES

We accept that the international system constrains a state's human rights activities and that there are, inevitably, trade-offs between rights and other foreign policy objectives. Nevertheless, there is, in our view, considerable room in which Canada can manoeuvre to minimize constraints and remain vigorous on human rights while tempering policy to accommodate other objectives. How the constraints are dealt with and trade-offs managed becomes a measure of Canada's seriousness about human rights.

Let us examine this point more fully. No democratic government can ignore the health of its economy and the security of its citizens, disregard threats to international peace, or turn a blind eye to the basic needs of the world's poor. These goals sometimes conflict with pursuit of human rights. By assigning high priority to attacking rights violations, a state may have to moderate its pursuit of other ends. Conversely, the search for realization of these other goals may involve downgrading human rights. In deciding policy a state must make trade-offs among a range of desirable national objectives.

To argue that states face conflicting interests and thus may have to restrain pursuit of human rights is one thing. It is quite another, however, to assert that because of these other pressing goals states cannot normally consider human rights in bilateral relations. There may be occasions when a government must sacrifice human rights policy for a more pressing goal: survival of a state (national security) or of the globe (world peace). But such occasions are rare. More frequently, conflicts will be less complete, forcing a state to modify rather than to cancel part of its foreign policy. Sometimes objectives may complement each other, thus permitting simultaneous pursuit of several goals (including human rights).

Canadian officials have most frequently cited international peace, international development, national security, and national prosperity as foreign policy goals conflicting with promotion of human rights. In the rest of this section we shall examine the prospects of conflicts between human rights and these goals and assess the trade-offs that the Canadian government has made.

International Peace and Security

The contemporary preoccupation with human rights grew out of the unspeakable policies and practices of Nazism during the 1930s and the resulting world war. The founders of the UN charter drew from that experience at least one lesson: peace and respect for human rights are inseparable: one was unattainable without the other. Hence article 55: "With a view to the creation of conditions of stability and well-being which are necessary for peaceful and friendly relations among nations based on respect for the principle of equal rights and self-determination of peoples, the United Nations shall promote ... universal respect for, and observation of, human rights and fundamental freedoms for all without distinction as to race, sex, language or religion."

In the long run, international peace and respect for human rights are clearly compatible, mutually reinforcing ends. In the shorter run, that need not be true. Short of a totally disarmed world, developed states, both capitalist and communist, have had to find ways of avoiding the nuclear cataclysm that threatens our survival. This in turn has produced such compelling intermediate goals as relaxation of tensions between the two major antagonists and their supporting alliances, reduction of nuclear and conventional arsenals, and development of an international régime to prevent horizontal proliferation of nuclear weapons.

While developing policies to achieve these middle-range goals, states may compromise their goal of promoting human rights. To reduce tensions between East and West, to secure agreement on arms control, or to divert a country from acquiring nuclear weapons depends on co-operation and close links with other states that are sometimes violators of human rights. Can human rights activists expect violators to respond favourably to appeals for co-operation on international peace while they denounce those states for the way they treat their own citizens? In effect, emphasis on human rights appears divisive; it tends to cause offence and confrontation between governments, touching as it does, "on the very foundations of a regime, on its sources and exercise of power, on its links to its citizens or subjects."[15] And thus, as international peace and security are certainly important, states may have to play down human rights.[16] The Soviet Union and a number of near-nuclear powers, South Africa, Pakistan, and Israel for example, have questionable human rights records.

Nevertheless, human rights are widely recognized as a matter of international concern. Thus it seems unlikely that relations with other states need be seriously impaired, to the point that co-operation on other matters is halted, just because one state criticizes another's performance in human rights. The argument that nuclear peace is of paramount importance cuts both ways. Even if one state moves beyond verbal censure, co-operation on an arms control treaty might still proceed, as both sides have an overriding common interest in reaching an agreement.

Whether relations will be damaged and other world-order goals placed in jeopardy will depend also on how the issue of human rights is broached. If human rights are used as a political weapon to embarrass an opponent or to gain an edge in a propaganda campaign, then co-operation on other ends may well be undermined. If, by contrast, a protest against violations is dealt with "in the proper forum, in reasonable terms, and is consistent with the policy pursued on similar matters towards other states,"[17] and if the emphasis is on universally acknowledged basic rights, then the risk is likely to be considerably less. We need conclude not that a genuine human rights policy must be abandoned, only that governments must exercise "prudence and skill in means."[18]

International Development

Encouragement of international development and promotion of human rights are, as Keenleyside has effectively argued, entirely compatible and indeed mutually reinforcing. The purpose of development is to ensure that all countries are able to meet the basic needs and to improve the general welfare of their people and, in the long run, to establish conditions for self-sustaining growth. A developed society is, at least in principle, one in which citizens fully enjoy political, social, and economic rights. Development, therefore, involves by its very nature the liberation of men and women from all forms of bondage.[19] By contrast, violation of basic rights is the opposite of development, its very denial. In certain circumstances, temporary curtailment of specific civil and political rights may be required in order to provide a minimum of order essential for effective economic development. However, in countries where basic rights are widely and persistently violated, the prospects of genuine development are slight, if not non-existent. Benefits from economic growth are likely to accrue to the government and the small urban élite, not to the poor and the oppressed.[20]

Contradictions or conflicts of purpose quickly emerge, however, in regard to the many countries that are neither gross and persistent violators nor exemplary defenders of rights. In those countries, people administering Canada's aid programs often judge that it is difficult to express with any effect their concern about states that violate human rights without doing harm to the poor and needy. This dilemma will certainly not be resolved either by ignoring violations or by cutting aid. Instead a careful combination of specific policies must be devised. Inducements, as well as sanctions and criticisms, and project selection focusing on the poor can improve human rights and help the neediest. Keenleyside's discussion of these issues is, we believe, nuanced, sensitive, and persuasive.

National Security

In a near anarchical world, in which there is little agreement among states and no authority above them, governments are preoccupied of necessity with national security. Defence against threats to a society's survival must be accorded highest priority. If the active pursuit of human rights is felt to weaken those defences, then the state will give human rights less prominence in its foreign policy.

Whatever the requirements of national security are judged to be – allies, co-operative relations with a "patron," access to strategic minerals, control of strategic sites, influence among the non-aligned – no state will readily antagonize countries on whose co-operation its security depends. To press human rights too strenuously with these states would seem to endanger national security. Anxieties of this sort have been particularly intense among those Western states that see the Soviet Union and "international communism" as intractably determined to undermine the security of their states. Such considerations seem to have provided justification for Portugal's NATO allies, Canada included, to mute criticism of its colonial policies and for the West to avoid criticizing too strenuously the Shah of Iran, the post-Sukarno régime in Indonesia, and several governments in Central and South America.[21]

These examples illustrate the danger of allowing the imperatives of alliances to overwhelm concern for human rights in countries with which one may be allied or have close relations. Continued support for any régime, no matter how friendly and closely aligned, that openly and persistently violates basic rights is likely in the long run to be counterproductive. Such régimes resort to increasingly repressive measures to stay in power, and foreign powers that identify with them will find their positions weakened. These powers risk having to choose between extending further support to their clients or facing a new and probably hostile régime.[22] Even with continued outside support, repressive governments may manage only to hang on for a while; their eventual collapse will leave foreign friends bereft of influence and, therefore, with national security presumably weakened.

Surely concerned states do not have to await the last moments of another régime's life before turning a critical eye to its human rights behaviour. Without seriously endangering their security they can often press home their concern. Quiet or public censure may be more easily accepted and more likely to be acted on if it comes from one's friends. Even if the action taken is stronger, involving cutting off of aid, for instance, the targeted country may still not undermine an alliance: it too may value that alliance or be unable to envisage a realistic alternative.

Aside from exploiting leverage over an offending régime – and that may not be insignificant – a concerned state could reconsider the relationship altogether. However important they may be for security purposes, allies are often expendable or replaceable; strategic resources can often be secured elsewhere or large supplies stockpiled for later use; and basing facilities can be relocated. Reorganization of a state's alliances will, undoubtedly, involve significant short-term costs, but a state genuinely interested in human rights should be willing to pay that price, especially as an alliance with an oppressive régime, as we have argued, is often short-lived.

In the final analysis, national security is a legitimate interest that may conflict with the human rights dimension in foreign policy. But the conflicts are less acute and less frequent than is generally assumed. And where they do occur, human rights need not be totally ignored. A government anxious to promote human rights abroad need not choose between doing all or nothing for human rights but should look for that particular policy or policies that most effectively exploit its leverage over an offending régime.

National Economic Growth

Governments are preoccupied, and rightly so, with the development and health of their national economies. No government, even an authoritarian one, can afford to neglect for too long a rising rate of unemployment or a slowdown in the growth of its GNP. No matter how well intended political leaders are, on judgment day it is their performance, particularly in economics, that is likely to count most.

Canadian foreign policy has clearly been influenced by fear that a strong human rights policy would damage our national economy. Such a policy may lead to cancellation of particularly valuable private-sector projects, reduction in economic relations with important commercial partners, or disinvestment abroad on a larger scale.

To avoid such consequences, Canada's interest in immediate economic advantages has at times constrained introduction of a more active policy. As the preceding studies suggest, Canadian policy has been marked by general reluctance to speak out against violators if economic interests are involved and by specific resistance to economic sanctions. An interesting recent illustration of resistance to sanctions is the Canadian government's preference even in 1986 for voluntary rather than mandatory sanctions against South Africa. Similarly, as Ernie Regehr shows, the Canadian government was reluctant even to enforce vigorously a policy of no arms sales to gross human rights violators.

A vivid example of the general reluctance to criticize where economic interests are involved occurred during Prime Minister Trudeau's trip to Asia in early 1983. Although the prime minister was unwilling to explain his silence on rights violations in the region, in spite of public pressure for him to speak out, one of his aides explained: "Canada cannot afford to increase unemployment in Sudbury to free a nun in the Philippines."[23] Similarly, Canada has skirted human rights in its dealings with the previous régime in Argentina and with the present régimes in South Korea and Chile, as it was unwilling "to take action against countries with which Canada has substantial and growing commercial relations, even though the seriousness of their human rights abuses is recognized."[24]

Perhaps the most persistent and revealing example of government responsiveness to commercial interests, even when they are slight and violations severe, is Canada's policy toward South Africa, carefully dissected by Rhoda Howard in chapter 14. We can understand Kim Nossal's disbelief that interests this insignificant can have been influential, but the bureaucracy in Ottawa has always tilted the trade-off between human rights in South Africa and Canadian commercial interests very much in favour of trading interests.[25] Our reading is that there is much evidence that this stance may at long last be shifting, partly, as Nossal argues, in order to safeguard the Commonwealth, but even more, we judge, because of the conviction of both the prime minister and the secretary of state for external affairs, against the advice of External Affairs, that Canada should assert a strong policy against racism in South Africa.

Despite this exception, Canada has frequently refrained from pursuing human rights out of fear of negative but minor economic consequences. This cautious approach is, in our view, unnecessary. That the trade-offs are made so consistently in this way reveals the inclination and bias of the policy-makers and the pressures to which they are most responsive. Most states have come to expect that human rights are a matter of international concern. If a state criticizes another because of the way it treats its own citizens, the repercussions will probably not be particularly harmful. Whether or not they are will depend in part on the manner in which objections are raised. And in those few cases of gross and persistent violators, where we would consider economic sanctions and other strong actions, such measures will carry an economic cost, but it is not self-evident why avoiding that damage would be in our national interest, properly understood. Indeed, the myopic pursuit of short-term economic interests at the expense of the long-run goal of an international environment in which human rights are promoted and protected may be self-defeating.[26] Certainly it is demeaning.

In the end, probably all states will build into their foreign policies "a cut off point at which principles must be sacrificed to preserve economic well-being."[27] How states define that point will vary and will reflect the relative importance of human rights concerns. For Canadians, this is a dismaying conclusion. The tendency of the Canadian government to promote national security, loyalty to alliances, and economic growth rather than human rights misrepresents Canadian values and misreads what in the long run is important. Worries about security, alliances, and growth are often exaggerated and misperceived, and conflict with rights issues can be moderated if one's concern is carefully expressed. Canada can find a fuller place for human rights in its foreign policy if the will to do so is genuine and the hesitations of officials are firmly contained.

Effectiveness

Politics is the art of the possible. While statesmen may, indeed should, concern themselves with the rightness of what they do, they cannot ignore the effects of their actions. Political leaders are therefore naturally preoccupied with effectiveness, which Allan MacEachen described as "the key guide to our actions, and the measure which determines how we proceed and in what ways."[28]

When applied to international politics, the principle of effectiveness may in some situations compel the internationalist and the moralist to moderate their idealism. This fact has been drawn on by some as an argument for doing nothing or, at least, very little in human rights. According to this view, even non-interventionist human rights policies will be viewed as hostile acts by government subjected to criticism; such states will appeal to their citizens' sense of pride and nationhood. The result, it is suggested, may be to strengthen the power of the oppressing régime rather than to undermine it. In addition, a government may sometimes give the appearance of amending its way by calling an election or removing a particularly oppressive piece of legislation, only to return to its old ways after a suitable lapse of time. In any event, it is argued, the effect is the same: human rights policies have been "a waste of energy, resources, and political capital."[29] Neither the offending government nor the oppressed have benefited from the human rights activities of other states. Worse yet, in pursuing human rights, states may do considerable harm, by provoking a tightening of repression and by undermining previously friendly interstate relations.[30]

Such a view is flawed in several ways. It is historically inaccurate: the record is far less gloomy than the one it portrays. While some oppressive states have clearly followed a pattern of resistance, refusing to change their ways, though occasionally making temporary gestures of conciliation toward their international critics, many others have improved their human rights performance, responding favourably, if begrudgingly, to international criticism and pressure.

This is surely a conclusion that can legitimately be drawn from the evidence in chapters by Foster (5), Miller (13), Nolan (6), and Skilling (8). There is a further, equally important point. In assessing the case for a strong human rights foreign policy, analysts and policy-makers alike must judge not only results but also whether the policy adequately expresses deeply held and widespread Canadian convictions about human rights. Thus, even failure of violators to change their behaviour as a result of international pressure should not in itself be reason to abdicate a strong policy. That might be concluded only if the sole purpose of a human rights policy were to induce change in countries where rights are severely violated. But if, as we have argued elsewhere, the goals included as well the need "to sustain the integrity of the society's commitment to these rights internationally and to contribute to an expanding international concern about human rights and an international capacity to act effectively,"[31] then the difficulty of influencing an oppressive régime would not be sufficient reason to abandon a human rights thrust altogether. At the most, it would be cause for caution in the choice of the goals, targets, and means of a human rights foreign policy.

SOME POLICY PRESCRIPTIONS

There are, we believe, three separable purposes of a human rights policy: to induce change in countries where rights are severely violated, to expand international concern about rights, and to contribute to an international capacity to act effectively to support human rights. Such an identification of purposes is particularly clarifying for discussion of the foreign policy of small or middle powers. If such powers, Canada included, conceive that the only purpose of a human rights policy is direct inducement of change, then it is deceptively easy for them to conclude that because they are unlikely directly to influence an oppressive régime, there is little point for them to have a strong policy. If, however, one recognizes the validity of the second and third purposes, then middle and small powers cannot abdicate this obligation.

On the basis of these fundamental purposes, it is possible to deduce as reasonable corollaries a number of broad foreign policy prescriptions, ranging from use of influence through to armed intervention, which should be closely considered by any government concerned about gross and persistent violations of basic rights.[32]

Use of Influence

Prescription 1. Governments ought to avoid actions that undermine basic rights anywhere else in the world and ensure that their citizens also avoid such actions. This single prescription, diligently implemented, would not only rule out direct acts of oppression but would also proscribe the arming and training of the military in oppressive régimes and the sustaining of such régimes economically. It would also apply to economic initiatives and technical innovations that weaken the capacity of the poor to provide for their own subsistence. Prescription 1 is a simple proposition which most people are likely to accept as undeniably compelling. Its consequences, however, if widely accepted internationally, would go a long way to transform international economic relations.

Prescription 2. Governments ought to minimize complicity with other governments that are gross and persistent violators of basic rights. To minimize economic, diplomatic and social links with a highly oppressive régime would remove whatever advantages are gained from these links, contribute to development of international pressure on these régimes, and give witness to the integrity of the government's commitment to human rights. Only if there are convincing reasons to believe that sustaining normal relations with oppressive states will significantly increase that state's responsiveness to international pressures should this prescription be set aside.

Prescription 3. In co-operation with like-minded states, governments should seek to correct those features of the international economic system that contribute to perpetuation of severe international economic inequities. Poverty and despair are not the sole environments in which brutality and oppression flourish. Nevertheless, both poverty and despair facilitate the emergence and full flowering of oppression and brutality. It does not stretch concern for human rights unreasonably to see this prescription as implying responsiveness to the requirements of Third World development and international equity.

Prescription 4. Governments should support international structures that expose severe abrogations of basic rights and place international pressure on oppressive régimes. Many governments have already taken this prescription seriously. We accept the criticism that the Canadian government has compartmentalized its concern for human rights and gives active expression to it primarily through activity in these international structures.[33] Nevertheless, this arena and this activity are important. The Second Report of the Parliamentary Sub-Committee on Canada's Relations with Latin America was, among other things, a high point of sensitive parliamentary scrutiny of human rights issues.[34] It gave priority to embodying human rights in international law and to strengthening the work of the UN Commission on Human Rights and the Committee on Human Rights. This fourth prescription reflects the same conviction.

Prescription 5. Governments ought to acknowledge, with other like-minded states if possible, the legitimacy of revolutionary struggles and régimes in countries where for decades there have been vast inequalities and sustained repression and where the revolutionary movements or régimes convincingly affirm their support for basic rights. There is a grave risk that many Western governments, including Canada, may increasingly value order, integration into the international economic system, and reliability within the East-West confrontation more highly than termination of existing oppression and injustice. This prescription is a reminder that many people live under highly repressive régimes offering no prospect of orderly and constitutional affirmation of their rights.

Prescription 6. The obligation of any country to act regarding grave violations of basic rights in another country is stronger in proportion to the closeness of the links between the two countries. This proposition follows from the argument that obligations increase with the degree of shared community with those whose rights are denied. Such obligations for state action are further increased if links with an oppressive régime are economically advantageous.

Prescription 7. The more universal the awareness of illegitimate oppression, and the wider the international support for initiatives to limit that oppression, the more legitimate in turn are external initiatives. International initiatives for rights not widely recognized are more likely to be ambivalent in consequences and in motivation. Attempts to influence allegedly in the interest of rights may be a cover for pursuit of geopolitical or ideological objectives. Internationalization of the effort to influence an oppressive régime diminishes this risk and increases the likelihood that the effort will be substantial enough and compelling enough to achieve success.

Prescription 8. The stronger the organized internal resistance to an oppressive régime, the more vigorous, in turn, ought to be external responses to appeals from that resistance for support and for international pressure upon that régime. This prescription may seem less self-evident than the earlier propositions. However, assuming that correction of injustice is the purpose, the stronger organized resistance, the more external sources can be sure of organized internal support for these international initiatives and the socio-political basis for a new régime. The reverse of this proposition, however, is unlikely to be true. A régime that has overwhelmed its critics, destroyed their structures, and imprisoned their leaders can hardly expect a lessening of international criticism. Nevertheless, without the existence of an organized and widely based opposition of nations, much less can be done by international action. Absence of organized opposition means that other countries may have to limit their efforts to applying economic and diplomatic pressure on the régime.

All the above prescriptions apply to efforts short of serious sanctions or the use of force to dissuade régimes whose human rights record is seriously deficient. This discussion is, therefore, still incomplete. Prescriptions are also needed concerning positive measures to encourage respect for human rights and direct interventions on their behalf.

Positive Measures

The requirements under this heading are straightforward and can easily be summarized in two additional prescriptions.

Prescription 9. Governments ought to make it evident that they regard with special favour states striving to improve their human rights record. There are many ways that this can be done. Such states can be favoured recipients of development assistance, special targets of cultural exchanges, the subject of a visit by the head of state or government. The point being made would be clear. Government would be demonstrating that they regard such states as meriting special favour.

Prescription 10. Governments ought in particular to be ready directly to assist the efforts of governments seeking to protect rights. In addition to generous development assistance, a range of measures can sometimes be helpful – specialized training for police, help with the work of an ombudsman or electoral commission, assistance with food storage and distribution. These actions can be valuable immediate contributions to strengthening of human rights and an additional demonstration of sympathetic support.

Direct Intervention

Some writers argue that no such intervention is legitimate. The most persuasive form of this argument accepts that states may legitimately seek to influence the policies of other states but that the importance of respect for the sovereignty of other states renders illegitimate any direct intervention with force in the internal affairs of another state.[35]

Two of the most subtle writers on the issue are Michael Walzer and Stanley Hoffmann.[36] Both agree that interventions in most cases will serve no humane and legitimate purpose. Each does concede, however, a few types of intervention that must be judged legitimate. These categories provide a good prelude to our own effort to define prescriptions in this regard.

Both Walzer and Hoffmann attach much importance to containing wars and to allowing peoples to settle their own fates without interference. This perspective leads them to accept certain interventions as legitimate because they are "corrective," offsetting previous interventions. Thus, for both, it is legitimate to extend military aid to a country that is invaded or to one that is facing a foreign-aided insurrection. Each case is clearly a counter-intervention. Neither Walzer nor Hoffmann sanctions intervention to aid a people struggling to rid itself of a dictator. Writes Hoffmann, "If there were an impartial arbiter capable of licensing legitimate interventions and of ruling out biased ones, one might choose a different guideline."[37] Both are afraid that to allow interventions to assist a struggle for self-government would provide a formula for hypocrisy and generalized war. Tyranny, they feel, is a legitimate target of domestic struggle but not of international intervention.

Yet each writer allows a few exceptions beyond counter-intervention. Walzer legitimizes intervention to help a people free itself from foreign rule, colonial or by another people within a multi-ethnic state. Hoffmann directly rejects this proposition but accepts intervention in civil or colonial wars, when, but only when, there have been large-scale atrocities. Finally, both accept the legitimacy of intervention when, to quote Walzer, "it is a response with reasonable expectations of success to acts that shock the conscience of the world."[38] These situations, the Cambodias and Ugandas of the modern world, are for them sui generis, lying outside the more nuanced guide-lines they had each evolved.

What we are now discussing, however, is precisely those exceptional cases that shock the conscience of the world. The final two prescriptions attempt a nuanced statement concerning the legitimacy of international and/or single-state intervention in these rare but crucial cases.

Prescription 11. Intervention can legitimately include military assistance to those resisting an oppressive régime when these five conditions are met: first, an active, organized resistance already exists; second, the régime nevertheless is itself able to command resources that will overwhelm those that this resistance is able to assemble; third, there seems no likelihood of meaningful change in other and less violent ways; fourth, there is near universal acceptance that the denial of human rights is particularly severe; and fifth, there is a reasonable likelihood that the armed resistance, if assisted, can overthrow the régime or win major reforms. This prescription is certainly rich in essential preconditions and may seem begrudging. Nevertheless, the arguments are certainly powerful against extending military assistance to a movement struggling against an oppressive government. Often it is impossible to be confident of the struggle's outcome, and, consequently, intervention may merely increase suffering without ensuring change. Intervention, moreover, is likely to increase the probability that the struggle will become more generally internationalized and thereby involve a much greater loss of life and the risk of more generalized war. Additionally, in many circumstances, the most important objective is likely to be halting external assistance to the oppressive régime rather than aiding the movement of the oppressed. In these cases, be it Afghanistan or El Salvador and Guatemala, championing non-intervention is very important. Any intervention unavoidably undermines the principle of non-intervention, which, as we are arguing, is an important check on less defensible intervention by strong states into the internal affairs of other, less powerful countries. For all these reasons, circumstances legitimizing armed support to a popular uprising need to be narrowly circumscribed.

To delimit narrowly, however, is not totally to exclude. This prescription accepts that there are circumstances in which military assistance to resistance movements is legitimate. We thus go beyond the position advocated by Walzer and Hoffmann, each of whom permits armed assistance only if the oppressive régime is also receiving such assistance or, in Walzer's case, is committing mass atrocities. We do so in recognition that there will be some circumstances in which an oppressive régime is able, from its own resources, to run a successful, technologically sophisticated police state which can overwhelm any internally organized opposition. For that reason one cannot rule out, in principle, military assistance to a liberation movement. Armed assistance is, in principle, legitimate where the denial of basic rights is severe and sustained, where the régime offers no alternative avenues of effective protest, and where the régime would be able to contain the liberation movement were the movement unassisted.

Prescription 12. Direct armed intervention is justified in those rare circumstances where either the oppression is so severe or the breakdown of order so complete that it is widely recognized that immediate humanitarian objectives justify intervention. In these circumstances it is much preferable that intervention be accomplished by an international force. This proposition may seem too hesitant. Why should not armed interventions be legitimate to correct abuses of human rights that are real but not as overwhelming as this proposition would require? There are, we think, two answers to this question. First, we are seeking ethical guide-lines for conduct in an international order where states are prone to intervene in other countries for ideological and political reasons and tend to present such intervention as motivated by human rights considerations. Non-intervention is therefore an important principle which should not be undermined unless the humanitarian considerations seeming to require intervention are incontrovertible. Second, and less important, if intervening powers apply sufficient force, it may be easy to overturn an oppressive régime or to secure a return to law and order. It is far less easy, however, to ensure the emergence of indigenous political forces able to rule more justly and more effectively – a consideration that should be set aside only when the humanitarian need for intervention is indeed compelling. In our present world, there can hardly be an intervention that will not be viewed by one or both superpowers as having geopolitical significance. For this reason, it becomes all the more important that the rest of the world work for the institutionalization of international action in cases that shock the conscience of the world.

These twelve policy prescriptions are corollaries of a serious commitment to promote basic rights internationally. Promotion of human rights, of course, can never be the sole objective of foreign policy. Moreover, other objectives have different implications, which will in part conflict with these. There is no rational way to resolve these contradictions. There is no common denominator to which the conflicting objectives can be reduced to compute the combination that will maximize the national interest. Determination of the weight to be given to competing objectives and the response to be made to differing prescriptions are therefore at the heart of the policy-making process. One state may give but little priority to human rights concerns, emphasizing instead economic or strategic interests. Another, in contrast, may value more highly such long-term goals as international equity. It is in the ordering of the priorities between various objectives of foreign policy that a country defines its international character and reveals the importance that it attaches to human rights internationally.

Notes

CHAPTER ONE

1 Judith Lichtenberg makes this distinction in her interesting chapter "National Boundaries and Moral Boundaries" in P.G. Brown and Henry Shue, eds. *Boundaries: National Autonomy and Its Limits* (Totowa, NJ: Rowman and Littlefield 1981).
2 Alan Gewirth, *Human Rights: Essays on Justification and Applications* (Chicago: University of Chicago Press 1982), 3, and Susan Moller Okin, "Liberty and Welfare: Some Issues in Human Rights Theory," *Nomos* XXIII: *Human Rights* (New York: New York University Press 1981), 325.
3 This is, we think, true even of Gewirth. He developed the argument that one must logically concede to others the rights that one must have if one is to engage in self-motivated purposive action. Yet he slipped into his analysis the key normative premiss that all humans are actual prospective or potential agents, a premiss essential to his whole argument and similar to the assumption identified in our argument above. The quotation from Gewirth is from his "The Epistemology of Human Rights," in Ellen Frankel Paul, Fred Miller, Jr, and Jeffrey Paul, eds., *Human Rights* (Oxford: Blackwell 1984), 18. See also Gewirth's *Human Rights: Essays on Justification and Applications Applications* (Chicago: University of Chicago Press 1982) and his *Reason and Morality* (Chicago: University of Chicago Press 1978).
4 The concept receives its fullest elaboration in Henry Shue, *Basic Rights: Subsistence, Affluence, and U.S. Foreign Policy* (Princeton, NJ: Princeton University Press 1980). The approach here is, we hope, faithful to his major emphasis. However, he adds to basic rights freedom of movement and political participation. We omit these. The first can reasonably be subsumed under freedom from arbitrary detention, and the second is better viewed as a likely prerequisite to sustaining government respect for basic

rights. It is, moreover, not the only such prerequisite. Think, for example, of freedom from deep communal, religious, racial, or class hostilities.

5 The philosophical and related literature on the basis and extent of our duties toward the human rights of those who live in other countries, though not extensive, is very good. We would refer readers to Brown and Shue eds., *Boundaries;* Jack Donnelly, "Human Rights and Development: Complementary or Competing Concerns," *World Politics* 36:2 (Jan 1983), 255–83, and "Human Rights, Humanitarian Intervention and American Foreign Policy: Law, Morality and Politics," *Journal of International Affairs* 37:2 (winter 1984), 311–28; James Fisk, *The Limits of Obligation* (New Haven: Yale University Press 1982); Richard Falk, *Human Rights and State Sovereignty* (New York: Holmes and Meier 1981); Stanley Hoffmann, *Duties beyond Borders: On the Limits and Possibilities of Ethical International Politics* (Syracuse: Syracuse University Press 1981); Henry Shue, *Basic Rights: Subsistence, Affluence and U.S. Foreign Policy* (Princeton, NJ: Princeton University Press 1980); Peter Singer "Famine, Affluence and Morality," in Peter Laslett and James Fishkin, eds., *Philosophy, Politics and Society, Fifth Series* (Oxford and New Haven: Blackwell and Yale University Press 1979); 3–33; Moorehead Wright, ed. *Rights and Obligations in North-South Relations* (London: Macmillan 1986).

6 In his "The Institution of Membership," in Brown and Shue, eds., *Boundaries,* 210.

7 *Independence and Internationalism: Report of the Special Joint Committee on Canada's International Relations* (Ottawa: Supply and Services Canada 1986), 100.

8 Gewirth, *Human Rights Essays,* 213. Gewirth's "basic goods" are in their coverage at least as wide as our basic rights.

9 James Fishkin, *The Limits of Obligation* (Cornell: Cornell University Press 1982), 23, 31.

10 Shue, *Basic Rights,* 122. Shue argues that we should do our part even if others do not do theirs. However, he does not deal directly with the harder question of whether we should not do more if others do nothing. See, in particular, 115 note 9.

11 Fishkin, *Limits of Obligation,* 31.

12 John Rawls, *A Theory of Justice* (Cambridge, Mass.: Harvard University Press 1971), 115.

13 Donnelly, "Human Rights, Humanitarian Intervention," 326.

14 For the influence of international organizations and their role in promoting and protecting human rights, see Jack Donnelly, "International Human Rights: A Regime Analysis," *International Organizations,* 40:3 (summer 1986), 599–642; David Forsythe, "The United Nations and Human Rights, 1945–1985;" *Political Science Quarterly,* 100 (summer 1985), 249–

70; Hurst Hannum, ed., *Guide to International Human Rights International Law: Legal and Policy Issues* (Oxford: Clarendon 1984); Karel Vasek and Philip Alston, eds., *The International Dimensions of Human Rights* (Westport, Conn.: Greenwood 1982).
15 John G. Ruggie, "Human Rights and the Future International Community," *Daedalus* (fall 1983), 104.
16 Evan Luard, "Human Rights and Foreign Policy," *International Affairs*, 56 (autumn 1980), 602.
17 One could not help being struck by the vehemence of domestic public reaction to the December 1985 visit to France by Poland's leader, General Wojciech Jaruzelski. The political costs for François Mitterand and his Parti socialist in the March 1986 elections are difficult to estimate but substantial.
18 Luard makes a strong case for fostering such contacts; "Human Rights and Foreign Policy," 600.
19 See Matthews and Pratt, "Human Rights and Foreign Policy Principles and Canadian Practice," *Human Rights Quarterly* (May 1985), 175–87.
20 Margaret Catley-Carlson, president of the Canadian International Development Agency, has argued that the ending of Canada's aid to Uganda had the indirect effect of contributing to starvation in northern Uganda.
21 Canada, Department of External Affairs, Statements and Speeches 83/6, Allan J. MacEachen, "Human Rights and Canadian Foreign Policy," 22 April 1983, 4.
22 Matthews and Pratt, "Human Rights," 167–75.

CHAPTER TWO

I am grateful to Jack Donnelly, University of North Carolina, and to Peter Russell, University of Toronto, for their constructive criticism and helpful suggestions on an earlier version of this chapter.
1 "Petition of the Quebec Traders," in W.P.M. Kennedy, ed., *Statutes, Treaties and Documents of the Canadian Constitution 1713–1927* 2nd ed. (Toronto: University of Toronto Press 1930), 56.
2 "Petition for House of Assembly, 24 November, 1784 to the King's Most Excellent Majesty," in ibid., 174, 172.
3 "Robert Baldwin to Glenelg, 1836," in ibid., 338–9, 341. See also "Baldwin on Responsible Government," in H.D. Forbes, ed., *Canadian Political Thought* (Toronto: Oxford University Press 1985), 31, 33.
4 "Joseph Howe to Lord John Russell," in Kennedy, ed., *Statutes*, 412. See also J. Murray Beck, *Joseph Howe: Conservative Reformer 1804–1848* (Montreal: McGill-Queen's University Press 1982), 198.
5 Sir John A. Macdonald, "Speech on the Quebec Resolutions," in Forbes, ed., *Canadian Political Thought*, 91–2.

6 Sir Wilfrid Laurier, "Political Liberalism," in ibid., 136, 150.
7 "Address of the French Citizens to the King Regarding the Legal System," in Kennedy, ed., *Statutes*, 64.
8 "Objections to the Requests Made to Our August Sovereign, December 1784," in ibid., 175.
9 "Mackenzie's Draft Constitution," in Forbes, ed., *Canadian Political Thought*, 38. Twelve of the eighty-one articles of the draft constitution refer to basic individual political rights and civil liberties. Particularly revealing of the contractarian assumptions underlying it is the first article: "Matters of religion and the ways of God's worship are not at all intrusted by the people of this State to any human power ... Therefore the Legislature shall make no law respecting the establishment of religion, or for the encouragement or the prohibition of any religious denomination."
10 'The Six Counties Address,' in ibid., 33–4.
11 According to Catherine L. Cleverdon, "The basic plea of the suffrage forces was for simple justice. Women were forced to pay taxes and obey laws; why not give them a share in making them?" See *The Woman Suffrage Movement in Canada* 2nd ed. (Toronto: University of Toronto Press 1974), 9–10. In 1913, in a special session on the right to vote, a leading Toronto suffragette, Mrs Leathes, told the annual convention of the National Council of Women: "Parliament is responsible to its electors only. Where women are not electors Parliament is not responsible to women, and their interests and wishes are not directly represented." Unlike men, who were concerned primarily with property interests, women were concerned with "life interests," and "to be able to protect human life from the onslaught of property interests we must today have the ballot." See *The Yearbook Containing the Report of the Twentieth Annual Meeting* (Toronto: Parker Bros 1913), 71,73.
12 An important exception would appear to be Pierre Trudeau, minister of justice responsible for the preparation of the 1968 draft charter of rights and prime minister during development and passage of the Canadian Charter of Rights and Freedoms. In 1958 Trudeau wrote a series of articles in the magazine *Vrai* under the general title "Les cheminements de la politique." In a discussion of "the right of protest" he began by citing the American Declaration of Independence and argued that a truly democratic state must listen to its citizens in order to attain the common good: "That is why certain political rights are inseparable from the very essence of democracy: freedom of thought, speech, expression (in the press, on the radio, etc.), assembly, and association. Indeed, the moment these freedoms suffer the smallest restraint, the citizens have lost their full power to participate in the organization of the social order. And so that each citizen may feel the benefit of the inalienable right to exercise his liberties – in spite of anyone, in spite of the state itself – to these rights two

317 Notes to Pages 27–35

more must be added: equality of all before the law, and the right not to be deprived of one's liberty or one's goods without recourse to a trial before one's peers, under an impartial and independent judicial system." See Pierre Elliott Trudeau, *Approaches to Politics* (Toronto: Oxford University Press 1970), 80. Trudeau noted that these rights are so basic to participation in a democracy that many states have bills of rights written into their constitutions but that, regrettably, this was not the case in Canada.

13 Salem Bland, "The New Christianity," in Forbes, ed., *Canadian Political Thought*, 219.
14 "The Regina Manifesto," in ibid., 241.
15 See Ronald Manzer, *Public Policies and Political Development in Canada* (Toronto: University of Toronto Press 1985), 187–8.
16 My summary of the post-war politics of human rights in Canada owes much to the research of Brian Howe, "The Human Rights Commission under Stress," doctoral dissertation, University of Toronto, forthcoming.
17 E.A. Partridge, *A War on Poverty: The One War That Can End War* (1926), quoted in John Richards, "Populism and the West," in Larry Pratt and Garth Stevenson, eds., *Western Separatism: The Myths, Realities and Dangers* (Edmonton: Hurtig 1981), 68.
18 G.A. Rawlyk and Doug Brown, "The Historical Framework of the Maritimes and Confederation," in G.A. Rawlyk, ed., *The Atlantic Provinces and the Problems of Confederation* (St. John's: Breakwater 1979), 30.
19 A similar argument was adopted by the Royal Commission on Dominion-Provincial Relations in its 1940 report. See Anthony Careless, *Initiative and Response* (Montreal: McGill-Queen's University Press 1977), 20.
20 Maurice Duplessis, "Confederation Has the Essential Ear-marks of a Compact," in J.M. Beck, ed., *The Shaping of Canadian Federalism: Central Authority or Provincial Right?* (Toronto: Copp Clark 1971), 42.
21 Doug Owram, "Reluctant Hinterland," in Pratt and Stevenson, eds., *Western Separatism*, 58.
22 Henri Bourassa, "Is the Compact between French and English-speaking Canadians to Be Abrogated?" in Beck, ed., *The Shaping of Canadian Federalism*, 35.
23 Lionel Groulx, "Tomorrow's Tasks," in Forbes, ed., *Canadian Political Thought*, 266.
24 Gilles Constantineau, "Letter from a Nationalist," in ibid., 312.
25 René Lévesque, "A Country That Must Be," in ibid., 398–9.
26 Quoted by George F.G. Stanley, *The Birth of Western Canada* (London: Longmans, Green 1936), 80–1.
27 See Michael Asch, *Home and Native Land: Aboriginal Rights and the Canadian Constitution* (Toronto: Methuen 1984), 125–8.
28 Beginning with Nova Scotia in 1758, the English common law, both

criminal and civil, was introduced in all the British North American colonies except Quebec, where French civil law was restored by the Quebec Act, 1774. The differences between English and French civil law and their implications for the protection of civil rights in Canada undoubtedly deserve a separate study. However, such a study probably would not modify significantly the general argument and conclusions stated here. To give one example, the common law case of *Rogers* v. *Clarence Hotel Co Ltd* was preceded in 1939 by a decision of the Supreme Court of Canada in *Christie* v. *York Corporation* that a licensed tavernkeeper had a right under the civil code of Quebec to refuse to serve a black man.

29 William Blackstone, *The Sovereignty of the Law: Selections from Commentaries on the Laws of England*, Gareth Jones, ed. (Toronto: University of Toronto Press 1973), 62.

30 Frederick Pollock, *The Expansion of the Common Law* (London: Stevens 1904), 52.

31 Jennifer Nedelsky, "Judicial Conservatism in an Age of Innovation: Comparative Perspectives on Canadian Nuisance Law 1880–1930," in D.H. Flaherty, ed., *Essays in the History of Canadian Law*, I (Toronto: University of Toronto Press 1981), 283–4. I am grateful to Professor Nedelsky for her help in developing the argument in this section.

32 See, for example, Morton Horwitz, *The Transformation of American Law 1780–1860* (Cambridge: Harvard University Press 1977); Grant Gilmore, *The Ages of American Law* (New Haven: Yale University Press 1977); and Patrick S. Atiyah, *The Rise and Fall of Contract* (Oxford: Clarendon Press 1979).

33 R.C.B. Risk, "The Law and the Economy in Mid-nineteenth Century Ontario: A Perspective," in Flaherty, ed., *Essays*, I, 100.

34 R.C.B. Risk, "'This Nuisance of Litigation': The Origins of Workers' Compensation in Ontario," in D.H. Flaherty, ed., *Essays in the History of Canadian Law*, II (Toronto: University of Toronto Press 1983), 432–6.

35 See D.A. Schmeiser, *Civil Liberties in Canada* (London: Oxford University Press 1964), 257–61, and Ian Hunter, "The Origin, Development and Interpretation of Human Rights Legislation," in R. St. J. Macdonald and John P. Humphrey, eds., *The Practice of Freedom* (Toronto: Butterworth 1979), 78–9.

36 Hunter, "The Origin," 79.

37 For a description and discussion of the development of public policies in these two periods, see Manzer, *Public Policies*.

38 See Canada, Department of the Secretary of State, *International Covenant on Civil and Political Rights: Report of Canada on Implementation of the Provisions of the Covenant* (Ottawa: Minister of Supply and Services Canada 1979), *International Covenant on Economic, Social, and Cultural*

Rights: Report of Canada on the Implementation of Articles 6 to 9 of the Covenant, August 1980 (Ottawa: Minister of Supply and Services Canada 1981), and *International Covenant on Economic, Social and Cultural Rights: Report of Canada on the Implementation of Articles 10 to 12 of the Covenant, December 1982* (Ottawa: Minister of Supply and Services Canada 1983).

39 Canada, *Report of the Royal Commission on Dominion-Provincial Relations*, Book II (Ottawa: King's Printer 1940), 33.

40 Ibid., 51.

41 See The Canadian Bill of Rights, 1960 (Canada, c 44, RSC 1970, Appendix III); Department of Justice, *A Canadian Charter of Human Rights* (Ottawa: Queen's Printer 1968); and Canada Act, 1982 (UK), c 11, Schedule B (Constitution Act, 1982). The Constitution Act, 1982, renamed the BNA Act the Constitution Act, 1867.

42 C.B. Macpherson, "Natural Right in Hobbes and Locke," in D.D. Raphael, ed., *Political Theory and the Rights of Man* (London: Macmillan 1967), 14.

CHAPTER THREE

1 James Eayrs, *Diplomacy and Its Discontents* (Toronto: University of Toronto Press 1971), 81.

2 Sheldon E. Gordon, "The Canadian Government and Human Rights Abroad," *International Perspectives* (Nov/Dec 1983), 9.

3 For a sample, see Robert Matthews and Cranford Pratt, "Human Rights and Foreign Policy: Principles and Canadian Practice," *Human Rights Quarterly* 7 (May 1985), 159–89; Douglas Roche, "Towards a Foreign Policy for Canada in the 1980s," *International Perspectives* (May/June, July/Aug 1979), 3–7; T.A. Keenleyside and Patricia Taylor, "The Impact of Human Rights Violations on the Conduct of Canadian Bilateral Relations: A Contemporary Dilemma," *Behind the Headlines* 42 (Nov 1984) 1–27; J.K. Fedorowicz, "Trudeau's Views on Domestic Developments in Poland," in Adam Bromke et al., *Canada's Response to the Polish Crisis* (Toronto: Canadian Institute of International Affairs 1982), 33–44; "Canadian Policy towards South Africa: Brief from the Taskforce on the Churches and Corporate Responsibility," *Canadian Journal of African Studies* 16 (1982).

4 For good discussions of the ultra-realist position, see Michael Walzer, *Just and Unjust Wars* (New York: Basic Books 1977), chapter 1; Stanley Hoffmann, *Duties beyond Borders: On the Limits and Possibilities of Ethical International Politics* (Syracuse: Syracuse University Press 1981), chapter 1. For shorter treatments from a Canadian perspective, see Eayrs, *Diplomacy and Its Discontents*, 166–77, and John W. Holmes, "Morality, Realism and Foreign Affairs," *International Perspectives* (Sept/Oct 1977), 20–5.

5 *Foreign Policy for Canadians*, United Nations booklet (Ottawa: Information Canada 1970), 26
6 Canada, Department of External Affairs, Statements and Speeches 77/5, "Human Rights: One of the Most Complex Foreign Policy Issues," 16 March 1977, 7. For a summary of the views of a succession of Canadian foreign ministers on this issue, see Keenleyside and Taylor, "Impact," 1–2.
7 See, for example, Flora MacDonald's address to the UN General Assembly: Statements and Speeches 79/16, 25 Sept 1979; likewise, the Mulroney government's green paper on foreign policy reiterated the government's commitment to human rights. While it devoted a mere seventeen lines to the issue, it did state that Canada has been "very active in the defence of human rights and in the search for political stability with human dignity. It is a moral and political imperative that we continue to work towards these ends." *Competitiveness and Security: Directions for Canada's International Relations* (Ottawa: Supply and Services Canada 1985), 15–16.
8 The following discussion is based on a survey of nine years of public statements on human rights by elected and bureaucratic officials. See Statements and Speeches: 78/13, 26 Oct 1978; 79/10, 11 June 1979; 81/3, 2 Feb 1981; 81/7, 27 March 1981; 82/23, 31 Aug 1982; 83/6, 22 April 1983; 84/4, 26 March 1984; 85/16, 29 March 1985.
9 Such perceptions may explain why in one study conducted in the mid-1970s human rights was accorded such low importance by Ottawa policy-makers. Officials were asked to rank foreign policy objectives in terms of both importance and Canada's ability to influence outcomes: human rights ranked last in a list of fifteen broad objectives. See Peyton V. Lyon and Brian W. Tomlin, *Canada as an International Actor* (Toronto: Macmillan 1979), chap. 3, especially 41, 52.
10 Margaret Doxey, "Human Rights and Canadian Foreign Policy," *Behind the Headlines* 37 (June 1979), 10.
11 See, for example, Cranford Pratt, "Canadian Policy towards the Third World: Basis for an Explanation," in *Studies in Political Economy* 13 (spring 1984), 27–56, and Linda Freeman, "The Effect of the World Crisis on Canada's Involvement in Africa," *Studies in Political Economy* 17 (summer 1985), 107–39.
12 Keenleyside and Taylor, "Impact," 24.
13 See John W. Holmes, *The Shaping of Peace: Canada and the Search for World Order, 1943–1957*, II (Toronto: University of Toronto Press 1982), 323–33.
14 Statement by R.A. MacKay to the Ad Hoc Political Committee, 9 Nov 1955, reprinted in Arthur E. Blanchette, ed., *Canadian Foreign Policy, 1955–1965: Selected Speeches and Documents* (Toronto: McClelland and Stewart 1977), 300.

15 Statement to the House of Commons, 26 Nov 1968, reprinted in Arthur E. Blanchette, ed., *Canadian Foreign Policy, 1966–1976: Selected Speeches and Documents* (Toronto: Gage 1980), 169.
16 Statements and Speeches 77/5, 16 March 1977, 2,3.
17 Ibid., 78/13, 26 Oct 1978, 1.
18 Ibid., 80/3, 4 Feb 1980, 1–2.
19 See Samual J. Nesdoly, "Changing Perspectives: The Ukrainian-Canadians' Role in Canadian-Soviet Relations," in Aloysius Balawyder, ed., *Canadian-Soviet Relations, 1939-1980* (Oakville, Ont.: Mosaic Press 1981), 121–2.
20 See "International Canada, December 1982 and January 1983," in *International Perspectives* (March/April 1983), 15; Gordon, "Canadian Government," 9.
21 Gordon, "Canadian Government," 9.
22 See, for example, the testimony of Marcel Massé on this question: Canada, Parliament, Senate, Standing Committee on Foreign Affairs, *Proceedings*, 33rd Parl., 1st Session, no. 7, 25 March 1986.
23 See, for example, the importance attached to strategic interests in my examination of Canadian policies toward Indonesia during the 1970s: "Les droits de la personne et la politique étrangère du Canada: le cas de l'Indonésie," *Etudes internationales* 11 (June 1980), 223–38.
24 For analyses of Canada's South African policy that reflect these macro-strategic concerns, see, inter alia, Robert Matthews and Cranford Pratt, "Canadian Policy towards Southern Africa," in Douglas Anglin et al., *Canada, Scandinavia and Southern Africa* (Uppsala: Scandinavian Institute of African Studies 1978), 164–78; Freeman, "Effect of the World Crisis," 107–39; and Freeman, "Canada and Africa in the 1970s," *International Journal* 35 (autumn 1980); Clarence G. Redekop, "Reconciling Canadian Objectives in Southern Africa, 1946–1980: The Search for Balance," paper presented to the Study Commission on US Policy toward South Africa, mimeo, July 1980.
25 Such was Robert O. Matthews's overly kind characterization of Canadian policy: see "Canada's Relations with Africa," *International Journal* 30 (summer 1975), 544.
26 From the beginning of the Timor incident, the Canadian government refused to engage in public criticism, abstaining, for example, on a 1975 UN resolution deploring the invasion. Nossal, "Droits de la personne et la politique étrangère du Canada," 234.
27 Though he is likewise loath to term Canada and the United States a "coalition," William T.R. Fox makes a comparable argument: see *A Continent Apart: The United States and Canada in World Politics* (Toronto: University of Toronto Press 1985).
28 For a discussion of how alliance membership shapes Canadian foreign policy, see John W. Holmes, *Life with Uncle: The Canadian-American*

Relationship (Toronto: University of Toronto Press 1981), chapter 4, "On Being an Ally." This issue is also dealt with by Denis Stairs, *The Diplomacy of Constraint: Canada, the Korean War and the United States* (Toronto: University of Toronto Press 1974), especially 322–6.

29 For a comparison of Canadian anti-apartheid measures with those of other states, see North-South Institute, *Review '85/Outlook '86: Multilateralism – Still the First Option for Canada* (Ottawa: North-South Institute 1986), 5–8.

CHAPTER FOUR

1 M.A. Molot and B.W. Tomlin, "The Conservative Agenda," in Molot and Tomlin, eds., *Canada among Nations 1985: The Conservative Agenda* (Toronto: Lorimer 1986), 3.
2 Canada's ratification in 1970 of the International Convention on the Elimination of All Forms of Racial Discrimination preceded most of this legislative development.
3 Cathal Nolan, "The Influence of Parliament on Human Rights in Canada's Foreign Policy," *Human Rights Quarterly* 7 (Aug 1985), 380–2.
4 Since then, this mechanism has become a focus for the sharing and generation of ideas. The Continuing Federal-Provincial Territorial Committee of Officials Responsible for Human Rights meets yearly in preparation for a bi-annual conference of ministers responsible for human rights. There is a link between domestic and foreign policy: through External Affairs, ministers receive information on obligations under international conventions that must be implemented nationally. At this time officials have an opportunity to influence positions to be taken by Canada in international forums. Further, the custom has evolved of including provincial human rights functionaries in Canadian delegations to multilateral meetings, particularly annual sessions of the UN Commission on Human Rights.
5 Efforts at expansion included both increased elaboration of rights (e.g. for women) and attempts to link Canada with international human rights measures within the Commonwealth and at the Council of Europe. A compilation of speeches and statements was distributed at the NGO–External Affairs "Consultation" held January 1988: Department of External Affairs, *Human Rights and Canadian Foreign Policy: Selected Statements and Speeches* (Ottawa: External Affairs Canada 1988).
6 See for example Canada, Department of External Affairs, Statements and Speeches 83/6, Allan MacEachen, "Human Rights and Canadian Foreign Policy," 22 April 1983; and Statements and Speeches 77/5, Don Jamieson, "Human Rights: One of the Most Complex Foreign Policy Issues, " 16 March 1977.
7 MacEachen, "Human Rights and Canadian Foreign Policy," and Jean-Luc

Pepin, "Human Rights in Canadian Foreign Policy," Statements and Speeches 84/4, 26 March 1984.
8 Jamieson, "Human Rights."
9 Statements and Speeches 82/23, Mark MacGuigan, "The Canadian Approach to the International Promotion and Protection of Human Rights," 31 Aug 1982.
10 Ibid., 2, 6.
11 Kim R. Nossal, *The Politics of Canadian Foreign Policy* (Scarborough: Prentice-Hall 1985), 150.
12 See, for example, Gerald Wright, "Bureaucratic Politics and Canada's Foreign Economic Policy," in Denis Stairs and Gilbert Winham, eds., *Selected Problems in Formulating Foreign Economic Policy*.
13 Ibid., 16, 18.
14 Ibid., 19.
15 John Kirton, "The Foreign Policy Decision Process," in Molot and Tomlin, eds., *Canada among Nations*, 45.
16 Ibid., 41.
17 Pierre Trudeau to the Rev. Clark Raymond, 7 March 1981.
18 See, for example, open letter from H. G. Pardy, director, South and Southeast Asia Division, Department of External Affairs, 3 Jan 1986.
19 See, for example, Martin Rudner, *Human Rights Conditionality and International Development Cooperation*, study prepared for CIDA (Ottawa: CIDA 1983); and "Briefing Notes for the Minister," for the Hon. Monique Landry, minister for external relations, Ottawa, 30 June 1986.
20 Department of External Affairs, Communiqué, 86, letter to Nelson Riis, 19 June 1985; House of Commons, *Debates*, 18 June 1985; External Affairs, Communiqué, "Export Controls Policy," 10 Sept 1986; *Globe and Mail*, 20 June 1985.
21 Department of External Affairs, *Competitiveness and Security: Directions for Canada's International Relations* (Ottawa: Minister of Supply and Services 1985); *Government Response to Independence and Internationalism: Report of the Special Joint Committee on Canada's International Relations* (Ottawa: Supply and Services Canada 1986). In the December 1986 document, Joe Clark reaffirmed that "human rights are and will remain a fundamental, integral part of Canadian foreign policy." There has been some tangible evidence of the resolve expressed by Clark. The first steps have been taken to implement the recommendation for establishment of courses in human rights for all External Affairs officers. The recommendation for establishment of an international institute for human rights and the development of democratic institutions led to a special inquiry and the publication of a report supporting the concept: Gisèle Côté-Harper and John Courtney, rapporteurs, *International Cooperation for the Development of Human Rights and Democratic Institutions* (Hull: CIDA 1987).

The latter report explains that there are many details left to be ironed out in establishment of an institute. This is not surprising. There has been no unanimity within the government or in the NGO community regarding the value of such an institution or its nature and priorities. Since Joe Clark is committed to the idea, it seems very likely that the proposed body will be established in 1988.

22 In November 1987, Joe Clark drew fire from the NGO community for announcing resumption of aid to Guatemala. Clark stated that there had been progress in human rights. NGO spokespersons countered that egregious and systematic abuses still plague Guatemala.

23 Most government officials interviewed were candidly informative, though none consented to be quoted or cited.

24 See, for example, "Canada's International Relations: An Alternative View: An Enhanced World Role for Canada," brief submitted by the Canadian Council of Churches to the Special Joint Committee on Canada's International Relations, 29 Nov 1985; and Donald Page, "Does Don Jamieson Read All Those Letters You Write?" *International Perspectives* (May/June 1978), 21–6.

25 Canada, House of Commons, Standing Committee on External Affairs and National Defence, *Canada's Relations with Latin America and the Caribbean* (Ottawa: Queen's Printer 1982).

26 *Independence and Internationalism*. This theme was reiterated by the "Winegard" report, which stated that countries judged by the international community to be the worst offenders should be deemed to be ineligible for government-to-government aid; nevertheless, basic needs assistance might be continued through NGOs working directly with the poor: *For Whose Benefit? Report of the Standing Committee on External Affairs and International Trade on Canada's Official Development Assistance Policies and Programs* (Ottawa: Queen's Printer 1987), 27–30. The government response to Winegard did not adopt its suggestion for a human rights country evaluation framework. It did, however, include "respect shown for human rights" as one of five criteria for core country aid eligibility; *To Benefit a Better World – Canadian International Development Assistance: Responses of Government of Canada to the Report by the Standing Committee on External Affairs and International Trade* (Ottawa: Supply and Services Canada 1987), 49–56, 75.

27 See, for example, Taskforce on Churches and Corporate Responsibility, "Proposal to Establish a Parliamentary Mechanism for Review of the Interrelationship between Canadian Foreign Policy and International Human Rights Observance," brief for the Special Committee on Reform of the House of Commons, Toronto, May 1985.

28 Nolan, "The Influence of Parliament," 280.

29 Kirton, "The Foreign Policy Decision Process," 34–5.

30 Cranford Pratt, "Canadian Policy toward the Third World: Basis for an

Explanation," *Studies in Political Economy* 13 (spring 1984), 41-4; Linda Freeman, "The Effect of the World Crisis on Canada's Involvement in Africa," *Studies in Political Economy* 17 (summer 1985), 123-31.

31 The Winegard report takes the type of sophisticated approach required: *For Whose Benefit?* 23-31 and 64-7.

32 CIDA's attempt to suffuse "women in development" criteria throughout its aid programs might provide some useful models. See Elizabeth McAllister, "Managing the Process of Change in Women and Development," presentation to President's Committee, Policy Branch, CIDA, Jan 1984.

CHAPTER FIVE

1 *The United Nations and Human Rights* (New York: UN 1984), 24.
2 For general descriptions of the functioning of the commission and the sub-commission, see, for example: ibid., 6-8, and Theo C. van Boven, "Protection of Human Rights through the United Nations System," in Hurst Hannum, ed., *Guide to International Human Rights Practice* (Philadelphia: University of Pennsylvania Press 1984), 46ff.
3 Theo van Boven, "Strengthening UN Human Rights Capacity," Working Paper l, Seminar on Human Rights in the United Nations, Geneva, 8-10 Sept 1986. Van Boven responds to the frequent professions of faith in human rights by governments and UN secretaries-general: "It is true that in 1982 the Division of Human Rights was elevated to the status of a Centre, but this up-grading of the human rights programme remained a cosmetic move inasmuch as it was not followed up by corresponding steps to strengthen the capacity of the United Nations to cope with the increased needs and demands in the field of human rights. It is no less than a scandal that, in spite of the large public interest in human rights and in spite of the immense problems many people are facing in this area, the resources of the United Nations allocated to the human rights programme amount to less than one percent of its total."
4 Van Boven, "Protection," 55.
5 "Report by Douglas Reichert, HRI Representative in Geneva," *Human Rights Internet Reporter* 7 (March/May 1982), 680. In the same issue, a joint statement (12 Feb 1982) by 32 international NGOs concluded: "We fear that the circumstances and pressures which led to Mr. van Boven's departure will serve to undermine the authority and credibility of the United Nations and belief in the integrity of its officers" (689).
6 See, e.g., *Report of the Sub-Commission on Prevention of Discrimination and Protection of Minorities* (Geneva 1985), UN E/CN.4/1986/5, E/CN.4/Sub. 2/1985/57, 4 Nov. 1985.
7 *The United Nations and Human Rights*, 7ff. See also Jakob T. Moller, "Petitioning the United Nations," *International Human Rights* (Oct/Dec 1979).
8 The variety of studies and initiatives undertaken by the sub-commission has

naturally created resistance among nations brought under review and guardians of budgetary or legal order. These concerns have led to critical comments and to a 1983 commission recommendation that the sub-commission review its work "to ensure complementarity and co-ordination" with the commission. See *The United Nations and Human Rights*, 8–9.

9 Author's notes from an address given by Philippe LeBlanc to Consultation on Canadian NGOs and International Human Rights Organisations, Ottawa, 13 and 14 Jan 1986.

10 Bill Fairbairn, *The United Nations Commission on Human Rights, 42nd Session: A Report by the Canadian Church Observer* (Toronto: Inter-Church Committee on Human Rights in Latin America [ICCHRLA] 1986). Fairbairn points out (p. 14) that "while Kooijmans at times refers specifically to a few states, in general he avoids naming countries."

11 Interview with Yvon Beaulne, Hull, Quebec, 6 Nov 1986.

12 The resolution for a special rapporteur on the issue was a priority project of the US delegation at the 42nd session.

13 Commission on Human Rights, 42nd session, "Annotations to the Provisional Agenda," E/CN.4/1986/1/Add. 1, 23 Dec 1985.

14 Fairbairn, *Commission*.

15 "Report by Douglas Reichert," 681.

16 Fairbairn, *Commission*.

17 David Kramer and David Weissbrodt, "The 1980 UN Commission on Human Rights and the Disappeared," *Human Rights Quarterly* 3 (Feb 1981).

18 Commission on Human Rights, 42nd session, "Report of the Working Group on Enforced or Involuntary Disappearances," E/CN. 4/1986/18, 24 Jan 1986.

19 *The United Nations and Human Rights*, 42-3; Fairbairn, *Commission*; John W. Foster, *The United Nations Commission on Human Rights, 38th Session: A Report by the Canadian Church Observer* (April 1982); and author's diaries on the 1983 sessions.

20 Foster, *Commission*, and *The United Nations and Human Rights*.

21 Interview with Theo van Boven, former director of the UN Centre for Human Rights, Maastricht, The Netherlands, 19 March 1986.

22 Ibid. I witnessed a sustained attack on a particular NGO spokesperson during the 38th session, when the Argentinian representative repeatedly interrupted the representative of the International Commission of Jurists, Dr Emilio Mignone, who was at the time playing an instrumental role in a legal documentation and investigation centre in Argentina that was active in the cases of the disappeared. Author's diary notes of 38th session, 1982.

23 On the participation of NGOs, see, for example, Menno Kaminga and Nigel S. Rodley, "Direct Intervention at the UN: NGO Participation in the Commission on Human Rights and Its Sub-commission," in Hannum, ed., *Guide*, 186ff.

24 Interview with delegate from a WEO country, New York, April 1986.
25 Interviews with delegates from a variety of WEO countries, Geneva, March 1986, and New York, April 1986, together with observations during sessions.
26 The limitations of the 1503 procedure received thorough and productive review at a September 1986 seminar sponsored by international NGOs in consultative status with the United Nations in Geneva. An evaluation of past activities along with proposals for reform resulted from remarks presented by Niall MacDermot, of the International Commission of Jurists, and Carlos Calero-Rodrigues of Brazil. Author's notes, 8-10 Sept 1986.
27 Howard Tolley, jr, "The Concealed Crack in the Citadel: The United Nations Commission on Human Rights' Response to Confidential Communications," *Human Rights Quarterly* 6 (Nov 1984).
28 Annual reports to the commission by the Working Group on Enforced or Involuntary Disappearances (since 1981) and the report to the 42nd session by the special rapporteur on torture show how a multilateral body like the commission can affect individual cases as well as country situations.
29 See, for example, David Weissbrodt, "Strategies for Selecting and Pursuing International Human Rights Matters," in Hannum, ed., *Guide*; Glenda de Fonseca, *How to File Complaints of Human Rights Violations* (Geneva 1975); Antonio Cassese, "How Could Nongovernmental Organizations Use UN Bodies More Effectively?," *Universal Human Rights* 1 (Oct–Dec 1979); John W. Foster, "In Praise of Plain Speaking," in ICCHRLA's *Newsletter* (March/April 1982).
30 The structure of External Affairs was revised at least twice during the period under study, leading to changes in names and reporting relationships. Delegations were organized by the office responsible for human rights or for human rights and humanitarian affairs (multilateral).
31 I have had the opportunity to follow concerns before the commission in consultation with delegation members such as Rod Bell and Jean-Paul Carrier through sessions in Geneva and the general assembly. Many Western governments adopt a pattern permitting first or second secretaries of their missions in New York to gain familiarity with thematic and situational issues of human rights. A number of such people stressed the need for the continuity and expertise that grow out of experience and persistence (interviews at permanent UN missions in New York, 1985 and 1986).
32 Interview with Yvon Beaulne.
33 This summary of activities draws on Beaulne's remarks at a consultation between representatives of External Affairs and the Canadian Council of Churches, Toronto, 8 September 1981; ICCHRLA's *Newsletter* (May 1981); diary notes by the author; and External Affairs, *Summary Report of the*

Canadian Delegation at the 37th Session of the United Nations Commission on Human Rights (Ottawa 1981).

34 As note 33. External Affairs, *Summary Report* (p. 12), reads: "The adoption of the Declaration was one of the high points of the session for the Canadian delegation and was in part a result of the Canadian representative's successful efforts over the years to engage Third World countries in the endeavour."

35 Why such priority was given to a rather ambiguously defined study and why so much energy was expended on the effort when clear and urgent country situations existed remain matters of concern to some observers.

36 External Affairs, *Summary Report*, 2.

37 Canada, Department of External Affairs, Statements and Speeches 79/16, "An Examination of Conscience at the United Nations," 25 Sept 1979, 3–4.

38 Iain Guest, "The U.S., the UN, and Human Rights," *International Herald Tribune*, 16 March 1981. Canadian patience with Guatemala exceeded what might be expected even of charity. By 30 November 1981, when Canadian delegate Julie Loranger spoke to the Third Committee of the general assembly, Guatemala was still delaying. While the secretary-general had initiated contacts, there was still "no agreement on modes of discussion." Nevertheless, the Canadian delegate appealed, "The United Nations is seeking to understand rather than to condemn." Similarly, on Chile, Loranger indicated that in Canada's opinion "the situation in Chile is no longer one that could be called urgent" and argued that it should be referred to the human rights committee and removed from the commission's agenda. External Affairs, Press Release 32, "Statement by Julie Loranger, Delegate of Canada to the Third Committee of the 36th General Assembly of the United Nations," New York, 30 Nov 1981, 3.

The Chilean situation has been persistent, with repeated moments of urgency, and the 1981 US project to get Chile off the agenda was only one of a series of such efforts. Whether Canada will become wiser or more independent remains to be seen.

39 The Australian delegation to the 42nd session included a representative of the non-governmental community. In an interview with the author, this man indicated that his experience made him hesitant to recommend such an initiative to NGOs in other countries. He cited as negative factors perfunctory delegation consultations on-site, confidentiality of some processes, and a general misconception among international NGO lobbyists at the commission as to his influence.

40 Philippe LeBlanc, "Silence Highly Regrettable," *Toronto Star* 17 March 1985, F1.

41 "Green book": External Affairs, Consultations between the Canadian NGOs

and Department of External Affairs in Preparation for the 42nd Session of the UN Commission on Human Rights, Jan. 1986.
42 Fairbairn, *Commission*, and LeBlanc, "Silence." See also Olivia Ward, "Low-key Canadian Voice on Human Rights Criticized," *Toronto Star* 17 March 1985.
43 *Independence and Internationalism: Report of the Special Joint Committee on Canada's International Relations* (Ottawa: Supply and Services Canada, 1986), 101–2.
44 The External Affairs assessment of conditions in Chile in the 1986 green book came under particular criticism by church coalition representatives for its lack of adequate analysis. For earlier criticisms, see, for example, ICCHRLA's "Submission to the Canadian Ambassador to the 40th Session of the United Nations Commission on Human Rights," 24–Jan 1984, 88–91.
45 For example, in 1985 a delegation of five from the Inter-Church Committee on Human Rights in Latin America held extensive meetings with UN Ambassador Stephen Lewis and with relevant mission staff. It also made representations to the delegations of Australia, France, Mexico, and Sweden.
46 I had conversations with the head of the Canadian delegation to the 39th session in which the forcefulness of the wording of telegrams from United Church of Canada congregations and Roman Catholic religious orders provoked his heated response. Both the executive secretary of the Inter-Church Committee on Human Rights in Latin America and I were repeatedly told by External Affairs officials that they were overwhelmed with correspondence from local church members regarding human rights.
47 Interviews with international human rights specialists in other WEO countries indicate that relations between External Affairs and NGOs with international human rights interests have a number of unique aspects.
48 A letter from Adolphe Proulx, chairperson, ICCHRLA, to Joe Clark, 24 Jan 1985, reads in part: "The churches have expressed concern that Canada has moved to an observer role within the Commission together with their hope that Canada will soon seek re-election for full membership." This view was transmitted as well in meetings with Stephen Lewis and departmental officials.
49 Philippe LeBlanc, "Canada at the UN Human Rights Commission," *International Perspectives* (Sept/Oct 1985); see also LeBlanc, "Silence."
50 "Notes for an Address to the Canadian Human Rights Foundation Conference on Human Rights and Canadian Foreign Policy," Ottawa, 29 March 1985, 4–6.
51 Interview with Theo van Boven.
52 Draft resolution on the "situation of human rights in Guatemala," Commission on Human Rights, 41st session, E/CN.4/1985/L.48, 7 March 1985.

53 Telephone conversation with former chairperson of the commission, 1 May 1986.
54 Interview with experienced senior staff person with the centre, 4 April 1986.
55 Hurst Hannum, "Gutting Human Rights at the United Nations," privately circulated article, April 1986.
56 Niall MacDermot, chair, Special Committee of International NGOs on Human Rights (Geneva), to Javier Pérez de Cuéllar, Secretary-General, United Nations, 26 March 1986, 2.
57 Hannum, "Gutting Human Rights," 4.
58 Telephone conversation with former chair of the commission.
59 See letter from Derek Evans, executive secretary, Canada-Asia Working Group, to Joe Clark, 20 May 1986, and the response of F.D. Pillarella, director, Human Rights and Social Affairs Division, External Affairs, 17 June 1986.
60 "Statement by Stephen Lewis to the General Assembly on the Financial Emergency," New York, 30 April 1986.
61 Stephen Lewis to Marjorie Ross, associate secretary, Canadian Council of Churches, 20 May 1986.
62 Fairbairn, *Commission*.
63 Special Committee of International NGOs on Human Rights (Geneva), Seminar on Human Rights in the United Nations, Geneva, 8–10 Sept 1986, Recommendations and Conclusions.

CHAPTER SIX

1 Strictly speaking, the Human Rights Committee is not a UN body. It was established by treaty (the International Covenant on Civil and Political Rights) and is linked to the UN only indirectly, through the Human Rights Secretariat in Geneva. It reports to the general assembly, but the assembly's directives are not binding in matters other than finance. The committee has formally asserted this independent status. See "Report of the Human Rights Committee," *Official Records* (United Nations General Assembly, 1977), A-322/44.
2 Ross Hynes, first secretary and consul, permanent mission of Canada to the Office of the United Nations at Geneva, July 1986.
3 The economic, social, and cultural covenant limits the obligation of states to "achieving progressively the full realization of rights recognized" within it. There is no such limitation in the civil and political covenant. Moreover, enjoyment of civil and political rights seems historically to have been an essential prerequisite to securing economic and social entitlements.
4 The International Labour Organization has a complaints procedure, but an individual cannot gain a hearing without the complaint being forwarded by a member union. The Committee on the Elimination of All Forms of Racial Discrimination (CERD) has introduced a complaints procedure in

the form of a declaration. Canada has not agreed to this for two reasons. First, CERD's requirement that racist organizations be made illegal would conflict with protection of freedom of speech. Second, the rights concerned are considered by Canadian officials to be adequately protected by the country's participation in the Optional Protocol. Interview with Coleen Swords, Legal Division, External Affairs, July 1986.

5 Canada was not among the first signatories, but after lengthy federal-provincial negotiations it finally acceded on 19 May 1986. From this point, Canada became one of the most active, co-operative, and important players. I have discussed the halting Canadian response to adoption of the covenants in "The Influence of Parliament on Human Rights in Canadian Foreign Policy," *Human Rights Quarterly* (Aug 1985), 79-80.

6 Since 1978 the committee has met three times per year, in the spring in New York and in the summer and autumn in Geneva. The final 1986 session was cancelled owing to cutbacks made necessary by a political and financial crisis in the United Nations.

7 Few countries respect the concept of an independent expert. Failure of the UN Centre for Human Rights to provide adequate support services has frequently forced members to fall back on their national missions. See Walter Tarnopolsky, untitled lecture, International Institute of Human Rights, Strasbourg, July 1984, 22.

8 Canada belongs to the West European and Others Group (WEOG). The United States, which has not ratified the civil and political covenant, participates in this group and in other human rights forums, such as the UN Human Rights Commission.

9 Farrokh Jhabvala, "The Practice of the Covenant's Human Rights Committee, 1976-82: Review of State Party Reports," *Human Rights Quarterly* (Feb 1984), 84.

10 Ibid., 85.

11 For a longer presentation of this debate see Glenn Mower, "The Implementation of the UN Covenant on Civil and Political Rights," *Revue des droits de l'homme* 10:1-2 (1977).

12 This effectively eliminated the proposal, which would have given teeth to the monitoring provisions. The state-to-state complaint procedure has been acceded to by a handful of Western states, including Canada. To date, it has not been used.

13 This idea was an extension of the original state-to-state complaints procedure. It too has yet to be used.

14 The Canadian report in 1979 was nearly 500 pages and included sections on the provinces and territories as well as the federal constitution and legal system; Canada filed a supplementary report in 1983. This record was singled out by UN officials as a model for other states. Interviews, UN Centre for Human Rights, Geneva, July 1986.

15 Quoted in Tarnopolsky, Strasbourg lecture, 25. Jhabvala discusses Soviet

tactics designed to evade accountability in "The Soviet-Bloc's View of the Implementation of Human Rights Accords," *Human Rights Quarterly* (Nov 1985). One Soviet official told the committee that there "were no objective reasons for emigrating [from the Soviet Union], since unemployment was non-existent and there were no problems of nationality because the peoples of the Soviet Union were all equal" (489 n,76).

16 When Third World members expressed their views on this issue, it became apparent that Soviet-bloc members were alone in their restrictive interpretation. Dana Fisher, "International Reporting Procedures," in Hurst Hannum, ed., *Guide to International Human Rights Practice* (Philadelphia: University of Pennsylvania Press 1984), 171.

17 Early examples are cited in M. Nowak, "The Effectiveness of the International Covenant on Civil and Political Rights – Stocktaking after the First Eleven Sessions of the UN-Human Rights Committee," *Human Rights Law Journal* 2:1-4 (1980), 149-51.

18 I recently prepared two reports on human rights and development for the Canadian International Development Agency. These involved a survey of Canadian NGO publications on human rights over the past five years. I uncovered almost no references to the committee, whereas the UN Human Rights Commission was discussed at length numerous times. Also, Canadian church groups have annually sent observers to commission sessions in Geneva, but not to the committee.

19 There has been experimentation with a "second round" of questions in which some members have tried to probe reports. Eastern-bloc countries have refused to participate, thereby prohibiting oversight beyond review of legal provisions of their constitutions. Fisher, "International Reporting Procedures," 170-2.

20 M. Nowak, "Civil and Political Covenant," 162-3.

21 However, in a few protocol cases, individual members attached dissenting opinions to the committee's "Final Views."

22 Louis Sohn, "Human Rights: Their Implementation and Supervision by the United Nations," in Theodore Meron, ed., *Human Rights in International Law: Legal and Policy Issues* (Oxford: Clarendon Press 1984), 392.

23 Nowak first made this observation in 1980 ("Civil Political Covenant," 142). It is still true today.

24 In addition to examples from Western countries, following communication with the committee laws have been changed, administrative practices altered, or prisoners released in Finland, Madagascar, Mauritius, Senegal, and Uruguay. Interviews, UN Centre for Human Rights, July 1986. The Uruguay and Madagascar cases are also referred to in "Report of the Human Rights Committee," *Official Records*, UNGA 39th session, supplement 40 (1984), 126.

25 "Report, " UNGA 39th session, 117.

26 Nowak, "Civil and Political Covenant," 160. In a minority opinion on one case, six members went further by "positively ascertaining" that the covenant had been violated.
27 At first they held press conferences. Later, critical comments were published in annual reports. Most recently, a volume of selected cases has been published as *Human Rights Committee Selected Decisions under the Optional Protocol*, CCPR/C/OP/1 (United Nations 1985).
28 Tarnopolsky, Strasbourg lecture, 32.
29 Interview with Julie Loranger, director general, International Organizations Bureau, External Affairs, July 1986. Justice may have been concerned also that Canada could be embarrassed by appeals to the committee.
30 Interview, July 1986. This praise might appear intended mainly to please an interviewer from Canada, but it was repeated during off-the-record conversations in which the performances of other countries were discussed frankly.
31 Interview with Loranger.
32 Tarnopolsky was appointed to the Ontario Court of Appeal in 1983; his unfinished term on the committee was completed by another highly qualified Canadian, Gisèle Côté-Harper.
33 The belief that Canada's nominee was blocked from re-election partly as a result of the country's activism was expressed by an official of the UN Centre. This is also the strongly held opinion of a number of officials at External Affairs. Interviews, July 1986.
34 Correspondence with Julie Loranger, Oct 1986.
35 Interview with M. Moller, chief, Communications Unit, UN Centre for Human Rights, Geneva, July 1986.
36 Ibid.
37 Interview with Swords.
38 *Chronicle Herald*, Halifax (8 Jan 1981).
39 Interviews, UN Centre for Human Rights, Geneva, July 1986.
40 Canada, Department of External Affairs, Statements and Speeches, 78-13.
41 External Affairs, Statements and Speeches, Stephen Lewis to UNGA, 25 November 1986.
42 General Comment 14, 23rd session, Human Rights Committee (1984); also cited in J. Gomez del Prado, "United Nations Conventions on Human Rights," *Human Rights Quarterly* (Nov 1985), 510, 513.
43 Interview with Swords.
44 Several countries have approached the committee for advisory assistance, but it has neither the resources nor the mandate to provide this; interview with Houshmand, July 1986. A number are apparently willing to ratify the covenant but lack the technical resources to report to the committee and respond to protocol complaints. Some fear international embarrassment over the poor reports they might produce; telephone interview with

Martin Low, Department of Justice, July 1986. Low was Canadian representative at an UNCTAD meeting on covenant reporting obligations, held in May and June 1985.
45 The Soviet bloc regards human rights advisory services as too Western in orientation. It has therefore worked to dissipate UN resources through general seminars. Interviews with officials from External Affairs, July 1986.
46 I have discussed this at greater length in "A Human Rights Advisory Service," *International Perspectives* (March/April 1987), 19-20.
47 Christian Tomuschat, "Evolving Procedural Rules: The United Nations Human Rights Committee's First Two Years of Dealing with Individual Communications," *Human Rights Law Journal* 1, 1/4 (1980), 255.
48 External Affairs, Statements and Speeches, 24 Sept 1986.

CHAPTER SEVEN

This chapter is based partly on the author's personal and direct experience with the ILO 1957–81.
1 *International Labour Standards* (Geneva: International Labour Office 1984).
2 Ernst B. Haas, *Beyond the Nation State – Functionalism and International Organizations* (Stanford, Calif.: Stanford University Press 1964).
3 Kalmen Kaplansky, "The International Labour Organization – Its Human Rights Components," Staff Discussion Paper 76-06, Department of Economics, Lakehead University.
4 K.T. Samson, "The Changing Pattern of ILO Supervision," *International Labour Review*, 118 (Sept/Oct 1979), 569–87.
5 Frank E. Burke and John A. Munro, *Canada and the Founding of the International Labour Organization* (Ottawa: Department of External Affairs 1969).
6 Allan Gotlieb, "The Changing Canadian Attitude to the United Nations Role in Protecting and Developing Human Rights," in Allan Gotlieb, *Human Rights, Federalism, and Minorities* (Toronto: Canadian Institute of International Affairs 1970), 17.
7 Ibid.
8 The conventions in question were: no. 1 – Hours of Work (Industry), 1919; no. 14 – Weekly Rest (Industry), 1921; no. 26 – Minimum Wage-Fixing Machinery, 1928.
9 Convention 27 – Marking of Weight (Packages Transported by Vessels), 1929, ratified in 1938; no. 32 – Protection against Accidents (Dockers) (Revised), 1932, ratified 1946; no. 58 – Minimum Age for Admission to Employment at Sea, 1936, ratified 1951; no. 63 – Statistics of Wages and Hours of Work, 1938, ratified 1946; no. 68 – Food and Catering (Ships' Crews), 1946, ratified 1951; no. 69 – Certification of Ships' Cooks,

1946, ratified 1951; no. 73 – Medical Examination (Seafarers), 1946, ratified 1951; no. 74 – Certification of Able Seamen, 1946, ratified 1951; no. 88 – Employment Service 1948, ratified 1950.
10 Convention 111 – Discrimination (Employment and Occupation), 1958, ratified 1964; no. 45 – Underground Work (Women), 1935, ratified 1966 (denounced by Canada May 1978); no. 122 – Employment Policy, 1964, ratified 1966; no. 87 – Freedom of Association and Protection of the Right to Organize, 1948, ratified 1972; no. 100 – Equal Remuneration, 1951, ratified 1972.
11 James E. Dorsey, " International Labour Conventions and the ILO: Application in British Columbia," paper presented to conference sponsored by Pacific Group for Policy Alternatives, Vancouver, 15–16 Feb 1985.
12 Kalmen Kaplansky, *Canada and the International Labour Organization* (Ottawa: Labour Canada 1980).
13 Report as quoted in Derek Fudge, "ILO Condemns Restrictive Labour Laws in Canada," *Canadian Labour* (31 Jan 1986), 14–15.
14 John Mainwaring, *The International Labour Organization: A Canadian View* (Ottawa: Supply and Services Canada 1986), 192.
15 Ibid., 53–4.
16 Ed Ratushny, "Contextual and Functional Dimensions of Human Rights: A Canadian Perspective," paper presented to international conference on peoples' rights, Zaguzig University, Cairo, Nov 1985.
17 Kaplansky, "Human Rights Components."
18 *Economically Active Population Estimates and Projections 1950–2025*, 3rd ed. (Geneva: International Labour Office 1986).
19 "The Changing World of Work: Major Issues Ahead," *Report of the Director-General*, Part I (Geneva: International Labour Office 1986).
20 *ILO Information* 22 (May 1986).
21 International Labour Conference, 72nd session, "Record of Proceedings," 1986.
22 Mainwaring, *The International Labour Organization*.
23 International Labour Conference, 70th Session, "Record of Proceedings," 1984.
24 *ILO Information* 22 (May 1986).
25 72nd session, "Record of Proceedings," 1986.
26 *Independence and Internationalism: Report of the Special Joint Committee on Canada's International Relations* (Ottawa: Supply and Services Canada 1986).

CHAPTER EIGHT

1 This background is fully created by Robert Spencer, "Canada and the Origins of the CSCE, 1965–73," in Spencer, ed., *Canada and the Con-*

ference on Security and Co-operation in Europe (hereafter *Canada and the CSCE*) (Toronto: Centre for International Studies 1984), 20–101. See also Hans-Adolf Jacobsen et al., eds., *Sicherheit und Zusammenarbeit in Europe (KSZE): Analyse und Dokumentation 1973–1978* (Cologne: Verlag Wissenschaft und Politik, 1978), 493–523. See also an earlier (1973) volume by Jacobsen under the same title.

2 For the Dipoli and subsequent Geneva negotiations, see Luigi Vittorio Ferraris, ed., *Report on a Negotiation: Helsinki-Geneva-Helsinki 1972–1975* (Alphen aan den Rijn: Sijthoff & NoordLoft 1979). See also the official record of the Geneva conference, limited in usefulness by the paucity of published documents: Igor I. Kavass, Jacqueline P. Granier, and Mary F. Dominick, eds., *Human Rights, European Politics, and the Helsinki Accord: The Documentary Evolution of the Conference on Security and Co-operation in Europe, 1973–1975*, 6 vols. (Buffalo: Wm. S. Hein 1981). See also Spencer, "The Curtain Rises: Canada in Stage One, Helsinki, July 1973," and Peyton V. Lyon, "Canada at Geneva, 1973–5," in Spencer, ed., *Canada and the CSCE*, 102–9, 110–33, respectively.

3 Ferraris, ed., *Report*, 43.
4 Spencer, "Canada and the Origins," 95.
5 For the texts of the final recommendations and the Final Act, see Spencer, ed., *Canada and the CSCE*, 351–402.
6 Spencer, "Canada and the Origins," 88.
7 Interview with Gaby Warren, member of the Canadian delegation responsible for basket I and the ten principles, 8 May 1985, Ottawa; also his notes for a speech at the Canadian Council on International Law annual conference, 27 Oct 1978 (typewritten). See also Ferraris, ed., *Report*, 101.
8 Text in Kavass et al., eds., *Human Rights*, I, 147–51, and Canada, Department of External Affairs, Statements and Speeches 73/17, 4 July 1973. Cf. Sharp's speech in the House 5 June 1972, in which he emphasized "freer movement of people, information and ideas"; Canada, House of Commons, *Debates*, 5 June 1972, 2830.
9 Kavass et al., eds., *Human Rights*, I, 391; Jacobsen et al., eds., *Sicherheit und Zusammenarbeit*, 697–8.
10 Ferraris, ed., *Report*, 302; Lyon, "Canada at Geneva," 117, 121.
11 Ferraris, ed., *Report*, 162–4; Lyon, "Canada at Geneva," 123–4. For a full discussion of the ten principles, see Harold S. Russell, "The Helsinki Declaration: Brobdingnag or Lilliput?," *American Journal of International Law* 70 (April 1976), 242–72.
12 Ferraris, ed., *Report*, 134–5, 139. See also Warren interview and notes for speech.
13 Russell, "Helsinki Declaration," 268.
14 Ibid., 268–9; Ferraris, ed., *Report*, 136–7.
15 The points of departure for each of the eight paragraphs were as follows:

para 1, the UN charter; 2, Romanian, Holy See, and Swiss texts; 3, Holy See text; 4, Yugoslav text; 5, charter and Yugoslav text; 6, Swiss text; 7, British text; 8, Soviet text.
16 Ferraris, ed., *Report*, 132, 137.
17 Ibid., 151–2. Canada actively supported the Holy See's efforts to secure para 3, on freedom of religion.
18 For a full discussion, see Vratislav Pechota, *The Right to Know One's Rights: A Road toward Individual Freedom* (New York: American Jewish Committee 1983).
19 Russell, "Helsinki Declaration," 269.
20 W. Tarnopolsky, "The Principles Guiding Relations between States: Human Rights and Non-intervention," in Spencer, ed., *Canada and the CSCE*, 170.
21 Text in External Affairs, Statements and Speeches 75/24, 30 July 1975, and Kavass, ed., *Human Rights*, VI, 26–9.
22 On Belgrade, see H.G. Skilling, "The Belgrade Follow-up," in Spencer, ed., *Canada and the CSCE*, 283–307; see also *Canada at Belgrade: Extracts from Speeches and Interventions by Canada* (Ottawa: Supply and Services Canada 1978).
23 Skilling, "Belgrade," 291–4.
24 For texts of these proposals, of the two NATO proposals, and of major Canadian speeches at Belgrade, see *Canada at Belgrade*.
25 For the Madrid conference, see H.G. Skilling, "The Madrid Follow-up," in Spencer, ed., *Canada and the CSCE*, 308–48; J. Szioo and R. Th. Jurrjens, *CSCE Decision-Making: The Madrid Experience* (The Hague: Martinus Nijhoff 1984); Herman Volle and Wolfgang Wagner, eds., *Das Madrider KSZE-Folgetreffen: Der Fortgang des KSZE-Prozesses in Europa* (Bonn: Verlag für Internationale Politik 1984). For an American view, see Max M. Kampelman (in conversation with George Urban), "Can We Negotiate with the Russians? (and If So, How?)," *Encounter* 64 (Feb 1985), 9–21, and (March 1985), 27–33.
26 Skilling, "Madrid Follow-up," 321–4, on human rights proposals, 327; also Sizoo and Jurrjens, *CSCE*, 85, 94, 96.
27 Text in Spencer, ed., *Canada and the CSCE*, 406–23; also Sizoo and Jurrjens, *CSCE*, 296–301.
28 External Affairs, Statements and Speeches 80/28, 12 Nov 1980.
29 For the texts of the two proposals, see conference documents CSCE/RM 16 and 21, xeroxed. See conference document CSCE/RM 48 of 9 Nov 1982, with more detailed proposals for a human rights meeting.
30 Interviews with Louis Rogers and his assistant, Murray Fairweather, Ottawa, 18 April 1985.
31 Sizoo and Jurrjens, *CSCE*, 222 and 260, and 246.
32 The author acted as a media representative and had access to the building and the delegates.

33 These were numbered CSCE/OME-P.2, 3, and 4, dated 25 April, 25 April, and 26 April, respectively. The agreed agenda was issued without number.
34 Most conference documents, as well as texts of major speeches, were regarded as "restricted" but eventually became available. Few have been published, but copies of most are available in the Thomas Fisher Rare Book Library at the University of Toronto. For speeches of US delegates and US reports on the meeting, see *Implementation of the Helsinki Accords: The Ottawa Human Rights Experts Meeting and the Future of the Helsinki Process,* Hearings before the Commission on Security and Cooperation in Europe, 25 June 1985, 100th Congress, 1st sess. (Washington: U.S. Government Printing Office 1985).
35 The texts of most speeches were made available by the delegations, usually in English, but sometimes only in French, German, Spanish, or Russian. Those available to the author are to be seen in the Fisher Library.
36 These proposals were released on a restricted basis as documents CSCE/OME/2–46, each dated by day of release.
37 CSCE/OME/47 and 48, respectively.
38 The Soviet proposal on religion recommended special attention to the elimination of discrimination on grounds of a person's attitude to religion, so as to ensure the right to profess or not to profess any religion, but made specific reference to legally prescribed limitations on the freedom to manifest one's religious beliefs (as in the international covenant on civil and political rights) (CSCE/OME/42). The proposal concerning co-operation in health and medicine urged action against "abuses" in medicine, such as experimentation on people without their consent, and condemned the politicization of the activities of certain psychiatric associations (CSCE/OME/41).
39 CSCE/OME/49 and 50, respectively.
40 Speech at the opening of the preparatory meeting by Monique Vézina, minister for external relations, Ottawa, 23 April 1985. See also the opening statement by the secretary of state for external affairs, Joe Clark, Ottawa, 7 May 1985. Cf. talks by Harry Jay, head of the Canadian delegation, at the Canadian Institute of International Affairs, Toronto, 11 March 1985, and at the Centre for International Studies, University of Toronto, 20 Sept 1985; his address to 8th annual conference of the Canadian Human Rights Foundation, Ottawa, 29 March 1985; my interview with him in Ottawa, 18 April 1985. For his major addresses to the meeting, see official typewritten copies, cited below by dates.
41 The sub-committee's final report, approved 7 May 1985, and the record of the hearings were published by the House of Commons, Standing Committee on External Affairs and National Defence, Minutes of Proceedings and Guidance, 33rd Parl., 1st sess., nos. 1 and 2 (30 April), 3 (1 May), and 4 (7 May). This committee was a temporary revival of the informal

Helsinki committee of both houses, which had functioned since 1977. Efforts by Senator Stanley Haidasz since 1978 to secure the appointment of a joint standing committee on human rights had not been successful.

42 Press conferences given by Richard Schifter, Sir Anthony Williams, Harry Jay, and others at the close of the conference and conversations with other delegates.

43 Vsevolod Sofinsky, "Post-Ottawa Reflection" (*Izvestia*, 11 July 1985), *From the Soviet Press*, no. 29 (30 July 1985); Sergei Kondrashov, "Human Rights: Double Standard" (from *New Times Weekly*, n.d.), ibid., no. 36, 5 Aug 1985. See also Sofinsky's letter to the *Globe and Mail* 7 Aug 1985.

44 The following was based on CSCE *Digest* (Washington) (Dec 1985–Jan 1986), 1–2; *Radio Free Europe Research* 10/49 (6 Dec 1985), part I; ibid., 10/35 (31 Jan 1986), part II: RAD Background Report no. 14, 22 Jan 1986; interviews in Ottawa with Canadian diplomats, including Michel Duval, delegation member. The opening speeches of all delegates were published in six languages: *Cultural Forum 1985, Budapest: Record of the Opening Statements 15–17 October 1985* (Budapest 1985).

45 See Timothy Garton Ash, "The Hungarian Lesson," *New York Review of Books*, 5 Dec 1985, 5–6, 8–10; *Washington Post* 16 Oct 1985; *New York Times* 16 Oct 1985; *The Times* (London), leader, 22 Oct 1985; *New York Times Book Review*, 3 Nov 1985 (including text of speech by Danilo Kis, a Hungarian from Yugoslavia).

46 On Canada's policy, see *Selection of Statements by the Delegation of Canada to the Human Contacts Experts Meeting of the Conference on Security and Cooperation in Europe (CSCE)*, Berne, 12 April–26 May 1968. Other briefer statements were available in xerox. The author also benefited from a letter from William Bauer, 24 June 1986, and from Bauer's briefing on Berne in Ottawa on 10 July 1986. On Romania, see *Radio Free Europe Research* 11/28 (11 July 1986), part II.

47 Bauer letter.

48 *Selection*, 81–7, 87.

49 Michael Novak, 27 May 1986, in CSCE *Digest* (June 1986), 6, 8.

50 William Bauer, 26 May 1986, in *Selection*, 89.

51 Letter to the *Wall Street Journal*, 8 May 1985, signed by Yuri Yarim-Agaev, V. Bukovsky, A. Ginzburg, Natalya Gorbanevskaya, Leonid Pliouchtch, and others. See also the testimony of Yarim-Agaev, former member of the Moscow Helsinki Committee, *Hearing before the Commission on Security and Cooperation in Europe*, 99th Congress, 1st sess., "Human Rights and the CSCE Process," 3 Oct 1985 (Washington: U.S. Government Printing Office 1986), 46–51 and passim.

52 Testimony at the hearings cited above by Jeri Laber, Rita E. Hauser, Leonard R. Sussman, and Ludmilla Alexeyeva, founding member of the Helsinki Watch Committee. All were ready to accept the doctrine of "link-

age" but wished to keep the CSCE process going. See also an article favouring continuance by Warren Zimmerman, head of the US delegation at the Vienna conference, *New York Times*, 1 Aug 1986. Both the Helsinki Committee in Poland and Charter 77 in Czechoslovakia issued statements in favour of the Helsinki process.

CHAPTER NINE

1 G.K. Helleiner, "Underutilized Potential: Canada's Economic Relations with Developing Countries," in John Whalley, research co-ordinator, *Canada and the Multilateral Trading System* (Toronto: University of Toronto Press 1985), 93.
2 Data on Canadian voting shares in IFIs from Department of Finance, July 1986.
3 Standing Senate Committee on Foreign Affairs, *Proceedings*, 33rd Parl., 1st sess., no. 11, 6 May 1986, 8–19. The remainder of the 1986 Canadian Official Development Assistance was distributed as follows (percentages):

Industrial co-operation	2
Multilateral technical co-operation	5
Humanitarian (emergency aid)	2
Voluntary (NGOs)	7
Multilateral food	7
Bilateral food	8
Petro-Canada International Assistance Corp	
International Centre for Ocean Development	11
International Development Research Centre	
and other	
Administration	3

4 Quoted in Margaret Conklin and Daphne Davidson, "The IMF and Economic and Social Human Rights: A Case Study of Argentina, 1958–1985," *Human Rights Quarterly* 8 (May 1986), 246.
5 Earl Drake, "Human Needs and Human Rights: Toward a Canadian Approach," address given at a North/South Institute Conference, 23–24 Oct 1978, 3.
6 W. Frick Curry and Joanne Royce, "Enforcing Human Rights: Congress and the Multilateral Banks," part three in a series on human rights and the international financial institutions, in *International Policy Report* (Feb 1985) 11, 14. During the first three years of the Reagan administration, these proportions have shifted to 31 per cent and 3 per cent respectively.
7 For details of the Harkin amendments, see ibid.
8 Quoted in ibid., 2.
9 Ibid., 17.

10 Ibid., 7.
11 "Address to the Board of Governors," Washington, 25 Sept 1972, 9, 18, 20.
12 World Bank, Operational Manual Statement 2.34, Feb 1982.
13 World Bank, Operational Manual Statement 2.38, Feb 1980.
14 World Bank, Operational Manual Statement 2.36, May 1984.
15 For a full legal examination see Victoria E. Marmorstein, "World Bank Power to Consider Human Rights Factors in Loan Decisions," *Journal of International Law and Economics* 13:1 (1978), 113–36.
16 As quoted in "A Victory over Apartheid," *International Policy Report* (April 1984), 2.
17 As quoted in ibid., 9.
18 Ibid., 9.
19 Richard Jolly, "Adjustment with a Human Face," The Barbara Ward Lecture 1985, mimeo, 5.
20 J.P. Grant, "Statement to the Global Meeting of UNDP Resident Representatives," Copenhagen, Nov 1985, 5.
21 Margaret Conklin and Daphne Davidson, "The IMF and Economic and Social Human Rights: A Case Study of Argentina, 1958–1985," *Human Rights Quarterly* 8:1 (May 1986), 262.
22 See chapter 10 (Keenleyside).
23 Cranford Pratt, "Canadian Policy towards the International Monetary Fund: An Attempt to Define a Position," *Canadian Journal of Development Studies* 6:1 (1985), 20.
24 TCCR, "Proposal to Establish Human Rights as a Co-determinant of Canada's Voting Decisions in the International Monetary Fund," accompanying letter to Marc Lalonde, 6 June 1983, and his response, 15 July 1983.
25 TCCR, "Bill C-30, Amendment to the Bretton Woods Agreement Act," Submission to the Standing Commons Committee on Finance, Trade and Economic Affairs, 16 April 1985, and *Proceedings* of the same date.
26 *Independence and Internationalism: Report of the Special Joint Committee on Canada's International Relations* (Ottawa: Supply and Services Canada 1986), 85.
27 Ibid., 103.
28 *United States Participation in the Multilateral Development Banks* (Washington: Department of the Treasury 1982), 48.
29 Ibid., 41.
30 Ibid., 61. The IMF continued to lend to Chile during the Allende period.
31 Ibid., 59.
32 Ibid., 65.
33 *Globe and Mail* (Toronto), 25 March 1986.
34 The loan was to finance land rehabilitation, construction of farm facilities, acquisition of machinery and agricultural tools, animal purchases, and working capital intended for small and medium-sized private farms.

35 The record of the events described here is based in part on telephone interviews with staff of the Center for International Policy, Washington, the centre's published research, unpublished documents, and telephone interviews with Canadian senior staff at the IDB. Where practicable, specific notes are given.
36 A copy of the set of documents quoted in this and the preceding paragraphs is in the possession of the TCCR, through the courtesy of the Center for International Policy, Washington.
37 Letter from Marc Lalonde to the TCCR, circa May 1984.
38 Caleb Rossiter, "The Financial Hit List," *International Policy Report* (Feb 1984), 4.
39 Telephone interview with senior Canadian staff at the IDB, March 1986.
40 J. Morrell, Center for International Policy, memo to the author, 7 May 1986. The memo also noted strong objections by the Netherlands, Sweden, and Switzerland.
41 Letter from Joe Clark, 21 May 1986.
42 Appendix to presentation by M. Catley-Carlson, president of CIDA, before Standing Senate Committee on Foreign Affairs, *Proceedings*, 6 May 1986, 19.
43 As quoted in TCCR, *Annual Report 1982–1983* (Toronto 1983) 47.
44 Telephone interview with staff of Center for International Policy, Washington, Dec 1982.
45 Jim Morrell and William Jesse Biddle, "Central America: The Financial War," *International Policy Report* (March 1983), 4.
46 Letter from Marc Lalonde to TCCR, 8 March 1984.
47 Morrell and Biddle, "Central America: The Financial War," 3.
48 Telephone interview with Department of Finance, May 1983.
49 *Le Devoir* (Montreal) 3 Dec 1983.
50 The IMF's assessment of South Africa still included Namibian data: it was the only UN agency that continued to treat the two countries as one. See David Gisselquist, "International Monetary Fund Relations with South Africa," submission to the Thirty-Sixth Session, Fourth Committee, United Nations, Oct 1981, unpublished.
51 Letter from Marc Lalonde to the TCCR, 8 Nov 1982, and from Allen MacEachen to the TCCR, 14 April 1983.
52 "A Victory over Apartheid," 4.
53 TCCR, *Annual Report 1983–1984*, 30; for the response in the US Congress to this decision, see 11–12.
54 International Monetary Fund, "South Africa: Staff Report for the 1983 Article IV Consultation and Review under Stand-By Agreement," 19 May 1983.
55 External Affairs, Speech to ASEAN foreign ministers, 27 June 1983.

56 A.W. Clausen, president, IBRD, "For Consideration on June 20, 1985," Executive Board Meeting, R85-104, 6 June 1985.
57 Letter from Michael Wilson, 31 July 1985.
58 Telephone interview with Canadian staff at World Bank, 10 July 1985.
59 "Aid Memo," Center for International Policy, 3 Dec 1986.
60 Letter from Michael Wilson to the TCCR, 2 Feb 1987.
61 *Independence and Internationalism*, 74.
62 *Canada's International Relations*, Response of the Government of Canada to the Report of the Special Joint Committee of the Senate and the House of Commons (Ottawa: Supply and Services Canada 1986), 74.
63 *For Whose Benefit? Report of the Standing Committee on External Affairs and International Trade on Canada's Official Development Assistance Policies and Programs* (Ottawa: Supply and Services Canada 1987).
64 Ibid., 30. "Human rights negative" and "human rights watch" denote the two most serious categories of human rights offenders.
65 CIDA, *To Benefit a Better World: Response of the Government of Canada to the Report of the Standing Committee on External Affairs and International Trade* (Ottawa: Supply and Services Canada 1987), 28.
66 Senate Committee, *Proceedings*, 6 May 1986, 26–7.
67 Sheikh Hamidou Kane, minister of planning and co-operation, Senegal, in the foreword to *Within Human Reach: A Future for Africa's Children*, United Nations Children's Fund, mimeo, 1985.
68 Albert Fishlow, "The State of Latin American Economics," *Economic and Social Progress in Latin America*, External Debt: Crisis and Adjustment, Inter-American Development Bank, 1985 Report, 147.
69 Tony Killick, *The Quest for Economic Stabilization: The IMF and the Third World* (London: Heinemann 1984), 198.
70 Senate Committee on Foreign Affairs, *Proceedings*, 33rd Parl., 1st sess., no. 7, 25 March 1986, 8.
71 Ibid., 17.
72 Senate Committee, *Proceedings*, 6 May 1986, 27.
73 See *Independence and Internationalism*, 85.
74 *Canada's International Relations*, 63.

CHAPTER TEN

I wish to thank Margaret Beddoe for her invaluable research assistance in connection with portions of this chapter.
1 Bernard Wood, in *Proceedings of the Eighth Annual Conference on Human Rights and Canadian Foreign Policy*, Canadian Human Rights Foundation, Ottawa, 29 March 1985, 126.
2 Paul Gérin-Lajoie, *The Longest Journey* (Ottawa: CIDA 1976), 15, 17, 22.

3 Canada, House of Commons, *Debates*, 3 March 1977, 3610, and 21 March 1978, 3989–96.
4 Final Report of the Sub-Committee on Canada's Relations with Latin America and the Caribbean, in Standing Committee on External Affairs and National Defence, *Minutes of Proceedings and Evidence*, 32nd Parl., 1st sess., no. 78, 23 Nov. 1982, 14-15; *Independence and Internationalism: Report of the Special Joint Committee on Canada's International Relations* (Ottawa: Supply and Services Canada 1986), 102-3; *For Whose Benefit? Report of the Standing Committee on External Affairs and International Trade on Canada's Official Development Assistance Policies and Programs* (Ottawa: Supply and Services Canada 1978), 27–30. For a fuller discussion of Parliament's consideration of human rights in the context of development assistance policy, see Cathal Nolan, "The Influence of Parliament on Human Rights in Canadian Foreign Policy," *Human Rights Quarterly* 7 (Aug 1985), 380–5.
5 See, in particular, Robert Matthews and Cranford Pratt, "Human Rights and Foreign Policy: Principles and Canadian Practice," *Human Rights Quarterly* 7 (May 1985), 186. See also Geoffrey Pearson, "Emergency of Human Rights in International Relations," *International Perspectives* (July/Aug 1978), 11; Douglas Roche, "Towards a Foreign Policy for Canada in the 1980's," *International Perspectives* (May/June, July/Aug 1979), 6; Robert Carty and Virginia Smith, *Perpetuating Poverty: The Political Economy of Canadian Foreign Aid* (Toronto: Between the Lines 1981), 176; Robert Carty, "Giving for Gain – Foreign Aid and CIDA," in Robert Clarke and Richard Swift, eds., *Ties That Bind: Canada and the Third World* (Toronto: Between the Lines 1982), 202; M.W. Conley, "Development Aid and Human Rights: The Canadian Position," address to the Sixth Annual Conference on Human Rights and Canadian Foreign Policy, Canadian Human Rights Foundation, Ottawa, 22 April 1983, 5-6; Sheldon E. Gordon, "The Canadian Government and Human Rights Abroad," *International Perspectives* (Nov/Dec 1983), 9; and Irving Brecher, "Foreign Aid and Human Rights," *International Perspectives* (Sept/Oct 1985), 23-6.
6 Martin Rudner, *Human Rights Conditionality and International Development Co-Operation*, study prepared for CIDA under contract 82-433/C335, project 083/00009 (Ottawa: CIDA 1983), 71.
7 See *North-South Relations 1980-85: Priorities for Canadian Policy*, a discussion paper prepared for the Special Committee of the House of Commons on North-South Relations (Ottawa: North-South Institute 1980), 65; E. Philip English, *Canadian Development Assistance to Haiti: An Independent Study* (Ottawa: North-South Institute 1984), 155, 162; Patricia Adams and Lawrence Solomon, *In the Name of Progress: The Underside of Foreign Aid* (Toronto: Energy Probe Research Foundation 1985), 160; "Public Statement of the Canadian Churches on Government Policy and

the Crisis in Central America," 31 March 1982, cited in Rudner, *Conditionality*, 57; Inter-Church Committee on Human Rights in Latin America (ICCHRLA), "Canadian Policy on Central America: A Brief Presented to the Honourable Allan MacEachen on 11 October 1983," 17. A number of individuals and groups also made representations before the special joint committee in 1985 and 1986 and before the standing committee on External Affairs and International Trade in 1986 and 1987 in support of an aid-rights link.

8 *Globe and Mail* (Toronto) 20 Aug 1984. See also 18 Nov 1982, 11 Jan 1983, 3 April 1984, 2 May, 27 May, and 12 July 1985.
9 White paper, *Foreign Policy for Canadians*, International Development booklet (Ottawa: Information Canada 1970), 12.
10 *Debates*, 2 March 1977, 3574.
11 Canada, Department of External Affairs, Statements and Speeches 78/13, 26 Oct 1978, 6.
12 "Canada in a Changing World – Part II: Canadian Aid Policy," in Canada, House of Commons, *Minutes of Proceedings and Evidence of the Standing Committee on External Affairs and National Defence*, no. 3, 10 June 1980, 176.
13 External Affairs, Statements and Speeches 83/6, 22 April 1983, 4.
14 *Debates*, 16 June 1981, 10654; External Affairs Statements and Speeches 81/21, 29 July 1981, 3.
15 See, for example, External Affairs Statements and Speeches 85/16, 18 Oct 1985, 6.
16 Ibid., 81/7, 27 March 1981, 5; and CIDA, *Elements of Canada's Official Development Assistance Strategy*. (Ottawa: CIDA 1984), 36.
17 Jack Donnelly, "Cultural Relativism and Universal Human Rights," *Human Rights Quarterly* 6 (Nov 1984), 404.
18 For articulate statements of this argument, see, inter alia, Peter L. Berger, "Are Human Rights Universal?" *Commentary* 64 (1977), 62; Evan Luard, "Human Rights and Foreign Policy," *International Affairs* 56 (autumn 1980), 592-3; Rhoda Howard, *Is There an African Concept of Human Rights?* Working Paper no. A 8 (Toronto: Development Studies Programme, University of Toronto); Rudner, *Conditionality*, 18, 59-60; Matthews and Pratt, "Human Rights and Foreign Policy," 163.
19 Carty and Smith, *Perpetuating Poverty*, 176.
20 Rudner, *Conditionality,* 64–5.
21 For arguments based on national interest, see ibid., 67, and Matthews and Pratt, "Human Rights and Foreign Policy," 164.
22 Rudner, *Conditionality*, 57.
23 Matthews and Pratt, "Human Rights and Foreign Policy," 163–4. As the Trudeau government in effect stated in the 1970 foreign policy review, basic Canadian values constitute a component of the national interest, so

that if Canadians aspire to a foreign policy that gives expression to humanitarian goals, then these goals require a place in its foreign policy. See *Foreign Policy for Canadians*, booklet 1, 10–11, 34. For a development of this idea, see James E. Hyndman, "National Interest and the New Look," *International Journal* 26 (winter 1970–1), 9–10.

24 Robert Matthews and Cranford Pratt, "Human Rights and Canada's Foreign Aid Policy," paper presented at the annual meeting of the Canadian Political Science Association, University of Guelph, 11 June 1984, 11.

25 Even multilateral action may, of course, be ineffective. Yet it may still be desirable to take an initiative on principle to avoid complicity in a state's repression.

26 This line of reasoning is particularly stressed by government officials and formed a central point in the Liberal government's opposition to the Foreign Aid Prohibition Bill of 1978, which, it was argued, would make Canadian development assistance policy a "hostage to only one factor." *Debates*, 21 March 1978, 3992. A CIDA policy document for the period 1982–3 to 1986–7 asserted that "the selection of countries of concentration for Canadian development co-operation assistance reflects" a "blend of humanitarian, developmental, political and commercial considerations"; human rights conditionality could be seen as conflicting with this goal of placing development "within a broader context of foreign policy objectives, governed by an overarching concept of the national interest." Rudner, *Conditionality*, 39.

27 See, for example, Margaret Doxey, "Human Rights and Canadian Foreign Policy," *Behind the Headlines* 37 (June 1979), 16; Rudner, *Conditionality*, 45.

28 See *Debates*, 21 March 1978, 3993. The problems in this regard are already apparent in the frequent differences of opinion expressed in Parliament about those countries where aid should be curtailed.

29 This argument was emphasized by some officials in interviews. See also Doxey, "Human Rights," 16.

30 Wood, in *Proceedings of Conference*, March 1985, 127.

31 See External Affairs, Statements and Speeches 78/13, 6; 81/7, 5; 82/23, 5; 83/6, 4; 84/4, 7; 85/16, 6; *Elements of Canada's Strategy*, 35.

32 Martin Rudner, "The Evolving Framework of Canadian Development Assistance Policy," in Brian W. Tomlin and Maureen Molot, eds., *Canada among Nations 1984: A Time of Transition* (Toronto: Lorimer 1985), 127.

33 Christian Bay, *Towards a Post Liberal World Order of Human Rights*, Working Paper no. A 7 (Toronto: Development Studies Programme, University of Toronto 1983), 5; Renate Pratt, *Human Rights and International Lending: The Advocacy Experience of the Taskforce on the Churches and Corporate Responsibility*, Working Paper no. A 15 (Toronto: Development Studies Programme, University of Toronto 1985), 12.

34 In support of such an approach, see Peter Baehr, "Concern for Development Aid and Fundamental Human Rights: The Dilemma as Faced by the Netherlands," *Human Rights Quarterly* 4 (spring 1982), 50.
35 On the devastating effects of many large-scale energy projects on those displaced by them without adequate compensation and a voice regarding implementation, see Adams and Solomon, *In the Name of Progress*.
36 A particular concern has been the neglect of women in development, despite their vital role in the process. In Africa, for example, it is estimated that 70 per cent of the work in rural areas is performed by women. David McKie, "Third World Women and Development," *International Perspectives* (July/Aug 1984), 13–16.
37 For a persuasive argument regarding the importance of civil and political rights, see Rhoda Howard, *The Full-Belly Thesis: Should Economic Rights Take priority over Civil and Political Rights? A discussion from Sub-Saharan Africa*, Working Paper A 3 (Toronto: Development Studies Programme, University of Toronto 1983).
38 The most appropriate model for Third World development has, of course, been a subject of considerable debate. The "basic needs" approach has been attacked by proponents of capital-intensive and export-oriented developmental strategies, who argue that only the latter will ensure that developing countries achieve sophisticated, self-sustaining economies. While not rejecting the role of large-scale capital projects and the enhancement of export performance in the developmental process, this chapter argues for a primary focus on aid targeted at the most disadvantaged groups in developing countries as that most compatible with a preoccupation with social justice. Among recent Canadian works advocating such an approach, see Richard Sandbrook, *The Politics of Basic Needs: Urban Aspects of Assaulting Poverty in Africa* (Toronto: University of Toronto Press 1982); and "Is There Hope for Africa?," *International Perspectives* (Jan/Feb 1983), 3–8; Peter Wyse, *Canadian Foreign Aid in the 1970's: An Organizational Audit* (Montreal: Centre for Developing-Area Studies, McGill University 1983); Carty, "Giving for Gain," especially 184.
39 In interviews, some officials have admitted this, while pointing out that only over the last few years has the government been developing a policy.
40 See Theodore Cohn, "Politics of Canadian Food Aid: The Case of South and Southeast Asia," in Theodore Cohn, Geoffrey Hainsworth, and Lorne Kavic, eds., *Canada and Southeast Asia: Perspectives and Evolution of Public Policies (Coquitlam,* BC: Kaen Publishers c. 1980), 43.
41 See, for example, *Debates*, 19 Nov 1964, 10301–2.
42 *Foreign Policy for Canadians*, Pacific booklet, 20.
43 Calculated from CIDA's annual reports, 1970–1 to 1985–6.
44 In the mid-1970s, the estimated number of detainees was over 55,000: *Indonesia: An Amnesty International Report* (London: Amnesty Interna-

tional Publications 1977), 43; *Amnesty International Report 1985* (London: Amnesty International Publications 1985), 215.
45 See *Torture in the Eighties* (London: Amnesty International Publications 1984), 189–91.
46 The Center for Defense Information in Washington ranks the East Timor conflict as the most violent in the world relative to population size: Derek Rasmussen, "East Timor: A Tragedy Ignored," *Globe and Mail* 7 Dec 1985. For further details of the situation in East Timor see *Amnesty International: East Timor Violations of Human Rights* (London: Amnesty International Publications 1985).
47 See Martin Rudner, "Advantages of Trading with Indonesia," *Canadian Business Review*, 11 (spring 1984), 26.
48 External Affairs, Statements and Speeches 81/16, 16 June 1981, 2.
49 Allan MacEachen, as reported in the Toronto *Star* 30 Sept 1976.
50 Cohn, "Politics of Canadian Food Aid," 49. For similar perspectives, see also Kim R. Nossal, "Les droits de la personne et la politique étrangère canadienne: le cas de l'Indonesie," *Etudes internationales* 11 (June 1980), 223–38; Lorne Kavic, "Innocents Abroad? A Review of Canadian Policies and Postures in Southeast Asia," and David Preston, "The Canada–Southeast Asia Aid and Trade Relationship: Evolution and Future Directions," in Cohn et al., eds., *Canada and Southeast Asia*, 28, 36–8; David Van Praagh, "Canada and Southeast Asia," in Peyton Lyon and Tareq Ismael, eds., *Canada and the Third World* (Toronto: Macmillan 1976), 334–5.
51 Interviews with the author.
52 Cohn, "Politics of Canadian Food Aid," 48.
53 *Country Profile: Uganda* (Ottawa: CIDA 1982), 2.
54 This was acknowleged by officials in interviews.
55 See, for example, *Debates*, 21 March 1978, 3991.
56 *Yearbook of the United Nations, 1979*, XXXIII (New York: UN Department of Public Information 1982), 259; *Canadians in the Third World: CIDA's Year in Review, 1980–81* (Ottawa: CIDA 1982), 21–2.
57 For more details, see, for example, Simon Baynham, "Equatorial Guinea: The Terror and the Coup," *World Today* 36 (Feb 1980), 65–71.
58 *Amnesty International Report 1981* (London: Amnesty International Publications 1981), 39.
59 *A Review of Canadian Development Assistance Policy in the Western Hemisphere* (Ottawa: CIDA 1974), 40–3, 43–7, as quoted in Carty and Smith, *Perpetuating Poverty*, 66.
60 Calculated from the EDC's annual reports, 1974–84, and from data provided to the author by the EDC for 1977–9 and 1985–6.
61 See Virginia Smith, "What's Good for Business," *Last Post* 6 (June/July 1977), 11.
62 External Affairs, Statements and Speeches 82/12, 31 March 1982, 3.

63 Carty and Smith, *Perpetuating Poverty*, 67.
64 Such funds, directed at improving the economic lot of poor black South Africans, have been disbursed since 1982–3. In April 1984, Canada also announced a contribution of $1.5 million over five years toward a scholarship program for non-white South African students: "International Canada: The Events of April and May 1984," supplement to *International Perspectives*. (July/Aug 1984), 11.
65 *Debates*, 9 March 1981, 8034.
66 *Canadians in the Third World: CIDA's Year in Review, 1981–82* (Ottawa: CIDA 1983), 26. See also Margaret Catley-Carlson, in *Minutes of Proceedings and Evidence of the Standing Committee on External Affairs and National Defence*, 33rd Parl., 1st sess., no. 22, 16 May 1985, 6. In interviews, officials acknowledged that the human rights rationale for these two suspensions was post facto.
67 James Guy, "El Salvador: Revolution without Change," *Behind the Headlines* 39 (October 1981), 4.
68 Indeed, in announcing the suspensions, the external affairs secretary praised the Duarte government for its efforts to bring order to the country and described it as a victim of violence by forces on the extreme left and right, while Duarte himself was seen as favouring reforms: *Debates*, 9 March 1981, 8034.
69 "International Canada: The Events of December 1984 and January 1985," supplement to *International Perspectives* (March/April 1985), 10; *Globe and Mail* 12 June and 10 July 1985; John Graham, "The Caribbean Basin: Whose Calypso?" notes for a speech by John Graham, director general, Caribbean and Central America Bureau, External Affairs, to the Canadian Institute of International Affairs, Foreign Policy Conference, 4 May 1985, 9.
70 *Globe and Mail* 1 April and 18 Dec 1985.
71 See Memorandum of Understanding between the Government of El Salvador and the Government of Canada, 2 April 1986. See also Meyer Brownstone, "Canadian Aid to El Salvador Gone Askew?," *Globe and Mail* 16 June 1986.
72 Graham, "The Caribbean Basin,"10.
73 Edgar J. Dosman, "Hemispheric Relations in the 1980's: A Perspective from Canada," *Journal of Canadian Studies* 19 (winter 1984–5), 57.
74 Ibid., 55; ICCHRLA, "Canadian Policy on Central America," 6–7; Cecilio J. Morales, "A Canadian Role in Central America," *International Perspectives* (Jan/Feb 1985), 12; Matthews and Pratt, "Human Rights and Foreign Policy," 179–80.
75 One encouraging exception to this general pattern of treating pro-Western and Communist states differently is Nicaragua. Despite the political orientation of the Sandinista régime (and charges of violations of political and

civil rights in particular), Canada continues to maintain a significant assistance program, justified on the grounds of its effective developmental impact at the grassroots level.

76 In interviews, some officials acknowledged this phenomenon and noted the difficulty of "taking on " countries where Canada has sizeable development programs and other important relationships.

77 Wood, in *Proceedings of Conference,* March 1985, 132–3.

78 Ottawa views human rights violations in Guyana as bad by Commonwealth Caribbean standards but not in global terms.

79 Information regarding aid to Sri Lanka has been obtained principally from interviews with officials in Ottawa.

80 *Globe and Mail* 29 Aug 1985, 12 June 1986.

81 "International Canada: The Events of October and November 1984," supplement to *International Perspectives* (Jan/Feb 1985), 8.

82 Compiled from CIDA annual reports, 1983–4, 1984–5, 1985–6.

83 Rudner, "The Evolving Framework," 134–5. See also *In the Canadian Interest? Third World Development in the 1980's* (Ottawa: North-South Institute 1980), 11, 56; Roger Young, *Canadian Foreign Aid Policies: Objectives, Influences and Consequences,* Working Paper no. A 10 (Toronto: Development Studies Programme, University of Toronto 1984), 9.

84 This problem is explored in Wyse, *Canadian Foreign Aid,* especially 47–69. See also *North-South Encounter: The Third World and Canadian Performance* (Ottawa: North-South Institute 1977), 122.

86 Instances of inappropriate Canadian aid as a result of tying provisions are legion: a fully automated bakery for Tanzania that led to reliance on imported fuel, spare parts, and hard grains; a satellite communications system for Bangladesh, used for international telephone communciations and the reception of television signals for the minuscule élite with television sets; water pumps for Ghana that immediately broke down under tropical conditions; redwood power poles for a transmission system in Botswana when cheaper eucalyptus trees were available in Swaziland; aircraft for a private airline in Indonesia; electrical power-generating projects where the principal beneficiaries have been urban companies and élites; and provision of Canadian food surpluses have often discouraged local agricultural production, deflated prices for homegrown produce, and, because of poor distribution, failed to reach those most in need. For a good recent account of the problems of tied aid, see G.K. Helleiner, "Canada, the Developing Countries and the International Economy: What Next?," *Journal of Canadian Studies* 19 (winter 1984–5), 18–19. See also English, *Assistance to Haiti*; Roger Erhardt, *Canadian Development Assistance to Bangladesh: An Independent Study* (Ottawa: North-South Institute 1983); Roger Young, *Canadian Development Assistance to Tanzania: An Independent Study* (Ottawa: North-South Institute 1983).

87 *North-South Relations 1980–85*, 53.
88 *Strategy for International Development Co-operation 1975–80* (Ottawa: CIDA 1975), 9, 23–5; External Affairs, Statements and Speeches 81/7, 5; 81/16, 3–4; 81/25, 3–5.
89 Carty, "Giving for Gain," 194; Young, "Canadian Foreign Aid," 34.
90 In April 1986, CIDA adopted an all-grant program.
91 Martin Rudner, "Trade cum Aid in Canada's Official Development Assistance Strategy," in Brian W. Tomlin and Maureen Appel Molot, eds., *Canada among Nations 1986: Talking Trade* (Toronto: Lorimer 1987), 136.
92 In February 1984, the government also announced creation of a new trade-aid fund. Half of the increase in aid over the next five years was to be allocated to this fund, to be used in conjunction with EDC loans to, in effect, cut loan rates for exports and thereby stimulate Canadian sales of capital goods, equipment, and related services to developing countries. For details, see *The Mulroney Program and the Third World* (Ottawa: North-South Institute 1985), 8; *Globe and Mail* 7 Oct and 2 Dec 1985; Rudner, "The Evolving Framework," 137–44. This proposed scheme was, however, shelved as a result of the expenditure cuts announced in the February 1986 budget.
93 The Mulroney government's green paper on foreign policy affirms this perspective: "Canadian understanding of the diversity and complexity of the Third World has deepened and become more sophisticated. So, too, has our appreciation of the interests we have at stake. Trade and investment, immigration, environmental conservation and international peace and security have been added to our original, largely humanitarian objectives"; *Competitiveness and Security: Directions for Canada's International Relations* (Ottawa: Supply and Services Canada 1985), 9.

CHAPTER ELEVEN

1 Ruth Leger Sivard, *World Military and Social Expendutres 1986* (Washington: World Priorities 1986), 25.
2 A comprehensive survey of current trends is provided by Michael T. Klare in *Journal of International Affairs*: "The State of the Trade: Global Arms Transfer Patterns in the 1980s" (summer 1986). The following description relies on this account, except as otherwise noted.
3 Michael Bzroska and Thomas Ohlson, eds., *Arms Production in the Third World* (London and Philadelphia: Taylor and Francis for the Stockholm International Peace Research Institute [SIPRI] 1986), 10. SIPRI tabulations regard both Israel and South Africa as Third World countries.
4 Figures reporting aggregate sales to non-European and non-US customers are provided annually by the Department of External Affairs.
5 The bureau is the office within the federal trade bureaucracy responsible

for administering the military trade effort. Currently it is a division of External Affairs; previously it was in Industry, Trade and Commerce.

6 For a full account of the Canadian military industry, exports, and government promotional efforts, see Ernie Regehr, *Arms Canada: The Deadly Business of Military Exports* (Toronto: Lorimer 1987).
7 *World Armaments and Disarmament: Sipri Yearbook 1985* (London and Philadelphia: SIPRI, Taylor and Francis 1985), 345–51.
8 See, for example, Michael T. Klare and Cynthia Arnson, *Supplying Repression: US Support for Authoritarian Regimes Abroad* (Washington: Institute for Policy Studies 1981).
9 For a detailed discussion of the political economy of arms exports, see Michael T. Klare, *American Arms Supermarket* (Austin: University of Texas Press 1985).
10 Quoted in *Ploughshares Monitor* 1 (Sept 1978).
11 Patrick Martin, "Ottawa's View of Saudis Shifting Gears," *Globe and Mail* 19 June 1986.
12 "Human Rights and the Regulation of Canadian Arms Sales," Churches' Brief to Special Joint Committee.
13 Traditionally, the ACL has included Warsaw Treaty states as well as Albania, Mongolia, North Korea, Vietnam, and the city of East Berlin. Since September 1986 Warsaw pact countries are not on the ACL; restrictions on sales to those states are dealt with through the ECL.
14 Department of External Affairs, communique 155, 10 Sept 1986, and accompanying Export Controls Policy Background Paper.
15 External Affairs, Notice to Exporters, serial no. 21 (18 July 1984, amended 1 March 1985).
16 Serial no. 21, 18 July 1984, amended 1 March 1985.
17 External Affairs, communique 86, 19 June 1985, text of a letter from Mr. Clark to Nelson Riis, MP.
18 SIPRI, *The Arms Trade with the Third World* (London: Paul Elek 1971), 35.
19 Notice to Exporters, serial no. 21, 6.
20 Clark letter to Riis, 19 June 1985.
21 The following analysis is based on data collected in the Project Ploughshares Military Industry Data Base and reported in Regehr, *Arms Canada*, chap 7.
22 Canada, House of Commons, *Debates*, 19 Jan 1987.
23 External Affairs, letter to the Taskforce of the Churches on Corporate Responsibility (TCCR), 12 Jan 1984.
24 External Affairs, letter to TCCR, 5 June 1984.
25 Clark letter to Riis, 19 June 1985.
26 Letter from External Affairs to TCCR, 5 June 1984.
27 Letter from External Affairs to TCCR, 5 Dec 1984.

CHAPTER TWELVE

1 Canada, House of Commons, Sub-committee on Canada's Relations with Latin America and the Caribbean of the Standing Committee on External Affairs and National Defence, *Final Report* (Ottawa 1982).
2 Canada, *Independence and Internationalism: Report of the Special Joint Committee on Canada's International Relations* (Ottawa: Supply and Services Canada 1986). Among its recommendations the committee suggested (p. 155): "The government should also strengthen Canada's capacity to monitor human rights situations in Central America, paying particular attention to the circumstances in each country."
3 Walter LaFeber, *Inevitable Revolutions: The United States in Central America* (New York: Norton 1984), 18.
4 Liisa North, *Negotiations for Peace in Central America: A Conference Report*, Proceedings of the Roundtable on Negotiations for Peace in Central America (Ottawa: Canadian Institute for International Peace and Security 1985), 11.
5 *Cepal Review* (Mexico City) no. 22 (April 1984); Cepal, "Centro America: notas sobre la evolucion economica en 1986," mimeo, Mexico City, 16 Jan 1987.
6 LaFeber, *Inevitable Revolutions,* chaps. 3 and 4.
7 Cynthia Brown, ed., *With Friends Like These: The Americas Watch Report on Human Rights and US Policy in Latin America* (New York: Pantheon 1985), 156. Americas Watch says human rights violations in Nicaragua are not attributable to a central policy but instead "have occurred in part as a result of the conditions of internal war and also because of the intolerance of dissent shown at times by high Sandinista officials."
8 Ibid., 175.
9 James Guy, "El Salvador: Revolution without Change," *Behind the Headlines* 39 (Oct 1981), 20.
10 *Settling into Routine* (New York: Americas Watch 1986). See also the Americas Watch report *The Continuing Terror* (New York: Americas Watch 1985).
11 *Free Fire: A Report on Human Rights in El Salvador* (New York: Americas Watch and Lawyers Committee for International Human Rights 1984), 1–3; Brown, ed., *With Friends Like These*, 130. Also see Martin Diskin and Kenneth E. Sharpe, "El Salvador," in Morris J. Blachman, William M. LeoGrande, and Kenneth Sharpe, eds., *Confronting Revolution: Security through Diplomacy in Central America* (New York: Pantheon 1986), 67: "These armed forces were the real government in El Salvador. They, and not the death squads, were responsible for most of the killings of non-combatants."

12 Kenneth E. Sharpe, "El Salvador Revisited: Why Duarte Is in Trouble," *World Policy Journal* 3 (summer 1986), 489. Also see Peter H. Smith, "The Origins of the Crisis," in Blachman et al., eds., *Confronting Revolution*, 16: "From only marginal involvement in 1979, Washington had become, by 1985, the principal architect, financier, and strategist for the Salvadoran government in general and the armed forces in particular."
13 Sharpe, "El Salvador Revisited," 479.
14 UN Economic and Social Council, "The Situation in El Salvador," resolution of the Sub-Commission on Prevention of Discrimination and Protection of Minorities of the Commission on Human Rights (E/CN.4/Sub.2/1985/L. 34), 27 Aug 1985. The sub-commission concluded: "The Salvadoran government continues to commit serious and massive violations ... as a result, primarily, of its non-observance of the Geneva Conventions." Also see Inter-Church Committee on Human Rights in Latin America (ICCHRLA), "Report to the 42nd Session of the United Nations Commission on Human Rights," *ICCHRLA Newsletter* nos. 1 and 2 (1986), 18–19.
15 *Settling into Routine*, 39–54.
16 *El Salvador: Human Rights Dismissed: A Report on 16 Unresolved Cases* (New York: Lawyers Committee for Human Rights 1986).
17 This linkage has been noted by the independent Committee for the Defence of Human Rights in Honduras (CODEH), by Americas Watch, and by the ICCHRLA. See *ICCHRLA Newsletter* nos. 1 and 2 (1986), 6; *Submission to the Canadian Ambassador to the 40th Session of the United Nations Commission on Human Rights* (Toronto: ICCHRLA 1984), 66–7; and Brown, ed., *With Friends Like These*, 146.
18 The US military build-up includes construction of 11 airstrips, six new radar installations, new Atlantic harbour facilities, a regional military training centre, and new military bases and associated infrastructure. "To put it bluntly, Honduras is doing Reagan's dirty work in Central America," according to a former assistant director of the Peace Corps Training Center in Honduras. Militarization "has become a means not to peace, stability, and development but to the very conditions militarization was presumably designed to avoid: Uncertainty, insecurity, violence, repression, and loss of freedom and well-being." See Philip L. Shepherd, "Honduras," in Blachman et al., eds., *Confronting Revolution*, 125–55.
19 Cited in *ICCHRLA Newsletter*, nos. 1 and 2 (1986).
20 *Foreign Policy for Canadians*, Latin America booklet (Ottawa: Information Canada 1970), 5–6.
21 Cited in Steven Baranyi, "Canadian Foreign Policy towards Central America, 1980–84: Independence, Limited Public Influence, and State Leadership," in *Canadian Journal of Latin America and Caribbean Studies* 10:19 (1985), 29.
22 For more analysis of Canada's commercial and aid relationship with Central

America see Robert Carty and Virginia Smith, *Perpetuating Poverty: The Political Economy of Canadian Foreign Aid* (Toronto: Between the Lines 1981), 69; Tim Draimin, "Canada and Central America: An Overview of Business and Governmental Relations," in *Central America: A Contemporary Crisis* (Toronto: LARU Studies 1982), 81–94.

23 Canada, Department of External Affairs, "Notes for a Speech by the Honourable Allan J. MacEachen, Deputy Prime Minister and Secretary of State for External Affairs, at a Seminar on Latin America and Its Relationship with Canada Sponsored by the United Nations Association of Canada and the Institute for International Cooperation, University of Ottawa, June 3, 1983."

24 The Montreal-based International Power Company brought the first electricity to El Salvador in the 1920s. In 1932, when the dictator, General Maximiliano Hernandez Martinez, began the bloody slaughter of 30,000 Salvadoran peasants, the Canadian navy was briefly deployed off the nation's coast to protect Canadian investments. See Tim Draimin, "Canadian Foreign Policy and El Salvador," in Liisa North, ed., *Bitter Grounds: Roots of Revolt in El Salvador* (Toronto: Between the Lines 1981), 99–110.

25 Canada, Office of the Prime Minister, "Joint Statement by the President of Mexico and the Prime Minister of Canada," 27 May 1980.

26 Since then, the Canadian government has had no comparable, high-level contact in Ottawa with the Salvadoran opposition, although Canadian diplomats do maintain contact with the FDR in Nicaragua. Unlike Mexico, however, Canada has not recognized the FDR/FMLN as a representative political force.

27 *Submission to the Canadian Ambassador to the 36th Session of the United Nations Commission on Human Rights* (Toronto: ICCHRLA 1980), 15–18.

28 William M. LeoGrande, Douglas C. Bennett, Morris J. Blachman, and Kenneth E. Sharpe, "Grappling with Central America: From Carter to Reagan," in Blachman et al., eds., *Confronting Revolution*, 304.

29 Quoted in Draimin, "Canadian Foreign Policy and El Salvador," 102.

30 In his 1982 testimony to the sub-committee, Sirrs did not volunteer any comments about human rights abuses in El Salvador, although death squad killings and military atrocities had been documented for over two years: see Sub-Committee on Canada's Relations with Latin America and the Caribbean, *Minutes of Proceedings and Evidence*, 32nd Parl., 1st sess., no. 24, 17 June 1982, 24–5, 52. For the department official's comment on trade promotion, see ibid., no. 15, 10 Feb 1982, 4.

31 Letter from the secretary of state for external affairs, Mark MacGuigan, to Archbishop Joseph N. MacNeil, president, Canadian Conference of Catholic Bishops (CCCB), 8 Sept 1980, in possession of author.

32 Letter from Msgr Dennis Murphy, general secretary, CCCB, to N.M. Stiles

(acting director, Caribbean Division, External Affairs), 13 January 1981, in possession of author.
33 Latin American Working Group (LAWG), Toronto, "Overview of Canadian Aid to Central America 1980–1985," *LAWG Letter* 9:3 (Feb 1986), 7–8. Also see *Globe and Mail* (Toronto) 29 Nov 1980.
34 Letter from N.M. Stiles to Msgr Dennis Murphy, 19 Dec 1980, in possession of author.
35 Alexander Haig, *Caveat: Realism, Reagan and Foreign Policy* (New York: Macmillan 1984).
36 John Dinges, "Wide Disparities between Haig's White Paper and Salvadoran Documents," in *Latinamerica Press*, 26 March 1981.
37 *Globe and Mail* 5 Feb 1981.
38 Letter from Mark MacGuigan to Adolphe Proulx, Bishop of Hull and chairperson of the ICCHRLA, 20 Feb 1981, in ICCHRLA archives. Also see Canadian Broadcasting Corporation, "Sunday Morning," documentary report on Canadian policy in Central America by Robert Carty, 26 June 1983.
39 Draimin, "Canadian Foreign Policy and El Salvador," 104.
40 Cited in Draimin, "Canada and Central America," 86.
41 Canada, Department of External Affairs, Statements and Speeches 81/16, "Canada and Third World Countries: A Statement by the Honourable Mark MacGuigan, Secretary of State for External Affairs, Ottawa, June 16, 1981," 5–8.
42 Interview with External Affairs official, June 1986. The volume of correspondence has been sustained: according to officials, the letters are characterized by their intelligence and quality of representation.
43 Letter from Mark MacGuigan to Adolphe Proulx, 20 Feb 1981.
44 *International Herald Tribune* (Paris) 6 March 1981.
45 Subcommittee on Canada's Relations with Latin America and the Caribbean, *Minutes*, no. 1, 8 June 1981, 14–44, and Standing Committee on External Affairs and National Defence, *Minutes of Proceedings and Evidence*, 32nd Parl., 1st sess., no. 48, 8 Dec 1981, 9–11.
46 John W. Foster, *The United Nations Commission on Human Rights, the 38th Session: A Report by the Canadian Church Observer* (Toronto: United Church of Canada 1982).
47 See Renate Pratt in this volume (chapter 9) as well as her *Human Rights and International Lending: The Advocacy Experience of the Taskforce on the Churches and Corporate Responsibility*, Working Paper no. A 15 (Toronto: Development Studies Programme, University of Toronto 1985), 8–9. Human rights criteria also seem to have been abandoned – along with technical criteria – in Canada's support for the 1983 loan from the Inter-American Development Bank to El Salvador for the reconstruction, with military specifications, of the strategic San Marcos bridge. US pressure seems to have been an overriding consideration in Canadian support.
48 *Central American Update* 3:4 (April 1982), 13.

49 Canada-Caribbean–Central America Policy Alternatives (CAPA), *Brief on Canada and Central America* (Toronto: CAPA 1984).
50 External Affairs, "Notes for a Speech by the Hon. Allan J. MacEachen," 3 June 1983, 9. For irregularities in the electoral process, see Brown, ed., *With Friends Like These*, 120–1.
51 According to Canada's San José–based ambassador, Francis Filleul, who served on the election observer team: "Our mandate was to observe and report upon an electoral process and not to make assessments or judgments about the internal political situation in the country": see ICCHRLA, *Nicaragua 1984: Democracy, Elections and War* (Toronto 1984), 40. Also see John W. Foster, "Central America and Canada under the Conservatives," paper presented at the 1984 CALACS conference, University of Toronto, 5–7 Oct 1984.
52 Patrick Martin, "U.S. Taking Wrong Road: MacEachen," *Globe and Mail* 17 April 1984.
53 Letter from Joe Clark to Robert Gardner, national co-ordinator, Inter-Church Committee for World Development Education, 10 Jan 1985, in author's possession.
54 External Affairs, Statements and Speeches 84/17, "Report to the Economic and Social Council: Statement by Dr. Jim Hawkes, Canadian Representative to the Third Committee at the Thirty-ninth Session of the United Nations General Assembly, New York, December 6, 1984"; letter from Joe Clark to Bishop Remi J. De Roo, chairman, Episcopal Commission for Social Affairs, CCCB, 29 April 1985; Michel Arseneault, "Salvador: Ottawa estime que Duarte poursuit une stratégie 'civilisée'," *Le Devoir* (Montreal) 3 Sept 1986.
55 "Superpower Moves in Central America Condemned by PM," *Globe and Mail* 16 Sept 1986.
56 External Affairs, Statements and Speeches 84/4, "Human Rights in Canadian Foreign Policy: An Address by the Hon. Jean-Luc Pepin, Minister of External Relations, to the Seventh Annual Conference on Human Rights and Canadian Foreign Policy, Canadian Human Rights Foundation, Ottawa, March 26, 1984."
57 External Affairs, "Consultations between the Department of External Affairs and Canadian NGOs in Preparation for the 42nd Session of the UN Commission on Human Rights," Ottawa, 23–4 Jan 1986, 12.
58 Rhea M. Whitehead, "The United Nations Commission on Human Rights: Report on the 40th Session" (Toronto: Canadian Council of Churches 1984), 4. Also see reports on the 38th and 39th sessions, published in *ICCHRLA Newsletter* (March/April 1982 and winter 1982–3); Olivia Ward, "Low-key Canadian Voice on Human Rights Criticized," *Toronto Star* 17 March 1985; and "At the Human Rights Commission," *Central America Update* 6:5 (March/April 1985).
59 Interviews with External Affairs officials, March and June 1986.

60 In a 1984 Gallup poll, Canadians who were interviewed opposed US militariz-ation of Central America by a 2–1 margin. See *Globe and Mail* 11 Oct 1984.
61 Stephen Clarkson, *Canada and the Reagan Challenge* (Toronto: Lorimer 1982), 283–4.
62 CBC, "Sunday Morning," 26 June 1983.
63 Standing Committee on External Affairs and National Defence, *Minutes*, 33rd Parl., 1st sess., no. 27, 3 Dec 1984, 27; *Globe and Mail* 24 Nov 1984.
64 Prime Minister Mulroney, for example, criticizes US policy by saying: "We do not approve of third-party intervention anywhere in Central America. Whoever the third party may be, and regardless of its legitimate interests in the area"; *Globe and Mail* 16 Sept 1986.
65 Cited in ICCHRLA, 'Canada in the Americas: Advocate of Peace: A Brief to the Special Joint Committee on Canada's International Relations,' 29 Nov 1985, 20. Also see *Mission for Peace: A Report: Canadians and the Search for Peace in Central America* (Toronto: Non-Intervention in Central America 1986), 11.
66 ICCHRLA, "Canada in the Americas," 20.
67 Cited in *Mission for Peace*, 9.
68 Letter to the editor from Michael R. Bell, assistant deputy director, Caribbean and Latin American Branch, External Affairs, *Globe and Mail* 25 April 1986.
69 *For Whose Benefit? Report of the Standing Committee on External Affairs and International Trade on Canada's Official Development Assistance Policies and Programs* (Ottawa: House of Commons 1987), 210.
70 *Submission to the Canadian Ambassador to the 40th Session of the United Nations Commission on Human Rights* (Toronto: ICCHRLA 1984), 88.

CHAPTER THIRTEEN

1 For documents on this period, see A. Kemp-Welch, trans., *The Birth of Solidarity: The Gdansk Negotiations 1980* (London: Macmillan 1983), and S. Persky and H. Flam, eds., *The Solidarity Sourcebook*. (Vancouver: New Star Books 1982).
2 For a discussion of the Roman Catholic church, see S.S. Miller, "Church and Catholic Opposition in the Polish Communist System," in A. Jain, ed., *Solidarity: The Origins and Implications of Polish Trade Unions* (Baton Rouge, La.: Oracle Press 1983). The influence of Catholic social thought on Solidarity's program is assessed in my "Catholic Personalism and Pluralist Democracy in Poland," *Canadian Slavonic Papers* 25 (Sept 1983), 425–39.

3 For documents and interpretation, see Peter Raina, *Poland 1981: Towards Social Renewal* (London: Allen & Unwin 1985), especially 229–53.
4 This aspect is developed in my chapter "Human Rights in Poland," in J. Donnelly and R. Howard, eds., *An International Handbook of Human Rights* (Westport, Conn.: Greenwood Press, 1987).
5 "The Solidarity Program," in Persky and Flam, eds., *Solidarity Sourcebook*, 205–25.
6 Stefan Olszowski's address in *Documents and Materials* no. 18 (Warsaw: Ministry for Foreign Affairs, 1982), 4.
7 Ibid.; also, in the same issue, see M.F. Rakowski, "Using the 'Polish Issue' for the Aggravation of East-West Relations," 26–38.
8 Olszowski address, 4–5.
9 The 1982 act is appended to *Documents and Materials* no. 18. Also see the ILO's assessment of this act in International Labour Office, *Official Bulletin: Special Supplement*, 67: Series B (1984), especially 38–40 (hereafter ILO Report on Poland).
10 UN Commission on Human Rights, "Question of the Violation of Human Rights ... Report on the Situation in Poland" (40th session, 1 March 1984), 7–8 and annex III (E/CN.4/1984/26) (hereafter CHR Report on Poland).
11 Ibid.; also see Jane Cave, "The Legacy of Martial Law," in *Poland Watch* no. 4 (1983), 1–20.
12 General Wojciech Jaruzelski's speech at a meeting with unionists in Katowice, 26 Aug 1983, in *Documents and Materials* no. 10/33 (1983), 16–46. In his address to the 17th plenum of the central committee of the PUWP, 27 Oct 1984, Jaruzelski stated: "Sensitivity to the dignity of man, to civil rights, is a great achievement of our system"; see *Contemporary Poland* 17:21 (Nov 1984), 33.
13 *Poland under Martial Law: A Report on Human Rights by the Polish Helsinki Watch Committee*, English edition distributed by US Helsinki Watch Committee 1983; *1984 Violations of Human Rights in Poland: Report by the Polish Helsinki Committee*, English edition distributed by the Committee in Support of Solidarity, United States, 1985.
14 *Documents and Materials* no. 18 (1982), 3–16, especially 23.
15 Ibid., 7.
16 United States, Department of State, *United States Participation in the UN: Report by the President to the Congress for the Year 1983* (Washington: Department of State Publications 1984), 201–2.
17 Ibid., 188.
18 See Howard Tolley jr, "Decision-making at the United Nations Commission on Human Rights, 1979–82," in *Human Rights Quarterly* 5 (Feb 1983), especially Table 7 indicating bloc voting, 51.

19 Jack Donnelly, "Recent Trends in UN Human Rights Activity: Description and Polemic," *International Organization* 35-4 (autumn 1981), 633-55.
20 ILO Report on Poland, 1-2; also see Jean-Michel Servais, "ILO Standards on Freedom of Association and Their Implementation," *International Labour Review* 123 (Nov/Dec 1984), 768.
21 CHR Report on Poland, 11-12.
22 The Polish Helsinki Watch Committee identified 50 victims who died "as a result of police action" between 1981 and 1983; four others "died in mysterious circumstances suggestive of foul play on the part of the police." See "Fatal Victims of Martial Law," and "The Helsinki Committee in Poland: Memorandum to the Human Rights Commission of the United Nations," in *Poland Watch* no. 6 (1984), 22-30 and 137-69, respectively. Also see *Poland under Martial Law*.
23 ILO Report on Poland, 137.
24 CHR Report on Poland, 11-12.
25 ILO Report on Poland, 131-50.
26 Ibid., 149; for Poland's response, see annex I.
27 For a general overview of Canada's relations with Poland in the 1980s, I have used the following: R.B. Byers, ed., *Canadian Annual Review of Politics and Public Affairs* (Toronto: University of Toronto Press, annually); Canada, Department of External Affairs, *Annual Report* (Ottawa, annually); M. Duval, External Affairs, "Direction des relations avec l'URSS et l'Europe de l'Est: les sanctions contre la Pologne" (Aug 1984) and "Outline of Bilateral Relations between Canada and Poland" (1984, copy sent by Duval); and House of Commons, *Debates*.
28 House of Commons, *Debates*, 4 Dec 1980, cited in *Canadian Annual Review for 1980*, 185.
29 As quoted in *Canadian Annual Review for 1981*, 291.
30 L.J. Cohen, "Soviet-Canadian Trade: Constraints and Opportunities," paper presented to Institute of International Relations, University of British Columbia, 1983, 28.
31 *Canadian Annual Review for 1981*, 292-3.
32 Ibid.; also see Paul Marantz, "Poland and East-West Relations," *Canadian Slavonic Papers* 25 (Sept 1983), 411-24; and Adam Bromke et al., *Canada's Response to the Polish Crisis* (Toronto: Canadian Institute of International Affairs 1982).
33 *Canadian Annual Review for 1982*, 158; Duval, "Les sanctions" and "Outline."
34 *Canadian Annual Review for 1982*, 158.
35 Duval, "Les sanctions."
36 *Canadian Annual Review for 1982*, 160-1.
37 Duval, "Outline."
38 This was especially evident during Pope John Paul II's 1983 visit to Poland.

39 See, in particular, A.H., "Proba Spojrzenia," *Polityka Polska* 1 (fall 1982), 8–41.
40 Interviews with External Affairs officials, Jan 1986; also see Duval, "Les sanctions."
41 Canada, House of Commons, *Sub-Committee on Human Rights in Eastern Europe of the Standing Committee on External Affairs and National Defence, Minutes of Proceedings and Evidence*, 33rd Parl., 1st sess., no. 1, 30 April 1985.
42 Interviews with External Affairs officials, Jan 1986.
43 In Bromke et al., *Canada's Response*; also see his *Poland: The Protracted Crisis* (Oakville: Mosaic Press 1981) and *Eastern Europe in the Aftermath of Solidarity* (New York: Columbia University Press 1985).
44 Cited in *Canadian Annual Review for 1982*, 189.
45 Ibid., 188.
46 In a background paper, preliminary to this volume.
47 Alexander M. Haig jr, *Caveat: Realism, Reagan and Foreign Policy* (New York: Macmillan 1984), 239–40.
48 Marantz, "Poland," 414–16, 422–4; also Haig, *Caveat*, 241.
49 Franz-Lothar Altman (Munich), "Presentation to the Kennan Institute," Oct 1985, in *Meeting Report of the Kennan Institute for Advanced Russian Studies* (Washington: Smithsonian Institution, Wilson Center, undated).
50 Jiri Valenta, "Soviet Use of Surprise and Deception," *Survival* 24 (March/April 1982), 50–61, and "Revolutionary Change, Soviet Intervention, and 'normalization' in East-Central Europe," *Comparative Politics* 16 (Jan 1984), 138–9.
51 Duval, "Outline."
52 Altman, "Presentation."
53 Duval, "Outline."
54 Altman, "Presentation."
55 Interview with Stanisław Długosz, deputy chairman, Council of Ministers Planning Commission, "The Cost of Western Restrictions: Who's Going to Foot the Bill?" in *Documents and Materials* no. 10/33 (1983), 60.
56 Ibid., 60–1.
57 Ibid., 61.
58 Poland's national traditions and deviations from the communist model are discussed in my "Human Rights in Poland."
59 Matthews and Pratt in this volume, 6–10.
60 *Independence and Internationalism: Report of the Special Joint Committee of the Senate and of the House of Commons on Canada's International Relations* (Ottawa: Supply and Services Canada 1986), 100. The report quotes the submission of the Canadian Council of Churches for a description of basic rights: "The churches assume that all people everywhere, regardless of their ideological, cultural, or political system, wish to be

362 Notes to Pages 262–9

free from disappearance, from arbitrary arrest, detention, torture and extrajudicial execution and from state-sponsored racial discrimination."

CHAPTER FOURTEEN

Except for minor editorial revisions, this chapter was completed on 10 October 1987 and does not take account of events since that time.

1 *Race Relations Survey 1985* (Johannesburg: South African Institute of Race Relations 1986), 3; *World Development Report* (New York: World Bank 1985), Table 23, 218.
2 *Apartheid: The Facts* (London: International Defence and Aid Fund 1983), 19.
3 Aziza Seedat, *Crippling a Nation: Health in Apartheid South Africa* (London: International Defence and Aid Fund 1984), 9; *World Development Report*, Table 23, 218 (combination of figures for infant and child mortality).
4 Seedat, *Crippling a Nation*, 84; Claude Meillassoux, *Apartheid, Poverty and Malnutrition*, FAO Economic and Social Development Paper 24 (Rome: Food and Agriculture Organization 1982), 91; *World Development Report*, Table 24, 220.
5 Seedat, *Crippling a Nation*, 20; *Accelerated Development in Sub-Saharan Africa* (Washington: World Bank 1981), Table 1, 143; *Race Relations Survey 1985*, 131.
6 Frederick Johnstone, "South Africa," in Jack Donnelly and Rhoda E. Howard, eds., *An International Handbook of Human Rights* (Westport, Conn.: Greenwood Press 1987), 348.
7 Seedat, *Crippling a Nation*, 19; Amnesty International, *South Africa: Imprisonment under the Pass Laws* (London: Amnesty International 1986), 1:1.
8 *Facts on File* 46 no. 2370 (25 April 1986), 291–2; *Christian Science Monitor* 28 Sept–4 Oct 1987, 7.
9 *Facts on File* 46 no. 2358 (31 Jan 1986), 53.
10 Rhoda E. Howard, *Human Rights in Commonwealth Africa* (Totowa, NJ: Rowan and Littlefield 1986), 70.
11 *Globe and Mail* 5 Nov 1985, A6.
12 Amnesty International, *Bulletin* (Canadian section) 13 (April 1986), 7–8.
13 Johnstone, "South Africa," 345.
14 *Apartheid: The Facts*, 59, 62.
15 Howard, *Human Rights*, 162.
16 Ibid., 130.
17 Ibid., 157–8.
18 Ibid., passim.
19 Letter to the *Hamilton Spectator*, 30 Aug 1985, A11.
20 Canada, Special Joint Committee of the Senate and the House of Commons

on Canada's International Relations, *Minutes of Proceedings and Evidence*, no. 24, 10 Dec 1985, 26.
21 Henry Shue, *Basic Rights: Subsistence, Affluence, and U.S. Foreign Policy* (Princeton, NJ: Princeton University Press 1980), 52.
22 Robert Matthews and Cranford Pratt, "Human Rights and Foreign Policy: Principles and Canadian Practice," *Human Rights Quarterly* 7 (May 1985), 163.
23 Harold Wolpe, "Capitalism and Cheap Labour-Power in South Africa: From Segregation to Apartheid," *Economy and Society* 1 (1972), 425–56.
24 Shue, *Basic Rights*, 170.
25 Robert O. Matthews, "The Churches and Foreign Policy," *International Perspectives* (Jan/Feb 1983), 19.
26 *World Development Report*, Table 24, 220, Table 25, 222; and *Accelerated Development*, Table 37, 180.
27 For a history of the conflict, see Edward Kannyo, "Uganda," in Donnelly and Howard, eds., *International Handbook*.
28 *World Development Report*, Tables 24, 25, 23, on 220, 222, 218 respectively.
29 Roger Young, *Canadian Development Assistance to Tanzania* (Ottawa: North-South Institute 1983), 104.
30 *World Development Report*, Tables 23, 24, 25, on 218, 220, 222.
31 Robert O. Matthews, "Canada and Anglophone Africa," in Peyton V. Lyon and Tareq Y. Ismael, eds., *Canada and the Third World* (Toronto: Macmillan 1976), 61.
32 *Foreign Policy for Canadians*, booklet 1 (Ottawa: Information Canada 1970), 26.
33 *Canada: Strategy for International Development Cooperation 1975–1980* (Ottawa: CIDA 1975), 26.
34 *International Canada*, 9 (March 1978), 69. See also the discussion of this bill in chapter 10.
35 Donald Barry, "Interest Groups and the Foreign Policy Process: The Case of Biafra," in A. Paul Pross, ed., *Pressure Group Behaviour in Canadian Politics* (Toronto: McGraw Hill-Ryerson 1975), 115–47. See also the discussion in chapter 3.
36 Matthews, "Canada and Anglophone Africa," 116.
37 Ibid., 121.
38 Douglas G. Anglin, "Canada and Africa: The Trudeau Years," in Colin Legum, ed., *Africa Contemporary Record*, 16 (1983–4), A182.
39 *International Canada*, 4 (Feb 1973), 65.
40 Ibid., 8 (June 1977), 135.
41 Howard, *Human Rights*, 135.
42 "International Canada (October and November 1983)," insert in *International Perspectives* (Jan/Feb 1984), 9.
43 *Foreign Policy for Canadians*, booklet on the UN (Ottawa: Information Canada 1970), 17–20.
44 Cranford Pratt, ed., "Canadian Policies towards South Africa: An Exchange

between the Secretary of State for External Affairs and the Taskforce on the Churches and Corporate Responsibility," *Canadian Journal of African Studies*, 17:3 (1983), 512–13.
45 See, for example, Canada, Department of External Affairs, Statements and Speeches 84/14, "Apartheid – A Violation of Fundamental Human Rights," 20 Nov 1984.
46 Ibid., 85/14, "Principles of UN Charter Signposts to Peace," 23 Oct 1985, 3.
47 *International Canada*, 7 (June 1976), 190.
48 Ibid., 9 (July and Aug 1978), 186.
49 The code of conduct is printed in Douglas G. Anglin, Timothy Shaw and Carl Widstrand, eds., *Canada, Scandinavia and Southern Africa* (Uppsala: Scandinavian Institute of African Studies, 1978), 156–8.
50 Clarence G. Redekop, "Commerce over Conscience: The Trudeau Government and South Africa, 1968–1984," *Journal of Canadian Studies*, 19 (winter 1984–5), 98.
51 Ibid., 99.
52 *International Canada*, 8 (Nov 1977), 256.
53 For details, see Anglin, "Canada and Africa"; Linda Freeman "The Effect of the World Crisis on Canada's involvement in Africa," *Studies in Political Economy*, 17 (1985), 107–39; Redekop, "Commerce over Conscience"; "Canadian Policy towards Southern Africa, Brief from the Taskforce on the Churches and Corporate Responsibility," *Canadian Journal of African Studies* 16:1 (1982), 113–26, and "Canadian Policy towards Southern Africa: A Brief Presented to the Right Honourable Joe Clark, Secretary of State for External Affairs," Toronto, TCCR, 16 May 1985.
54 See chapter 9.
55 *Facts on File* 45 no. 2329 (12 July 1985), 516, and 45 no. 2345 (1 Nov 1985), 821; *Globe and Mail* 13 June 1986, A1–A2.
56 *Globe and Mail* 6 Sept 1986, A2; 11 Sept 1986, A8.
57 Ibid., 5 Aug 1986, A1; 30 Sept 1986, B22; 8 Oct 1986, B9.
58 Testimony of Linda Freeman in Special Joint Committee, *Minutes*, no. 24, 12.
59 *Globe and Mail* 13 June 1986, A2; 30 Sept 1986, B3; 11 Nov 1986, A1.
60 *Independence and Internationalism: Report of the Special Joint Committee of the Senate and the House of Commons on Canada's International Relations* (Ottawa: Queen's Printer 1986), 108–11; *Canada's International Relations: Response of the Government of Canada to the Report of the Special Joint Committee of the Senate and the House of Commons* (Ottawa: Supply and Services Canada 1986), 77.
61 *Globe and Mail* 13 June 1986, A2.
62 Paul Ladouceur, "Canada's Humanitarian Aid for Southern Africa," in Anglin, Shaw and Widstrand, eds., *Canada, Scandinavia and Southern Africa*, 85–102.

63 *Globe and Mail* 31 Jan 1987, A1; 10 Sept 1987, A1.
64 Statistics Canada, *Imports by Countries January–December 1985* (Ottawa 1986), Table 3, *Exports by Countries January–December 1985* (Ottawa 1986), Table 3, *Canada's International Investment Position 1981 to 1984* (Ottawa 1986), Table 4.
65 Robert Matthews and Cranford Pratt, "Canadian Policy towards Southern Africa," in Anglin et al., eds., *Canada, Scandinavia and Southern Africa*, 168.
66 See Cranford Pratt, "Dominant Class Theory and Canadian Foreign Policy: The Case of the Counter-Consensus," *International Journal* 39 (winter 1983–4), 99–135.
67 Ibid., 118.
68 Canadian Institute of Public Opinion, *Gallup Poll Report* 2 June 1983; Gallup Omnibus Study Conducted for the Minister of State for Multiculturalism, Nov 1981.
69 *Gallup Poll Report* 4 Nov 1985.
70 Anglin, "Canada and Africa," A179.
71 Freeman, "Effect of the World Crisis," 122
72 Pratt, "An Exchange," 503; for a discussion of extraterritoriality, see chapter 3.
73 Statistics Canada, *Exports 1985*, Table 3, and *Imports 1985*, Table 3.
74 *Globe and Mail* 13 June 1986, A10.
75 Ibid., 17 Aug 1987, A5.
76 Ibid.
77 Ibid., 11 Sept 1985, B1; 29 Aug 1985, B4; 21 March 1986, B6; 29 May 1986, A1; 10 Feb 1987, B7.

CHAPTER FIFTEEN

1 Stanley Hoffmann, *Duties beyond Borders: On the Limits and Possibilities of Ethical International Politics* (Syracuse: Syracuse University Press 1981), 157.
2 *Independence and Internationalism: The Report of the Special Joint Committee on Canada's International Relations* (Ottawa: Supplies and Services 1986), 100.
3 These reasons are more fully discussed in our "Human Rights and Foreign Policy: Principles and Canadian Practice," *Human Rights Quarterly*, 7:12 (May 1985), 4–5.
4 Louis Henkin, "Human Rights and Domestic Jurisdiction," in Thomas Buergenthal, ed., *Human Rights, International Law and the Helsinki Accord* (Montclair, NJ: Allenheld, Osman 1977), 21.
5 Ibid., 26.
6 Jack Donnelly, "Human Rights, Humanitarian Intervention and American

Foreign Policy," in *Journal of International Affairs* (winter 1984), 311. R.J. Vincent defines intervention as "that activity undertaken by a state, a group within a state, a group of states or an international organization which interferes coercively in the domestic affairs of another state," *Nonintervention and International Order* (Princeton: Princeton University Press 1974), 13.

7 Louis Henkin, *The Rights of Man Today* (Boulder: Westview Press 1978), 125.
8 This view is hotly disputed. For the supporting case see Hoffmann, *Duties beyond Borders*, and Michael Walzer, *Just and Unjust Wars* (New York: Basic Books 1977). For the opposing view see Donnelly, "Human Rights."
9 Neo-realism is a theoretical approach to the study of international relations that is largely the product of American scholarship. Its most sophisticated application to the study of Canadian foreign policy is by David DeWitt and John Kirton, *Canada as a Principal Power* (Toronto: Wiley 1983). Dominant class theory is primarily about the relation between economic and political power; the most authoritative application to Canadian affairs is still Leo Panich, ed., *The Canadian State: Political Economy and Political Power* (Toronto: University of Toronto Press 1977). The theory has not been much applied to the study of foreign policy. For examples see Cranford Pratt, "Canadian Policy towards the Third World: Basis of an Explanation," in *Studies in Political Economy* 13 (spring 1984), 27–56; Tom Keating, "The State, the Public and the Making of Canadian Foreign Policy," paper presented to the Canadian Political Science Association, June 1985; and J. Rochlin, "Theoretical Aspects of Canada's Relations with Central America," Canadian Institute for International Peace and Security, 1987, mimeo.
10 This distinction is developed and used with much effect by Peter Katzenstein, John Goldthorpe, and Robert Keohane in their essays in John Goldthorpe, ed., *Order and Conflict in Contemporary Capitalism: Studies in the Political Economy of Western European Nations* (Oxford: Clarendon Press 1984).
11 On Canada's position with respect to the place of human rights in the new world order established in 1954, see John W. Holmes, ed., *The Shaping of Peace: Canada and the Search for World Order*, I (Toronto: University of Toronto Press 1979) 242, 290–5.
12 Ibid., 242.
13 Quoted in ibid., 293.
14 See *Independence and Internationalism: Report of the Special Joint Committee on Canada's International Relations* (Ottawa: Supplies and Services 1986); *For Whose Benefit? Report of the Standing Committee on External Affairs and International Trade on Canada's Official Development Assistance Policies and Programs* (Ottawa: Queen's Printer 1987);

and CIDA, *To Benefit a Better World: Response of the Government of Canada to the Report of the Standing Committee on External Affairs and International Trade* (Ottawa: Suppply and Services Canada 1987).
15 Stanley Hoffmann, "The Hell of Good Intentions," *Foreign Policy*, 29 (winter 1977–8), 8.
16 According to American officials, at the recent Soviet-American summit in Geneva, "the Americans decided not to denounce the Russians publicly on human rights, largely on the recommendation of former President Richard M. Nixon, who had said that public criticism would stiffen Soviet resistance"; *International Herald Tribune*, 25 Nov 1985. Presumably, the Americans feared that a frontal attack on behalf of human rights would damage the chances of making any progress with the Soviets on political conflicts, arms control, cultural exchanges, and human rights.
17 Evan Luard, "Human Rights and Foreign Policy," *International Affairs*, 56: 4 (autumn 1980), 585, 584.
18 Hoffmann, "Reaching for the Most Difficult: Human Rights as a Foreign Policy Goal," *Daedalus* (fall 1983), 44.
19 While he was president of CIDA, Paul Gérin-Lajoie argued that "the main objective of development" was "to liberate man from all types of bondage"; *The Longest Journey ... Begins with the First Step: Thoughts on International Development* (Ottawa: CIDA 1976), 22.
20 In mounting a case for a US boycott of Uganda's coffee during the Amin years, Richard Ullman notes that benefits from sale of coffee accrued to the Amin régime, not the peasant farmers. As most Ugandans rely on subsistence agriculture, "an effective boycott of Uganda's coffee would thus seriously curtail the livelihood only of the country's small urban sector, including Amin's army and police." Ullman, "Human Rights and Economic Power: The United States versus Idi Amin," *Foreign Affairs* (April 1978), 532–3.
21 In his challenging discussion in chapter 3, Kim Nossal emphasizes the inhibiting impact on any state's concern for human rights of the need to be sensitive to the interests of the major coalitions to which it belongs.
22 See Hoffmann, "Reaching," 47.
23 Quoted in *Le Devoir* 18 Jan 1983.
24 T.A. Keenleyside and Patricia Taylor, "The Impact of Human Rights Violations on the Conduct of Canadian Bilateral Relations: A Contemporary Dilemma," *Behind the Headlines*, 42:2 (1984), 24.
25 Department of External Affairs, Statements and Speeches 83/6, Allan MacEachen, "Human Rights and Canadian Foreign Policy," 1983, 2.
26 In his recent study, *After Hegemony: Cooperation and Discord in the World Political Economy* (Princeton: Princeton University Press 1984), Robert Keohane drew an interesting parallel (p. 24) between conflicts over short-run and long-run objectives and conflicts between "consumption on the

one hand and savings or investment on the other." Governments can, he argued, maintain high levels of consumption without investing in the long run. In the end, such a policy will catch up with them: they will find the basis of their influence eroded.

27 Garth Legge, Cranford Pratt, Richard Williams, and Hugh Winsor, *The Black Paper: An Alternative Policy for Canada towards Southern Africa* (Toronto: CIIA 1970), 11.
28 MacEachen, "Human Rights," 3.
29 Luard, "Human Rights," 583.
30 In his evaluation of Jimmy Carter's human rights record, Ernst Haas concludes: "There has been some marginal improvement in behavior on the part of a few countries. Nobody can tell how permanent that change may be, but past experience with similar waves of relaxation in repression strongly suggests that, unless the régime changes basically, people released from prison can always be rearrested. The skills of the torturer, though perhaps not used for a while, are never forgotten." "Human Rights: To Act or Not to Act?" in Kenneth A. Oye, Donald Rothchild, and Robert Lieber, eds., *Eagle Entangled: U.S. Foreign Policy in a Complex World* (New York: Longman 1979).
31 Matthews and Pratt, "Human Rights and Foreign Policy," 163.
32 This entire final section is a slightly modified version of parts of ibid.
33 This argument is made in Renate Pratt, "The Compartmentalization of the Promotion of Human Rights," Taskforce on the Churches and Corporate Responsibility, Toronto, 1983.
34 Second Report of the Parliamentary Sub-Committee on Canada's Relations with Latin America and the Caribbean, *Minutes of Proceedings and Evidence of the Standing Committee on External Affairs and National Defence*, Issue no. 48, House of Commons, Ottawa, 1981.
35 A sustained and vigorous but finally unconvincing representation of this view or one very close to it has recently been offered by Jack Donnelly. See his "Human Rights, Humanitarian Intervention and American Foreign Policy: Law, Morality and Politics," *Journal of International Affairs*, 37:2 (winter 1984), 319.
36 Hoffmann, *Duties beyond Borders*, and Walzer, *Just and Unjust Wars*.
37 Hoffmann, *Duties beyond Borders*, 69.
38 Walzer, *Just and Unjust Wars*, 107.

Index

Aboriginal rights, 33-5, 41, 43, 163
Aga Khan, Sadruddin, 86, 91
Agriculture, Department of, 63
Aitken, Margaret, 90
Amin, General Idi, 199, 267, 268, 272, 275, 276
Amnesty International, 89, 95, 96, 197, 235
Apartheid, 83, 266, 267, 276, 279
Argue, Senator Hazen, 253
Arms trade, Canada: characteristics of, 211, 216-17; constraints on, 213, 215; determinants of, 216, 217; and foreign policy, 213-14; major recipients of, 218; policy toward, 215, 218-20; promotion of, 213; regulation of, 214-17; to Third World, 210-12. *See also* Guide-lines; Military industry
Assembly of First Nations, 34-5
Axworthy, Lloyd, 253

Baldwin, Robert, 24
Basic needs, 133-4, 196 n 38, 205-8

Basic rights; centrality of, 262, 264, 274, 285-8; definition of, 6, 9, 190, 192; and ILO, 129-30; and IMF, 179-81; and international debt, 179-82; participation, 187-8; violations of, 47, 84, 194, 265-8
Bauer, William, 155-6
Beaulne, Yvon, 83, 91-3, 96, 243
Biafra, 275
Black Africa: Canada's policy toward, 274-5, 281-2
Blackstone, Sir William, 35
Bland, Salem, 27
B'nai Brith, 28
Bourassa, Henri, 32-3
Boven, Theo van, 80, 82, 89
Brezhnev Doctrine, 136
Bromke, Adam, 257
Bush, George, 225

Cabinet, 63, 64, 74
Cadieux, Rita, 90
Canada's International Relations, on human rights and IFIs, 178-9, 184
Canadian Civil Liberties Association, 28

Canadian development assistance; and basic economic rights, 195-6, 205-7, 350 n 86; as instrument of foreign policy: punishment, 196-203, reward, 203-5; and linkage in practice: Chile, 200, Cuba, 200-1, El Salvador, 201-2, 230-4, Equatorial Guinea, 199, Guatemala, 201-2, 236, Guyana, 203-4, Honduras, 202, Indonesia, 196-8, Kampuchea, 198, Sri Lanka, 203, Suriname, 202, Uganda, 199, 275-6, Vietnam, 198; and linkage with human rights: government policy on, 189-90, ideal standard, 193-6, public support for, 188, rationale for, 17-18, 60, 68, 74, 187-8, 190-3. *See also* Canadian International Development Agency
Canadian foreign policy: competing objectives: commerce, 48-9, 209-10, 241, 242, 292-3, development, 189, 193,

300, growth, 302-4, security, 53-4, 192, 239-40, 252-4, 257-8, 261, 284, 300-2; constraints on, 295-7, 297-304, consistency, 192, 195, effectiveness, 192, 304-5, international coalitions, 54-7, sovereignty, 191, 290-3; and foreign aid, 171-8, 196-207; and human rights: bilateral, 13-18, British heritage, 296, business lobbies and, 174-5, 302-4, civil and political emphasis, 285-8, compartmentalization of, 296-7, and IFIs, 171-9, 238, 277, 297, multilateral, 12-15, policy to 1970, 294, policy since 1970, 51-2, 60, 61-2, 294-7, prescriptions regarding, 270-4, 305-11; instruments of, 16-20, 252-9, 260-2, 275, 276-80, 280-2; and NGOs, 19-20, 245, 280-4; theoretical approaches to, 293-4. *See also* External Affairs

Canadian Human Rights Foundation, 60

Canadian International Development Agency (CIDA), 63, aid-trade fund of, 351 n 92; human rights courses at, 323 n 21; relations with IFIs, 161, 180-2; types of aid, 340 n 3. *See also* Canadian development assistance

Canadian Jewish Congress, 28

Canadian Labour Congress, use of ILO, 123-6

Carty, Robert, 190

Catley-Carson, Margaret, 180, 315 n 20

Central America: Canada's interest in, 221, 227-9; Canadian policy toward, 222, 236-40; human rights violations in, 223-4, 227; US intervention in, 221, 222

Cerezo, Vinicio, 226

Charter 77 (Czechoslovakia), 138, 141, 151

Charter of Rights and Freedoms, 29, 40-2, 127-8

Chile: Canadian policy: on foreign aid to, 200; on loans, 174-5, 177-8; military sales to, 69, 219; at the UNCHR, 84, 87, 89, 92

Civil and political rights: British heritage of, 24-6, 42, 44; in Canada 23-7, 40, 295; constitutional protection of, 40-2; emphasis on, 285-6; policy toward, in Soviet Union, 286-7; US influence regarding, 37; Western bias for, 147

Clark, Joe, 99, 113; on Central America, 233, 234, 239; on Helsinki forum, 150, 153; on human rights, 47, 51, 69; on human rights and aid, 189, 201; on military sales, 213, 218; on South Africa, 74-5, 278-9; on structural adjustment, 182

Clarkson, Stephen, 238

Coalitions, as policy determinant, 54-7

Cohen, L., 253

Cold War: effects on Canadian policy: aid, 198-8, 201, Central America, 222, 231, 238, 240, Poland, 246, South Africa, 282; and Helsinki process, 135-58; and human rights, 3, 289; impact on Committee on Human Rights, 103, 104-5, 110; impact on UN Commission on Human Rights, 84, 250, 251, 260, 264

Collective rights, 5, 8; demands for, in Canada, 29-35, 43; *See also* Aboriginal rights; French Canada

Committee against Racial Intolerance, 29

Committee of Experts on Applications of Standards (ILO), 118, 129, 131

Committee on Freedom of Association (ILO), 118-19, 125, 131

Common law and human rights, 35-9; compensation, 36; independent judiciary, 35; racism, 36, 38-9; security and liberty, 35-6; trade unions, 36

Commonwealth, 197, 204, 244, 265, 276, 278, 279, 282, 283

Competitiveness and Security (1985 green paper), 64, 71

Conference on Security and Cooperation in Europe (CSCE), 13, 54, 60, 135. *See also* Helsinki Process

Conflicts, definition of, 217

Contras (Nicaragua), 224, 227, 235

Co-operative Commonwealth Federation (CCF), 27-8

Crofton, Patrick, 269

Cuba, Canadian aid policy toward, 200-1

Debt, international: and human rights, 179-82; ILO on, 133; role of IMF, 179-80. *See also* Inter-

371   Index

national Monetary Fund: structural adjustment
Declaration of Human Rights. *See* Universal Declaration
Deschenes, Judge Jules, 90
Division of Human Rights. *See* United Nations Human Rights Centre
Donnelly, Jack, 11-12, 368 n 35
Doxey, Margaret, 48
Drake, Earl, 161
Duarte, José Napoleon, 224, 225, 226, 234
Duncan, Sir Andrew Rae, 32
Duplessis, Maurice, 32

East-West relations. *See* Cold War
Eayrs, James, 46
Economic sanctions, 49, 196-203, 250, 253-6, 260, 276-9, 282-4, 292, 302
Economic, social, and cultural rights, 3; early claims in Canada, 27-9; and ILO, 116-17; legislative protection of, 38-9; Soviet bias for, 147; and structural adjustment, 180-1; weakness in Canada, 123-5, 126-8, 295-6; World Bank and, 162-4
El Salvador, Canadian policy toward: aid, 201-2; Clark years, 234-5; at IFIs, 173-4; MacEachen years, 233-4; MacGuigan years, 229-33; public opposition to, 231-2; since 1979, 224-5; at UNCHR, 297; on US military assistance, 225. *See also* Central America
End use certificates, 218
Energy, Mines and Resources, Department of, 174-5
Export Development Corporation (EDC), 188, 194, 200, 206, 236, 277-8
External Affairs, Department of: decision-making in, 62-4, 75-6; human rights and, 65-8, 70-1; ideology of, 46-8, 293-4; and NGOs, 60, 70, 71-2, 94-5; organization of, 62-3, 69-71, 90, 91, 237, 242-3, 296; and other departments, 62-3; role of minister in, 61, 68-9; sources of information of, 66-7, 242; sources of policies of, 61-2, 291, 293-4. *See also* Canadian foreign policy

Fairweather, Gordon, 90, 98
Finance, Department of, 63, 160
Fishkin, James, 10
French Canada, 25, 32-3, 43

Gérin-Lajoie, Paul, 187
Gewirth, Alan, 6, 10
Goldberg, Arthur, 140
Goldschlag, Klaus, 141
Gorbachev, Mikhail, 158
Gordon, Sheldon, 47, 51
Gotlieb, Allan, 119-20
Guatemala: Canadian investment in, 227; Canadian policy toward, 173, 201, 202, 235-6; coup in, 224; criticism of Canadian policy toward, 22, 69; escalating violence in, 226. *See also* Central America
Guide-lines: Canadian, on military sales, 215, 219; implementation of, 215-16; narrow interpretation of, 218-19

Guyana, 241-2, 243

Haig, Alexander, 231, 242, 258
Hardy, J.E.G., 154
Harkin Amendments, 162-3
Helsinki process, 135-58; Belgrade, 140-1; Canada's role at, 140-1; Cultural Forum, Budapest, 153-5; Helsinki Final Act: Canada's contribution to, 136-40, origins, 135, 136-40; Human Contacts Experts Meeting, Berne, 155-6; Human Rights Experts Meeting, Ottawa (1985): Canada's role, 142-3, 144, debate at, 145-6, final outcome of, 148-9, 152-3, preparatory meeting for, 143-5, proposals of, 146-8, purpose of, 143; Madrid: 141-2, Canada's role, 142-3, 144, Polish issue at, 252, 254, 258; prospects for, 157-8; role of neutral states, 140, 146-8, 153-4, 156-7; Vienna, 156-7
Herndl, Kurt, 80, 82, 98
Hoffmann, Stanley, 286, 308, 318
Holmes, John, 50
Honduras: after 1981, 226-7; Canadian policy toward, 235. *See also* Central America
Howe, Joseph, 24
Human rights: arms sales and, 209, 213-14, 215, 218, 276, 277; in Chile, 84, 89; convention on torture, 82-3; in Cyprus, 84; definitions of, 3-6, 9-10; disappearances, 85, 89, 91, 93; in El Salvador, 224-6; in Guatemala, 226; in Honduras, 227;

mass exodus and, 86; in Nicaragua, 224; obligations toward: beyond borders, 4-6, 7-11, 306-11, domestically, 4, 5; non-basic: importance of, 262-4, obligations regarding, 8-10; in Poland, 247-52; religious intolerance and, 83, 91; rights of child, 83; in South Africa, 83-4, 265-7, 268; summary executions, 85-6; violations: causes of, 229, competing hypotheses concerning, 288-90. *See also* Canadian foreign policy: and human rights
Humphrey, John, 80

In Whose Benefit?, 63, 188, 245
Indian Brotherhood, 34
Indonesia: arms sales to, 217; Canadian aid policy toward, 197-8; rights violations in, 54
Institute for human rights and democratic development (proposed), 323 n 21
Inter-American Commission on Human Rights, 228, 229
Inter-American Development Bank (IDB): Canadian policy re human rights at, 171-5, 297; Chile loan 1983, 174-5; Chile loan 1986, 178; El Salvador loan, 173; Guatemala loan, 173; structure of, 160-1; US politicization of, 168-70
Inter-American Treaty of Reciprocal Assistance, 228
Inter-Church Committee on Human Rights in Latin America (ICCHRLA), 72,

89, 96, 229, 240, 245
International Bill of Human Rights, 82
International Court of Justice, 103
International Covenant on Civil and Political Rights, 9, 39, 41, 42, 101, 155, 248, 249, 252; Canadian accession to, 60, 90; Optional Protocol under, 79, 82, 102, 106-7, 112, 151, 241, 257
Intenational Covenant on Economic, Social and Cultural Rights, 9, 29, 41, 79, 82, 117, 275; Canadian accession to, 60, 90
International debt. *See* Debt, international
International financial institutions (IFIs): Canadian policy toward, 171-9, 181-2, 183-4; human rights and, 161-8, 179; politicization of, 168-70, 171-5; structure of, 159-61; US policies toward, 162, 168-70. *See also* Debt, international; International Monetary Fund; World Bank
International Labour Organization (ILO): complaints machinery, 123-4; implementation instruments, 118-19, 128-9, 130-2; limitations of, 128-30; and Poland, 246-7, 249, 251-2, 257, 262-3; structure and functions, 115-19, 119-20, 128-30; and unemployed, 129-30
International Labour Organization (ILO) and Canada: attitudes to, 126, 130-3; federal complications regarding, 120-2,

influence on, 125-8; involvement with, 118-19, 123-5, 128-9, 130-2; ratification by, 120-2, 126-7
International Monetary Fund (IMF): Canadian policy regarding, 179-82; constitution and organization of, 159-60, 166; credits to South Africa by, 164-5, 175-6; and human rights, 130, 180-2; and structural adjustment, 130, 165-6, 180
Intervention: in Central America, 211-12, 235; and international law, 191, 291-2; potential for, in Poland, 252-4, 263; prescriptions regarding, 308-11

Jamieson, Donald, 47-8, 51, 110, 189
Jay, Harry, 143, 149, 150-3
Jolly, Richard, 165-6

Kampuchea, 47, 57, 295
Kaplan, Robert, 109
Keenleyside, T., 49
Kilgour, David, 97, 98
King, W.L. Mackenzie, 26, 126
Kooijmans, P., 83

Labour, Department of, 126-7
Labour Conventions case (1937), 120-1
LaFeber, Walter, 221
Lalonde, Marc, 171, 174
League of Nations, 79
LeBlanc, Philippe, 97, 98
Léger, Raoul, 235
Lévesque, René, 33
Lewis, Stephen, 94, 100, 111

MacDonald, David, 74
Macdonald, Flora, 93

Macdonald, Sir John A., 25, 34
MacEachen, Allen: on Central America, 233-4, 238-9; on effectiveness, 304; on human rights in foreign policy, 48, 51, 61, 228; on Vietnam, 176; role in External Affairs, 69
MacGuigan, Mark: on aid to Cuba and Vietnam, 189; on Central America, 229-31, 232-3, 237, 242; endorses Human Rights Experts Meeting, 142; on human rights, 51; on Polish crisis, 253, 255
MacKinnon, Richard, 91
McLean, Walter, 97
McNamara, Robert, 163
Macpherson, C.B., 42
Massé, Marcel, 181
Media, role of, 71-2
Mercier, Honoré, 31
Métis Association, 34
Middle East, arms sales to, 217
Middleton, Robert, 90
Militarization and human rights violations, 224, 226, 235, 244
Military assistance and human rights violations, 223, 225, 227
Military industry (Canada), 211-12
Military sales. *See* Arms trade
Montt, Rios, 86, 173
Morse, David, 129
Mowat, Oliver, 31
Mulroney, Brian: on Central America, 235, 240; on human rights, 47, 189-90; on South Africa, 74-5, 276, 278-9, 284

Nguena, Macias, 199
Nicaragua: Canadian policy toward, 234-5, 241-2; IDB loan to, 169-70; Sandinista revolution, 224. *See also* Central America
Nigeria: Canada's obligations toward, 272-3; Canada's policies toward, 275; as violator of human rights, 267-9
Non-governmental organizations (NGOs): as channel for aid, 194; consultations of, with External Affairs, 60, 94-5; as lobbyists, 19, 28, on Central America, 245, on Poland, 256-7, on South Africa, 272, 280-4, at UNCHR, 81, 85, 87-9, 95-6, 99; at Ottawa 1985, 150; as source of information, 66, 105
North Atlantic Treaty Alliance (NATO), 54, 137, 142, 144-8, 153, 246, 248, 250, 252, 254-6, 259, 264. *See also* Cold War
Nyerere, Julius, 213

Obote, Milton, 199, 267, 268, 272, 276
Olszowski, Stefan, 248, 250
Ontario Human Rights Code, 38
Organization for Economic Co-operation and Development (OECD), 54
Organization of American States (OAS), 228
Parliament, 69, 73-4, 183-4; and ILO conventions, 121-2
Participation as a basic right, 287-8
Partridge, E.A., 31
Pérez de Cuéllar, Javier, 81
Poland: Canada's response to rights violations in, 252-7; discussion of human rights in: at ILO, 251-2; at UN, 247, 250, at UNCHR, 84, 250-1; martial law in, 247-52
Police and military training, 204
Political parties, Canadian, and human rights, 20, 30
Portillo, President Lopez, 229
Prime minister: and foreign policy, 63-4, 74-5; Office of, 63, 74
Privy Council Office (PCO), 63
Project Plowshares, 219
Provinces: and ILO complaints, 123-5, 126-7; and ILO conventions, 121-2; rights thereof, 31-2, 43; role re human rights, 57

Rawls, John, 11
Reagan, Ronald, 225, 231, 254, 255, 257
Restrictive arms sales, 216-17
Right to know about rights, 288
Rights, basic. *See* Basic rights
Rights, human. *See* Human rights
Riis, Nelson, 69
Rogers, Louis, 144
Romero, Archbishop, 228, 230
Royal Commission on Dominion-Provincial Relations (1940), 39
Rudner, Martin, 188, 191, 193

Sakharov, Andrei, 151, 153
Sanabria, Herbert Anaya, 244
Saskatchewan Bill of Rights, 38

Scharansky, Anatoly, 151, 153
Schifter, Richard, 145, 250
Schmidt, Helmut, 254
Secretary of State, Department of the, 60, 90, 109
Security interests and human rights, 300-2
Sharp, Mitchell, 50, 137
Shue, Henry, on basic rights, 6, 285; on delimiting obligations, 10-11, 270-2, 274
Shultz, George, 169
Sirrs, R. Douglas, 229-30, 243
Sivard, Ruth Leger, 209
Six Counties Address (1837), 26
Smith, Virginia, 190
Sohn, Louis, 106
Solidarity (Polish trade union), 141, 247-9, 251-2, 254-6, 260, 263
Somoza, General, 224, 235
South Africa: Canada's obligations toward, 271-2; Canadian policy: to 1977, 56, 276-7, 1977-84, 52, 56-7, 74-5, 276-7, since 1984, 56-7, 74-5, 276, 278-9, 303, UK influence on, 57; compared with black Africa, 269-70; as gross violator, 265-8, 295; IMF credits to, 164-5, 174-6; sanctions against, 276-9, 292, 302
Sovereignty: and human rights, 46, 49-53, 89, 191, 241, 290-3; intervention despite, 310-11
Soviet bloc. *See* Warsaw Treaty Organization
Soviet Union, 286, 288; as primary threat to rights, 288-90
Space Research Corporation, 277

Special Joint Committee on Canada's International Relations, 64, 73; on basic rights, 7, 287; NGO briefs to, 95, 269; report of, 134, 167, 188, 221, 262; response to, 69, 179-80; on rights and IFIs, 167-8, 178, 184, 297
Sri Lanka, 68
Stackhouse, Reginald, 149
Standing Committee on External Affairs and International Trade, 73, 188; policy on IFIs, 179, 184, 297
Stockholm International Peace Research Institute (SIPRI), 216
Strategic interests and human rights, 53-4, 292-3
Structural adjustment, and the poorest, 132, 165-6
Sub-Committee on Canada's Relations with the Caribbean and Latin America, 73, 188, 221, 232, 306
Subsistence, rights to, 165-6

Tambo, Oliver, 279
Tanzania: and Canada, 273-4; as violator of human rights, 267-8
Tarnopolsky, Walter, 108, 139
Taskforce on the Churches and Corporate Responsibility (TCCR): on Chile, 178; proposals re IFIs, 167, 172, 175
Taylor, P., 49
Trades and Labour Congress, 27
Trades Union Act (1872), 36
Tripartite Committee (ILO), 118
Trudeau, Pierre Elliot: on Biafra, 275; on civil and political rights, 316 n 12; on compartmentalization, 67, 302; foreign policy review of (1970), 47, 189, 276; on Helsinki Final Act, 135, 139; on Indian policy, 34; on non-intervention, 229, 241; on Polish crisis, 252-4, 257, 259

Uganda: Canada's obligations toward, 272; Canada's policies toward, 57, 93, 275-6; Canadian aid to, 199; criticism of Canada's policies, 95; gross violator, 47, 84, 267, 268; US sanctions against, 367 n 20
United Nations charter, 79, 137, 291, 298-9
United Nations Commission on Human Rights (UNCHR), 79-100; Canadian role in, 90-8, 228, 232, 233, 236, 243, 296, 306; and the child, 83; and gross and systematic violators: Chile, 84, 89, Cyprus, 84, Poland, 246, 250-1, 257, 261, 263, South Africa, 83-4; and involuntary disappearances, 85, 89, 91, 93; and mass executions, 85-6; and mass exodus, 86; NGOs' role in, 81, 85, 87, 88-9, 95-6, 99; and religious intolerance, 83, 91; resolution 1503 of, 83, 88-9; structure and history of, 9, 80-6, 87-8; sub-commission on minorities of, 80, 81, 99; and summary/arbitrary executions, 85-6; and torture, 82-3; US role in, 87-8, 92; and WEO group, 88; and Working Group on Communications, 81, 88

United Nations Economic and Social Council (ECOSOC), 80, 81, 83, 98, 103, 111, 117, 118

United Nations Human Rights Centre, 80, 89, 98, 102, 108, 112

(United Nations) Human Rights Committee, 82, 101-14, 296, 306; Canada's early involvement, 107-8; Canada's implementing of the covenant, 108-10; Canada's interest in, 110-11; human rights advisory role for, 111-12; importance of, 101-2; and Optional Protocol, 101-2, 106-7, 112; origin and role of, 102-4; state reports to, 104-6

United States: arms sales disclosures, 214; Congress on rights, 162-3, 165; policy on human rights, 60, 171; politicization of IFIs by, 168-70, 172, 173-4

Universal Declaration of Human Rights, 9, 79, 82, 137-9, 291; and ILO, 116; influence in Canada of, 28, 41

Walzer, Michael, 7, 308, 310

Warren, Gaby, 137

Warsaw Treaty Organization (WTO), 87, 144-5, 148, 150, 152-8, 248, 255, 257-9, 263, 286. *See also* Cold War

Winegard Report. *See In Whose Benefit?*

Winnipeg General Strike (1919), 27

World Bank: Chilean loans, 176-8; emphasis on poorest, 163; organization of, 159-61; voting power within, 160

World Employment Programme (ILO), 129, 133

Women's rights, 316 n 11

Contributors

Frances Arbour is a Toronto-based human rights and refugee consultant. From 1977 to 1985 she was executive director of the Inter-Church Committee on Human Rights in Latin America, a national, ecumenical body concerned with Canadian policy in Latin America. In 1985 she was awarded the Letelier-Moffitt Human Rights Award in Washington, DC. She continues to travel frequently to Central America and is a member of the Refugee Status Advisory Committee.

Victoria Berry is executive secretary to the Commission of the Churches on International Affairs, World Council of Churches, Geneva. She has worked on human rights and international relations for, among others, the United Church of Canada and the Human Rights Research and Education Centre of the University of Ottawa.

John W. Foster is staff officer for economic justice and ecumenical coalitions in the Division of Mission in Canada, United Church of Canada. He is also chairperson of the Roundtable on Negotiations for Peace in Central America. He formerly chaired the Inter-Church Committee on Human Rights in Latin America and was Canadian church observer at five sessions of the United Nations Commission on Human Rights. He is author of many articles, briefs, and essays on Canadian–Latin American relations, human rights, and Canadian economic justice.

Rhoda E. Howard is professor of sociology at McMaster University. She is the author of *Colonialism and Underdevelopment in Ghana* (1978) and *Human Rights in Commonwealth Africa* (1986) and co-editor of *An International Handbook on Human Rights* (1987). Her interests include Canadian refugee policy, women's rights, and theory. Professor Howard is also an editor of the *Canadian Journal of African Studies*.

Kalmen Kaplansky served for 12 years as director of the Canada Branch Office of the International Labour Organization and special adviser to its director-general, retiring October 1980. As the first director of international affairs of the Canadian Labour Congress (1957–67), he attended as a member of the Canadian delegation the annual International Labour Conference in Geneva and served for 7 years as a member of the ILO governing body. As senior fellow of the University of Ottawa Human Rights Research and Education Centre, he has been closely associated with human rights activities and institutions in Canada since 1946.

T.A. Keenleyside is professor of political science at the University of Windsor, where he has been teaching since 1971. He was previously a foreign service officer in the Department of External Affairs, serving abroad in Thailand and Indonesia. Professor Keenleyside is the author of a number of articles on Canadian foreign policy, including several related to human rights.

Allan McChesney is a lawyer, consultant, and educator. His human rights research and publications concern foreign policy, development assistance, non-governmental organizations, human rights laws, and the Canadian Charter of Rights. From 1981 to 1983 he was director of legal aid in the Northwest Territories. As a research associate of the University of Ottawa Human Rights Centre, he has helped plan and present the first comprehensive human rights courses for Canadian foreign service officers. He wrote the chapter on Canada in *International Handbook of Human Rights* (1987).

Ronald Manzer teaches public policy administration at the University of Toronto. He is author of *Teachers and Politics in England and Wales* (1970); *Canada: A Socio-Political Report* (1974), which includes analysis of social indicators of equality and liberty in post-war Canada; and *Public Policies and Political Development in Canada* (1985), which has a chapter on the development of provincial and federal policies on human rights.

Robert O. Matthews is associate professor of political science at the University of Toronto, co-editor of *International Journal*, and chair of the International Affairs Committee of the Canadian Council of Churches. He is the author of several articles on Canada's foreign policy relating to human rights.

Stefania Szlek Miller is assistant professor of political science at McMaster University. She wrote a chapter on human rights in Poland in *International Handbook of Human Rights* (1987) and edited a special issue on Poland of the *Canadian Slavonic Papers* (September 1983). She was president 1985–6 of the Canadian Association of Slavists.

Cathal J. Nolan is currently completing a doctorate in international relations at the University of Toronto. His thesis is on the relationship between national security policies and human rights concerns in the United States and Canada since 1945. For three years he was a researcher in human rights with the Development Studies Program of the University of Toronto. He has acted as a consultant on human rights and development to CIDA and written on Canadian foreign policy.

Kim Richard Nossal is professor of political science at McMaster University. He is the author of *The Politics of Canadian Foreign Policy* (1985) and a number of articles on Canada's external relations.

Cranford Pratt is professor of political science at the University of Toronto. For several decades he was primarily an Africanist and, as such, has written or edited four books and numerous articles. More recently he has worked on Canadian foreign policy. He has written on human rights and foreign policy, on Canadian policies toward North-South issues, and on the emergence of a counter-consensus to Canadian foreign policy.

Renate Pratt is a former vice-president of the Young Women's Christian Association of Canada. From 1975 to 1986 she was co-ordinator of the ecumenical Taskforce on the Churches and Corporate Responsibility. She is a member of the Council of Trustees, International Defence and Aid Fund for Southern Africa, and of the Advisory Board, International Defence and Aid Fund for Southern Africa (Canada).

Ernie Regehr is research director for Project Ploughshares. He is the author of *Arms Canada: The Deadly Business of Military Exports* (1987), an examination of Canadian military export policies and practices. He has worked as a writer/researcher in southern Africa and is author of *Perceptions of Apartheid: The Churches and Political Change in South Africa* (1979).

H. Gordon Skilling is professor emeritus, political science, and former director, Centre for Russian and East European Studies, University of Toronto. He was chairman, Committee on Freedom of Science and Scholarship, Royal Society of Canada. He is the author of *Charter 77 and Human Rights in Canada* (1981) and *Samizdat and an Independent Society in Central and Eastern Europe* (forthcoming) and with Vilém Precan edited *Ten Years of Charter 77* (forthcoming).